1987

Science Year

The World Book Annual Science Supplement

A Review of Science and Technology
During the 1986 School Year

World Book, Inc.

a Scott Fetzer company

Chicago London Sydney Toronto

Preface

New theories about ancient rivers on Mars . . . how monarch butterflies migrate distances of up to 4,000 miles . . . fresh insights on the mysterious practices of the ancient Aztecs . . . the explosion of the *Challenger* spacecraft and the nuclear accident in Chernobyl . . . these and other notable developments are captured in the 1987 *Science Year.*

Each edition of *Science Year*—The World Book Annual Science Supplement—provides *World Book* owners with an ongoing record of advances in science and technology. Special Reports give in-depth treatment to timely topics. The Science File, arranged alphabetically like *World Book,* reports on the year's major developments in wide-ranging fields. The World Book Supplement reprints new and completely revised articles from the latest edition of *World Book.* And a three-year cumulative index provides ready access to the wealth of information in the current and two previous editions.

Now a new feature makes it even easier to use *Science Year* in updating *World Book*'s coverage of science and technology. The *Science Year* Cross-Reference Tabs, found between pages 16 and 17 of this volume, are designed to be placed in your *World Book.* By affixing the gummed tabs to the appropriate *World Book* article, your search for information can proceed smoothly from *World Book* to related information in subsequent editions of *Science Year.*

Updating your *World Book* with the latest developments in science—that's the role of *Science Year.* And now, with the *Science Year* Tabs, it's even easier than before.   [A. Richard Harmet]

Contents

See page 178.

See page 367.

A tear-out page of cross-reference tabs for insertion in *The World Book
Encyclopedia* appears after page 16.

Staff

Editorial Advisory Board

Contributors

Adelman, George, M.S.
Editorial Consultant and Editor
[*Neuroscience*]

Alderman, Michael H., M.D.
Chairman
Department of Epidemiology & Social
Medicine
Albert Einstein College of Medicine
[*Public Health*]

Alsofrom, Judy
Free-Lance Writer
[Science You Can Use, *Home
Medical Tests: What You Should
Know*]

Anderson, Don L., Ph.D.
Director
Seismological Laboratory
California Institute of Technology
[Special Report, *Exploring Earth's
Inner Space*]

Andrews, Peter J., M.S.
Free-Lance Writer, Chemist
[*Chemistry*]

Auerbach, Stanley I., Ph.D.
Senior Staff Adviser,
Environmental Sciences Division
Oak Ridge National Laboratory
[*Ecology*]

Ballard, Robert D., Ph.D.
Senior Scientist
Woods Hole Oceanographic
Institution
[*Oceanography* (Close-Up)]

Bell, William J., Ph.D.
Professor of Biology
University of Kansas
[*Zoology*]

Belton, Michael J. S., Ph.D.
Astronomer
National Optical Astronomy
Observatories
[*Astronomy, Solar System*]

Bierman, Howard, B.E.E.
President
Paje Consultants, Inc.
[*Electronics; Computer Hardware;
Computer Software*]

Black, John H., Ph.D.
Associate Professor of Astronomy
Steward Observatory
University of Arizona
[*Astronomy, Galactic*]

Brett, Carlton E., Ph.D.
Associate Professor
Department of Geological Sciences
University of Rochester
[*Paleontology*]

Brower, Lincoln Pierson, Ph.D.
Professor of Zoology
University of Florida
[Special Report, *The Migrating
Monarch*]

Covault, Craig P., B.S.
Space Technology Editor
Aviation Week magazine
[*Space Technology; Space
Technology* (Close-Up)]

Dewar, Robert E., Ph.D.
Associate Professor of Anthropology
University of Connecticut
[Special Report, *The Lemurs and
Other Wonders of Madagascar*]

Dorozynski, Alexander
Free-Lance Writer
[People in Science, *The Max Planck
Society at 75*]

Dressler, Alan, Ph.D.
Astronomer
Mount Wilson and Las Campanas
observatories of the Carnegie
Institution of Washington
[Special Report, *Galaxies—Islands in
the Universe*]

Fisher, Arthur, M.A.
Science and Engineering Editor
Popular Science
[Special Report, *The Fabulous Laser*]

Francis, Donald P., D.Sc.
AIDS Adviser to the State of
California
Centers for Disease Control
[Special Report, *Unraveling the
Secrets of AIDS*]

Gary, Norman E., Ph.D.
Professor of Entomology
University of California, Davis
[*Agriculture* (Close-Up)]

Gates, W. Lawrence, Sc.D.
Professor and Chairman
Department of Atmospheric Sciences
Oregon State University
[*Meteorology*]

Gazzaniga, Michael S., Ph.D.
Professor of Psychology
Cornell Medical College
[Special Report, *Our "Two" Brains:
Facts and Myths*]

Goldhaber, Paul, D.D.S.
Dean and Professor of Periodontology
Harvard School of Dental Medicine
[*Dentistry*]

Hartl, Daniel L., Ph.D.
Professor of Genetics
Washington University School of
Medicine
[*Genetic Engineering; Genetics*]

Hay, William W., Ph.D.
Professor of Natural History and
Director
University of Colorado Museum
University of Colorado, Boulder
[*Geology*]

Hellemans, Alexander, B.S.
Book Review Editor
Physics Today magazine
[*Physics, Fluids and Solids*]

Herzog, David B., M.D.
Director, Eating Disorders Unit
Massachusetts General Hospital
[Special Report, *Dangerous Eating
Habits*]

Hester, Thomas R., Ph.D.
Professor of Anthropology and
Director
Center for Archaeological Research
University of Texas, San Antonio
[*Archaeology, New World*]

Jennings, Feenan D., B.S.
Director
Sea Grant Program
Texas A&M University
[*Oceanography*]

Jones, William G., A.M.L.S.
Assistant University Librarian
University of Illinois at Chicago
[*Books of Science*]

Kalson, David, M.A.
Manager, Public Information Division
American Institute of Physics
[Special Report, *Creating Images with Computers*]

Katz, Paul, M.D.
Associate Professor of Medicine
Georgetown University Medical Center
[*Immunology*]

King, Lauriston R., Ph.D.
Deputy Director
Sea Grant Program
Texas A&M University
[*Oceanography*]

Kolata, Gina, M.S.
Senior Writer
Science magazine
[People in Science, *Grace M. Hopper*]

Liuzzo, Joseph A., Ph.D.
Professor of Food Science
Louisiana State University
[*Nutrition* (Close-Up)]

March, Robert H., Ph.D.
Professor of Physics
University of Wisconsin
[Special Report, *Mind-Boggling Mysteries of Matter; Physics, Subatomic*]

Matos Moctezuma, Eduardo
Archaeologist
[Special Report, *The Great Temple of the Aztecs*]

McGee, Harold, Ph.D.
Free-Lance Writer
[Science You Can Use, *Matching Pots and Pans to Your Cooking Needs*]

Merbs, Charles F., Ph.D.
Professor of Anthropology
Arizona State University
[*Anthropology*]

Merz, Beverly, A.B.
Associate Editor
Journal of the American Medical Association
[*Medical Research; Medicine*]

Meyer, B. Robert, M.D.
Chief, Division of Clinical Pharmacology
North Shore University Hospital
[*Drugs*]

Murray, Stephen S., Ph.D.
Astrophysicist
Harvard/Smithsonian Center for Astrophysics
[*Astronomy, Extragalactic*]

Olson, Maynard V., Ph.D.
Professor
Department of Genetics
Washington University School of Medicine
[*Molecular Biology*]

Ott, Ingrid L., B.A.
Research Coordinator, Eating Disorder Unit
Massachusetts General Hospital
[Special Report, *Dangerous Eating Habits*]

Patrusky, Ben, B.E.E.
Free-Lance Science Writer
[Special Report, *Nature's Fireworks*]

Pennisi, Elizabeth, M.S.
Free-Lance Science Writer
[*Zoology*]

Reed, Christopher, A.B.
Managing Editor
Harvard Magazine
[*Botany* (Close-Up)]

Richard, Alison F., Ph.D.
Professor of Anthropology
Yale University
[Special Report, *The Lemurs and Other Wonders of Madagascar*]

Salisbury, Frank B., Ph.D.
Professor of Plant Physiology
Utah State University
[*Botany*]

Sever, Thomas L., M.A.
Archaeologist and
NASA Remote Sensing Specialist
NASA
[Special Report, *Archaeology's New Eyes in the Sky*]

Sherman, Spencer E., M.D.
Ophthalmologist
[Science You Can Use, *Contact Lenses: Keeping an Eye on New Advances*]

Soderblom, Laurence A., Ph.D.
Geophysicist
United States Geological Survey
[*Astronomy, Solar System* (Close-Up)]

Squyres, Steven W., Ph.D.
Research Scientist
NASA Ames Research Center
[Special Report, *Changing Visions of Mars*]

Stammer, Larry B.
Environmental Writer
Los Angeles Times
[*Zoology* (Close-Up)]

Stern, Jennifer, B.A.
Free-Lance Writer
[Science You Can Use: *What to Look for in a Videotape; Video Systems: New Choices for Home Moviemakers*]

Trotter, Robert J., B.S.
Senior Editor
Psychology Today magazine
[*Psychology*]

Visich, Marian, Jr., Ph.D.
Associate Dean of Engineering
State University of New York
[*Energy*]

Wenke, Robert J., Ph.D.
Associate Professor
Department of Anthropology
University of Washington
[*Archaeology, Old World*]

Westman, Walter E., Ph.D.
Research Associate
NASA Ames Research Center
[*Environment*]

Wittwer, Sylvan H., Ph.D.
Director Emeritus
Agricultural Experiment Station
Michigan State University
[*Agriculture*]

Yager, Robert E., Ph.D.
Professor of Science Education
University of Iowa
[*Science Education*]

Young, Eleanor A., Ph.D.
Associate Professor
Department of Medicine
University of Texas Health Science Center at San Antonio
[*Nutrition*]

Special Reports

Fourteen Special Reports give in-depth treatment to major advances in science and technology. The subjects were chosen for their current importance and lasting interest.

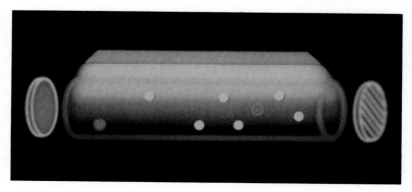

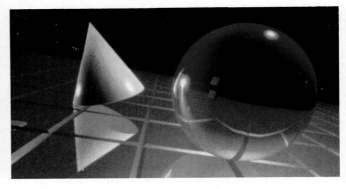

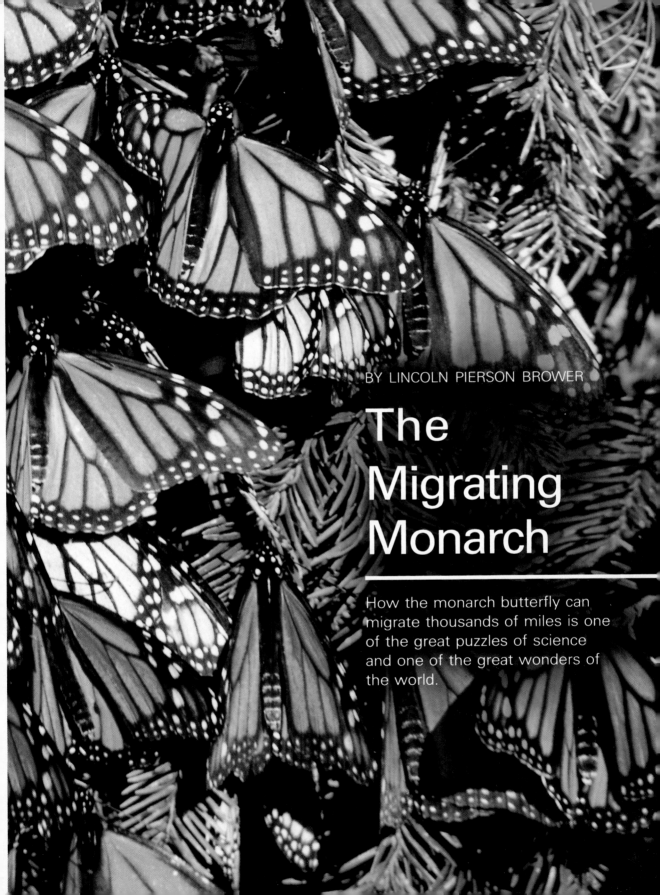

BY LINCOLN PIERSON BROWER

The Migrating Monarch

How the monarch butterfly can migrate thousands of miles is one of the great puzzles of science and one of the great wonders of the world.

I had studied the monarch butterfly for years and knew many details about its life—including the fact that these butterflies migrate up to 4,000 miles. But nothing prepared me for what I witnessed when I first saw the monarchs at one of their Mexican wintering sites. It was late afternoon, and we had just set up camp in a magnificent fir forest in central Mexico. We decided to explore a little before dinner, and while walking along a narrow path we suddenly noticed that the trees before us were no longer green. Instead, they were gray. I realized that we were looking at a wall of trees covered with monarch butterflies whose folded wings showed their gray underside. Numbering in the tens of millions, the monarchs were totally immobilized by the cold—mysterious and magnificent.

My first glimpse of the wintering monarchs took place in January 1977 during an expedition with William Calvert, who, like me, is a zoologist at the University of Florida in Gainesville specializing in the study of the monarch butterfly. We had traveled to an 11,000-foot-high fir forest in the rugged and majestic Sierra Chincua, about 80 miles west of Mexico City. The Sierra Chincua is an isolated range in the center of a huge volcanic mountain system known as the Volcanic Axis that runs across Mexico from east of Mexico City to the Pacific coast. Hundreds of millions of monarch butterflies from the United States and Canada migrate every year to about 30 overwintering colonies in this and nearby mountain ranges that extend over 1,500 square miles. Here they spend the winter far from the freezing temperatures that would surely kill them.

We had come to the area to collect samples of monarchs in order to learn more about this butterfly's remarkable chemical defense against birds. When birds try to eat monarchs, they become violently ill from poisons the monarchs carry. We wanted to study how this chemical defense would protect the monarch during the overwintering period. But it was now obvious that the millions of monarchs we were seeing were a biological wonder of great importance. During dinner that first night, we reviewed our research plans and decided to change them. Why do so many monarchs migrate to this isolated region, and how do they behave during their overwintering period? Since that day in 1977, much of my research has been devoted to these questions.

Monarchs migrate to two principal overwintering regions—the one in Mexico's Sierra Chincua and nearby mountains belonging to the Volcanic Axis and another along the coast of California between San Francisco and Los Angeles. Monarchs west of the Rocky Mountains migrate to the sites spread along the California coastline. The most famous of these sites is at Pacific Grove on the Monterey Peninsula, where monarchs cling to leaves and the bark of eucalyptus trees by the tens of thousands.

Some of the monarchs that live east of the Rockies and as far north as Canada overwinter along the Gulf Coast of Florida. Most of these eastern monarchs, however, migrate by the hundreds of millions to Mexico. Although overwintering sites in California were

The author:
Lincoln Pierson Brower, wearing cap, is distinguished professor of zoology at the University of Florida in Gainesville.

first described by naturalists as early as 1869, the location of the sites in Mexico remained a mystery to scientists until 1975.

In the early 1950's, Canadian zoologist Fred A. Urquhart of the University of Toronto, along with his wife, Norah, and other colleagues, began the first systematic study of the monarch's migration. They enlisted the aid of hundreds of amateur volunteers and began tagging monarchs in order to monitor the migration. The tags were ordinary pressure adhesive labels, such as those used as price tags on merchandise. The tags were harmless to the butterflies and adhered to their wings even when soaked in water. They carried identifying codes along with the message, "Send to Zoology University Toronto Canada." Throughout the 1950's and 1960's, people who recaptured some of the hundreds of thousands of tagged monarchs reported the locations of their captures to Urquhart. By tracking these reports, it became clear that most of the monarchs passed through Texas during their migration, seemingly on their way to Mexico. But where in Mexico did the monarchs go? In 1972, Urquhart began writing to newspapers in Mexico, asking for volunteers to help look, and in 1973, he received an offer from a salesman named Kenneth C. Brugger, a United States citizen living in Mexico City. Brugger searched the Mexican countryside for the next two years and finally located one of the colonies in 1975.

Data from the recaptured tagged butterflies have revealed that some monarchs migrate as far as 1,900 miles south to Mexico and up to 2,200 miles north during the return migration the following spring. Considering that each monarch is less than one-sixth the weight of a United States penny—about a hundredth of an ounce—their ability to fly a distance of more than 4,000 miles in their lifetime is quite a feat.

The monarch is one of 157 butterfly species belonging to a group known as *milkweed butterflies*. They are so named because the caterpillars of most of these 157 species feed only on milkweed plants. Most of these species live in Africa and Asia. Only four species live in North America, and only one of these—the monarch—migrates.

Milkweed plants play a crucial role in the monarch's life cycle. Beginning in the spring, monarchs leave their overwintering grounds and fly northward until they encounter budding milkweed plants. The butterflies seem to have an uncanny ability to locate isolated patches of milkweeds. After the male and female monarchs mate, the females lay their eggs on the milkweed leaves.

During the cool spring weather, each monarch egg takes about one week to hatch into a tiny *larva* (caterpillar). The new caterpillar gorges itself on milkweed leaves for two to three weeks. While it is eating, the caterpillar is also accumulating poisons that will protect it and, later, the adult butterfly from birds. These poisons come from chemicals in milkweed leaves known as *cardiac glycosides*, which can cause birds to vomit. Monarch caterpillars, however, are able to

Life Cycle of a Monarch

The monarch butterfly's life cycle begins as a tiny, white egg, *below,* deposited on a milkweed plant by a female monarch. The caterpillar that emerges from the egg, *bottom* (right), multiplies its weight 3,000 times (left), as it feeds on the milkweed plant, *right.*

eat these poisons and store them in their tissues without suffering any harm themselves. The monarch retains these cardiac glycosides as it passes from the caterpillar to the adult butterfly stage. Birds that eat monarchs get sick because of the poisons and learn to avoid the monarch, which has a distinctive orange and black pattern on its wings. In fact, birds learn to avoid any butterfly with similar colors, such as the viceroy.

The caterpillar periodically stops eating in order to shed its skin. After the old skin is shed, the caterpillar can grow larger. After the caterpillar has done this four times over a period of two to three weeks, it has multiplied its birth weight 3,000 times. It then forms a *chrysalis* (hard shell), which hangs from a milkweed leaf or other vegetation. About one week later, the monarch emerges from the chrysalis as an adult butterfly. The first spring generation of monarchs is thus born. After a day or two, their soft new bodies harden, and males court and mate with the females. After mating, the females of this first spring generation likewise lay their eggs on milkweeds. This first generation lives for three or four weeks, the normal life span for adult butterflies, and a single female can lay about 500 eggs during that time. By the time they die, a new generation has been born.

When warm summer weather arrives, offspring develop more

The cycle continues when the caterpillar forms a chrysalis, *left,* inside which it is transformed into a butterfly, *below.* It emerges as an adult, *bottom,* after one week. The entire cycle—from egg to butterfly—takes about a month.

rapidly, though the life span of the adult remains the same. Therefore, as new generations of monarchs are born, their numbers increase to many millions. By midsummer, monarchs can be found throughout the continental United States and southern Canada. Monarchs have been found as far north as James Bay in Ontario, Canada, but most of the monarch population in Canada lives near the border with the United States.

The monarch's normal life cycle undergoes changes as summer draws to an end. The last generation of the summer—which emerges from the chrysalis between late August and early September—differs greatly from previous generations both in behavior and in physical makeup. This is the generation that will migrate south to the overwintering sites. These monarchs live up to nine months, unlike butterflies of the previous generations, and they do not begin mating after they emerge from the chrysalis. This change in behavior is related to the physical changes that the monarchs of this generation undergo. During this period, female monarchs do not develop the mature *ovaries* that are responsible for producing eggs. Also at this time, males do not develop the mature *sperm duct* that enables them to fertilize the female's eggs.

Since the early 1970's, when scientists first learned of these physical changes, they have been conducting experiments to see if some-

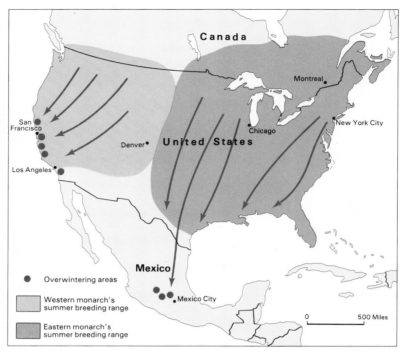

A butterfly, *above,* bears an adhesive tag asking that whoever finds the butterfly report its location to the scientist listed on the tag. Recaptured tagged butterflies helped scientists determine the monarch's two main migration routes, *right.* Monarchs that breed west of the Rockies migrate to overwintering sites along the California coast. Those that breed east of the Rockies journey mainly to sites near Mexico City.

thing in the butterfly's environment may trigger them. Zoologist William S. Herman of the University of Minnesota in Minneapolis-St. Paul placed monarchs in incubators where he could vary the temperature and light. By controlling the length of time that the lights in the incubator were on, Herman imitated the length of a late summer day. He also changed the temperature, gradually lowering it just as the average temperature of late summer days becomes lower. Herman placed adult butterflies, chrysalises, caterpillars, and eggs in the incubator at separate times to see which stage in the monarch's life cycle was sensitive to changes in daylength and temperature. His experiments suggested that either the egg or the caterpillar of this late-summer generation is sensitive to declining daylength. Declining daylength—signaling that summer is drawing to a close—apparently triggers changes in the egg or caterpillar that suppress the adult butterfly's *juvenile hormone,* the substance responsible for the development of the ovaries and sperm duct. As a result, the adult butterfly that emerges from the chrysalis in late summer does not have the mature reproductive organs necessary for mating and reproducing. So the butterfly will not develop mature reproductive organs and reproduce until the spring, when days again grow longer.

Although the monarchs of late summer do not mate and reproduce, they become extremely social. As they begin their migration, they spend much of their time feeding together upon nectar from

the abundance of fall flowers. They alternate these feeding bouts with periods of flying and soaring on wind currents as they move southward. By mid-September, the migration is well underway.

As the monarchs approach the overwintering sites, they spend more and more time eating, an activity that is crucial to their survival. An organ in the butterfly's abdomen converts the sugar in flower nectar to fats. When monarchs hatch from the chrysalis, about 14 per cent of their body weight consists of stored fats that provide energy as the need arises. During the fall migration, the monarchs increase their fat content to 42 per cent of their body weight. Because there are no sources of nectar at the overwintering sites in Mexico, all of the butterflies' activities for nearly five months depend upon these energy reserves. Monarchs that arrive with insufficient fat reserves starve to death.

One of the mysteries that fascinates zoologists is how the migrating monarchs find their way to the overwintering sites. The monarchs that migrate south in the fall are several generations removed from their ancestors who migrated north in the spring. Thus, their southward migration cannot be the result of learned behavior, as seems to be the case with most birds that migrate in groups. Instead, the monarch migration must be the result of an inherited behavior pattern. Somehow, the monarch's pinhead-sized brain manages to guide its flight over a course of thousands of miles to a precise location that it has never before visited.

In November, monarchs arrive by the hundreds of thousands at their overwintering colonies in the mountains of central Mexico. By the end of the migration, hundreds of millions of monarchs will have arrived. Ever since the discovery of these colonies in 1975, scientists have been studying the winter survival behavior of the monarch.

The Monarch in Winter

During the overwintering period, monarchs cling to the branches of fir trees in such dense numbers that the trees appear to change color.

During the dry season toward winter's end, monarchs replenish lost moisture by flying off to drink water along the edges of streams.

On cool days, monarchs must bask in the sun to raise their body temperature to the point where they are able to fly.

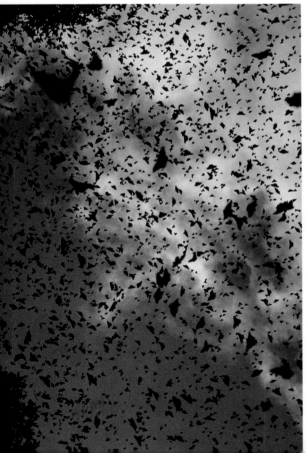

Scientists have proposed a number of theories to explain this phenomenon, but none has been proven. One theory maintains that the butterflies migrate by using the sun as a guide while adjusting their course as the sun moves across the sky. Using an "inner clock," the monarch maintains a southwesterly direction by periodically adjusting the angle of its flight to coordinate with the sun's movement. Many scientists have also proposed this theory to explain bird migration. Still other scientists theorize that the monarch could keep on a southwesterly course—the general direction to the overwintering sites—simply by following the sun during the hours of the day when the sun is in the southern sky. Another and possibly more promising theory is that the monarchs orient to Earth's magnetic field. In 1982, scientists discovered magnetic material in the monarch's head and *thorax* (the middle section of a butterfly's body between the head and abdomen), suggesting that the monarch is sensitive to Earth's magnetic field. In the same year, scientists also discovered an unusually strong magnetic field at the Mexican overwintering area. This suggested that magnetism could play a significant role in guiding the migrating monarchs to the isolated area in Mexico. But this theory, like the others, remains mere speculation.

Scientists have a better understanding of why the California and Mexico sites provide ideal conditions for the wintering monarchs. Both areas have relatively cool and moist climates where temperatures rarely dip below the freezing mark of 32°F. If the butterflies wintered in a dry, hot region, they would lose moisture and have to fly about in search of water. This expenditure of energy could cause them to use up the fat reserves needed to survive the long winter and still make the return migration in the spring. The foggy seaside groves of California and the mountainous Mexican sites, however, stay relatively cool and moist, enabling the monarchs to remain largely inactive, thereby conserving their fat reserves.

Clouds blocking light and warmth from the sun prompt monarchs to take flight, an apparently instinctive reaction that may protect them from frost.

21

Birds quickly learn that monarchs taste terrible and thus leave them alone. A blue jay that eats a monarch, *top,* soon becomes ill, *above.* This chemical defense is due to poisons the butterfly acquired during its caterpillar stage from eating the milkweed plant.

Ever since I first saw the millions of monarchs in the Sierra Chincua in 1977, my colleagues and I have been studying the monarch's behavior at the Mexico sites. These sites are at least 11,500 feet above sea level. Because of the high altitude, these mountains are colder than their tropical surroundings and are covered with dense evergreen forests of the Oyamel fir. In fact, these forests resemble fir tree forests in Canada.

Our studies have shown that the delicately balanced weather conditions in the Oyamel forests are a critical factor in enabling the butterflies to survive the nearly six-month-long overwintering period—from November to April. The forests must be cold enough for the butterflies to remain largely inactive, but they must be warm enough to prevent the butterflies from freezing. We have found that temperatures at the overwintering sites are usually just right for the monarchs, ranging from just above freezing to 60°F., though subfreezing temperatures and snow sometimes occur.

During the summer rainy season, which lasts from May to October, rain and hailstorms deluge the forests, which are covered by clouds most of the time. By October, the dry season has begun. Many brilliantly sunny days gradually dry out the forest, though it never becomes too dry.

The arrival of the monarch butterflies begins in November, when wave after wave of migrants appear. The early arrivals settle on the branches of the firs along the top of mountain ridges and attract others to them. At the peak of the migration into the area, my colleagues have observed what appears to be an actual arrival ceremony. Huge clouds of butterflies swirl above the mountains several times a day, as if to signal their location to butterflies that are still arriving.

As the days pass and the migration appears to be completed, the monarchs move down from the mountain ridges into protected valleys along the southwestern side of the Sierra Chincua. Gradually, millions of butterflies cover the trunks and branches of the fir trees. By mid-December, densely packed colonies have formed. We know of about 30 colonies, ranging in size from less than 1 acre to more than 8 acres. We estimate that the largest colonies contain about 30 million monarchs. In comparison, the largest colonies in California consist of only about 120,000 butterflies. By the end of December, all of the butterflies have clustered into the various colonies. Their total population in Mexico, according to our estimates, ranges from 100 million to 500 million.

Monarch activity at the overwintering sites centers around the butterfly's need for water and warmth. As the dry season progresses, there is less moisture in the air. Dry winds rob the butterflies of moisture, and as they gradually dry out, they must fly off to locate a source of water, usually a small stream. Before a monarch can fly, however, its body temperature must be warm enough. The muscles responsible for flight cannot move if they are too cold. The butterfly is an *ambient* creature—that is, its body temperature is determined by the surrounding air, unlike the fixed, constant body temperature of a healthy human being. If the air temperature is below 55°F., as often happens during the dry season, the butterflies must raise their body temperature by basking in the sun before they can fly. Once warmed, they fly distances of up to a mile to drink along streams. As the dry season advances and the days become warmer, increasingly greater numbers of butterflies take flight to the local watering holes.

The wintering monarchs must be careful to avoid exposure to frost. On cool, clear nights, frost often forms on both the upper portions of the fir trees that are exposed to chilly winds and the surface of the ground in open treeless areas. The forest canopy, however, traps heat and reduces heat loss so frost seldom forms on the lower branches of the fir trees. If butterflies that have been out in the open fail to return to the blanketing protection provided by the forest, dew will condense and freeze on their bodies. Ice crystals will invade their tissues and destroy their internal cells, killing or permanently damaging them.

Monarchs have evolved an instinctive behavior that reduces the danger of their being trapped in the open. We first discovered this while watching them drink water on a partly cloudy day. When a cloud blew across the sky and obscured the sun, all the butterflies immediately took to the air and headed back to the colony. By using a *thermistor probe*, a tiny needlelike device that measures temperature, we were able to find out how these clouds affect the butterflies' body temperature. We inserted thermistor probes into the abdomens of captured butterflies and found that within four minutes of being in the shade, their body temperatures dropped below 55°F.

Scientists conduct experiments on monarchs in the laboratory and in the field. In a laboratory test, a scientist, *below right,* prepares a monarch for analysis of the chemicals that make birds ill. At an overwintering colony in Mexico, two researchers, *below left,* use a device called a thermistor probe to check a butterfly's body temperature.

Occasional winter storms in the mountains of central Mexico can be devastating to monarchs, knocking them to the ground and causing many to freeze to death. In 1981, a severe storm killed about 2½ million butterflies.

So on cold days when clouds block sunlight, butterflies have less than four minutes before their body temperature drops too low to permit flight. Consequently, the farthest that monarchs can safely fly from their colonies during these cool periods is limited to the distance they can cover in four minutes, or about 1 mile.

This instinctive behavior seems to occur whenever clouds darken the skies overhead—often for no apparent reason, such as when butterflies are basking on branches in the evergreen forest. As a cloud passes over, so many monarchs fly up into the air that they nearly blacken the sky. As they hover, they produce a sound like that of gently falling rain. Then, in three to four minutes, they settle back down into the clusters. As you watch from the vantage point of a cliff overlooking the colony, it appears that a golden mist of monarchs rises out of the forest and then settles mysteriously back into it.

The monarchs cannot avoid every danger, however. The storms that occur in the overwintering area are a mixed blessing for the monarchs. Although the precipitation helps to prevent the forest from drying out, the storms can be very damaging to the monarch colonies. In January 1981, for example, a strong cold front roared down from Canada and produced stormy weather at the overwintering sites in Mexico. Temperatures plunged to 23°F. and over a period of 12 days, gale-force winds, heavy rain, and snow knocked several million butterflies from the forest branches. Some 2½ million monarchs were either buried by the snow or left immobilized on the surface, where they froze to death.

During a visit to the overwintering areas, one of my students, James Anderson, tested the ability of monarchs to survive low temperatures. He placed monarchs in a special type of refrigerator that lowered the temperature slightly every minute. He found that a temperature of approximately 18°F. would kill about half of the wintering monarchs. A temperature of 5°F. would kill the entire colony. In contrast, other butterflies, such as the mourning cloak, which spends the winter hibernating inside hollow tree trunks as far north as Canada, can survive temperatures lower than −22°F.

By late February, as spring arrives and the days in Mexico grow longer, the butterflies become more active, flying to water and sucking nectar from the millions of fresh spring flowers. By the end of March or the first few days in April, the great exodus begins—the monarch's return migration to the United States and Canada. Wave upon wave of monarchs fly out of the valleys and head northward. The departure is spectacular. By the end of the first week in April, only a single monarch may remain where a week before there had been millions. Having survived for about six months, the monarchs now fly northeast across the great Sierra Madre Oriental mountain range of Mexico and enter the United States.

Scientists still do not completely understand how the spring mi-

Some birds appear to be unaffected by the monarch's poisons. Two species—the black-headed grosbeak, center, and the black-backed oriole, top—eat at will as the monarchs cling to fir trees, immobilized by the cold. Each winter, such birds kill more than 1 million monarchs.

gration is accomplished. We know that the monarchs do not fly in large groups, as they do during the fall migration. But it is unclear whether the generation that migrated and overwintered in Mexico flies all the way back to their summer breeding range. Butterflies tagged at the overwintering colonies in Mexico have been found as far north as North Dakota and New York. But most evidence suggests that the return migration largely ends in the South, in the row of states that stretch from Texas to Florida. There, the overwintering monarchs, whose reproductive systems are now functioning, breed and die out, leaving the next generation to continue the journey northward. By June, all of the overwintering monarchs have died, having completed one of the most remarkable cycles in the annals of life. Succeeding generations then appear to continue flying in a generally northern direction as the days continue to lengthen and milkweed plants sprout in the Northern states. By summer, monarchs once again can be seen over most of North America.

To understand better how the monarchs complete their return migration, my colleagues and I have been trying to refine a new technique that will provide more extensive evidence than has the recapturing of tagged butterflies. Relying on tagged butterflies to map the return migration has involved an immense amount of work with little to show for it. Of the several hundred thousand butterflies that scientists have tagged in Mexico, only about 20 have been recaptured in North America. Our new technique involves the study of the cardiac glycosides found in both milkweed plants and monarch butterflies.

Along with chemists James N. Seiber of the University of California at Davis, Carolyn Nelson of the University of Sydney in Australia, and our students, I have investigated the chemistry of cardiac glycosides in monarch butterflies since the mid-1970's. We have found that most species of milkweed plants have slightly differing types of cardiac glycosides. Because each monarch stores the glycosides of the milkweed plant that it ate as a caterpillar, the adult

"Protect the butterfly," reads a sign in Spanish at an overwintering site in Mexico, reminding visitors that the fate of the monarch is ultimately in human hands.

The gravest threat to the monarch comes from human activities. Logging near the overwintering sites threatens to thin out the forests, exposing the butterfly colonies to cold and dry winds.

butterfly ends up carrying a cardiac glycoside "fingerprint." By studying the types of glycosides in each monarch, we can tell what milkweed species the butterfly ate. Because the various milkweed species sprout and mature at different times and grow in different geographic areas, we can also examine these "fingerprints" from a sample of monarchs and tell where most of the butterflies originated. We hope this technique will help us determine whether the first monarchs arriving in the Northern states in the spring migrated there directly from Mexico or are offspring of the butterflies that overwintered in Mexico. If they are offspring of the overwintering butterflies, for example, their "fingerprints" should indicate that they were born in the South in the early spring.

The life history of the monarch butterfly is thrilling to people of all ages. Because of its complexity, the monarch harbors secrets that when unlocked will probably expand our basic biological knowledge. For example, how the monarch manages to find its overwintering sites is a mystery that once solved may tell us much about animal navigation. And understanding how it can store poisons in its body without harming itself may one day provide medical benefits for humankind.

These and the sheer beauty of its migration are reasons enough why the conservation of this remarkable creature is so important. The monarch is not considered an endangered species because its numbers are so great. Its migration and overwintering behavior, however, is a phenomenon that is definitely threatened by human activities. Because the monarchs gather in such great numbers in relatively concentrated areas, they are particularly vulnerable to any human or natural forces that threaten these habitats. In view of this, conservation groups, such as the World Wildlife Fund, have created a special category for the monarch—Endangered Phenomenon—in recognition of the monarch's unique migration.

One very subtle effect that humanity has had on the overwintering monarchs in Mexico is the weakening of the monarch's chemical defense against birds. Extensive cultivation of land for farming and the use of *herbicides* (weedkillers) in the United States and Canada have killed off wild flowers and altered the balance of milkweed species east of the Rocky Mountains. Many milkweed species have been destroyed, greatly increasing the numbers of a species known as the *common milkweed*. The common milkweed contains cardiac glycosides that are much less toxic than those that occur in other species of the milkweed family. Our studies at the overwintering sites strongly suggest that two species of birds in Mexico—black-backed orioles and black-headed grosbeaks—have partially broken through the monarchs' now-weakened chemical defense. The grosbeaks appear mostly unaffected by the poisons, while the orioles eat parts of the monarch's body that contain the least amount of poisons. These birds kill more than 1 million butterflies each winter.

The most immediate threat to the monarch migration, however, is logging near the monarch colonies in Mexico. Logging thins out the forests, exposing the butterflies to cold and dry winds and to more sunlight. Sunlight and dry conditions make them more active and cause them to use up their fat reserves, while the cold increases their risk of freezing. In California, many overwintering areas—including one of the most famous sites in Pacific Grove—have been destroyed by real estate development, and many others face the threat of destruction. Fortunately, several California sites are located in state parks and so fall under the protection of the state government. In Mexico, the fir forests that harbor the overwintering monarchs are few and fragile. A Mexican conservation group, Monarcha, is working to preserve the fir forests. But it is also urgent for the Mexican government to take steps to prevent further logging near the monarch colonies.

Unless such action is taken, we may very soon—possibly in the next 20 years—lose one of the most spectacular biological wonders on our planet.

For further reading:

Brewer, Jo. "A Visit with 200 Million Monarchs." *Defenders*, Summer 1982.

Brower, Lincoln P. "Monarch Migration." *Natural History*, June/July 1977.

Menzel, Peter. "Butterfly Armies Are Now Under Guard in Annual Bivouac." *Smithsonian*, November 1983.

Pyle, Robert Michael. "Migratory Monarchs: An Endangered Phenomenon." *The Nature Conservancy News*, September/October 1983.

Urquhart, Fred A. "Found at Last: The Monarch's Winter Home." *National Geographic*, August 1976.

BY EDUARDO MATOS MOCTEZUMA

The Great Temple
of the Aztecs

The excavation of the Great Temple of the ancient
Aztecs in Mexico City is leading to a better
understanding of the Aztec people and their culture.

A human skull pierced with a stone knife was one of many skulls found buried in the Great Temple of the Aztecs during a five-year excavation project near Mexico City's main plaza. The ruins of the temple, with metal roofs protecting the more fragile sections, are now open to the public.

At exactly 7:18 A.M. on Sept. 19, 1985, as I sat in the bedroom of my Mexico City house watching the news on television, everything around me began to shake violently. The same thing was obviously happening at the TV studio—the image on the screen was swaying crazily from the movement of the camera. The alarmed newscaster said, "It's an earthquake—but please stay calm." Then the screen went blank as the tremors knocked out the city's electricity.

The earthquake was the first of two that rocked the city on September 19 and 20. When it was over, as I was saddened to learn, thousands of people were dead or injured and some 250 buildings in downtown Mexico City lay in ruins. But in the first moments after the quake had subsided, one of my greatest concerns was the condition of the Great Temple of the Aztecs next to the city's central plaza. The temple had been the major religious center of the Aztec people. Most of the structure was torn down by the conquering Spaniards in 1521, but its remains had recently been excavated, a task that I directed. I feared that the temple had now been destroyed for a second time, this time by nature. Anxious to see if the historic remains had been damaged, I drove through rubble-strewn streets to the center of the city. When I reached the temple grounds, I was relieved to see that, aside from a few cracks in the walls and floors, the structure was unscathed. Our five-year project of excavation and restoration had not been a wasted effort.

That project got its start on the morning of Feb. 21, 1978. In the predawn hours, electrical workers were digging a ditch near Constitution Plaza—or the Zócalo, as most Mexicans call it. Suddenly, the diggers struck an expanse of carved stone 6 feet below street level. As soon as it received word of the discovery, the National Institute of Anthropology and History, the major institution for the study of Mexico's early civilizations, sent a team of archaeologists to the site. Under the scientists' supervision, workers continued to clear the dirt away from the stone, and within a week it lay exposed to view. The object was a huge stone disk 11 feet in diameter and 12 inches thick. It was sculpted with the image of a partially nude woman whose head, arms, and legs had been separated from her body. The archaeologists recognized the sculpture as a likeness of an Aztec moon goddess named Coyolxauhqui (*koh yohl SHAU kee*), sister of the Aztecs' most important deity, the war god Huitzilopochtli (*weet see loh POHCH tlee*). In Aztec mythology, Huitzilopochtli defeated his sister in a long-ago battle for possession of the sacred mountain where the war god was born. He then tore her limb from limb and threw the pieces of her corpse to the foot of the mountain.

There was little doubt that the stone disk had been a part of the Great Temple of the Aztecs. The temple, as archaeologists had long known from Spanish chronicles of the 1500's, had been dedicated to Huitzilopochtli and to another important Aztec deity, Tláloc (*TLAH lok*), the god of rain and agriculture. And the disk was found within an area that small-scale excavations earlier in the 1900's had shown to be the former boundaries of the temple complex.

The author:
Eduardo Matos Moctezuma is general director of the Center for Investigations and Advanced Studies in Social Anthropology in Tlalpan, Mexico.

The discovery of the disk stimulated renewed interest in the Great Temple. The Mexican government quickly authorized a full-scale excavation of the buried remnants of the structure by archaeologists of the National Institute of Anthropology and History, and I was named director of the project. Before starting the dig, my colleagues at the institute and I studied all the known historical and archaeological records relating to the Great Temple. Guided by this information, we were able to devise a plan for the systematic unearthing of the temple ruins. The excavation began in March 1978 and was completed in November 1982. The final phase of the project, which is still in progress, consists of studying the remains of the temple and the thousands of *artifacts* (handcrafted articles) and other objects we found there. This continuing part of our investigation is shedding new light on the Aztecs and their culture.

The Aztecs were the last in a series of great Indian civilizations that flourished in Mexico and northern Central America from about 1000 B.C. through the time of the Spanish conquest. These civilizations had much in common with one another. They shared many cultural traditions, and they worshiped many of the same gods. Those gods included Tláloc; Quetzalcóatl (*ket sal ko AH tl*), the god of learning and civilization, who was often represented as a feathered serpent; and dozens of others. Indian culture in Mexico reached a high point from A.D. 250 to 900—a time known as the Classic Period—when the civilizations of the Maya, mainly in Central America, and the Zapotec in southern Mexico were in flower. The end of the Classic Period saw the rise of several new warlike nations—the Mixtecs, the Toltecs, and, finally, the Aztecs.

The Aztecs originated in northern Mexico in a place they called

An archaeologist clears dirt from the details of a mammoth stone disk found beneath the streets of Mexico City in 1978. The discovery of the almost perfectly preserved disk encouraged archaeologists to launch the Great Temple excavation project. The disk represents an Aztec moon goddess who, according to myth, was slain and dismembered by her brother, the war god Huitzilopochtli.

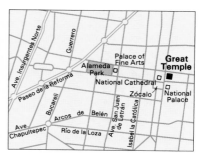

The Aztecs once ruled over a large area of central Mexico, *above left.* After the Aztecs were conquered by the Spanish in 1521, Mexico City was built on the ruins of the Aztec capital, Tenochtitlán. The remains of the Great Temple of the Aztecs were discovered in the central part of Mexico City, *above, center and right,* close to the National Palace and the National Cathedral.

Aztlan, from which they got their name. The Aztecs worshiped the ancient gods, but they paid greatest reverence to Huitzilopochtli, an ancestral hero who was their special guardian. The Aztec belief in the war god probably stemmed from a dim tribal memory of an actual person and an actual event—most likely a mighty warrior who defeated his sister in a power struggle. If so, that individual's exploits were recounted and magnified by generations of storytellers and priests, who finally transformed Huitzilopochtli into a powerful god mystically associated with the sun.

Aztec legends relate that Huitzilopochtli told his chosen people to leave Aztlan and find a new home. Why the Aztecs really left their original homeland is unclear, but we know that they wandered for many years before settling in the high Valley of Mexico sometime in the 1200's. A lowly and despised people at that time, the Aztecs were forced to submit to the will of powerful Indian groups who controlled the valley. But that soon changed as the Aztecs organized themselves and began to fight for supremacy of the area. After a decisive war in 1427, the Aztecs controlled most of the valley, and by 1450 they were masters of nearly all central Mexico.

The Aztecs ruled their new empire from the city of Tenochtitlán (*tay nohch TEE tlahn*), which they had founded in the mid-1300's. Judging from descriptions made by the Spanish conquerers, Tenochtitlán was a dazzling sight. Constructed on an island in shallow, salty Lake Texcoco (*tesh KOH koh*), it was a metropolis of colorful temples, plazas, municipal buildings, and private homes. The population of Tenochtitlán may have been more than 250,000, larger than that of any European city of the time. The centerpiece of the capital, towering 200 feet into the air, was the Great Temple. This impressive pyramid was topped by dual shrines—one dedicated to Tláloc, the other to Huitzilopochtli, the Aztecs' principal gods.

To modern eyes, the Aztec religion, with its multitude of gods and emphasis on human sacrifice, was a thing of horror. The Aztec priests periodically drowned children as an offering to the rain god, cut off women's heads to appease goddesses within the earth, and burned people alive to gain the favor of the god of fire. But it was to the god of war that the greatest number of victims were sacrificed. Aztec sources relate that when the Great Temple was rededi-

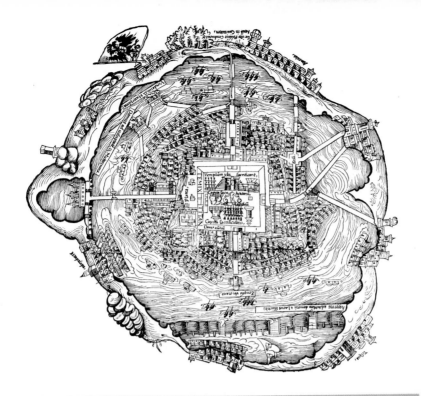

A map published in 1524, *left,* shows Tenochtitlán with the Great Temple at the center. The conquered Aztecs made many drawings of their vanished culture and their gods. In a drawing of a sacrifice to the war god Huitzilopochtli, *below left,* a priest cuts out a victim's heart. A drawing made before the conquest pictures Huitzilopochtli, *bottom,* as a warrior in feathered armor. A representation of the rain god Tláloc, *below,* shows the god producing a gushing stream of water.

52.

A Coronation in Tenochtitlán

As priests, nobles, and the people of Tenochtitlán look on, the newly crowned Montezuma II, the last Aztec emperor of pre-Spanish Mexico, is carried to the Great Temple where he will offer drops of his blood. The temple, topped by shrines dedicated to the gods Tláloc and Huitzilopochtli, was the main religious center of the Aztec capital. Throughout the year, the temple priests offered human sacrifices to the gods and displayed victims' skulls on a huge rack, at left center. Today, nothing remains of the upper part of the temple, which was destroyed after the conquering Spaniards crushed the Aztec empire in 1521.

cated in 1487, at least 20,000 people were slain in front of the Hui-tzilopochtli sanctuary in just four days. In other years, the number of people sacrificed to the war god was smaller, but the ritual seldom varied. Each victim was seized by four priests at the top of the pyramid and stretched, face up, across a small carved slab of volcanic rock. With a sharp stone knife, a fifth priest cut out the person's heart and placed it, still throbbing with life, into a sacred fire. The priests then threw the torn body down the temple steps. Later, the victims' skulls were displayed on a huge rack next to the temple.

Many of the people sacrificed to Huitzilopochtli were slaves, but prisoners of war were the most prized offerings. The Aztecs often engaged neighboring Indian groups in ceremonial combat called *flowery wars*, in which the primary objective was to take captives. Such prisoners never had any doubt about what end awaited them.

As repulsive as these religious practices may seem to us, we must understand that the Aztecs were not motivated by hatred or cruelty. The Indians of Mexico had a much different view of the world than we do. To them, the world was an unstable place that could come to an end at any time if the gods became displeased. The Aztecs thought of human life as the greatest gift they could offer to the gods, and they showed a strange mixture of respect and affection toward their sacrificial victims. Moreover, because death on the altar was considered a sure path to the realm of the sun—the Aztec equivalent of heaven—many of the condemned went willingly to their fate.

The gods not only preserved the world but also maintained the Aztecs' position of power within it. Because the Aztecs considered themselves so utterly dependent on the gods, people at every level of society were required to take part in the innumerable religious ceremonies that were held at specific times of the year or in connection with important events. Members of the ruling class, especially, were expected to publicly demonstrate their devotion to the gods. Immediately after his coronation, for example, a new emperor was carried in a spectacular procession to the Great Temple, where he offered drops of his blood to Huitzilopochtli.

In 1502, the newly crowned Montezuma II, the last ruler of pre-Spanish Mexico, took part in this ceremony. As he was borne on his throne to the temple by richly clad nobles and military officials, Montezuma (also spelled *Moctezuma* or *Motecuhzoma*) must have felt that the gods were smiling on the Aztec empire. That empire, however, was brought to its knees just 19 years later by a few hundred Spanish soldiers commanded by Hernando Cortés and aided by Indian enemies of the Aztecs. The Spanish conquerers leveled all the buildings in Tenochtitlán and built a new city on the ruins. Within a couple of generations, the glories of the Aztec capital, including the Great Temple, were almost totally forgotten. But not everything had been destroyed. Remnants of the Aztec past lay buried for cen-

Workers use shovels to clear dirt and rubble away from the temple ruins. The canopy protects temple walls that could be damaged by rain and sunlight. In the background is the National Cathedral, a landmark of Mexico City's main plaza, the Zócalo.

turies beneath the streets and plazas of Mexico City, waiting to be rediscovered by archaeologists—or, as in 1978, ditchdiggers.

Our effort to bring the Great Temple back into the light of day was one of the most ambitious archaeological projects ever undertaken in Mexico. It was complicated by the fact that the excavation site was in one of the oldest and busiest parts of Mexico City, an area that includes the National Palace and the National Cathedral. Before proceeding, we had to analyze the buildings that stood on the dig site to make sure that we would not demolish any structures from the Spanish colonial period. Only 2 of the 13 buildings we eventually removed were found to be of colonial origin. We photographed those two buildings and then painstakingly took them apart, numbering each piece as we removed it. The disassembled buildings were sent to Mexico's National Bureau of Monuments, which may someday reconstruct them at another location.

The next step was to mark the site with a gridwork of ropes, dividing the work area into squares 2 meters on a side. We identified each square with a letter and a number. We also set up a marker, corresponding to street level, from which depth measurements could be made. This system, a standard method used at most archaeological sites, enabled us to record the exact location of every artifact and temple part we unearthed.

Once we started digging in earnest, we created quite a mess in the area around the plaza. Frequent traffic jams caused by the closing of two streets led to loud protests from many drivers and shopkeepers. Despite such criticism, however, the government stood firmly behind the project, and the excavation continued without interruption. Each day, some 100 workers, under the supervision of 10 archaeologists, swarmed over the site, carefully removing earth from the ruins and searching for artifacts. The work continued year-round for almost five years. Finally, in late 1982, the remains of the temple were fully revealed.

The excavation showed that the Aztecs repeatedly enlarged the temple over a span of more than 100 years. We were not surprised by this finding. Aztec historical records tell us that rulers often tried to surpass the achievements of their predecessors, while preserving a sense of the past, by building new temples atop existing ones. Archaeologists have discovered temples in other parts of Mexico that were constructed in just this way, like a series of progressively larger boxes fitted one over the other. Each level, or layer of construction, of such a temple is therefore not only taller, but also wider, than the one beneath it. The builders filled in the spaces between the various levels with dirt and rubble.

In Tenochtitlán, the custom of erecting new structures over older ones was also a practical necessity. The island the city was built on was marshy and subject to flooding, so heavy buildings such as the Great Temple slowly sank into the ground. (Present-day Mexico City, much of which sits on the drained bed of Lake Texcoco, is still plagued with the problem of sinking buildings.) We now know that the temple was enlarged at least seven times on all four sides and

An archaeologist makes notes in one of the best-preserved parts of the temple, dating from A.D. 1390—the earliest level that could be excavated. The painted sculpture, situated outside the shrine of Tláloc, is a *chacmool,* a messenger who carries offerings to the god.

The shrine of Tláloc in the 1390 level of the temple, *left,* still has some of its original colors. Many objects found in the dig represent Tláloc. Others represent water, such as a huge sculpted sea shell, *above,* symbolizing the waters of the ocean.

four other times on just the main facade. The temple seen by the Spanish was thus actually a shell enclosing about 10 layers of construction from earlier periods.

The marshy soil of Tenochtitlán was a problem for the Aztecs but a boon for archaeologists. Older, smaller levels of the Great Temple had settled as much as 20 feet into the ground by the time of the Spanish conquest and so escaped total destruction. We found that the first two temple levels were almost completely intact, though the earlier of the two—the original temple—was submerged beneath ground water and could not be excavated. Large outer sections of more recent versions also remained, but their upper structures were gone. The outermost level—the final stage of construction—which was entirely aboveground in 1521, was demolished by Cortés down to the last stone. Of that level, nothing was left except traces of the foundation.

The second version of the temple, the oldest level that we were able to excavate, contains a stairway bearing a carved Aztec inscription that translates as "2 Rabbit." This is a date in the Aztec calendar corresponding approximately to the year 1390. We concluded from this finding that the second version of the temple was completed about 1390 and that the original temple—the level now underwater—was built sometime before that date.

In the 2-Rabbit level of the temple, we found two sanctuaries, side by side, in remarkably good condition. Outside the sanctuary on the right, we discovered a sacrificial stone set into the floor. The stone had almost certainly been used for sacrifices to Huitzilopochtli. Outside the sanctuary on the left, we found a painted statue of a reclining figure known as a *chacmool*—a divine messenger who carries human offerings to Tláloc. These findings confirmed that even the earliest temple levels were dedicated to the gods of war and rain.

The next level of the temple contains an inscription that means "4 Reed," a date corresponding to the year 1431. We think the Aztecs enlarged the temple at that time to celebrate their decisive victory in 1427 that gave them control over central Mexico. The triumphant Aztecs probably forced people under their rule to build this and later versions of the temple.

Some of the temple's most impressive decorative elements are part of the next version of the temple, a level inscribed with the date "1 Rabbit" (1454). This date fell within the reign of Montezuma I, the great-grandfather of Montezuma II. The remains of this temple include a platform ornamented on all four sides with *braziers* (containers for burning charcoal) and serpent heads, all carved from stone. The braziers on the Tláloc side of the temple are sculpted with the rain god's face; those on the Huitzilopochtli side are carved with a knot, a symbol of the war god. The next emperor made a number of additions to Montezuma I's temple. These included a small altar with a pair of stone frogs and two large stone sculptures of wriggling snakes. Images of frogs and snakes were associated by the Aztecs with the two gods.

The enormous stone disk of the moon goddess Coyolxauhqui that was uncovered in 1978 is also a part of this level, another probable addition by Montezuma I's successor. The disk was set into the floor

The subtle colors and textures of alabaster, a stone similar to marble, give a warm look to the carved sculpture of a deity—an unidentified goddess thought to be associated with water and the earth. The figure was placed in the temple by the Aztecs as an offering to Tláloc.

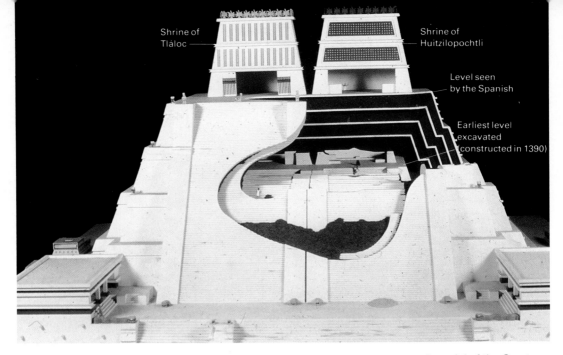

Shrine of Tláloc

Shrine of Huitzilopochtli

Level seen by the Spanish

Earliest level excavated (constructed in 1390)

A model of the Great Temple shows how the Aztecs repeatedly enlarged it over a period of many years. The outer temple walls—the level seen by the Spanish conquerors—enclosed about 10 other layers of construction. The structure at the center of the model represents the 1390 level of the temple. There is at least one other level below the 1390 level, but it is submerged in ground water and could not be excavated.

at the base of a stairway leading to Huitzilopochtli's shrine. The shrine is gone, but the bottom of the stairway remains, with the disk in its original position. The Aztecs completed the next version of the temple in 1487, a labor they commemorated with the mass sacrifices at the rededication ceremony. During the construction of that level, the Coyolxauhqui stone was covered with earth and masonry along with everything else as the Aztecs filled in the space between the old and new walls. A new stone disk was most likely made for the enlarged temple, but it has been lost—presumably destroyed by the Spanish.

After 1487, the temple was altered twice more, reaching its final dimensions during the reign of Montezuma II. From what we can tell, though, these last two additions did not greatly change the size of the structure. Part of a stairway and a wall decorated with three serpent heads are all that are left of the earlier of these two temples. And of course, virtually nothing remains of the final temple.

During the course of our excavation, we uncovered more than 7,000 objects that the Aztecs had offered to Tláloc and Huitzilopochtli during periods of temple construction. The items ranged from human skulls to finely modeled statues and figurines. Some objects were placed in special offering boxes or chambers, while others were simply tossed onto the dirt and broken rocks used to fill the spaces between walls.

Most of the offerings we recovered were images of Tláloc or symbols that the Aztecs associated with the rain god, water, or fertility. These included many handmade articles, such as stone or ceramic pots bearing Tláloc's likeness, and a variety of natural objects. Among the latter were sea shells, coral, and the bones of fish, birds,

The sacrificial stone knife, *above,* was one of many such offerings to Huitzilopochtli found buried in the temple ruins. A deity of carved alabaster, *above right,* was probably associated with the god Tláloc. The polished stone receptacle atop the figure may have been intended for offerings such as bits of grain or turquoise—symbols of agriculture and water.

turtles, and snakes, even jaguars and crocodiles. There was also an offering box containing the bones of several dozen children sacrificed to the rain god.

We found no images of Huitzilopochtli among the offerings, but many objects were symbolic of the war god. For example, we unearthed a number of ceremonial knives similar to those used for sacrifices. We often found these knives embedded in human skulls, undoubtedly the remains of sacrificial victims.

Many of the offerings were meant to convey deeper symbolic meanings, which we are still trying to decipher. For one thing, the Aztecs apparently felt that the placement of objects in an offering box was as important as the objects themselves. We found, for instance, two offering boxes containing sea shells, crocodile remains, and representations of Tláloc and a fire god. In each case, the sea shells were placed at the bottom, the crocodiles in the middle, and the gods on top. This arrangement may have symbolized the mystical levels of creation.

A number of stone artifacts found in the temple, including more than 300 masks, had been sent to Tenochtitlán by peoples living under Aztec rule. We are trying to determine the areas these objects came from to establish more precisely the boundaries of the Aztec empire. We are also studying the bones of the children sacrificed to Tláloc. We hope to learn exactly how the children were killed. That information would increase our knowledge of the sacrificial rituals associated with the rain god.

From our study of the temple and its contents, we learned that the temple was more than just an imposing structure for worship and sacrifice. It was also a highly symbolic structure that embodied historical myths and expressed the Aztecs' awe of the forces of nature. We discovered that the temple represented the joining of two mountains: the mountain birthplace of Huitzilopochtli and the mountain (or mountains) from which rain clouds descended into the Valley of Mexico.

Part of this symbolism became clear when we excavated the area around the Coyolxauhqui disk and found that the disk was positioned at the foot of the Huitzilopochtli stairway. This discovery made it quite plain that the Huitzilopochtli side of the temple pyramid represented the mythical mountain where the war god defeated his sister. The stone sculpture of her dismembered body at the base of the pyramid commemorated that dramatic episode. We now think the sacrificial ritual, in which the victim's body was thrown to the bottom of the pyramid, was a symbolic reenactment of the moon goddess's violent death.

Our conclusion that the Tláloc side of the pyramid also represented a mountain was based on different kinds of evidence, including excavations at other Aztec sites. For example, archaeologists have found Aztec temples dedicated to Tláloc in the mountains east of Tenochtitlán. The highland setting of the temples illustrates the Aztecs' reverence for the mountains as places where rain clouds form. It was only natural, therefore, that they built their own "water mountain" in the city to honor the rain god.

We can thus interpret the Great Temple as both a mirror of history and a mirror of nature. The war god's side of the temple commemorated the beginnings of Aztec history and the migration that eventually led to the founding of Tenochtitlán. The rain god's half of the temple paid homage to the aspects of nature that the Aztecs held most sacred: the gift of water and the continual regeneration of living things.

We cannot ignore the fact that the Great Temple was a place of terrible suffering. As our excavation has shown us, however, the Aztecs were not bloodthirsty savages whose only joy was killing. Like their temple, the Aztecs had a dual character. They did kill, yes. But they were also the civilized heirs of a complex and sophisticated system of beliefs dating back at least 2,500 years. In that religious system, humanity was seen as a part of the larger, living organism of the natural world, a world that could be preserved only through constant human effort. This revised, and more sympathetic, view of Aztec culture is the most important result of the Great Temple excavation project. Perhaps future excavations will shed still more light on the Aztecs and their civilization.

For further reading:

Matos Moctezuma, Eduardo. "New Finds in the Great Temple." *National Geographic*, December 1980. "The Great Temple of Tenochtitlán." *Scientific American*, August 1984.

McDowell, Bart. "The Aztecs." *National Geographic*, December 1980.

Nicholson, H. B. "Revelation of the Great Temple." *Natural History*, July 1982.

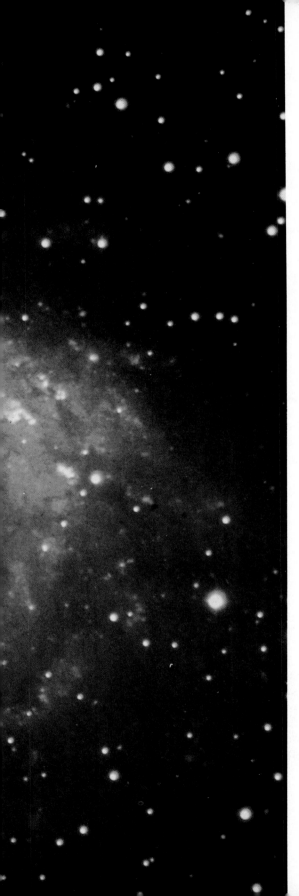

Astronomers are unraveling
many mysteries surrounding the
collections of stars called galaxies.

Galaxies–
Islands in
the Universe

BY ALAN DRESSLER

We spend our lives learning that the world is
much bigger than we first realized. When we were
infants, our world was our crib. Our universe extended as far as we could crawl. Then we found
there were other rooms in our home, and one day
we discovered that there were other buildings and
even other streets.

Similarly, humanity itself has passed from infancy to childhood in its perception of our universe. With telescopes, we have peered out the
windows of our little corner of the universe, and
we have seen to distant worlds. With space missions, we have even opened our front door and
dared to step outside.

We have learned that Earth is only one of nine
known planets that orbit our sun. We learned that
our sun is a star—one of 100 billion stars that together make up a larger world, our Galaxy. We
learned that beyond our Galaxy are hundreds of
billions of other galaxies, that galaxies are bound
together in clusters, and that these clusters, in
turn, seem part of even larger groupings called
superclusters. Now the instruments of modern astronomy are helping us learn more about the na-

An optical telescope in Australia captured the image
of a spiral galaxy, *left,* in the constellation Antlia.

ture of these galaxies that populate our universe—how they began and how they evolved.

My colleagues and I at the Mount Wilson and Las Campanas observatories in Pasadena, Calif., and northern Chile, along with thousands of other astronomers, have been introduced to bizarre and wonderful mysteries in our study of galaxies. We have found evidence that as much as 90 per cent of all the matter in the galaxies may be "invisible," made up of strange particles unlike anything we have ever known. We have observed powerful energy sources at the centers of galaxies that some astronomers think may be due to massive *black holes*—areas where matter is so densely packed and gravity is so intense that even light cannot escape.

Thousands of years ago, long before these discoveries were even imaginable, sky watchers peered out at the heavens and saw a glowing band of light that stretched across the night sky. The ancient Greeks thought this band of light resembled a stream of milk, and they named it *galaxias kyklos* (*Milky Way*) from the Greek words *gala*, meaning *milk*, and *kyklos*, meaning *circle*. In the early 1600's, the Italian astronomer Galileo Galilei used the newly invented telescope to reveal for the first time that this cloudlike band was actually the light of stars "so numerous as to be almost beyond belief." This enormous collection of stars came to be called the Galaxy.

The first hint that there might be other galaxies came in the late 1700's, when British astronomer William Herschel made the first systematic study of the stars, using a more powerful telescope. Herschel was particularly interested in objects in the sky known as *nebulae*. In his telescope, nebulae appeared as hazy, fuzzy objects, rather than as pointlike stars. Herschel noted that many of these nebulae were spiral-shaped. He thought they might be separate star systems far from our Milky Way. But he could not be certain, because his telescope was not powerful enough to reveal stars in the spiral nebulae. At that time, astronomers also had no accurate way of calculating distances to the stars, and so they could not determine if the spiral nebulae were part of the Milky Way or outside it.

Finding an accurate method of calculating distances to the stars was of key importance to understanding our Galaxy and to the eventual discovery that there were other galaxies besides our own. It was not so easy to do, however.

In 1837, the German astronomer Friedrich W. Bessel published the first calculations of the distance to a nearby star. Bessel used a method known as *parallax measurement*. Parallax is the angle a star appears to move in relation to more distant stars when viewed from two different vantage points—in this case, from two different points in Earth's orbit around the sun, which can be accomplished by taking the measurements at two different times of the year. Knowing the distance that Earth travels in its orbit around the sun and knowing the parallax angle, Bessel was able to calculate the distance to

The author:

Alan Dressler is an astronomer with the Mount Wilson and Las Campanas observatories of the Carnegie Institution of Washington.

the star. Bessel's findings were eye-opening for his time. Astronomers of the 1800's were amazed to learn that the nearest stars were trillions of miles away, far more distant than they had thought.

Astronomers can use parallax to measure distance only to the closest stars. Beyond about 300 *parsecs* (1 parsec equals 19.2 trillion miles), a star's apparent motion in relation to other stars as Earth orbits the sun is negligible, and its parallax cannot be measured. So distances to only a few thousand stars have been measured by parallax, and only a few hundred with great accuracy.

In the late 1800's, astronomers began to explore other ways of measuring distances by relying on comparisons of the brightness of stars. This is known as the *standard candle method* for measuring astronomical distance. To understand the standard candle method, imagine that you must figure out the dimensions of a football field when you are tied to a goal post. Here's the trick: Wait until dark and cover the football field with 100 people, each holding identical flashlights pointed toward you, all of which give off the same amount of light. Knowing that the flashlight of a closer person will appear brighter than one farther away, you could estimate the length of the field. Astronomers do similar calculations using starlight. Just like the flashlights, stars can have what astronomers call the same *true brightness*. The light from stars with the same true brightness will appear different to an observer on Earth depending on distance. A star that is farther away will appear fainter, while closer ones will appear brighter. Astronomers can measure these differences in *apparent brightness* with a sensitive instrument known as a *photometer*, which is attached to a telescope. Then, by comparing the apparent brightness of stars known to have the same true brightness, astronomers can calculate their distances.

The trick was to find a kind of star that reveals its true brightness so that it would serve as a standard candle. In the early 1900's, astronomers found a type of star known as a *Cepheid variable*, which varies in brightness at regular intervals. They discovered a direct relationship between this type of star's true brightness and the length of the period when it varied in brightness. For example, studies showed that Cepheids with longer variation periods had a greater true brightness than those with shorter periods. Determining the true brightness of a Cepheid star, then, was simply a matter of measuring its period of variation. Once its true brightness was known, its distance could be calculated.

During the early 1900's, some of the findings made with the standard candle method renewed the debate over whether there were other galaxies. Heber D. Curtis of Lick Observatory on Mount Hamilton near San Francisco argued that the spiral nebulae Herschel had observed in the 1700's were other galaxies, far distant from our own Milky Way. Astronomer Harlow Shapley of Harvard University argued, however, that our Galaxy was the dominant

Galaxy center

Our sun

Spiral arm

Star-forming regions

27,700 light-years

Central bulge

Disk

Our sun

The Milky Way

Our Galaxy, the Milky Way, is a spiral galaxy. The spiral arms, top, contain regions where new stars are forming. Our sun lies on a spur of a spiral arm, about 27,700 light-years from the center of the Galaxy. Like all spiral galaxies, the Milky Way consists of a central bulge surrounded by a disk, above, each containing billions of stars. From the side, this gives it a "flying saucer" shape.

structure of the universe and so incredibly huge that the spiral nebulae were well within it. Shapley based his measurements of the Galaxy's size on a study of Cepheid variables in the Milky Way, but he was unaware that starlight is absorbed by dust in the space between the stars. This flaw distorted Shapley's brightness measurements and led him to exaggerate the size of the Galaxy.

Neither side had enough evidence to prove their case until 1924, when astronomer Edwin P. Hubble of the Mount Wilson Observatory broke the deadlock. Using the observatory's 100-inch telescope, Hubble took photographs showing recognizable stars in a spiral nebula known as Andromeda. Hubble found Cepheid variables in Andromeda that enabled him to calculate their distance based on their brightness, after taking into account the absorption of starlight by interstellar dust. When he determined that these Cepheid stars in Andromeda were thousands of times fainter than Cepheids

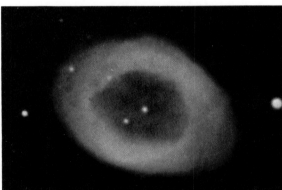

Galaxies are constantly changing and evolving as new stars are born and old stars die. In our Galaxy, the Great Nebula of Orion, *above,* is a "stellar nursery," a region of gas and dust where new stars are forming. The doughnut-shaped ring of gas in the Ring Nebula, *left,* formed when the outer gas layers were blown off a dying star, still visible at the center of the ring. Eventually, this gas may become part of another stellar nursery where new stars will form in a continuing cycle of star birth and death.

known to be in the Milky Way, he proved that they lay far beyond our Galaxy, and therefore, were part of another galaxy.

In the years that followed Hubble's discovery, astronomers found many more galaxies and classified them into four main categories, according to their shapes. The two most common are *spiral* and *elliptical* (round to oval-shaped). The others are *lenticular* (lens-shaped) and *irregular*.

Spiral galaxies have two distinct parts—a bright round bulge containing billions of stars surrounded by a flat plane or disk also containing billions of stars. Spiral galaxies resemble a huge pinwheel, with stars in the disk outlining several spiral arms that seem to rotate around the bright central bulge. When seen from the side, spiral galaxies have a "flying saucer" shape.

Elliptical galaxies have a round shape similar to the central bulge of a spiral galaxy, but no flat disk or spiral arms.

The Varieties of Galaxies

Astronomers classify galaxies according to their shapes. In addition to spiral galaxies, there are elliptical galaxies, *right,* which have a round shape like the central bulge of a spiral; lenticular galaxies, *opposite page, left,* which have a lens shape like the flat disk of a spiral; and irregular galaxies, *opposite page, right,* which have bizarre shapes that defy any neat category. The way galaxies are shaped may be related to how they evolve and interact with one another. An elliptical shape may be due to the merger of two spiral galaxies; a lenticular shape, to gravitational interactions with other galaxies; and an irregular shape, to colliding galaxies.

Lenticular galaxies resemble spirals in that they have a disk of stars surrounding a central bulge, but they have no spiral arms. Irregular galaxies have no special shape. They belong to a catchall classification that includes galaxies with bizarre shapes that defy any neat category. Many astronomers think that some irregular galaxies resulted from the collision of two or more galaxies.

The Milky Way is a spiral galaxy, and our sun lies in one of the spiral arms, about 27,700 light-years from the central bulge. (A *light-year* is equal to about 5.9 trillion miles, the distance that light travels in a year at the rate of 186,000 miles a second.) Our Galaxy stretches about 85,000 light-years across.

In the 1930's, Hubble observed that some galaxies seemed to be clumped or clustered together, as if they were part of some larger system. More evidence for such a system came in the 1950's, after astronomers took a complete survey of the sky. Astronomer George O. Abell of the University of California, Los Angeles, using the results of the survey, showed that there were so many clusters of galaxies that clustering could not happen by pure chance. Abell counted more than 2,700 clusters of galaxies, finding that many clusters contain hundreds and even thousands of galaxies. His observations led astronomers to conclude that about 10 to 20 per cent of all galaxies are bound together in clusters by gravity.

A good way to think about the distribution of galaxies is to imagine that the surface of the Earth is the whole universe and that each galaxy is a house. If you covered the Earth with farmhouses, say one for each square mile, this would be something like the number and density of galaxies in space. But just as houses are not spread out this evenly on Earth, so galaxies are not spread out this way in the universe. Galaxies are clumped in space just as, for example, farms are grouped together around small towns.

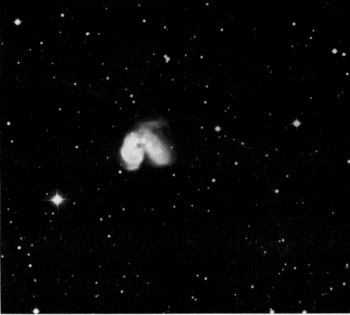

Most galaxies are found closer to their neighbors than you might expect by pure chance. Our own Milky Way belongs to such a group—called the Local Group—which includes the Magellanic Clouds; the Andromeda galaxy; and M33, another spiral galaxy. Like a small suburban community, our group of galaxies sits on the edge of a much larger "metropolitan area," and an enormous grouping of galaxies, a "major city," can be found only 50 million light-years away. The major city is a dense cluster called the Virgo Cluster, and the metropolitan area, the Local Supercluster. Galaxies found in dense clusters are crowded together at a density thousands of times greater than in our "suburban area group." Nevertheless, only a few per cent of all galaxies are found in dense clusters. Most galaxies are out in the suburbs like we are.

Among galaxies, city dwellers are easy to distinguish from their suburban cousins. The suburban galaxies are mainly spirals and ir- regulars. Ellipticals and lenticulars represent only 10 per cent of the suburban galaxies, but they dominate the dense clusters. This is a clear sign that a galaxy's shape is related to its *environment*.

To calculate distance beyond our nearest neighboring galaxies, astronomers had to use a distance measure other than the standard candle. They could not use Cepheid variables because the light of these stars is too faint to be seen in very distant galaxies. So astron- omers turned to another Hubble discovery, made in 1929.

Hubble observed that the light arriving from distant galaxies was systematically shifted toward the red, or longer, wavelengths of the *electromagnetic spectrum*, the radiant energies that range from gamma and X rays through visible light and radio waves. Hubble knew that this *red shift* indicates the galaxies are moving away from Earth. The greater the red shift, the faster the speed away from Earth.

Astronomers soon realized that the explanation for this was that

A Universe of Galaxies

As telescopes have probed farther out into the universe, we have learned that the universe is far more vast and complex than we ever thought possible. Stars are part of galaxies. Galaxies are part of clusters, and clusters are part of superclusters.

Milky Way

Gravity holds stars together in groups to form the galaxies. The Milky Way Galaxy, *left,* for example, is made up of about 100 billion stars.

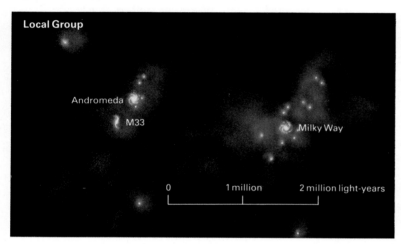

Local Group

Andromeda

M33

Milky Way

0   1 million   2 million light-years

Galaxies in turn are grouped together by gravity to form large structures called clusters. Our Galaxy is a member of a small clusterlike system called the Local Group, *left,* which includes Andromeda, M33, and 30 other galaxies. Galaxy clusters are pulled together in even larger structures, enormous clusters of clusters called superclusters. Some 50 clusters make up the Local Supercluster, *below.* At its center is the enormous Virgo Cluster.

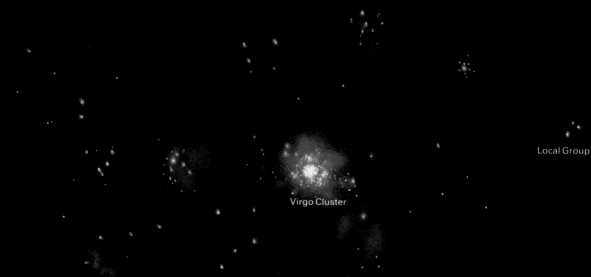

Local Supercluster

Local Group

Virgo Cluster

0   10 million   20 million light-years

the universe is expanding. Actually, the galaxies themselves are not moving away, but the space between the galaxies is increasing. It is as though the people holding flashlights on the football field remained in place while the space between the yard lines increased.

As astronomers were learning about the expansion of the universe, they were also discovering that galaxies are not static collections of stars but dynamic places—constantly evolving and producing new stars. Astronomers know that stars are born from clouds of gas—mainly hydrogen, the lightest element. As these gas clouds condense, gravity causes them to collapse in on themselves. The more they collapse and condense, the hotter they become until nuclear reactions begin and a new star is born.

The nuclear reactions cause the fusion of atomic nuclei, creating heavier elements. In stars more massive than the sun, these heavy elements include silicon, magnesium, and iron. After billions of years, a star exhausts its nuclear fuel and dies. Some of these dying stars, especially the massive ones, end in a violent explosion known as a *supernova*, spewing layers of gas containing heavy elements back into space where, sometime in the future, they will collect in another gas cloud to produce more stars. So as old stars die, new stars are born, and in this way, a galaxy continues to evolve.

Astronomers can learn much about the evolution of galaxies by finding the relative ages of stars within the galaxies. The first step in determining the relative ages is to find out whether the stars have been enriched with the heavy elements. The first stars to form in a galaxy must have had no heavy elements at all because these elements were yet to be produced. Only later generations of stars formed from gas enriched with these heavy elements.

To determine whether stars contain heavy elements requires the use of *spectroscopy*, a method that astronomers have used since the late 1800's to detect chemical elements in an object by analyzing the spectrum of light it gives off. Finding a lot of heavy elements in a star, however, tells us only that the star is probably younger—that is, it formed more recently—than one with fewer heavy elements.

Fortunately, astronomers have found groups of stars that formed from the same gas cloud at about the same time. Astronomers can determine the ages of various stars in the group because all the stars do not evolve at the same rate, even if they are born about the same time. The brightest, most massive stars exhaust their fuel and disappear more quickly than less massive stars. We know that certain massive stars have a lifetime of 3 billion years, and if we cannot see any in the group but we can see fainter, less massive stars with a lifetime of 4 billion years, then we can assume the group is between 3 billion and 4 billion years old.

Surrounding the central bulge of the Milky Way are many such star groups called *globular clusters*, each containing about 10,000 stars. Astronomers have determined that the ages of these clusters are between 10 billion and 20 billion years. In fact, the globular clusters in all nearby galaxies are about the same age. This leads us to think that all galaxies formed at about the same time, between 10 billion and 20 billion years ago. Astronomers have not yet found any galaxies that are entirely made up of young stars, indicating that none of the galaxies formed relatively recently.

Astronomers are fortunate to have their very own "time machines" that allow them to look at galaxies of the distant past. The farther out we look in space, the farther back we look in time. Many galaxies are so far away that their light has taken almost 10 billion years to reach Earth. This means that we are now seeing these galaxies as they were 10 billion years ago. These distant galaxies appear only as fuzzy blobs with Earth-based telescopes, but when the *Hubble Space Telescope* is launched into space in the late 1980's, with its view undistorted by Earth's atmosphere, we will be able to compare the shapes of these galaxies from ancient times with relatively nearby galaxies whose light has taken only a few million years to reach us. By comparing them, we may learn how these nearby galaxies evolved their present shapes and star populations.

Until then, I and my colleagues are using the largest telescopes on Earth to obtain spectra of very distant galaxies to chart the course of star formation. This is a new field and so the results of our studies are few. But from our observations it appears that long ago galaxies went through "fits" of star formation, making many stars in a relatively short period of time. Few of the nearby galaxies

Radio telescopes, such as the Very Large Array near Socorro, N. Mex., *below,* have probed the heart of our Galaxy, which is hidden from the view of optical telescopes by interstellar dust. Radio waves, however, penetrate the dust, revealing streams of hot gas, *below right* (yellow), spiraling around the Galaxy's center (red spot), and suggesting to some astronomers that a massive black hole may lurk there.

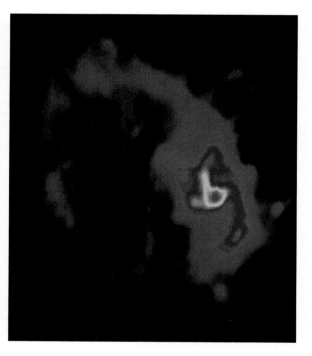

seem to do this. Instead, these nearer and presumably older galaxies make stars steadily and slowly at a pace that has been unchanged for billions of years. Why such bursts of star formation were more common in the past is still a mystery.

The way in which galaxies evolve probably has something to do with why they have different shapes. Astronomers think, for example, that the disks of spiral galaxies are younger than ellipticals. They point out that the arms of a spiral galaxy are regions where new stars are forming, and that spiral galaxies have a great deal of the hydrogen gas needed to form new stars. Star-producing regions and spiral patterns may go hand in hand. According to one theory, spiral arms originate when an invisible wave of pressure, much like an ocean wave, sweeps through a galaxy, compressing hydrogen gas as it passes. Stars form as a result of the compression, and their light, in turn, outlines a spiral pattern.

Elliptical galaxies, with no disk or spiral arms, have few—if any— new stars and seem to have exhausted their supplies of hydrogen gas. This indicates that they are old and at the end of their star-producing careers.

Some astronomers think that the shape of an elliptical galaxy— like that of some irregular galaxies—is due to the merger of two galaxies that have "collided" with each other. The stars of the two galaxies do not physically collide, but the gravitational pull of each

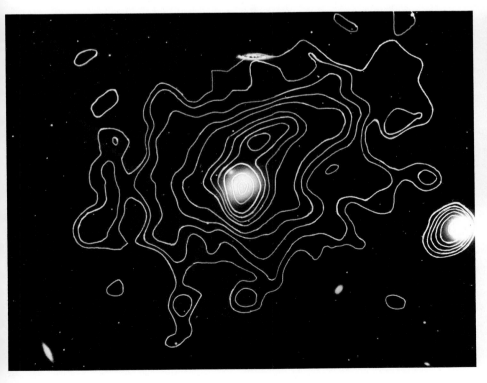

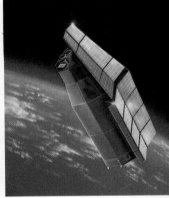

X-ray telescopes, such as the orbiting *Einstein Observatory, above,* have collected data showing that some galaxies, *left,* are surrounded by X-ray-emitting halos. Such halos may contain dark matter, the "missing matter" of the universe.

galaxy disrupts the normal motions of the stars. Studies of some colliding galaxies indicate that they are beginning to take the shape of elliptical galaxies.

Lenticular galaxies are shaped somewhat like spirals because, according to some astronomers, they were spirals when they were younger. These astronomers reason that when a spiral galaxy uses up the hydrogen gas responsible for making new stars, it will lose its arms and evolve into a shape like that of a lenticular galaxy. Other astronomers, however, believe that the shape of lenticular galaxies is related to their location in the universe. Most lenticular galaxies are found in regions crowded with other galaxies. Interactions with those galaxies may have swept away a lenticular galaxy's hydrogen gas, and with it, the spiral arms.

But where did galaxies come from in the first place? Most scientists believe that between 10 billion and 20 billion years ago, the entire universe came into being when an event of unimaginable energy, known as the *big bang*, created space and began its rapid expansion, which continues today. For the first million years or so after the big bang, the universe was a fireball of hot gas and light. There were no galaxies or stars. Slowly, as the expanding gas began to cool, gravity began to pull the gas into clumps that would eventually form the stars and galaxies.

Astronomers have proposed at least two theories to describe exactly how galaxies may have begun. One theory, proposed in the 1970's by astrophysicist P. James E. Peebles of Princeton University in New Jersey, says that initially there were clumps of gas that condensed to form a few million stars. Eventually, these stars and the surrounding gas merged to form the galaxies we see today. Later, the pull of gravity drew galaxies together to form clusters and then superclusters.

Another theory, proposed in 1972 by Russian astrophysicists Yakov B. Zel'dovich and Rashid Sunyaev of the Institute of Applied Mathematics in Moscow, states, essentially, that the opposite occurred. Enormous gas clouds the size of clusters or even superclusters were the first structures to take shape in the early universe. As time went on, gravity pulled together smaller and smaller sections of these large clouds, eventually forming "galaxies" of gas and dust and, finally, stars.

We may not be able to understand how the galaxies were born, however, until we have more knowledge about the nature of the matter within them. Astronomers are puzzled by observations that indicate there is more matter in galaxies than can be detected with any kind of telescope, including X-ray, infrared, and radio.

Astronomers know that there must be unseen matter because of calculations based on the force of gravity. First, we observe the speed at which stars rotate as they orbit the center of a galaxy. From this, we can deduce the amount of mass that controls the orbital speed—just as the mass of the sun determines the orbital speed of the planets. We compare this mass with the amount of matter we can actually see in various wavelengths of the spectrum. Since we observe more matter at the center of the galaxy, we expect that stars far from the center will rotate more slowly than stars close to the center because the force of gravity should be less as the distance from the center increases.

Since the 1960's, however, these observations and calculations have been done for many spiral galaxies and always with the same astonishing result: Stars far out toward the edge of a galaxy rotate at the same speed as stars near the center. The simplest, though baffling, explanation for this is that there is more mass exerting more gravitational force in a galaxy than we can see. In fact, it seems that there may be 10 times as much matter in a galaxy than can be observed. Astronomers refer to this as the *dark matter*, or *missing mass*, problem.

Calculations suggest that the dark matter exists in huge halos surrounding galaxies. The gravitational force of this unseen halo keeps the rotational speed of the stars from decreasing at distances far from the center of the galaxy.

The existence of halos may explain where the missing mass is located, but astronomers are still puzzled about what it is made of. It may be unlike any known form of matter. Since we have not seen it in any band of the electromagnetic spectrum, it apparently does not give off or reflect electromagnetic radiation. This means that it might not be made of atoms, the building blocks of matter as we know it.

Increasingly, astronomers suspect that this dark matter is some strange material—perhaps ghostlike particles left over from the violent birth of the universe. Physicists have observed such particles for brief instants in experiments using giant *particle accelerators* (atom smashers). Some such strange particle may turn out to be the major building block of the universe. What we see when we look at galaxies with our telescopes may be like glimpsing a city skyline at night. We see the lights that outline the buildings, but the buildings themselves remain shrouded in darkness. (In the Special Reports section, see MIND-BOGGLING MYSTERIES OF MATTER).

Through the study of galaxies and their evolution, astronomers may eventually learn what the very early universe was like, in the same way that geologists have learned about the early Earth by studying rocks and the fossil record. Because the Milky Way is our home, we are especially curious about how this galaxy formed and what its final destiny will be. But we cannot help wondering whether there are other civilizations in other galaxies that have embarked on a similar search. When we gaze at the sky, perhaps we see the lights of other "houses." The lights are on, but the most perplexing question remains: Is anybody home?

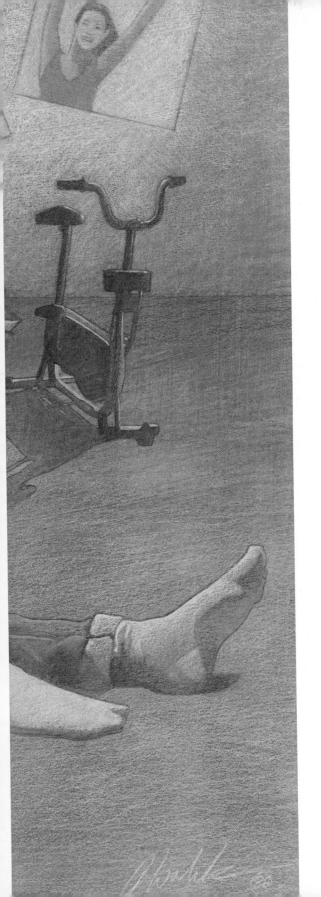

We are learning more about anorexia nervosa and bulimia—eating disorders that afflict millions of young people.

Dangerous Eating Habits

BY DAVID B. HERZOG
AND INGRID L. OTT

Cathy and Laura are two high school students who have a great deal in common. Both come from good families. Both are doing well in school. And two years ago, both developed dangerously unhealthy eating habits.

Cathy was starving herself. She was obsessed with food and ate as little as she could. She lost about 30 pounds in just a few months and was terribly thin. Yet she believed she was still too fat.

Laura, on the other hand, has maintained normal body weight for many years. But she, too, was preoccupied with food. Nearly every afternoon, Laura shut herself up in her room and devoured enormous quantities of junk food. Then she would make herself vomit.

Both Cathy and Laura suffered from eating disorders—Cathy from anorexia nervosa and Laura from bulimia. Medical researchers do not know just how many people suffer from eating disorders. But they do know that anorexia and bulimia have become much more common since the mid-1970's. They also know that 90 to 95 per cent of those suffering from eating disorders are female. Researchers estimate that 5 to 10 per cent of the adolescent girls and young women in the United States suffer from eating disorders. Bulimia is far more common than anorexia nervosa. Recent studies suggest that between 4.5 and 18 per cent of female high school and college students suffer from bulimia.

Self-imposed starvation

Cathy's case demonstrates many of the primary features of anorexia nervosa. Cathy had always been a shy, well-behaved child who earned straight A's in school. Other students teased her about being a bookworm, but she claimed that their ridicule didn't bother her. She was, however, very sensitive to her classmates' comments about her weight. In gym class, she began to feel embarrassed about her body, which was developing much faster than most other girls'. Cathy decided that, to avoid being teased, she would go on a strict diet and lose 10 pounds. She began counting calories. At first, she ate only half of her lunch and claimed that she was too full to finish dinner. In a couple of months, Cathy had lost 8 pounds, and her diet began to gain momentum. She started skipping lunch altogether and dropping pieces of food onto a napkin on her lap at the dinner table while her parents weren't looking.

Every morning, Cathy would examine her body in a full-length mirror. Although she was pleased that her breasts had become smaller, she wanted her chest, stomach, and hips to be completely flat. Cathy was determined to lose 10 more pounds. Cathy's parents began to worry about her weight loss and her eating habits. Whenever they succeeded in getting her to eat, however, Cathy would count the number of calories that she had eaten and then burn them off in a long walk around town.

Cathy's weight had dropped from 118 to 88 pounds when her parents insisted that she see a pediatrician. The doctor told Cathy that her weight was dangerously low for her height of 5 feet 4 inches. She had begun to show signs of severe malnutrition—her body temperature was only 96°F. (98.6°F. is normal), and her pulse was only 43 beats per minute (the normal rate is 50 to 85 beats per minute). The pediatrician decided to hospitalize Cathy until her weight had risen to at least 100 pounds. She spent several months in the hospital before admitting that she had an eating problem.

After her release from the hospital, Cathy saw a psychologist for almost two years. The psychological counseling helped her understand how and why she had developed an eating problem and helped her restore healthy eating habits and a healthy body image.

Although anorexia nervosa has received widespread public attention only in recent years, it has been recognized as a specific disorder since the late 1600's. In 1694, Richard Morton, an English physician, wrote the first medical description of anorexia nervosa, which

The authors:
David B. Herzog is director of the Eating Disorders Unit at Massachusetts General Hospital and assistant professor of psychiatry at Harvard Medical School. Ingrid L. Ott is research coordinator at the Eating Disorders Unit at Massachusetts General Hospital.

he called "a Nervous Consumption" that had come about through "Sadness and Anxious Cares." The Greek term *anorexia nervosa*, which means "a nervous loss of appetite," was coined in 1874 by English physician William W. Gull.

During the early 1900's, many physicians thought that anorexia was caused by a malfunctioning of the pituitary gland, which secretes hormones that control many body functions. By the 1940's, researchers had discovered that pituitary malfunction and anorexia nervosa were separate disorders. The belief in a physical cause of anorexia nervosa was then replaced by a psychological theory that focused on fasting as an act of repentance and dieting as a method of purification. The overwhelming drive for thinness was not considered an essential part of anorexia until the 1960's. Psychiatrist Hilde Bruch of Baylor College of Medicine in Houston contributed a great deal to our understanding of eating disorders. Her work on anorexia nervosa explored the fundamental disturbances in the patient's self-image, emphasizing the struggle to achieve an identity and selfhood.

Understanding anorexia

Physicians now understand anorexia nervosa as a psychiatric disturbance with severe physical and psychological consequences. It commonly begins in a teen-ager, like Cathy, who starts dieting to lose some weight. Often the teen-ager is not overweight, though she sees herself as being fat. In some young women, such a diet leads to an obsession with being thin and a profound change in eating habits. Some people with anorexia make themselves vomit, or take laxatives or other medicines to *purge* (eliminate) whatever food they have eaten from their body. Others exercise excessively to burn off calories. Like most people with anorexia, Cathy had high expectations of herself, was a perfectionist, and denied that she had an eating problem. Such denial of the problem often makes it difficult to convince a person who is suffering from anorexia that she needs professional help.

The medical consequences of anorexia nervosa are complicated and may be severe enough to result in death. Some of the physical effects of anorexia are similar to the symptoms of people who are starving. In females, *amenorrhea* (cessation of menstrual periods) and a deficiency of *estrogen* (a hormone partially responsible for sexual characteristics and growth) are two of the most common consequences of anorexia nervosa. The estrogen deficiency may eventually lead to *osteoporosis*, a disease that causes the bones to become weak and brittle. During the first stages of weight loss, a person with anorexia may feel energetic, but after long-term weight loss, she will feel weak and tired. Her skin, nails, and hair may become dry, and a fine and downy hair called *lanugo* may start to grow on her body in order to conserve body heat. Other common medical consequences include a slowed heart rate, low body temperature, in-

Anorexia Nervosa

People suffering from anorexia nervosa often have a distorted image of their body. Although they are dangerously underweight, they still see themselves as being too fat. Part of the treatment of anorexia nervosa involves helping the patient achieve and accept a more accurate body image.

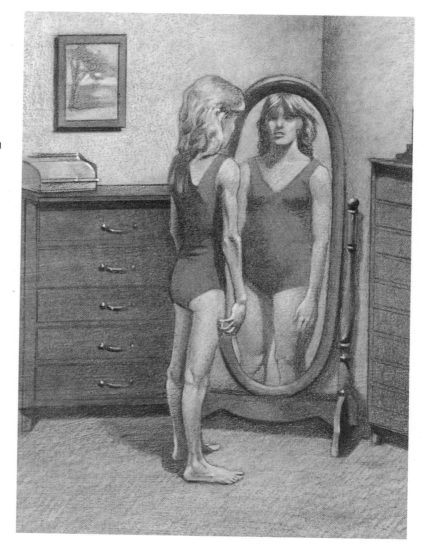

Characteristics of Anorexia Nervosa

Anorexia nervosa is an eating disorder characterized by:

- Refusal to maintain at least the minimum normal body weight
- Extreme weight loss, usually exceeding 15 per cent of a person's original total body weight and not explained by the presence of another illness
- Intense fear of becoming fat
- Disturbed body image—seeing oneself as too fat even though one is extremely thin
- Loss of menstrual periods in women

Physical effects of anorexia nervosa include:

- Chills and low body temperature
- Dry skin and hair
- Increased growth of fine hair over the body
- Constipation
- Anemia
- Slow, irregular heartbeat
- Low blood pressure
- Thinning of the heart muscle
- Loss of bone mass
- Kidney stones

creased sensitivity to cold, slow passage of food from the stomach (leading to a sensation of fullness), constipation, and mild *anemia* (decrease in the number of red blood cells). People with anorexia can also suffer from decreased resistance to infection.

Out-of-control eating

In many ways, Laura's story illustrates the typical pattern of the other eating disorder—bulimia. Laura always admired her older sister Liz, who was one year ahead of her in high school. Laura's grades were just as high as Liz's, but Laura felt that she would never succeed in becoming as thin and popular as her older sister. After much hard work, Laura earned a spot on the junior varsity gymnastics team during her sophomore year. She was thrilled. If she practiced every day and lost 5 pounds, perhaps she could even earn a varsity letter. With time and practice, Laura's gymnastics skills improved, but her diet was less successful. Every day on her way home from practice, Laura promised herself that she would have an apple and only three cookies for a snack. Much to Laura's horror, the snack would often become an apple and a whole bag of cookies.

The feelings of guilt and depression that came from breaking her diet were intensified when she began to put on weight. Laura started sneaking food out of the kitchen and devouring it in the privacy of her room. Her afternoon snacks soon became hourlong binges, during which she would consume a quart of ice cream, eight pieces of toast with butter and jam, a box of crackers, four chocolate bars, and a dozen cookies. Laura felt so miserable and nauseated after these binges that she began forcing herself to throw up. Although the vomiting prevented her from gaining any more weight, Laura was still afraid that someone would discover her secret. She tried to stop bingeing several times without success. Finally, Laura broke down and told her parents the whole story. With the assistance of her physician and a psychologist, Laura and her family worked together to restore her life to normal.

The earliest medical reports of bulimic symptoms appeared in the 1800's in connection with anorexia nervosa. It was not until 1944 that a case of bulimia—separate from anorexia nervosa—was described in medical literature. Bulimia was first listed in psychiatric manuals as a distinct eating disorder in 1980.

Bulimia's dangerous results

The term *bulimia* comes from a Greek word meaning *ox hunger*. The primary feature of bulimia—binge eating—may have little to do with actual hunger, however. A binge is not defined solely by the number of calories consumed, but also by the anxiety, guilt, and sense of helplessness that a person feels during and after a binge. A young woman with bulimia typically sets aside time each day for solitary bingeing on junk food that is high in carbohydrates. To counteract the effects of a binge, she may vomit, take laxatives, *diuretics* (medicines that increase urine production), or diet pills, or severely restrict her intake of food for long periods of time. Some people with bulimia also exercise rigorously to burn off the calories consumed during a binge. After bingeing and purging, a person suffering from bulimia often makes a renewed commitment to control her eating habits. The inevitable disappointment that results from not meeting her own high expectations nearly always leads to a resumption of the cycle of bingeing and purging. The preoccupation with food often interferes with personal relationships and ability to function at school or work. A person with bulimia is usually distressed by her eating problem and willing to accept help.

The medical consequences of bulimia result largely from purging. Purging by means of vomiting or the use of laxatives or diuretics reduces the body's supply of *potassium*—a chemical that plays an important role in regulating body fluids. A loss of potassium may result in muscle weakness or paralysis, an irregular heartbeat, and kidney disease. Repeated bingeing and purging may result in rupture of the esophagus, stomach cramps and ulcers, a constantly sore throat, and difficulty in breathing and swallowing. In addition, the acid from vomit may erode the enamel that protects teeth from decaying. The disturbances of body chemistry that accompany bulimia may cause dizziness, fatigue, and decreased resistance to infection.

Why people develop eating disorders

Although research has increased our understanding of anorexia nervosa and bulimia, we still have no clear answers to the question of how eating disorders develop. An adequate explanation of the cause of eating disorders must take into account cultural, psychological, and physiological factors.

No one can live in Western society without coming into contact with the notions that fat is bad and thin is good. We receive these messages from television shows and commercials, magazine advertisements, our friends, and even our families. Overweight people are often stereotyped as lazy, uncoordinated, ineffective, and out of control. On the other hand, being thin often implies "having it all together," being motivated, active, and in control. Many theorists have proposed that the pressure to be thin is directed particularly at women. Since 1970, the women featured in *Playboy* centerfolds and the winners of the Miss America Pageant have been progressively thinner, while Americans on the average have become heavier. Psychologists Marlene Boskind-Lodahl and William C. White, formerly of Cornell University in Ithaca, N.Y., argue that our society teaches girls and women to define themselves in terms of how men see them. The resulting overemphasis on thinness may lead to a tendency in young women to develop abnormal eating patterns.

Just as there are social values associated with weight, so are there values and rituals that society associates with food. From our earliest

Bulimia
People suffering from bulimia may eat thousands of calories of food in a single, solitary binge and then make themselves vomit. Many people with bulimia feel extremely isolated and fear that they have lost control of their eating behavior.

Characteristics of Bulimia

Bulimia is an eating disorder characterized by:

- Repeated episodes of binge eating
- Following binges by fasting, using diuretics or laxatives, or making oneself vomit
- Eating in secret during a binge
- Repeated attempts to lose weight
- Fear of not being able to stop bingeing

Physical effects of bulimia include:

- Irregular menstrual periods in women
- Erosion of tooth enamel by stomach acid associated with frequent vomiting
- Dangerously low levels of potassium caused by excessive vomiting or use of laxatives
- Stretching and rupture of the stomach and esophagus

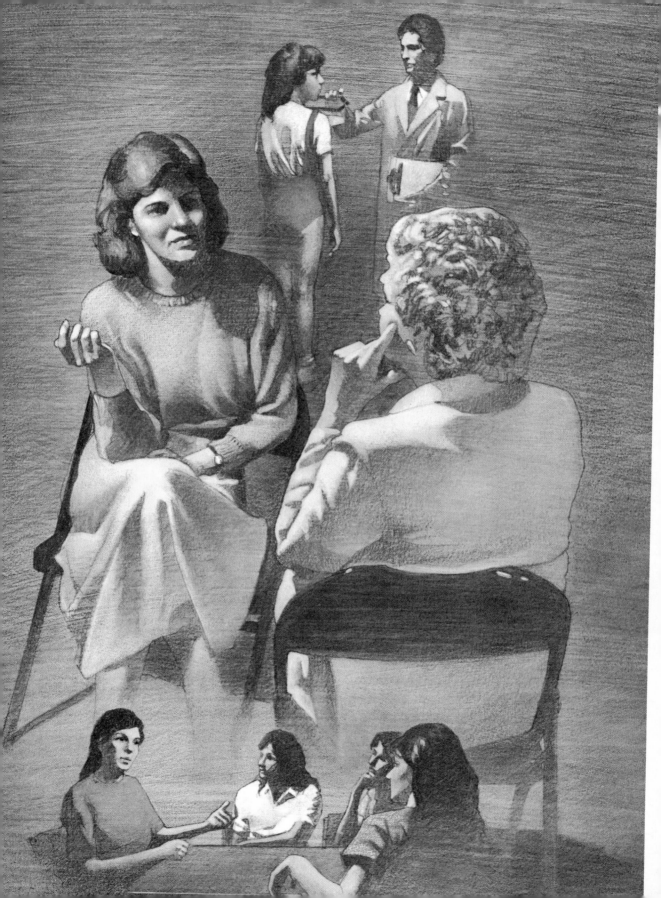

years, we associate food with feelings and emotions. A child may be rewarded with a candy bar for behaving well. But a child who misbehaves may be sent to bed without dinner. Thus, food can be associated with celebration, anxiety, guilt, or depression.

Many people with eating disorders suffer from some other psychological problems as well. They tend to have low self-esteem despite a constant drive for perfection. Initially, they may have turned to food in response to depression, stress, loneliness, or anxiety, just as someone else might turn to alcohol or drugs. On the other hand, they may have become completely preoccupied with food as a way of avoiding other personal or family problems.

Many of the problems that people with eating disorders face are similar to those experienced by people who are depressed. Both types of patients report disturbances in their sleep habits, poor concentration, fatigue, loss of interest in their usual activities, and feelings of helplessness and hopelessness. Both groups also display some of the same abnormalities of *metabolism*—the body's use of food to produce energy and body tissues. Some researchers believe that the eating-related behaviors of people with anorexia or bulimia are actually signs of depression. Other experts believe that the signs of depression are caused by the eating disorder.

The treatment of anorexia nervosa or bulimia often is long and difficult, requiring the teamwork of a medical doctor and a psychiatric therapist. Medical treatment, *opposite page, top,* is aimed at correcting any physical problems associated with these disorders. Psychiatric care may include individual therapy, center, family therapy, or group therapy, bottom. Group therapy is often helpful in combating the feelings of isolation felt by many people suffering from bulimia.

The search for physical links

Although scientists now believe that bulimia and anorexia nervosa are psychiatric disorders, the search for physiological explanations of eating disorders continues. This search is complicated by the fact that the physiological symptoms of anorexia are similar to those of starvation. Researchers have discovered several physiological differences between anorexia nervosa and starvation, however. For example, some female patients with anorexia nervosa cease menstruating before they begin losing weight. In starvation, however, menstruation ceases only after the woman has lost weight. In addition, starving people produce the hormone *cortisol* at a reduced rate, but people with anorexia produce it at an increased rate.

In 1982, Walter H. Kaye and his colleagues at the National Institute of Mental Health (NIMH) in Rockville, Md., reported finding an increase in the activity of *endogenous opioids* in some people with anorexia. Endogenous opioids, the body's natural painkillers, have effects on the body similar to those of opium. When a person does not get enough to eat, such as during a diet, his or her endogenous opioid activity increases. This causes a feeling of well-being that may lead to an addiction to dieting. Further research by Kaye and others has shown that some people with anorexia nervosa have low levels of certain *neurotransmitters*—chemicals that transmit signals along nerves. These neurotransmitter abnormalities persist long after the patient has returned to normal weight. Scientists have not yet determined whether these abnormalities contribute to the development of anorexia or are caused by it.

Studies of bulimia suggest that the desire to binge may be in some way related to the neurotransmitters serotonin and norepinephrine. Serotonin causes the sensation of satiation or fullness. Research at NIMH suggests that people with bulimia may have a low level of serotonin, which may make them feel like bingeing. Norepinephrine stimulates rats to eat. An elevated level of norepinephrine in people with bulimia may increase their desire to binge.

Treating eating disorders

The treatment of eating disorders is highly complicated. People with anorexia often deny that they have a problem and consequently resist treatment. Although patients with bulimia are more likely than those with anorexia to seek treatment, they often become frustrated and quit if the treatment does not produce results quickly. Furthermore, some people with eating disorders and their families are reluctant to receive treatment because of the shame they associate with mental illness and psychiatric care. People may struggle with their eating disorder for years before seeking professional help. Even those who pursue treatment may fight their eating disorder for years before feeling that they have recovered.

In the treatment of eating disorders, hospitalization is generally recommended only for patients whose physical or emotional states severely threaten their health. Most people with an eating disorder, however, are treated as outpatients.

Teamwork is crucial in the treatment of eating disorders. The patient should be seen by both a psychiatrist or psychologist and a general medical physician. Medical treatment aims at correcting any physical problems associated with the disorders. Psychological treatment may include individual psychotherapy, behavioral therapy, family therapy, or group therapy. The goals of individual psychotherapy are to help patients restore normal eating habits, increase self-esteem, and become more aware of—and able to express—their thoughts and feelings. Behavioral therapy differs from psychotherapy in that it makes use of rewards and punishments to help individual patients gain control of their eating behavior and change thinking patterns associated with eating disorders. Family therapy is directed at improving family relationships and communication. Group therapy is often effective for people who feel isolated and believe that no one else understands their eating problem.

Researchers also have tested a variety of *psychotropic drugs* (medicines such as antidepressants that affect the patient's psychological state) in the treatment of eating disorders. Experiments with several antidepressants have shown a reduction in the symptoms of bulimia.

Although our understanding of eating disorders has increased over the past 25 years, many questions remain to be answered. One such question is how to define recovery. Have patients recovered from anorexia when they gain weight? Have people with bulimia recovered when they stop bingeing and purging? It is not uncommon for people with anorexia to lose the weight they struggled to gain, or for people with bulimia to start bingeing and purging after having eaten normally for several months. Furthermore, some people with anorexia develop bulimia, and some with bulimia develop anorexia.

Some people who seek treatment for anorexia or bulimia recover completely after only a short period of treatment. Many patients, however, suffer from eating disorders for many years. About 80 per cent of the patients that we see at the Eating Disorders Unit at Massachusetts General Hospital in Boston have been treated previously for an eating disorder or other psychiatric problem. Five years after beginning treatment, 30 to 40 per cent of the patients with anorexia still suffer from the disorder, and about 35 per cent of those treated for bulimia still show some symptoms of bulimia.

Preventing eating disorders

What steps can parents, teachers, and friends of young people take to prevent eating disorders? First, we can help young people feel good about themselves and accept their bodies. We should be particularly careful of what we say about a person's weight. A change in our society's attitudes toward food, weight, and body shape may help prevent eating disorders. We should also be alert to the crises and stress in a young person's life and offer emotional support. Helping people deal with their problems may keep them from turning to a preoccupation with food.

The prevention of anorexia and bulimia can also be assisted by educating people about diets, exercise, eating disorders, and nutrition. Young people must be encouraged to discuss their attitudes toward food and weight. If a young person wants to begin a diet, we should encourage him or her to talk about the reasons for dieting, and any diet to lose weight should be supervised by a physician. Finally, the early detection and prompt treatment of abnormal eating behavior may prevent the development of anorexia or bulimia. People who are developing or suffering from an eating disorder should consult a physician. If you suspect that someone has an eating disorder, the best thing you can do is offer understanding support and encourage him or her to seek medical help.

For further information:

The following organizations provide printed material about anorexia nervosa and bulimia and about local self-help groups for people suffering from eating disorders.
American Anorexia/Bulimia Association,
   133 Cedar Lane, Teaneck, NJ 07666. (201) 836-1800
Anorexia Nervosa Aid Society (ANAS),
   Box 213, Lincoln Center, MA 01773. (617) 259-9767
National Anorexic Aid Society,
   P.O. Box 29261, Columbus, OH 43229. (614) 895-2009
National Association of Anorexia Nervosa and Associated Disorders
   (ANAD), Box 7, Highland Park, IL 60035. (312) 831-3438

Using specially equipped rockets and aircraft,
scientists are triggering lightning on command to
learn more about this awesome and mysterious force.

Nature's Fireworks

BY BEN PATRUSKY

As a handful of scientists huddled around the instruments in a nondescript van at the John F. Kennedy Space Center at Cape Canaveral, Florida, the countdown began. Outside, the August sky was gray with storm clouds. Only a slight breeze disturbed the warm still air. It was a perfect day for this type of launch.

Near the van, a row of 3-foot-tall rockets rested on a mobile platform. Suddenly surging to life, one of the small rockets began its rise to its target—a billowing thundercloud overhead. As the rocket shot skyward, it trailed a hair-thin metal wire attached to a spool on the ground. Within moments, the wire exploded as lightning flashed upward from the tip of the rocket, causing the cloud to throb with an eerie glow. Fractions of a second later, a series of brilliant electric flashes raced between the cloud and the ground along a channel made by the vaporized wire.

Grinning, the scientists clapped one another on the back. Once again, they had succeeded not only in triggering lightning almost at will but also in guiding it to exactly where they wanted it—a site heavily rigged with testing and measuring equipment.

It may seem strange that scientists studying lightning would need to create flashes artificially when naturally occurring lightning is so common. Lightning strikes Earth about 100 times each second—more than 8 million times each day. These bolts often have a devastating impact. Every year, lightning kills from 100 to 200 people in the United States alone, more than tornadoes and hurricanes combined. Lightning also sparks 10,000 brush and forest fires in the

In a dangerous experiment in 1752, Benjamin Franklin flew a home-made kite during a thunderstorm and attracted an electric current, proving that lightning is electricity.

United States annually and causes an estimated $1 billion in property damage as well as numerous electric power failures.

Despite their frequency, however, lightning strikes are difficult to predict. So in order to study lightning, scientists are triggering strikes by launching rockets into thunderclouds, flying specially equipped airplanes into thunderclouds, or re-creating thunderstorms in the laboratory. These projects are part of an intense effort to unravel the many mysteries still surrounding this beautiful and deadly phenomenon and to reduce the damage it causes.

The rockets being launched at Cape Canaveral can be thought of as a modern version of the first aerial device used to study lightning—a kite. In 1752, Benjamin Franklin flew a homemade kite during a thunderstorm and proved that the atmosphere in and around thunderclouds is electrically charged and, therefore, that the lightning that comes from them is electricity.

To protect himself during the experiment, Franklin held on to a silk ribbon, a poor conductor of electricity, which was tied to the end of the kite string along with a metal key. The kite also was equipped with a metal rod. When Franklin flew the kite during the thunderstorm, it attracted an electric current, which traveled down the string to the key, then sparked to the fingers of Franklin's free hand—and through his body to the ground. As it turned out, Franklin was very lucky. Had lightning actually struck his kite, he almost certainly would have been electrocuted. The silk ribbon would have provided no protection at all.

Despite Franklin's work and the work of other early lightning researchers, it wasn't until the early 1900's that scientists developed the instruments that allowed them to examine closely how lightning forms and what happens during a lightning flash. In the early 1900's, Scottish physicist and Nobel Prize winner Charles T. R. Wilson used an electric-field detector positioned on the ground to examine thunderclouds that produce lightning. An electric-field detector reveals the presence and strength of electrically charged

The author:
Ben Patrusky is a free-lance science writer and a media consultant to several scientific institutions.

particles. Wilson's experiments led him to theorize that thunderclouds have two electrically charged regions—a negatively charged bottom and a positively charged top. In 1937, British meteorologists George C. Simpson and F. J. Scrase confirmed Wilson's theory by flying weather balloons equipped with electric-field detectors into thunderclouds. Once scientists discovered the separation of charges in thunderclouds, they could determine how lightning forms.

As with the poles of a magnet, similar electric charges repel, while opposite charges attract. When positive and negative charges flow violently toward each other in the air, they create a spark. A lightning flash is actually a very large spark created by the flow of many positive and negative electric charges.

The most common type of lightning flash takes place within a thundercloud. But lightning may also strike from the cloud to the surrounding air or from the cloud to the ground. Only about 20 per cent of lightning flashes are cloud-to-ground, but they are the most dangerous to people and the most destructive to property.

Earth's surface normally carries a negative charge. But as a thunderhead moves along, the negative charge in the base of the cloud repels the negative charge on the ground below, creating a positively charged area. Air is a poor conductor of electricity, so for a while it prevents an electric current from flowing between the negative base of the storm cloud and the positive area on the ground. But eventually, the growing difference in charges overcomes the resistance of the air and lightning flashes between them.

The Paths of Lightning
Lightning can travel in several paths. The most common path is within a cloud (1). Lightning may also flash from the cloud to another cloud or to the surrounding air (2), from the bottom of the cloud to the ground (3), or from the top of the cloud to the ground (4).

73

Lightning can take many strikingly beautiful forms. Streak lightning appears as a single jagged bolt.

In the 1930's, scientists were finally able to get a close look at the structure of a cloud-to-ground lightning bolt. The key to their success was a special high-speed camera. The lightning bolt turned out to be far more intricate than anything the naked eye could ever see. The photographs also helped resolve the controversy about whether lightning moves down from the cloud or up from the ground. The answer was—both.

What the photographs helped show was that lightning begins when a nearly invisible line of negative charge, called a *stepped leader*, moves downward from the bottom of a thundercloud in a series of jumps or steps. Each step, which is about 150 feet long, takes about one-millionth of a second. As the stepped leader moves toward Earth's surface, it establishes the channel along which the lightning bolt will travel. This channel, which is about 1 inch in diameter, is not straight because the stepped leader encounters resistance in the air and is halted—for about 50-millionths of a second—until it receives more negative charge from the cloud.

As the stepped leader zigzags its way toward Earth, it often forms branches. When the main branch comes within 30 to 300 feet of the ground, it attracts streamers of positive charge from trees, tall buildings, and other elevated objects on the ground. Usually, the streamer from the tallest object in the area is the first to meet the stepped leader and to establish a flow of electric current.

With the circuit between cloud and ground now completed, a huge blinding surge of current, called the *return stroke*, races upward along the channel created by the stepped leader. Often, a second stroke, called a *dart leader*, moves down from the cloud along the same channel. When the dart leader reaches the ground, a second return stroke flashes skyward. A lightning flash normally consists of four such down-and-up strokes, though as many as 26 strokes have been recorded.

The "band" of ribbon lightning occurs when the wind blows apart the successive strokes of a single flash, causing the parallel streaks to appear as a wide line.

Forked lightning, the most spectacular form of lightning, occurs when different strokes of a flash break away from the main channel and strike the ground at different places.

This down-and-up movement explains why lightning often seems to flicker. Between strokes, the lightning channel is dark. The longer the period between strokes, the greater the flickering effect. But if the strokes occur rapidly—perhaps 10-thousandths of a second apart—the flash appears to be continuous.

Thunder is produced by the return stroke. Packing enormous energy, the stroke heats the air in the lightning channel, causing this air to expand rapidly and push against the surrounding cooler air. This creates *shock waves* (vibrations in the air that move faster than the speed of sound). After traveling outward from 30 to 300 feet from the lightning channel, the shock waves slow down and become sound waves, which we hear as thunder. Because light travels about 900,000 times faster than sound, thunder always lags behind the lightning flash. The first sound of thunder you hear after a lightning flash is from the part of the lightning channel nearest you. The last sound comes from the part farthest away. Eventually, the sound waves become too weak to be heard.

Until the 1950's, scientists thought downward-moving stepped leaders were always negative. Researchers now know that some leaders are positive.

Scientists believe that positive lightning may represent anywhere from 1 to 10 per cent of all flashes. Mysteriously, positive lightning becomes more frequent the farther north you go and occurs far more often in winter than in summer. Positive lightning is also more powerful than negative lightning. In Japan, for example, winter lightning disrupts power-transmission systems far more often than summer lightning does.

How does positive cloud-to-ground lightning happen? One theory states that violent winds may cause electrified clouds to "tilt," thereby bringing positively charged top areas of a thundercloud closer to the ground. The positive charge now at the base of the thundercloud creates a negative area on the ground below, replacing the positively charged area normally found beneath the thundercloud. This sets the stage for the formation of a positive flash.

Sometimes, cloud-to-ground lightning is actually ground-to-cloud lightning. In such cases, lightning flashes are initiated by stepped leaders that originate at the top of a very tall structure, such as a skyscraper, and travel upward to an electrified cloud. Scientists believe this may occur when lightning within the cloud reduces the charge level in the cloud. As a result, charged particles from the building are the first to break down the resistance of the air, and they then race upward toward the cloud.

As it crackles through the sky, lightning can take a variety of spectacular visual forms. *Streaked* lightning is a single jagged bolt with little or no branching. *Forked* lightning occurs when different leaders in the flash break away from the main channel and strike the ground at different places.

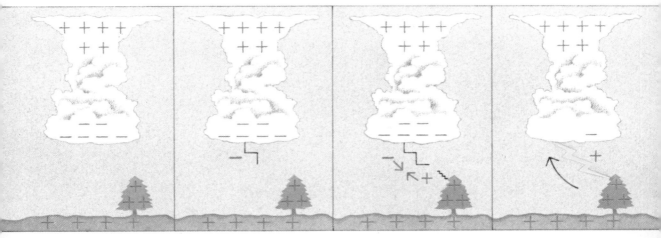

1. 2. 3. 4.

How Lightning Strikes
Cloud-to-ground lightning, like other types of lightning, originates in thunderclouds that have become positively charged at the top and negatively charged at the bottom. The negative charges in the cloud attract positive charges on the ground below (1). A lightning strike begins when a negative streamer moves downward from the cloud in a series of steps (2). When the streamer comes close to Earth, it attracts a positive streamer from elevated objects on the ground (3). When the two streamers meet, negative charges rush to Earth along the path created by the upward-moving streamer. A lightning flash is a return stroke of current that races upward, leaving the channel positively charged (4).

Sheet lightning is actually lightning inside a cloud that illuminates a large area of the cloud but produces no visible bolt. *Heat* lightning, which occurs on warm summer evenings, is lightning that is too far away for the accompanying thunder to be heard.

Two relatively rare forms of cloud-to-ground lightning are *ribbon* and *bead* lightning. Ribbon lightning occurs when wind blows apart the successive return strokes of a single flash. As a result, the parallel streaks appear as a wide line rather than as the usual pencil-thin channel. The channel of bead lightning, or chain lightning, appears to be broken up into unconnected fragments, like beads on a string. No one knows for certain what causes bead lightning. One theory suggests it may be due to the angle at which a lightning flash is viewed while another attributes it to the presence of clouds along the lightning channel that block out some of the flash.

Some instances of bead lightning, however, may be related to *ball* lightning, the most mysterious and least understood of all types of lightning. Ball lightning has never been photographed, but thousands of people say they have seen it. They say it usually consists of a luminous red or yellow sphere about the size of a grapefruit that often floats close to the ground. After lingering for a few seconds, it disappears, sometimes with a pop or boom. Ball lightning occurs

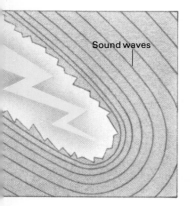

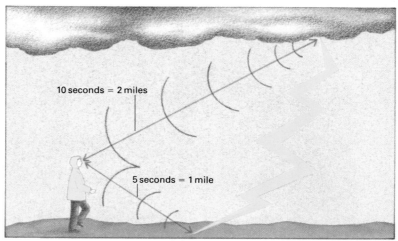

Sound waves

10 seconds = 2 miles

5 seconds = 1 mile

Thunder's Rumble and Roll

Thunder is produced when lightning heats the air in the lightning channel, causing it to expand rapidly and push away the surrounding cooler air, *above left*. This creates waves, or vibrations, in the air. At first, these waves move faster than the speed of sound, but after traveling about 30 feet, they slow down and become sound waves that we hear as thunder. You can determine how far you are from a lightning flash, *above,* by counting the seconds between the flash and the first sound of thunder, then dividing by five. The result is the distance in miles. Thunder rumbles and peals because lightning bolts are jagged. The first sound of thunder you hear is from the part of the bolt nearest you; the last sound is from the part farthest away.

only during thunderstorms. But why it forms and exactly what it consists of are still a mystery.

St. Elmo's fire, which is often confused with ball lightning, is not really lightning at all but a halolike glow caused by a steady discharge of very low-intensity current by pointed objects, such as the mast of a ship or even the horns of cattle. It occurs only in total darkness and only in an area of electrified clouds.

All types of lightning have the same source—thunderclouds. These clouds form when moist air, warmed by the sun, expands and begins to rise. The rapidly rising column of air, called an updraft, cools as it rises. Eventually, the air becomes so cool and so saturated with moisture that the moisture *condenses*—that is, the water vapor changes into microscopic water droplets or tiny ice crystals—and piled-up masses of white clouds form. As the moisture condenses, it releases heat, making the air warmer and lighter, so that it continues to rise. The updraft can be very powerful, reaching speeds of nearly 60 miles per hour. As more moisture condenses, the cloud grows bigger and can reach heights of 60,000 feet or more.

Whirled about violently by gusts in the updraft, the tiny water droplets and ice crystals collide and combine. Some form raindrops. Others, swept toward the top of the cloud, form hail and large ice crystals. When the heavier particles grow too heavy to be supported by the updraft, they fall and precipitation begins.

The main question baffling lightning scientists today is how thunderheads become electrified. Most scientists believe that the cloud becomes electrically charged because of the collision of heavier, falling particles with lighter particles rising in the updraft. The process is similar to the one by which you may become electrically charged by walking across a carpet on a dry day. As you walk, the friction strips electrons from atoms in the carpet, making the carpet positively charged. You gain electrons and become negatively charged. Within a cloud, the heavier particles become negatively charged and the lighter particles positively charged. As the heavier particles fall, the bottom of the cloud becomes negatively charged. Meanwhile, the top of the cloud, with its lighter particles, acquires a positive charge. At this point, the scientists say, the conditions in the cloud are ripe for lightning.

Other scientists, however, have proposed an altogether different theory. In their view, molecules of air become electrically charged outside the thundercloud and then are swept into the cloud by winds circulating in and around the cloud.

All of the efforts to unravel the mysteries surrounding lightning will undoubtedly provide practical benefits. Knowing how clouds become electrically charged would, for example, give meteorologists the ability to predict which clouds will become thunderstorms, and they could then warn electric power companies and air-traffic controllers to beware of potential dangers from lightning striking power lines or aircraft. In fact, right from the very start, most lightning research has had a very practical goal—protection.

In 1752, Benjamin Franklin invented a device that has been the main source of lightning protection for more than 200 years—the lightning rod. Before that, people relied mainly on prayer and church bells for protection. For centuries, during thunderstorms, men rang church bells in the belief that the clangor would chase away the evil spirits causing the lightning or break up the lightning.

Franklin's lightning rod changed all that. It is a simple device—a long metal pole mounted atop a building and connected by wire to the ground. Lightning headed for the building strikes the rod first and is diverted harmlessly to the ground.

Not much has changed since Franklin established the basics. Even the technologically advanced space shuttle is protected by a long wire that acts as a lightning rod. Once in flight, however, all spacecraft and aircraft, including the shuttle, are vulnerable to lightning strikes. Just how vulnerable became frighteningly clear in 1963 and again in 1969.

Before 1963, airplanes were thought to be relatively safe from lightning damage because their all-metal bodies acted as lightning rods, rapidly diverting the current across the outside of the aircraft and discharging it back into the air. But on Dec. 8, 1963, a Boeing 707 was hit by lightning over Elkton, Md., and crashed, killing all 81 people on board. An investigation concluded that lightning had probably ignited the plane's reserve fuel tank.

On Nov. 14, 1969, just 30 seconds after lifting off for the moon, the *Apollo 12* rocket was hit by lightning. Sixteen seconds later, it was struck by a second bolt. The strikes caused surges of electric current that knocked out a power supply and guidance system and destroyed a number of other instruments. Fortunately, the astronauts quickly regained control of the spaceship and went on to complete their mission successfully.

These incidents got the National Aeronautics and Space Administration (NASA) and the Federal Aviation Administration (FAA) deeply involved in lightning research. New developments in aircraft materials and equipment have also spurred research. Modern aircraft made with plastic, fiberglass, and other composite materials, are lighter, faster, and more fuel-efficient than all-metal aircraft, but they are also more vulnerable to lightning.

Unlike metals, composite materials are poor electrical conductors and therefore more likely to heat up, melt, or explode when struck by lightning. In addition, electric currents entering the plane when it is struck by lightning are more likely to build up larger electric charges. These charges can seriously interfere with the technologi-

An engraving from the 1700's shows lightning running down a bell rope to strike a French bell ringer. Until the invention of the lightning rod in 1752, people relied on prayer and church bells for protection against lightning. They believed the clangor of bells chased away the evil spirits that caused lightning and broke up the lightning bolt.

Interesting Facts About Lightning

The peak temperature of lightning can reach 50,000° F., five times the temperature on the surface of the sun.

Lightning can strike the same object more than once. The Empire State Building in New York City is struck an average of 23 times per year. Lightning once hit the skyscraper 8 times in just 24 minutes.

Trees are struck by lightning more than any other object. Oak trees, perhaps because of their great height, are struck more often than any other type of tree.

The return stroke of a lightning flash can reach speeds of up to 87,000 miles per second.

Straightened out, lightning bolts can measure up to 90 miles long.

Lightning strikes most often in the United States during July.

Florida experiences more lightning strikes than any other state.

The greatest number of people killed by a single bolt of lightning is 21. They were killed on Dec. 23, 1975, in the southeast African country of Zimbabwe (then Rhodesia) when lightning struck a hut.

The late Roy C. Sullivan of Virginia holds the world's record for being struck by lightning most often. Sullivan, a former United States national park ranger, who died in 1983—not from lightning—was struck seven times between 1942 and 1977. In his encounters with lightning, he lost a toenail, his eyebrows, his left shoe, had his hair set on fire twice, and was once tossed 10 feet from his car.

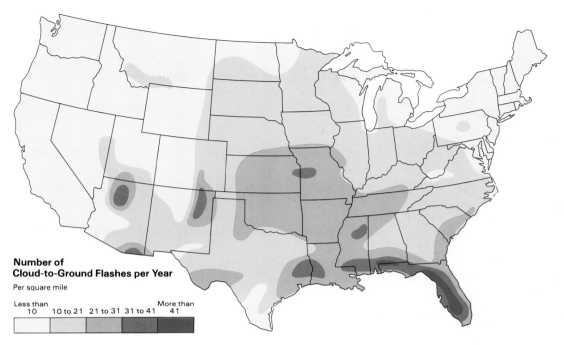

**Number of
Cloud-to-Ground Flashes per Year**

Per square mile

Less than 10	10 to 21	21 to 31	31 to 41	More than 41

cally advanced computer systems and electronic equipment increasingly used in aircraft. Such systems operate on very low current and can be severely damaged by power surges. Thus, they are far more susceptible to disruption than mechanical or hydraulic systems.

To find out what happens when a plane gets hit by lightning, scientists have been flying specially reinforced planes, armed with measuring equipment, into thunderstorms to rendezvous with lightning bolts. At the Langley Research Center in Hampton, Va., for example, NASA pilots have flown an F-106 jet fighter into thunderstorms nearly 1,400 times since 1980. During these flights, the plane was struck by lightning about 700 times. Using computer simulations based on the data gathered from these and similar missions, scientists hope to learn which aircraft designs provide the best protection against lightning.

The lightning research rockets launched into thunderclouds at Kennedy Space Center and other sites are also helping scientists study how lightning affects composite materials. In addition, the launches are providing valuable information on the ways in which flying aircraft trigger lightning strikes that might not have occurred otherwise. From these investigations, scientists may find ways to reduce the number of such potentially hazardous events. Finally, the rockets help scientists test lightning protection systems designed to prevent power surges from damaging electric power lines.

The newest technique for minimizing lightning damage—and perhaps helping to prevent it altogether—are automated lightning

Where Lightning Strikes
In the United States, cloud-to-ground lightning flashes occur most often in the lower Midwest; in the Southeast, especially Florida; and along the Gulf of Mexico. In these areas, hot, humid weather conditions favor the formation of the thunderstorms that produce lightning.

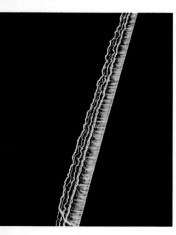

A rocket, *top,* attached by wire to instruments on the ground, speeds toward an electrified cloud in an effort to trigger a lightning strike where and when researchers want it. The many strokes of a single lightning flash triggered by a rocket race along an airborne wire, *above.*

detection systems that locate lightning storms, as they are happening, with great precision. The key to these early-warning systems is a "smart" magnetic direction finder developed in the early 1970's by E. Philip Krider of the University of Arizona in Tucson and Martin A. Uman of the University of Florida in Gainesville. According to Krider, the device responds only to those electrical signals characteristic of cloud-to-ground return strokes. All other sources of electrical interference—whether from lightning within a cloud or from radio stations, automobile ignitions, or copying machines—are filtered out. The device has a range of 250 miles. Using two such devices, positioned at different locations, scientists are able to pinpoint the site of a lightning strike.

The first such lightning detection system went into operation in the late 1970's. Established by the Department of Interior's Bureau of Land Management, the system, which covers 11 Western states and Alaska, has sharply reduced damage caused by forest fires and brush fires ignited by lightning strikes. The system picks up just about every cloud-to-ground lightning flash occurring within its range. Automated sensors positioned throughout the area transmit the information to a data-collecting center in Boise, Ida., where specialists using computers assess the hazard. If, for example, lightning strikes a region where rainfall has been scarce—and, where the risk of fire is high—the center immediately dispatches a plane to the area. If a fire is spotted, fire fighters are sent into action. Getting to fires right away makes fire fighting easier, safer, and less costly.

An electric power company in Tampa, Fla., uses information from a lightning-detection system to position repair crews along the track of the storm. If lightning downs wires or causes other power failures, the crews can then restore service quickly.

Installation of another detection network, designed by atmospheric scientist Richard Orville of the State University of New York at Albany and based on the magnetic direction finder, began in 1982. By early 1986, it included 30 detecting stations, equipped with automated sensors, that spanned the entire East Coast, from Maine to Florida, and extended as far west as Ohio.

The purpose of the system, according to Orville, is to determine in great detail where and how often lightning strikes. Power companies planning routes for new electric lines use the information to avoid areas where lightning strikes frequently. The FAA's Air Route Traffic Control Center in Leesburg, Va., also uses the system to warn pilots of quickly developing thunderstorms.

Clearly, the story of lightning is far from finished. Many chapters have been written since Franklin flew his kite 234 years ago. Many questions remain. Yet we need not fear that by solving age-old mysteries we will lose our sense of awe at lightning's beauty and power. In fact, each new flash of insight, each new piece of knowledge, seems only to add to the measure of our wonderment.

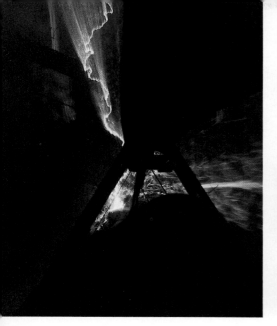

A multiple-exposure photo—more than 125 exposures in less than a tenth of a second—shows lightning striking the nose of a NASA jet specially equipped to serve as a lightning research laboratory, *above left*. A jet used in such research shows the scars of its encounters with lightning's awesome power, *above*.

The National Oceanic and Atmospheric Administration (NOAA) offers these tips to avoid getting struck by lightning:

■ Stay away from isolated trees or telephone poles. You could be electrocuted if lightning struck the tree or pole. In addition, the lightning could send electric currents across the ground toward you. The closer you are to the tree or pole, the stronger—and more dangerous—those currents could be. Take cover under a group of trees of about the same height.

■ Don't rise above the landscape by standing on a hill, on a beach, or in an open field. Drop down into a gully or other depression. If you feel a tingling in your feet or on your scalp, and the hair on your arms stands up, lightning may be about to strike you. Drop to your knees and bend forward, putting your hands on your knees.

■ Stay out of and away from water.

■ Avoid metal objects, such as drainpipes and metal fences. Get away from metal motor scooters, bicycles, tractors, and golf carts.

■ Get to a car, if you can. If you're already in a car, stay put, unless it's a convertible. If the vehicle is struck, the body will divert the current into the ground. But avoid touching any metal in the car.

■ If you're indoors, don't use the telephone, except in emergencies. Avoid touching the television, electric appliances, radiators, plumbing, or anything else connected to the outside of the house or to the electric wiring system.

For further reading:

Garelik, Glenn. "Different Strokes." *Discover*, October 1984.
Keen, Martin L. *Lightning and Thunder*. Simon & Schuster, 1969.
Uman, Martin A. *Understanding Lightning*. Bek Technical Publications, 1971.

Isolated on an island off the African coast, Madagascar's plants and animals, such as the lemur, evolved into forms found nowhere else.

The Lemurs and Other Wonders of Madagascar

BY ROBERT E. DEWAR AND ALISON F. RICHARD

On a clear night when the moon is full, the desertlike spiny forest of southern Madagascar turns silver and we feel as though we are exploring another planet. Our group casts long, dark shadows on the sandy soil, which glows strangely white underfoot. Above us loom the *fansilotra*, cactuslike trees specially adapted to desert conditions. Their twisting limbs, rising 30 to 40 feet into the night sky, resemble fistfuls of gigantic silver snakes. Dressed warmly against the chilly night air, we pad silently across the sand, the beams of our headlamps playing on the fansilotra limbs and the bushy shrubs growing beneath them. In the bright moonlight, we could find our way through the forest without headlamps, but we need them to find the animals we are looking for—lemurs. Lemurs are relatives of monkeys, apes, and human beings. When a lemur is caught in a lamp's beam, its eyes glow like two small embers.

We walk on. Suddenly, one of our blanket-swathed guides hisses softly and stops. We peer into the clump of bushes he is pointing at and there, less than 6 feet away, sits a furry little animal with a grayish-brown back and a creamy-white chest. It is a mouse lemur, and would fit in the palm of your hand. It stares at us with huge round eyes. We stare back. Then all at once, the spell is broken and the tiny creature leaps off into the dark safety of the thickets behind it. We had just seen a species of animal found nowhere else in the world, and we had seen it in a forest made up almost completely of trees and shrubs found nowhere else.

The eerie magic of the forest at night disappears when the sun

Opposite page: A tiny mouse lemur—one of Madagascar's many rare species—prowls in the nighttime forest.

85

comes up, and daytime grays and greens replace the silvery tones of the moonlit landscape. But by day or by night, the forests of Madagascar are both beautiful and fascinating, their wildlife enormously diverse and much of it unique. This island in the Indian Ocean is like a vast natural laboratory, and scientists have learned more about evolutionary processes the world over by studying its plants and animals.

Madagascar is the fourth largest island in the world. With a surface area of 227,000 square miles, it is about twice the size of Arizona. Madagascar is located south of the equator, about 250 miles east of the African nation of Mozambique. As anthropologists with an interest in the people and animals of Madagascar, we have visited the island many times since the 1970's. Our research, conducted with other scientists from both Madagascar and the United States, has included gathering data on the behavior of the sifaka, another variety of lemur. We have also studied the tremendous ecological changes that have occurred on the island during the 1,500 years that people have lived on the island. Those changes are threatening to wipe out many of Madagascar's plant and animal species—indeed, many species have already become extinct. As research in Madagascar is revealing, the effects of human habitation can quickly destroy the results of millions of years of evolution.

Madagascar was once part of Gondwanaland, an enormous ancient continent. During the Age of Dinosaurs, perhaps 175 million years ago, Gondwanaland began to break apart, forming the continents of Africa, Antarctica, Australia, and South America, and the Indian subcontinent. Many geologists think that Madagascar is a piece of Africa that broke away about 125 million years ago and drifted slowly eastward. Eventually, Africa joined Europe, India joined Asia, and South America joined North America. But Madagascar, like Australia, remained separated from all other land masses.

As the continents drifted slowly apart, the plants and animals of Madagascar evolved in isolation. The laws of nature are of course the same in Madagascar as everywhere else on Earth. But the environment and the "cast of characters" have differed during much of the island's history—and so, therefore, do the evolutionary results we see today. Nature has provided scientists with thousands of species of plants and animals—great numbers of them unique—to study and to compare with similar species on other continents. Because of the sheer volume of work to be done, many of those species have as yet received little attention, and almost none have been thoroughly studied. That is unfortunate because the wildlife of Madagascar has much to tell us about the workings of evolution.

In the process of evolution, species of plants and animals undergo changes over millions of years. New characteristics in a species arise from alterations in the *genes*—the molecular units of heredity—of

The authors:
Robert E. Dewar is associate professor of anthropology at the University of Connecticut at Storrs. Alison F. Richard is professor of anthropology at Yale University in New Haven, Conn.

individual members of the species. Some members of a species inherit from their parents genes that differ from those inherited by other members of the species and, as a result, they have recognizably different characteristics. These characteristics make an individual better adapted to its environment if they help it survive longer and produce more offspring than individuals that lack the new traits. The process of change in species through differences in the survival and reproduction of their individual members is called evolution by *natural selection*. When the environment changes, traits—both new and old—with the greatest survival value spread among the members of a species, and the species thus remains well adapted to its surroundings. When plants and animals change in this way in response to the environment, new species may arise from older ones. Sometimes, however, environments change too fast and too dramatically, and some species become extinct because they cannot adapt quickly enough through the process of natural selection.

Plant life in Madagascar, as in any environment, reflects the abundance and seasonal distribution of water. In the island's humid eastern and northern coastal areas, there are lush rain forests, with a tremendous diversity of trees and other plants. In the south, which is very dry except along rivers, the desert vegetation of the spiny forest prevails. Woodlands called gallery forests grow near the rivers of the south, while the central highlands support vast grasslands dotted with wooded areas.

Thousands of plant species found nowhere else evolved in these areas, including the fansilotra, several of its spiny, cactuslike relatives in the plant family *Didiereaceae*, and more than 1,000 species of orchids, all but a few of which are found only in the rain forests of Madagascar.

The animals of Madagascar are also diverse. For instance, about half of the world's approximately 100 species of chameleons—small lizards that can change their skin color to match their surroundings—are unique to the island. Madagascar's insects include more than 800 species of moths and butterflies. The island has fewer kinds of birds than most other tropical countries, but,

Island of the Lemurs

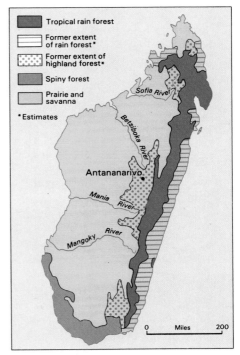

Madagascar lies in the Indian Ocean about 250 miles east of Africa. Since the coming of human inhabitants about 1,500 years ago, large areas of forest have been cut or burned down to make way for farms and grazing land. "Spiny forests"—areas of cactuslike vegetation—cover much of the dry southwestern part of Madagascar.

In eastern Madagascar, the trees of a surviving tract of rain forest, *left,* grow to the very edge of a river. The rain forest is home to many species of lemurs and many unique plant species, including various types of white orchids, *below.*

The arid southwestern part of Madagascar is home to the cactuslike plants of the spiny forest, *left.* Among the plants that grow in this parched environment are various forms of a cactuslike species in the plant family *Didiereaceae, below.*

again, many of the species are found nowhere else in the world. In all, Madagascar has perhaps 175,000 animal species.

Many kinds of plants and animals were already present on Madagascar when it broke away from Africa. For example, there were a number of species of reptiles—including dinosaurs—and birds on the island at that time. A few of those early reptiles evolved into Madagascar's present-day snakes, and a bird species evolved into the recently extinct elephant birds, which were related to ostriches. Other plants and animals made their way from Africa to Madagascar over the next 100 million years or so. It seems likely, for example, that all of the island's mammals made the overwater journey from Africa. We speculate that they did so—quite by accident—by floating on driftwood or tree branches. But a great number of Africa's animal species never made it to Madagascar. There are, for example, no buffaloes, antelopes, giraffes, or deer on the island—in fact, no four-legged grazing mammals at all. Neither are there any monkeys or apes. And happily for those who like to explore the wilds, there are no poisonous snakes.

As the animals of Madagascar evolved, they came to occupy distinct ecological roles in the natural habitat—with each species developing characteristics that enabled it to satisfy its needs by using the environment in a unique way. Animals everywhere have largely similar needs, however, such as the need for food. And since there is a limited range of kinds of resources in the world, animals in different parts of the world playing similar ecological roles often have similar characteristics. For example, a group of species called *insectivores* have evolved physical characteristics that are specializations for capturing and eating insects and worms. Members of this group include such animals as moles and hedgehogs. In Madagascar, the role of insect-eater is occupied by insectivores called tenrecs, some of which closely resemble hedgehogs, though they are only very distantly related.

Among the lemurs, which are some of the most interesting of Madagascar's animals, there is one species that plays an unusual ecological role for a mammal. This is the aye-aye, a strange lemur with big ears like a bat that is one of the rarest animals in the world. The bushy-tailed aye-aye eats insect larvae that it digs out of tree branches with its spindly middle fingers. This and other specialized features allow the aye-aye to occupy the ecological role played elsewhere by woodpeckers, birds not found in Madagascar.

Lemurs are members of the animal group called the *primates*, which also includes monkeys, apes, and human beings. All modern primates are descended from lemurlike animals that inhabited much of the world from 40 million to 50 million years ago, when even Europe and North America were covered with tropical forests. Those early primates gave rise to two major subgroups of primates. Lemurs belong to the subgroup called *prosimians*, which also in-

A tenrec, *right*, searches under a log for insects. In Madagascar, some tenrecs fill the ecological role—that of burrowing insect-eater—that hedgehogs and moles occupy in other parts of the world.

A brightly colored chameleon, *top*, one of some 50 chameleon species unique to Madagascar, crawls across a leaf in search of prey. The island also has about 800 species of moths and butterflies. Many of them, including this rainbow-hued moth, *above*, are found nowhere else.

cludes several kinds of small forest-dwelling animals in Africa and Asia. Apes, monkeys, and human beings belong to the other major subgroup, the *anthropoids*.

After anthropoids became common about 35 million years ago, prosimian primates began to disappear. Less intelligent and often slow-moving, prosimians were apparently not able to compete successfully with monkeys and apes, and many became extinct. Those prosimians, however, that were *nocturnal* (moving about and feeding at night) did not compete directly with anthropoids. Those prosimians evolved into galagos (bush babies), lorises, pottos, and tarsiers—the present-day prosimians of Africa and Asia. Meanwhile, a few prosimian ancestors of the lemurs floated on driftwood to Madagascar where, untroubled by monkeys or apes, they flourished. Because some present-day lemurs still resemble the early prosimians from which the anthropoids evolved, visiting Madagascar is, for *primatologists* (scientists who study primates), almost like going back millions of years in time.

Today, there are 22 species of lemurs in Madagascar. They range in size from the gray mouse lemur—at a mere 2 ounces, the smallest primate anywhere—to the tailless black-and-white indri, the largest of all prosimians, weighing about 20 pounds. The indri and its cousin the sifaka get around by bounding from one tree trunk to another and can cover more than 30 feet in a single leap.

Some lemurs, such as the aye-aye, are nocturnal, while others, like the indri, are *diurnal*—active during the day. The smallest species, the mouse and dwarf lemurs, are night feeders, roaming through tree branches in search of insects, tasty leaves, and other morsels. Their eyes have an internal layer of reflective cells that magnify the dim light of the nighttime forest. Most of the larger species of lemurs are diurnal. In addition to the indri and sifaka, these include

The Primate Family Tree

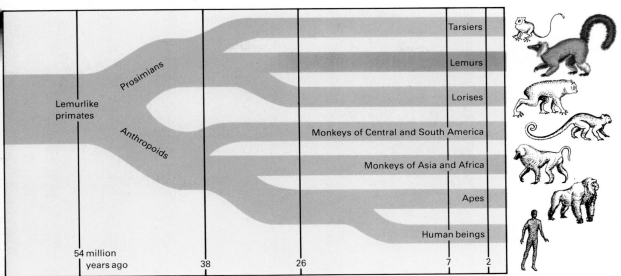

	54 million years ago	38	26	7	2

Labels in figure: Lemurlike primates; Prosimians; Anthropoids; Tarsiers; Lemurs; Lorises; Monkeys of Central and South America; Monkeys of Asia and Africa; Apes; Human beings

Lemurlike primates that lived between 40 million and 50 million years ago gave rise to two major subgroups of primates—prosimians and anthropoids. Lemurs belong to the prosimian subgroup. The anthropoid subgroup includes monkeys, apes, and human beings. Scientists believe lemurs developed from earlier prosimians that made their way to the island from Africa, most likely by floating on pieces of driftwood, about 35 million years ago.

the ring-tailed lemur, so named for the bold black and white rings around its tail. The ring-tail is the only lemur that usually travels on the ground rather than in the trees. They can often be seen sitting in forest clearings on chilly mornings, warming themselves in the rays of the sun.

The diets of all lemurs include leaves, fruits, flowers, insects, and insect larvae. The amounts and kinds of plants and insects eaten by a particular species depend on the animal's body size and the environment in which it lives. Large species like the indri and the sifaka need bulky foods, and so most of their diet consists of leaves and fruit. Small species, for whom every bite counts, tend to eat more insects, a source of easily digested, high-quality protein. Of the larger-bodied species, only the aye-aye gets most of its nutrition from insects.

The eating habits of one small lemur, the 10-ounce forked lemur, represent an interesting evolutionary specialization. This species, named for the stripe on its back that forks into two stripes over the top of its head, is the only lemur we know of that is biologically equipped to digest the gum secreted by trees. This adaptation helps the forked lemur survive the dry season in western Madagascar, when fruit is scarce and many trees lose their leaves. The animal obtains gum by scraping it off the surface of branches and trunks with its *dental comb*—long, forward-pointing lower-front teeth. All lemurs except the aye-aye have a dental comb, which, despite its fragile appearance, is quite sturdy. They use it for grooming themselves and one another and also for harvesting various kinds of food. Thirsty sifakas, for example, use their dental combs during

The strange aye-aye, *right*, is one of Madagascar's rarest lemurs. The aye-aye has spindly middle fingers that it uses to scoop out insect larvae from under the bark of tree branches.

A family of ring-tailed lemurs relaxes beside a fallen tree. Ring-tails are the most thoroughly studied lemurs. Scientists have found that ring-tails live in close-knit groups dominated by females.

The sifaka, *above,* and the indri, *left,* are large lemurs that live in the trees. They get around by leaping from one tree trunk to another. Like all lemurs, except the aye-aye, they have long lower-front teeth that form a "dental comb," *below,* which is used for various purposes, such as grooming or gouging moisture-laden wood out of trees in dry months.

the dry season to gouge moisture-laden wood out of tree trunks.

Lemurs exhibit a wide range of social organization. Among the mouse and dwarf lemurs, mothers move about and feed with their maturing young, but adults otherwise lead mostly solitary lives. Scientists once thought that mouse and dwarf lemurs did not establish social relationships at all, but we now know that adults of these species do in fact regularly communicate with one another from a distance, using sounds and scent marks.

The most complex forms of social organization are found among some of the larger lemurs. The best-studied species to date is the ring-tailed lemur, which lives in groups ranging from 5 to more than 20 individuals. In research done in Madagascar in the 1960's, biologist Alison Jolly, currently of Rockefeller University in New York City, found that females form the stable core of the group, whereas males move from group to group, perhaps several times in their lives. In addition, female ring-tails are *dominant* over males. This means that females invariably win disputes with males. Such disputes might involve, for example, who gets an especially choice clump of leaves or fruit, or who is entitled to sit in a particular patch of sunshine. Jolly observed that sometimes a simple glare is sufficient to intimidate the male. Other times a cuff or a lunge may be necessary, and on occasion a chase breaks out. Members of each sex within a social group, however, can also be ranked according to their dominance, and it is between males that we find the most elaborate form of dominance interaction, the "stink fight." During a

Madagascar's forest habitats of lemurs and other unique animals and plants are being destroyed by fires, *below,* set to clear land for farms and pastures. Trees are also cut down in large numbers for firewood or for the production of charcoal, *below right.*

stink fight, each combatant rubs scent onto his tail with glands located on his wrists. The opponents then hold their tails above their heads and shake them threateningly at each other.

Recent research by biologists Linda Taylor and Robert Sussman with captive lemurs at the Duke University Primate Center in North Carolina has revealed that a female's dominance rank is determined by the rank of her mother. A female ranks beneath her mother and above all other females over whom her mother is dominant. When a mother has more than one daughter, the younger daughter, surprisingly, ranks above the elder.

Lemurs establish and maintain social relationships with one another in several ways: by calls, touching—particularly while grooming one another's fur—body posture, a limited range of facial expressions, and scent marks. They seem able to communicate particularly well by smelling one another's scents. Lemurs make scent marks by rubbing tree trunks or branches with secretions from glands located on the throat or wrists or in the genital area. This is a difficult subject for study, however, because scent marks are invisible. Much remains to be learned about how lemurs communicate, just as we still have a great deal to learn about many other aspects of lemur behavior, biology, and evolution.

There is one fact about lemurs, though, that is beyond dispute: They are in danger of extinction. These unique and fascinating creatures—along with many other animals and plants on the island—are succumbing to the pressures of human habitation.

The deforestation of Madagascar is causing severe erosion problems. Eroded red soil turns a river's water the color of blood.

The black-and-white ruffed lemur, *right,* is becoming extremely rare. Rarer still is the angonoka tortoise, *above,* which is now the world's most endangered reptile. The fate of these and other animals in Madagascar depends on efforts to save the island's natural land areas.

About 1,500 years ago, merchants from Indonesia and Africa became the first people to settle in Madagascar. Since then, the island has experienced great ecological turmoil. The newcomers mined the earth for minerals and burned down forests to make way for cropland and pastures. Over time, Madagascar was remade, as people turned an untouched landscape into a countryside of villages and farms.

As the number of human inhabitants on the island grew, the number of animals declined. At least 14 species of lemurs, including 1 species the size of orangutans, were driven to extinction. Other animals also vanished, among them giant tortoises with 4-foot-long shells, and a pygmy hippopotamus. Madagascar's extinct animals also include the 10-foot-tall, 1,000-pound elephant bird, the largest bird ever known to exist. Hunting may have hastened the extinction of some of these animals, but the destruction of natural habitats was probably the major cause of their disappearance.

And today, the damage continues. In central Madagascar, the once-lush grasslands have become sparse. On the eastern side of the island, large tracts of rain forest are gone, cleared away to grow food for the ever-increasing population. The people of Madagascar, like most of those in the developing countries of the tropics and subtropics, depend on firewood as a source of energy and cut down many trees to produce firewood or charcoal. With so much of its grass and forest cover removed, the land is now eroding rapidly. The reddish soil is being washed away so fast that many of Madagascar's rivers look as if they are running with blood, and from the air one sees red stains on the ocean before sighting the island itself.

The ongoing destruction of Madagascar's vegetation is jeopardizing many of the remaining animal species, including a native eagle and two large tortoises. Adding to this sad situation is the plight of the lemurs. Some species, notably the mouse lemur, are still fairly abundant. Others, however, such as the indri, the aye-aye, and the hairy-eared dwarf lemur are becoming increasingly rare. And with the population of Madagascar expected to soar from 10.2 million in 1986 to 24 million by the year 2020, the outlook for the survival in the wild of any of the lemurs is not good.

Clearly, the present ecological situation in Madagascar is grave— but it is not yet hopeless. Although it is among the world's poorest nations and the achievement of economic well-being is a top priority, Madagascar is not willing to sacrifice its natural treasures in the pursuit of material prosperity. The government has enlisted international help in a concerted effort to develop a stronger economy while protecting the island's natural heritage. Conservation has never been totally neglected. There are, for example, 34 wildlife preserves, and the hunting of lemurs has been illegal since 1927. But conservation is now, more than ever, regarded as an essential part of economic development.

Emphasizing its commitment to conservation, the government of Madagascar in 1984 adopted a National Conservation Strategy. The goals of the program include educating the population about the need for conservation; restoring woodlands; eliminating soil erosion; and protecting endangered animals. To help put those policies into effect, the government in November 1985 hosted a nine-day conference attended by experts from many nations and by representatives of the major international conservation and development organizations. Momentum is gathering for the protection and rational development of Madagascar's natural environment and for the conservation of its unique species. The road ahead will be a long and bumpy one. There will be work to do for years to come, and there may never be a time when the task is finished. But there is reason to believe that conservation efforts in Madagascar are turning a corner.

For further reading:

Jolly, Alison. "Some Tall Tales: Remarkable Lemurs of Madagascar." *Smithsonian*, November 1978. *A World Like Our Own: Man and Nature in Madagascar*. Yale University Press, 1980.

Kavanagh, Michael. *A Complete Guide to Monkeys, Apes, and Other Primates*. Viking Press, 1983.

Tattersall, Ian. *The Primates of Madagascar*. Columbia University Press, 1982.

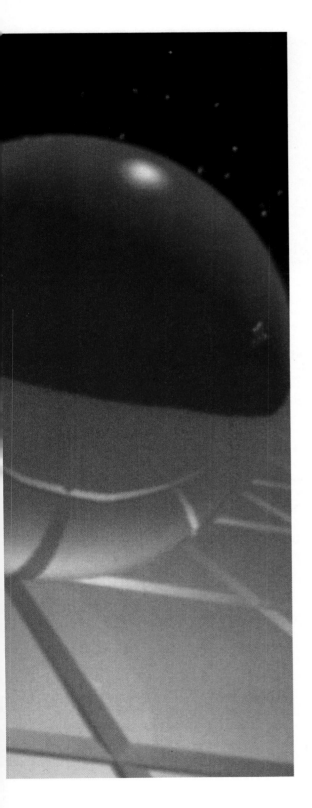

The computer has become an animation machine, a drafting tool, and even a new kind of science laboratory.

Creating Images with Computers

BY DAVID KALSON

Now clearly visible, an enemy jet fighter bobs and weaves through white clouds 50,000 feet above Earth. A United States pilot maneuvers his F-15 fighter closer to the enemy aircraft, then squeezes off a burst of cannon fire. He hears the deep chatter of guns over the engine's whine. Instantly, the enemy's wing bursts into flame. The F-15 pilot twists to his left and presses his face against the canopy. He catches sight of the burning jet, now below and behind him, as it rolls belly-up and begins to tumble helplessly. In seconds, the plane seems to be swallowed by Earth.

Happily, this was not a scene from a real war, and no one died, though the F-15 pilot does feel jittery. He has just experienced an elaborate and

A computer and a TV-like screen are the "paint-brush" and "canvas" for such new works of art as this gleaming image of a geometrical world.

99

A military pilot, *above left,* learns how to maneuver a jet fighter in combat without leaving the ground. The illusion of flight is created by a flight simulator, *above right,* an elaborate, computer-controlled device that projects realistic moving images onto screens positioned around a real jet control panel.

The author:
David Kalson manages the Public Information Division of the American Institute of Physics.

costly illusion—a computer simulation of air combat. The enemy jet, the clouds, and Earth were images created by computers at the St. Louis, Mo., laboratory of McDonnell Douglas Corporation, manufacturer of the F-15.

The pilot climbs out of his cockpit and looks at the devices that created the illusion. He is standing on a small platform next to a modified F-15 cockpit located in the center of a 40-foot-wide plastic bubble. The images that seemed so real were projected like ordinary movies onto the bubble.

Several companies and government agencies use such simulators to train commercial and military pilots. These machines can simulate every sort of weather condition, flight tactic, and airfield. The effect is so convincing that one experienced fighter pilot tore the ejection lever out of its mounting after he was "shot down."

Although they are immensely more complicated and costly, these flight simulators share four basic pieces of equipment with arcade and home video games: a computer to generate the pictures, a display unit such as a TV screen to show the computerized images, a computer memory in which to store images, and one or more input controls. But while an input control for a video game might be only a keyboard or a lever called a *joystick,* a training simulator has a jet cockpit fully equipped with the same kinds of buttons, levers, dials, and other controls that would keep a real plane flying.

Both the video games and the flight simulators are based on *computer graphics,* the creation and manipulation of pictures with the aid of a computer. Computer graphics devices are making major contributions in a wide variety of fields. They perform tedious drafting chores for machine designers and architects; produce financial charts for businesses in an instant; serve teachers as visual aids; and function as computerized paintbrushes for artists.

Computer graphics has even provided a new "laboratory" for science. Physicists use this laboratory to study subatomic particles—nature's smallest objects. Astronomers employ it to unravel mysteries of clusters of galaxies—gigantic collections of matter in the universe. Biologists use it to investigate processes of life.

And computer graphics is an integral part of such new medical techniques as magnetic resonance imaging (MRI) and computerized tomography (CT) scanning for taking pictures of the inside of the body. Computer graphics displays help doctors locate tumors and blocked arteries. Surgeons even use computer graphics before operating to help them design new body parts such as artificial hip joints.

The science of computer graphics had its beginnings in the early 1960's, when electrical engineer Ivan E. Sutherland of the Massachusetts Institute of Technology, shown above, wrote a computer program to manipulate simple geometric forms on a television screen.

The rise of computer graphics began with the linking of two devices that are of central importance to all industrialized nations—television and the computer. In 1950, scientists at the Massachusetts Institute of Technology (MIT) in Cambridge first programmed a computer to create television pictures. One program solved certain mathematical equations and displayed the solutions on the TV screen as the movements of a bouncing ball. In the late 1950's and early 1960's, scientists used computers to make crude animated drawings of air circulating in the atmosphere, satellites orbiting Earth, molecules in motion, and other physical phenomena. The animation process, however, was agonizingly slow and wildly expensive. The computers used for animation ran at about 2 per cent of the speed of today's machines, and they cost more than 100 times as much.

In 1962, computer graphics reached another milestone, one that led to the development of *interactive computer graphics*, the instantaneous manipulation of pictures with the aid of a computer—as in the flight simulator. That year, Ivan E. Sutherland, an MIT graduate in electrical engineering, wrote a prophetic doctoral thesis, *Sketchpad, A Man-Machine Graphical Communication System*. Sutherland's thesis described computer programs that he had written to manipulate simple geometric forms, such as triangles and hexagons, on a TV screen. He ran the programs on MIT's TX-2, an experimental computer.

The computer display unit was much like an ordinary black-and-white TV set. A TV screen is made up of an orderly grid of about 250,000 tiny dots that glow to form pictures. Built into the back of the set is a device called an electron gun that scans back and forth across the screen, firing electrons at certain dots to make them glow. The scanning process creates a *raster*—a pattern of parallel lines—as it builds a picture out of glowing dots.

Sutherland's programs contained short cuts that made the TX-2 somewhat interactive. When Sutherland wanted to produce a picture of a group of interconnected hexagons, for example, he did not give the computer step-by-step instructions for each hexagon.

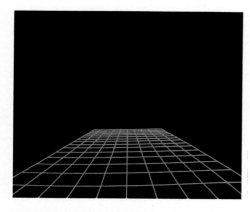

A modern computer-graphics image takes shape in stages. First, the computer "draws" the major parts of the picture as meshlike patterns made up of basic forms such as straight lines, *top*, and ellipses, *center*. The computer then fills in the gaps within the mesh and adds color, highlights, and texture to give the image a realistic look, *bottom*.

Instead, he began by drawing one hexagon on the TV screen with a device called a *light pen*, which was shaped like a fountain pen but worked somewhat like a flashlight. As Sutherland moved the light pen about on the computer's TV screen, light-sensitive devices in the screen transmitted electrical impulses to the computer, indicating—moment by moment—the location of the pen-point. The TX-2 translated the impulses into the 0's and 1's that are the basic "alphabet" of computer language, and then processed these symbols to produce instructions for the display's electron gun. The TX-2 instructed the electron gun to "draw" a hexagon on the screen. Sutherland then pushed buttons and flipped switches to activate computer programs for duplicating the hexagon and moving the duplicates into new positions. Again, the computer manipulated millions of 0's and 1's, "drawing" the duplicates where Sutherland wanted them.

Sutherland's display system had two major drawbacks. First, the TX-2 did not have the computing speed and memory to calculate and "remember" the positions of glowing dots very well. Consequently, after displaying only a few hundred dots, Sutherland's raster would flicker. Second, curves and diagonal lines showed a jagged, staircaselike effect—"the jaggies"—a result of the orderly grid pattern.

Nonetheless, computer graphics caught on after Sutherland's pioneering work. Research facilities dedicated to computer graphics were soon set up by such organizations as MIT, Bell Telephone Laboratories, General Motors Corporation, and Lockheed Aircraft Corporation. Manufacturers of products as varied as electronic components and airplanes used the new technology to develop *Computer-Aided Design* and *Computer-Aided Manufacturing* (CAD/CAM) systems. CAD, besides displaying pictures with the accuracy of blueprints, acts as an information storehouse that analyzes a design, perhaps checking the ability of a mechanical part to bear weight or the ability of an electronic circuit to conduct electricity. CAM controls the machinery that manufactures components. The efficiency of CAD/CAM has proved to be a major factor in continually reducing the

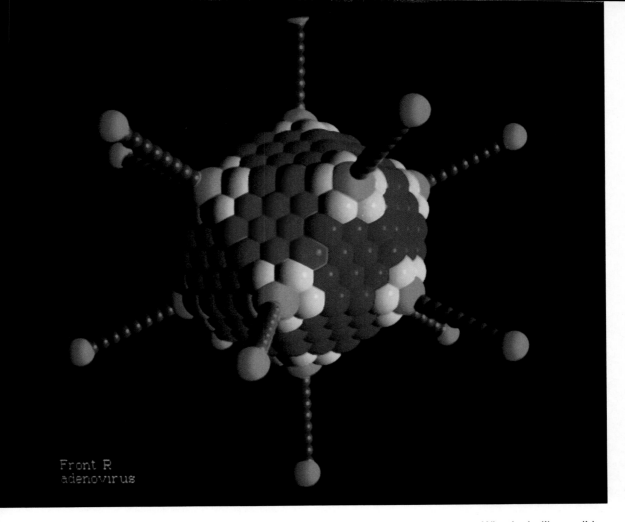

Front R
adenovirus

What looks like a solid model of a virus is actually an image that a computer "drew" on a televisionlike screen. Such images can be moved around on the screen, enabling medical researchers to study complex biological structures without building and manipulating solid models.

cost of most kinds of electronic equipment, including computers.

During the mid-1960's, researchers worked to get around the problems of limited computing power and the jaggies. A different kind of display system solved these problems. Called a *vector display*, it gained prominence in the 1960's and 1970's.

No staircasing effect can occur in a vector display because the screen has no dots. Instead, material that glows when electrons hit it completely covers the screen. To create an image, the electron gun traces the image the way a pencil is used to draw a picture on paper. Because the gun does not scan back and forth across the screen, the computer does not have to use valuable time telling the gun not to fire at parts of the screen that are supposed to remain dark. The computer simply ignores these parts.

Vector display systems made huge amounts of extra computing power available for other tasks such as rotating a picture, zooming in for a close-up, and automatically displaying perspective in a three-dimensional drawing. Individuals who rely on drafting, such as mechanical and electrical engineers, caught on quickly to the new line-making tool, writing programs that could give them various views of machinery and parts.

Biological researchers were among the first scientists to take advantage of vector displays. Many biochemical reactions take place between pairs of complex molecules that fit together like a lock and a key. Before the development of vector displays, a scientist studying these reactions had to build ball-and-stick models of a pair of molecules and then move the two models around, looking for "locks" and "keys." This was a laborious, time-consuming process. With vector displays, a researcher could draw pictures of the molecules rapidly, then manipulate the pictures so that they fit together.

Biomedical researchers also reaped great benefits from the fertile ground of vector displays, designing medicines that do not cause undesirable side effects, such as addiction, allergic reaction, and even poisoning. A molecule that would work well as a medicine because of one lock-and-key arrangement with a harmful bacterium may have an undesirable side effect because of another lock-and-key arrangement with a substance needed by the body. Vector displays helped researchers design molecules that have the first type of lock-and-key arrangement but not the second.

A wire-mesh image drawn by a computer-assisted design program shows how the various parts of the front end of an automobile fit together. A designer can manipulate the image to see how certain parts would react to actual driving conditions—for example, how the suspension system would absorb shock as the car traveled on a bumpy road.

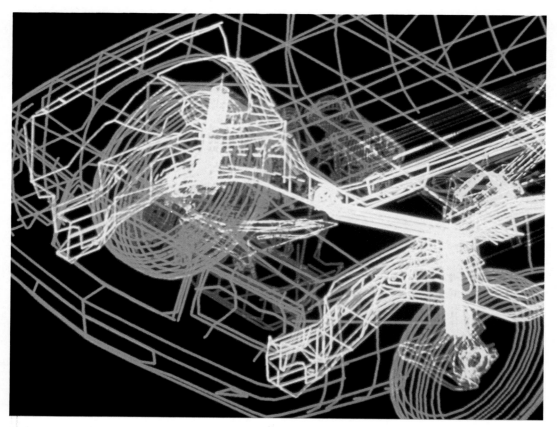

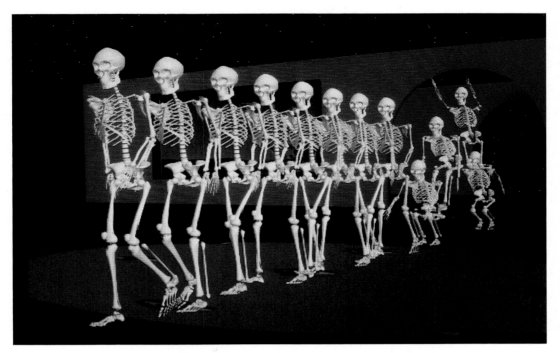

Computer-generated images are a big hit in the film industry. A computer can make a figure move on a screen, *above,* just as a cartoon animation artist can. Lucasfilm used highly sophisticated computer graphics to create a realistic scene in the movie *Young Sherlock Holmes, left.*

These activities gave rise to new input controls now familiar to everyone who uses computer graphics. One such control is the *mouse*—a handheld device the size of a bar of soap, which can be moved around on a desk top to produce instant effects on the screen. Another helpful device is called a *menu*, a listing on the screen of the various functions the computer can perform. By moving an indicator called a *cursor*, usually the image of a square on the screen, the user can choose a particular function on the menu. In some cases, the mouse and the menu work together. To rotate an image, for example, a user might move the mouse to make the cursor line up with the appropriate command on the menu—"rotate." Then with the press of a button, the mouse would command the computer to rotate the graphics image.

But vector displays had a major problem. Vector systems could make only line drawings. Therefore, solid objects were shown as a sort of three-dimensional wire mesh that could only hint at what the objects looked like.

The solution to this problem came about through improvements in raster displays for TV sets and the development of more powerful computers with larger memories. Manufacturers of displays for computer graphics borrowed the improved raster technology from broadcast TV, producing screens that provided clear, sharp images.

An astrophysicist, *below,* uses computer graphics to study a representation of a ring of gas orbiting a black hole—an object in outer space so dense that not even light can escape its gravitational pull. The scientist feeds data about black holes into a terminal connected to an extremely powerful computer. The computer uses the data to construct an image of the gas ring on a color monitor. The computer can also produce detailed images of the gas, including a cross section, *right*.

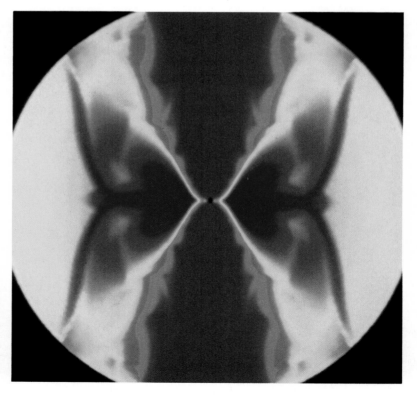

The manufacturers built large memories called *frame buffers* into the displays, enabling displays to "remember" the positions of glowing dots from moment to moment. Now, computers could display images on rasters without flickering. The new rasters could even produce images in vivid color.

A color raster requires more power and memory than does a black-and-white raster because each picture unit is not a single dot but a trio of red, green, and blue dots. The computer varies the intensity of these dots to make the trios glow in all the colors of the rainbow.

The new equipment ushered in a golden age of computer graphics. In the early 1970's, several centers for raster-based graphics emerged. Sutherland, now at the University of Utah in Salt Lake City, teamed up with electrical engineer James F. Blinn and several other colleagues to create programs that made images look more realistic. Their programs blurred the sharp edges of the jaggies and added reflections, shading, shadows, and even texture to images. General Electric Company engineers developed flight simulator graphics in Syracuse, N.Y., and researchers at Mathematical Applications Group, Incorporated, of Elmsford, N.Y., created a design program that could produce realistic images of machinery on a raster display. The wire-mesh effect of a computer-generated car body, for example, gave way to a smooth, gleaming automobile surface that could even cast shadows.

The computer graphics revolution spread throughout the world, spurred on not only by improvements in raster technology and the computer's increased power but also by the lower prices and reduced sizes of displays and computers. The newly developed *microprocessor*—a computer on a silicon chip about the size of a fingernail—led the way. The revolution was ready to envelop the masses. Video games and home personal computers were born.

In 1972, Nolan Bushnell, who became president of Atari Corporation, invented a tennislike game called Pong—the "granddaddy" of the multitudes of beeping, flashing video games common in homes and arcades today. Pong was about the size and shape of today's arcade games. Built into the front of the game were a TV-like screen about 12 inches wide and two dials—one for each of two players. The screen showed a square representing a ball; and thin, vertical rectangles representing racquets. For each position of a player's dial, a racquet position was fed—as 0's and 1's—into a built-in computer. The computer calculated where the racquet should be located on the screen, calculated the ball's rebound angle, and transmitted the results of these calculations to the screen's electron gun. All modern video games—and even sophisticated flight simulators—operate in much the same way.

The computer graphics revolution soon spread to motion-picture studios. With rasters containing more than 1 million trios of dots to

Nature by the Numbers

By the mid-1970's, many users of computer graphics were frustrated. The lines and basic geometrical shapes produced by their computers worked fine for simple engineering drawings of machine parts and electric circuits. But they proved useless for making images of complicated natural objects such as trees and mountains.

Suddenly, in 1975, a new kind of geometry enabled computers to draw realistic pictures of natural objects. The developer of the new geometry, mathematician Benoit B. Mandelbrot, an International Business Machines Corporation (IBM) fellow now teaching at Harvard University, named it *fractal* geometry, from the Latin word for *broken*, because it can represent irregular or fragmented objects. Mandelbrot developed the concept of fractals in the 1960's and early 1970's while working at IBM's Thomas J. Watson Research Center in Yorktown Heights, N.Y.

Fractals bring together several mathematical ideas concerning randomness. The ideas had been known since the end of the 19th century, but most mathematicians scorned them as mere curiosities. Mandelbrot, however, applied these ideas to many apparently random phenomena such as static on a telephone line and fluctuations in cotton prices. Where others saw only chaos, Mandelbrot found elusive yet detectable patterns.

Nature often reveals a subtle repetition. A tree looks like its branch, which looks like its twig, for example. Trees are considered fractal because they are *self-similar* at different scales.

A fractal constructed in 1904 by German mathematician Helge von Koch shows self-similarity clearly and is easy to sketch. First, draw an *equilateral* (equal-sided) triangle. Next, add to the center of each side another equilateral triangle with sides one-third the length of that side. Then, to the center of each side of the new triangles, add an equilateral triangle with sides one-third the length of the sides of the new triangles. By repeating this process two or three times, you would produce a snowflakelike figure.

If you could continue this process indefinitely and view any part of the figure up close, you would see that all the patterns of triangles on triangles—from the largest to the smallest—were alike.

Mandelbrot acknowledges that few people would ever have cared about this new development in mathematics except for one fact. Fractal computer programs can generate realistic, even breathtaking pictures of natural and imaginary objects. With his colleague at IBM, physicist Richard F. Voss, Mandelbrot created some of the most stunning images of natural objects ever seen on a computer screen—rugged mountains, billowy clouds, islands and continents, and even planets. He showed that the outline of a tiny, jagged pebble could be made to grow into a mountain, if one repeated its pattern over and over.

Computer graphics users are not the only fractals enthusiasts. Physicists see fractal patterns in randomly structured materials such as glass. Chemists use fractals to characterize certain chemical reactions. Biologists have observed that tissues grow fractally.

Today, with fractal geometry still in its infancy, no one can predict where the use of fractals will take us. But in the foreseeable future, wherever computer graphics goes, fractals will be there.   [D. K.]

Complex patterns of fractal geometry, rich in intricate detail along their edges, repeat themselves endlessly in a dazzling array of sizes and colors, producing what looks like abstract art.

A fractal program generates irregular shapes that mimic those of nature, enabling a computer artist to produce *Fractal Planetrise,* a vision of an imaginary planet viewed from its moon.

As the science of computer graphics becomes more sophisticated, computer scientists are looking for more realistic ways to move the images around. Joystrings allow a scientist to move images in three dimensions. The wires connected to the computer controls send signals telling the computer how to manipulate an image. They also feed back information about forces in the image through the sense of touch.

provide even greater picture clarity, and with enormously powerful computers to operate the rasters, Hollywood filmmakers saw the advantages of the new technology. Some animations, traditionally drawn by hand one frame at a time, could now be created automatically by computer. Instead of building expensive movie sets or shooting movies at distant locations, filmmakers found they could simply superimpose studio shots of actors over futuristic background images generated by computer graphics. Walt Disney Productions' *Tron* (1982) was the first movie to use this technique.

Generating computer graphics images to fill the wide screens found in most theaters today requires tremendous numbers of dots and extremely powerful computers. *The Last Starfighter*, a Lorimar-Universal film made in 1984, for example, contained computer-generated pictures of battles in space produced by Digital Productions of Los Angeles on a raster containing 24 million trios of dots, with each trio controlled by up to thirty-six 0's and 1's. The "screen" containing all these dots is amazingly small—about 2 inches wide by 1 inch high—so that Hollywood animators can easily transfer raster images to film, which is about the same width. They then project the film for viewing. A \$12.6-million supercomputer, which performs 400 million calculations per second, ran day and night for a month to generate 25 minutes of *Starfighter* film.

Computer-generated film is extremely expensive. Computer animators charge from \$2,000 to \$6,000 per second of film. At those rates, 25 minutes would cost about \$3 million to \$9 million. To decrease costs, animators are developing short cuts for computer graphics. Animators sometimes build their own computer circuits to automatically perform certain tasks that formerly had to be programmed. Also, they create computational techniques that greatly speed up production and enable computers to draw complicated natural objects such as trees and mountains. One such technique uses *fractal geometry*, a branch of mathematics developed in the mid-1970's by mathematician Benoit B. Mandelbrot, an International Business Machines Corporation (IBM) fellow now teaching at Harvard University in Cambridge, Mass. (See NATURE BY THE NUMBERS on page 108.)

A computer animator follows three basic steps. First, the animator draws a model—usually a wire-mesh picture—of the objects that will appear in the scene. This is accomplished by tracing a blueprint of the object with a mouse, by freehand light-pen drawing, or with mathematical equations. The animator then moves the objects, usually by typing commands on the computer keyboard. Finally, additional keyboard commands give everything realistic textures, lighting, and shadows, while minimizing the jaggies.

Although the general public is better acquainted with computer-generated animation in TV commercials and in movies, CAD/CAM is by far the most widely used application for highly sophisticated computer graphics. The annual market for movie and TV computer graphics is a relatively small $25 million to $50 million compared with $2 billion for CAD/CAM.

A great deal of computer graphics activity today centers on making input controls easier to use. Scientists at Carnegie-Mellon University in Pittsburgh, Pa., for example, are developing image controls that will respond to hand gestures. A video camera will send electrical impulses representing gestures to a computer, which will translate the impulses into 0's and 1's to manipulate an image. Other researchers are trying to do this with voice commands.

Richard J. Feldmann, a computer specialist at the National Institutes of Health in Bethesda, Md., and electrical engineer and computer specialist John Staudhammer of the University of Florida in Gainesville helped to develop controls called *joystrings* that are used to manipulate images of molecules and to feed back information to the user through the sense of touch. The joystring device consists of a hand-sized, T-shaped object connected by wires to plates above, below, and behind it. When the user changes the arrangement of a molecule, the wires even transmit a feeling of the forces within the molecule resisting the change.

Displays also may change down the road. Several researchers are attempting to replace ordinary screens with true three-dimensional displays called *holograms* that are projected in space.

Someday, a biochemist may be able to walk around—and even through—a gigantic holographic display of a molecule in a medical research laboratory. Using only hand gestures and spoken commands, the biochemist may change the positions of individual atoms in the molecule, rotate the entire structure, and fit it into the image of, for example, a cancer cell as a key fits into a lock. Perhaps in this way, after years of difficult research, computer graphics will help scientists develop cures for the deadliest diseases.

So the future of computer graphics seems to be limited only by our imaginations. And wherever our imaginations go, computer graphics will make the journey faster and easier.

For further reading:

Artwick, Bruce A. *Applied Concepts in Microcomputer Graphics.* Prentice Hall, 1984.

Byte (computer graphics issue), September 1984.

Dewdney, A. K. "Computer Recreations." *Scientific American*, August 1985.

Hammer, Signe. "The Image Maker." *Science Digest*, March 1985.

Kerlow, Isaac Victor, and Rosebush, Judson. *Computer Graphics for Designers and Artists.* Van Nostrand Reinhold, 1986.

Mandelbrot, Benoit B. *The Fractal Geometry of Nature.* W. H. Freeman, 1982.

McDermott, Jeanne. "Geometrical Forms Known As Fractals Find Sense in Chaos." *Smithsonian*, December 1983.

Scott, Joan, ed. *Computergraphia: New Visions of Form, Fantasy, and Function.* Gulf, 1984.

West, Susan. "The New Realism." *Science '84*, July/August 1984.

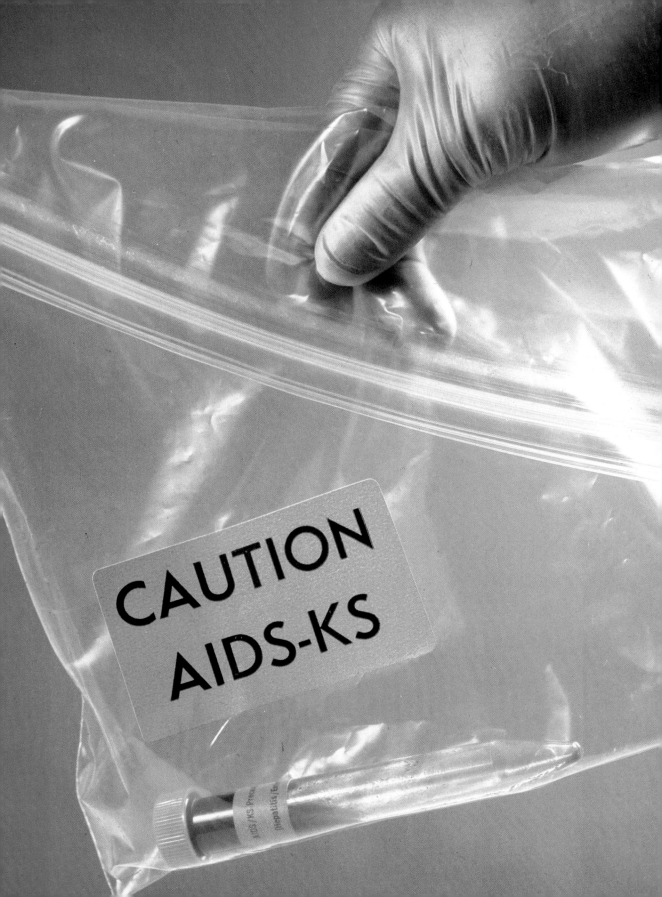

Never has so much been learned about a disease in so short a time as scientists, using the tools of biotechnology, have learned about AIDS and its cause.

Unraveling the Secrets of AIDS

BY DONALD P. FRANCIS

During the summer of 1981, physician Michael S. Gottlieb of Los Angeles noticed an unusual disease in several of his patients. It was *Pneumocystis carinii* pneumonia (PCP), a rare kind of pneumonia that usually occurs only in patients with severe diseases of the immune system or in cancer patients receiving powerful drug treatment. But Gottlieb's patients were young, otherwise healthy men. At almost the same time, on the other side of the United States, dermatologist Alvin E. Friedman-Kien of New York City had several patients with an unusual form of skin cancer, Kaposi's sarcoma, which usually strikes only elderly men of Mediterranean descent. But Friedman-Kien's patients were also otherwise healthy young men.

As we know now, Gottlieb and Friedman-Kien were seeing the first known cases of a new and terrible disease—AIDS (*a*cquired *im*mune *d*eficiency *s*yndrome). Even though the patients complained about very different symptoms, their underlying disease was the same. Both groups of patients were suffering from a severe weakness of the immune system, the body's defense against all types of diseases.

From the beginning, the results of AIDS were tragic. Despite heroic efforts, physicians could do nothing to save their AIDS patients.

Glossary

Antibody: An immune-system molecule that locks onto a microbe's antigens and helps other parts of the immune system destroy the microbe.

Antigen: A molecule on the surface of a microbe or other invader that identifies it as foreign to the body.

B cell: A type of white blood cell that produces antibodies.

Deoxyribonucleic acid (DNA): The molecule that makes up the genes of all plants, animals, and some viruses and carries the instructions for an organism's life processes.

Gene: A segment of DNA that contains coded instructions for the production of a single protein.

Helper T cell: A type of white blood cell that orders B cells to produce more antibodies.

Retrovirus: An RNA virus that can insert its genes into those of the cell it invades.

Ribonucleic acid (RNA): The molecule that is a copy of DNA and carries out DNA's instructions. The genes of some viruses are made of RNA.

The author:
Donald P. Francis is a physician with the Centers for Disease Control, serving as AIDS adviser to the state of California.

The patients not only contracted PCP and Kaposi's sarcoma but also fell victim to a host of other infections and cancers. If one of the infections or cancers was successfully treated, then another would follow. Sometimes the patients survived for a year or more, and sometimes there were periods when the patients appeared normal. But inevitably, another infection or cancer followed, and the patient ultimately died.

The disease spread at an alarming rate. By mid-1983, there were more than 1,400 diagnosed cases in the United States; by mid-1986, there were more than 20,000.

What was causing this horrible disease? The first step in answering this question was to collect information: Who were the victims, where did they live, what factors did they have in common? At the U.S. Centers for Disease Control (CDC) in Atlanta, Ga., doctors called *epidemiologists* began to investigate the outbreak by reviewing medical records and interviewing the patients. Their first finding was that the outbreak was indeed new. The CDC doctors were able to find one or two cases as far back as 1978, but none before that.

The CDC investigators and researchers at a number of other laboratories also wanted to know what had gone wrong with the immune systems of AIDS patients. They soon found that a single type of white blood cell known as the *helper T cell* was at the center of the problem.

The immune system is responsible for protecting the body from invasion by foreign intruders, such as bacteria and viruses. It is a complex system consisting of several types of white blood cells and various kinds of molecules, each with a particular job to do. When something foreign invades the body and attempts to set up residence, the immune system rallies to eliminate the intruder. This immune reaction occurs in several stages. The foreign invader is recognized by a type of white blood cell called a *B cell*, which produces molecules called *antibodies*. Each invader carries on its surface *antigens* that identify it as foreign to the body. Antibodies lock onto these antigens and help the other cells of the immune system kill the foreign invader.

The helper T cells are crucial players in this immune response. They direct the attack. One of their most crucial functions lies in ordering B cells to produce great quantities of antibodies. When all parts of the immune system are working effectively, the foreign invader is eliminated and the body continues to thrive. If for some reason the immune system falters, then the invader can defeat the body's defenses, and disease or death may follow.

The researchers found that this is what happens with AIDS. They discovered that the AIDS patients had few, if any, helper T cells in their bloodstreams. Without helper T cells to order the attack, infections, such as PCP, or cancer cells, such as Kaposi's sarcoma, can grow unchecked. In September 1982, after this defect in the immune system was discovered, the disease was named acquired immune deficiency syndrome.

By late 1982, some 500 AIDS cases had been diagnosed in the United States, and the CDC epidemiologists had found that the cases did not occur randomly. They were concentrated primarily in New York City, San Francisco, and Los Angeles. Almost all the victims of the disease were men, and most of them were white. In addition, three-fourths of the patients were homosexual. Many others were intravenous drug users or emigrants from the Caribbean island of Haiti.

Armed with this information, the investigators proposed several possible causes. One theory suggested that the disease was caused by some toxic drug. Another theory suggested that the immune systems of AIDS patients were being overwhelmed by some substance to which they were exposed because of their life styles. But the most probable theory proposed that some infectious microbe, such as a virus or bacterium, was behind it all. Those who favored the infectious-agent theory pointed out that new AIDS cases arose mainly among male homosexuals and intravenous drug abusers, two groups known to be at risk for several other infectious diseases, such as hepatitis B.

Researchers soon found important evidence that supported the infectious-agent theory. In late 1982, they discovered AIDS in individuals who belonged to none of the known risk groups. These new patients had only one thing in common: They had been treated with blood or blood products. Some of them were *hemophiliacs*, people whose body lacks the ability to make an essential factor for clotting blood. Hemophiliacs are treated with injections of this factor manufactured from human blood plasma. The other new AIDS cases were adults and children who had received blood transfusions. The CDC investigators found that the supplies of blood used to treat these patients included blood donated by either homosexual men or intravenous drug users.

Not only did this discovery provide more indirect support for the infectious-agent theory but it also pointed toward a virus as the culprit. The antihemophiliac clotting factor was manufactured by a process that filtered out larger organisms such

The Frightening Rise of AIDS
Since 1981, the number of new AIDS cases diagnosed in the United States has roughly doubled every year. The 8,551 new cases diagnosed in 1985 brought the total to almost 18,000 cases. The Centers for Disease Control estimate there will be between 14,000 and 15,000 new cases diagnosed in 1986.

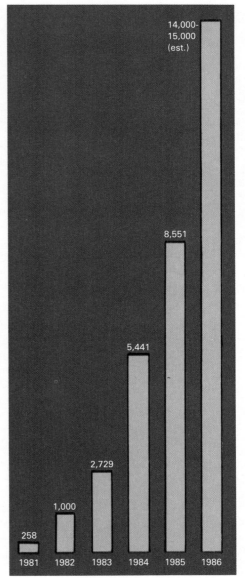

Source: Centers for Disease Control.

AIDS and the Immune System

The immune system, the body's defense against disease, consists mainly of white blood cells that circulate in the bloodstream. There are several kinds of these immune system cells, each with its own assignment in the battle against disease. Early in their investigation of AIDS, scientists noticed that AIDS victims have weakened immune systems.

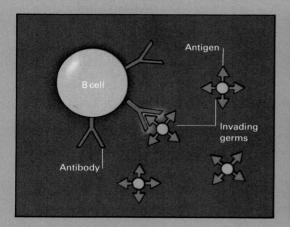

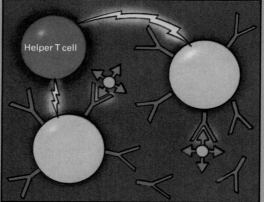

A normal immune system goes into action when special white blood cells called B cells notice invaders, such as germs or cancer cells. Invaders betray their presence with molecules called antigens, which identify the invaders as foreign to the body. B cells produce disease-fighting molecules called antibodies that help destroy the invaders by locking onto their antigens.

Next, another kind of white blood cell, called the helper T cell, directs an all-out attack against the foreign invader. One of the duties of the helper T cell is to order the B cells to increase antibody production until—with the aid of other immune system cells—the foreign invaders are overwhelmed and destroyed.

as bacteria. Only a virus would be small enough to slip through the microscopically fine filters.

The AIDS researchers knew that searching for an unknown virus would be difficult. These tiny organisms do not grow by themselves outside of living cells. In order to study them, researchers must grow viruses in laboratory animals or laboratory cell cultures. To make matters worse, many viruses are very picky about which animals or cultured cells they will grow in. So the researchers called upon their understanding of the AIDS disease process for clues to where the virus might lurk. Because the disease is caused by the destruction of white blood cells, the investigators reasoned that the virus they were looking for must grow in and destroy white blood cells.

In late 1982 and early 1983, teams of researchers at several major laboratories in the United States and France were examining viruses in white blood cells. In May 1983, a research team headed by virologist Luc Montagnier at the Pasteur Institute in Paris published a report indicating they may have identified the actual virus that

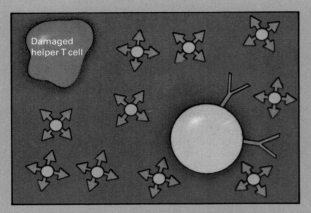

Damaged helper T cell

An AIDS victim's immune system does not have functioning helper T cells. Therefore, when an invader strikes, the B cells do not receive an order to step up antibody production and no other immune system cells are called into action, *left.* Thus, invading germs and cancer cells are free to overwhelm the body, causing AIDS patients to suffer a range of illnesses, such as the rare skin cancer called Kaposi's sarcoma, *below left,* or an equally rare form of pneumonia, *below,* caused by parasites in lung tissue (arrow).

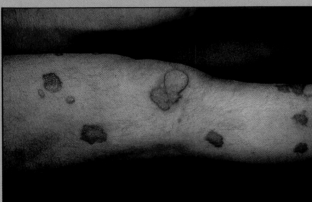

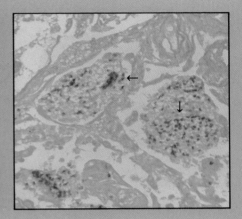

causes AIDS. Montagnier and his colleagues found the virus in cells taken from an AIDS patient's *lymph nodes* (small organs in the body where white blood cells, including helper T cells, grow). The French researchers named their virus lymphadenopathy-associated virus (LAV).

From this point, it took almost a year to prove that this virus was indeed the cause of AIDS. During this time, dozens of different strains of the virus were found in patients with AIDS and AIDS-related conditions. In the United States, researchers at the National Cancer Institute headed by virologist Robert C. Gallo called the virus they found human T-lymphotropic virus, Type 3 (HTLV-III); a team at the University of California, San Francisco, headed by virologist Jay Levy, called their virus AIDS-associated retrovirus (ARV). All these turned out to be variations of the same virus. Other researchers developed tests for antibodies to the virus; the tests showed that all patients with AIDS and related conditions had been infected with the same type of virus.

Thus, it took less than three years from the discovery of a new disease in 1981 until scientists had positively identified the virus that causes it. Never had so much been learned about a disease and its cause in so short a period of time—thanks to the tools of modern microbiology and biotechnology. And since it was identified in 1983, scientists have learned a great deal more about the AIDS virus, which in May 1986 was renamed Human Immunodeficiency Virus (HIV).

Like all viruses, the AIDS virus is so small that it can be seen only through electron microscopes. And also like all viruses, it has no ability to multiply on its own. Viruses are built up in layers and contain very few parts—perhaps a dozen. They have so few parts because they have very little genetic material and thus can *code for* (specify the production of) only a few proteins. But they are champions of biological efficiency. With this limited genetic material, and the help of the cells they invade, viruses can gather the proteins necessary to make up new offspring, reassemble themselves, and exit the cell to go after additional cells and repeat the cycle.

The outer layer of the AIDS virus is made of protein. This protein coat determines what cells the virus will infect. For example, certain areas of the AIDS virus protein coat fit into proteins called

The virus that causes AIDS was found independently in 1983 and 1984 by three research teams led by: Robert Gallo of the National Cancer Institute in Bethesda, Md., *right,* who named the virus HTLV-III; Jay Levy of the University of California, San Francisco, *below,* who named it ARV; and Luc Montagnier of the Pasteur Institute in Paris, *below right,* who named it LAV.

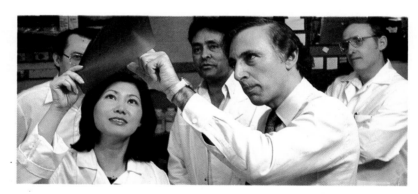

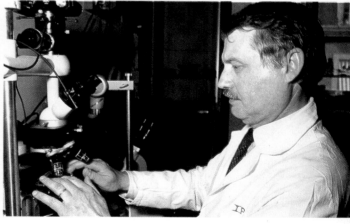

receptors on the surface of helper T cells and some cells in the brain. These receptors act like "locks" into which the virus can fit its "key" to enter the cell. And this explains why certain viruses infect only certain cells. For example, cold and flu viruses infect the respiratory tract, never blood cells, because they fit into receptors found only on respiratory cells. On the other hand, the AIDS virus infects only helper T cells and certain brain cells, never cells in the respiratory tract.

The lock-and-key arrangement of cell receptors and viral protein coats also determines how the virus can be transmitted. The AIDS virus must enter the bloodstream somehow and directly infect white blood cells. Medical evidence indicates it is spread in limited ways—through sexual contact with an infected person, through contaminated needles shared by drug users, or through contaminated blood or blood products. In addition, babies born to infected mothers can be infected with the AIDS virus. Although the virus has occasionally been found in saliva, no one is known to have contracted AIDS by casual contact, even kissing. Because the AIDS virus cannot attach to and enter cells of the respiratory tract, spread of this virus by coughing and sneezing is very unlikely.

As with all viruses, the outer proteins of the AIDS virus are important in immunity, because this is the part of the virus that is recognized by the immune system. The virus's identifying antigens are protein molecules that stick out of the coat like little spikes.

Inside another protein layer called the core lies the genetic material of the AIDS virus. The genes of plants, animals, and many viruses are constructed of deoxyribonucleic acid (DNA). The genes of some viruses, however, are constructed of ribonucleic acid (RNA). Some of these viruses with RNA genes are called *retroviruses*. The AIDS virus is a retrovirus. Retroviruses can insert their genes into the genetic material of the cells they infect, and some are known to cause cancers in animals. *Retro* means *backward*, and, from the standpoint of genetic material, this is exactly how retroviruses, including the AIDS virus, behave.

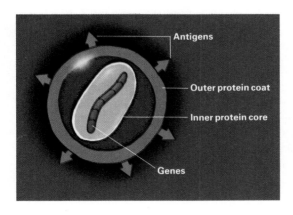

The AIDS virus consists of genetic material (RNA), an inner protein core, an outer protein coat, and identifying antigens. Because its genes are made of RNA instead of the usual DNA, the AIDS virus is classified as a retrovirus, a type of virus that can insert its genes into the genes of the organism it infects.

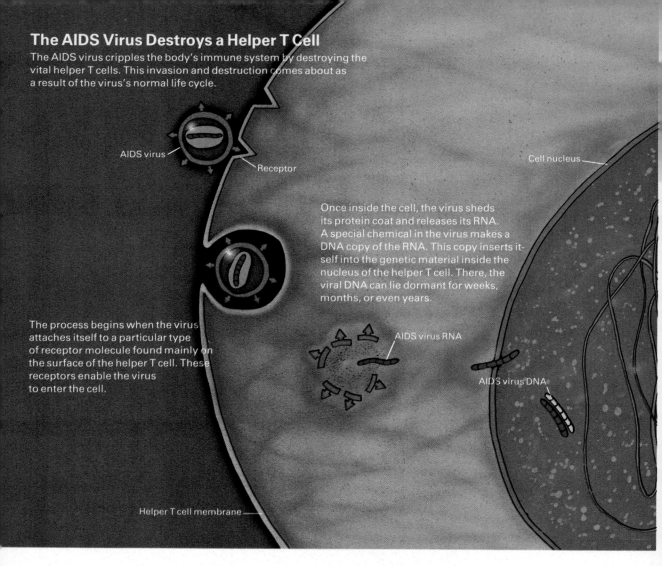

The AIDS Virus Destroys a Helper T Cell

The AIDS virus cripples the body's immune system by destroying the vital helper T cells. This invasion and destruction comes about as a result of the virus's normal life cycle.

AIDS virus

Receptor

Cell nucleus

Once inside the cell, the virus sheds its protein coat and releases its RNA. A special chemical in the virus makes a DNA copy of the RNA. This copy inserts itself into the genetic material inside the nucleus of the helper T cell. There, the viral DNA can lie dormant for weeks, months, or even years.

The process begins when the virus attaches itself to a particular type of receptor molecule found mainly on the surface of the helper T cell. These receptors enable the virus to enter the cell.

AIDS virus RNA

AIDS virus DNA

Helper T cell membrane

All organisms require both DNA and RNA to process genetic information. In organisms whose genes are made of DNA, the DNA contains the instructions for all the organism's functions, which are carried out by the various proteins for which the DNA codes. When a cell needs to make a particular protein, it begins by making an RNA blueprint of the part of the DNA molecule containing the appropriate genes. This RNA copy then directs the assembly of the protein. So, in these organisms, the flow of genetic information goes from DNA to RNA.

In retroviruses, the genetic information flows the opposite way, from RNA to DNA. In order for a retrovirus to reproduce, it must first make a DNA blueprint of its RNA genes. This backward flow of genetic information gives retroviruses, such as the AIDS virus, the dangerous ability to insert themselves into the DNA genes of the cells they invade.

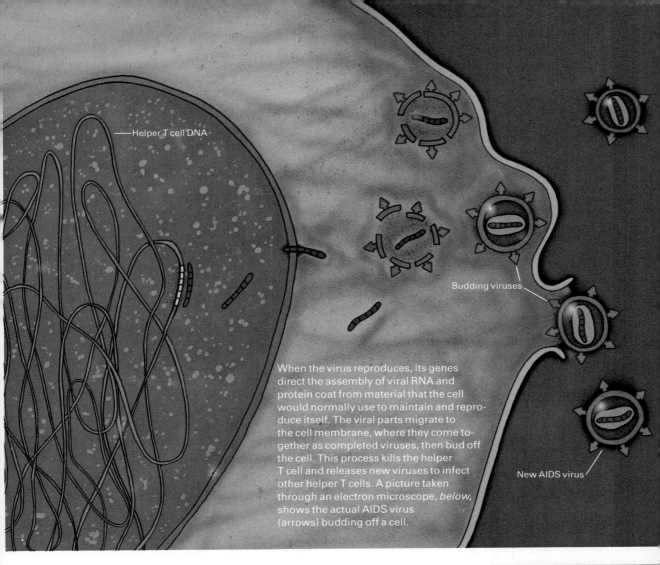

—Helper T cell DNA

Budding viruses

When the virus reproduces, its genes direct the assembly of viral RNA and protein coat from material that the cell would normally use to maintain and reproduce itself. The viral parts migrate to the cell membrane, where they come together as completed viruses, then bud off the cell. This process kills the helper T cell and releases new viruses to infect other helper T cells. A picture taken through an electron microscope, *below*, shows the actual AIDS virus (arrows) budding off a cell.

New AIDS virus

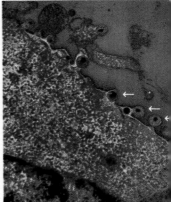

When the AIDS virus invades a helper T cell, the virus breaks up, shedding its protein coat and releasing its RNA to be copied into DNA. The copying is done by a special biochemical called *reverse transcriptase*, which the AIDS virus makes.

The DNA copy of the AIDS virus genes inserts itself into the genetic material inside the nucleus of the helper T cell. There, the viral genes can remain for weeks or months—perhaps even five years or more—without causing symptoms.

Scientists do not yet know what causes the virus to become active. But when it does, an RNA copy of the AIDS virus DNA hidden among the cell's genes moves out of the nucleus and directs the assembly of more AIDS virus parts. The new AIDS viruses line up along the infected T cell's outer membrane and form bulges, or buds, from which the new viruses burst out to infect other helper T cells. This process of infection and replication saps the resources of

Tracking Down the Origin of AIDS

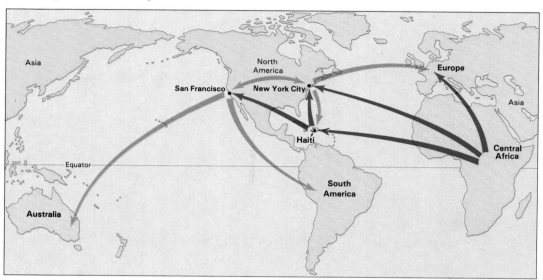

Epidemiologists have found evidence that the AIDS virus originated in central Africa. Travelers may have carried the disease to Europe, Haiti, or both, then to the United States, *top.* The virus now has spread to many areas of the world. The AIDS virus is similar to a virus found in the African green monkey, *above,* and researchers have speculated that one virus may have developed from the other.

the helper T cells and kills them, thus crippling the immune system.

People infected with the virus but having no signs of disease are known as "healthy carriers." Epidemiologists estimate that about 1 million to 2 million people (between one-half and three-fourths of the people infected with the AIDS virus) are healthy carriers and potential transmitters of infection to others. The disease could be passed along if some of the infected T cells entered the bloodstream of another person.

While virologists were studying the structure and behavior of the AIDS virus, epidemiologists were trying to answer other questions: Where did the AIDS virus come from? Was it imported from faraway lands, or is it a new mutation of an old virus?

An important clue to the answer came from Europe. In the early 1980's, Belgian physician Nathan Clumeck noticed that some of his patients from central Africa suffered from a disease that had many similarities to the new disease being reported in the United States. On learning of this, investigators wondered whether these patients had contracted the disease at home in Africa or while traveling in Europe. Studies now underway point toward the AIDS virus being present in Africa before 1960.

Meanwhile, scientists discovered an AIDS-like disease in monkeys at both the California Regional Primate Center in Davis and at the New England Regional Primate Center in Southborough, Mass. Other researchers found a virus similar to the AIDS virus in monkeys in central Africa, particularly the African green monkey. This caused some scientists to wonder whether the monkey virus had been passed to human beings, perhaps through bites or scratches.

Once in humans, the virus might have changed into the form that causes AIDS. This is possible, but much further study is required to be sure.

AIDS is on the increase in Africa much as it is in Europe and the United States. In Africa, however, men and women appear to be equally at risk. Prostitutes are especially likely to have AIDS in Africa and may be a major factor in spreading the infection.

Some epidemiologists speculate that AIDS could have traveled from Africa by two routes—to Western Europe by one route; to Haiti and the United States by another. Exactly how Haiti fits into the puzzle is still unclear. Haiti has been a popular vacation site for homosexual men, especially from New York City. Whether Haitians were first infected by visiting Americans or by Africans is a question that is difficult or impossible to answer.

From wherever the AIDS virus originated, it has now spread to many nations of the world. People infected with the AIDS virus appear to be concentrated in urban areas, probably because of the ways in which the disease is transmitted. The greatest risk factors are large numbers of sexual contacts or the sharing of needles among drug users. And in some nations, the number of AIDS cases has reached truly epidemic proportions. The CDC estimates that by mid-1987 the United States will have almost 40,000 cases of AIDS and Western Europe about 3,000 cases. There are no accurate estimates of the number of AIDS cases in Africa, but the disease appears to be taking an increasing toll, especially in the central area from Zaire to Kenya.

The virus was apparently introduced into the homosexual communities of New York and San Francisco in the mid-1970's. The CDC has been able to trace its rise at least in one group of homosexual men by analyzing blood samples from volunteers who participated in hepatitis studies in San Francisco beginning in 1978. The CDC tested these blood specimens for evidence of AIDS virus and found that in 1978 less than 3 per cent of the homosexual men had antibodies to the AIDS virus, thus indicating they had been infected with the virus. By 1981, this figure had risen to 25 per cent; by 1984, to 65 per cent.

Scientists have learned that not everyone infected with the AIDS virus comes down with the disease. They have followed a small number of infected people for between two and five years. Of these, between 14 and 34 per cent have developed AIDS and approximately 25 per cent have developed what are called AIDS-related conditions (ARC). Patients with ARC usually have enlarged lymph nodes, often in the neck, armpits, and groin. Many patients have no other symptoms, but others have considerable discomfort, including fevers, night sweats, and diarrhea. Most AIDS-related conditions are mild, but some are severe and others have progressed to AIDS. Patients are said to have AIDS if they have one of several diseases,

The Search for Prevention or Cure

Scientists are mapping the genes of the AIDS virus and studying the various stages of its life cycle for clues that may lead to the development of a vaccine against the disease or drugs that might provide a cure.

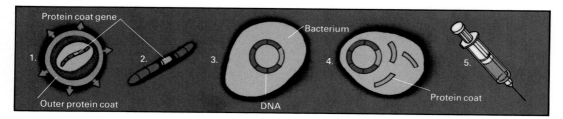

A vaccine against AIDS probably would contain only part of the virus, perhaps the outer protein coat (1). With sophisticated genetic engineering techniques, scientists could remove the gene that codes for this area (2) and splice it into the DNA of another organism, such as a bacterium (3). Acting like biological factories, bacteria would produce pieces of AIDS virus protein coat (4), which could be extracted and purified to create a vaccine (5).

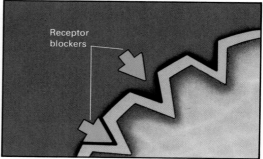

There are several points in the virus's life cycle where drugs might intervene. For example, tailor-made antibodies, *above,* might be injected to attack the virus directly, or a receptor-blocking molecule, *above right,* could prevent the virus from entering the cell. Other types of drugs might prevent the viral RNA from changing into DNA or block the assembly of new virus parts.

mainly PCP and Kaposi's sarcoma, that reflect a severe weakness in their immune system. Increasingly, however, physicians are noticing the AIDS virus's ability to damage tissue in the brain and nervous system.

There are specific treatments for some of the diseases resulting from AIDS, but there is not yet an effective treatment for the underlying weakness of the immune system. All that has been learned about AIDS so far, however, may someday lead to the prevention or cure of this devastating disease. And progress has been made in eliminating the risk of transmitting AIDS through blood transfusions or blood products.

Soon after the AIDS virus was identified, researchers developed a test that could detect the presence of antibodies to the virus, which would mean that the immune system had been activated against the virus. Beginning in March 1985, this antibody test was used to check all donated blood in the United States, and in July, the U.S. Food and Drug Administration announced that the national blood supply was AIDS-free. Blood products used by hemophiliacs are now heat-treated to kill the AIDS virus.

Scientists have not yet had as much success in the search for drugs or a vaccine to prevent or lessen the effects of AIDS. Researchers are experimenting with several drugs. Some are looking for drugs that will boost the function of the immune system or prevent the virus from entering the helper T cells. Other researchers are trying to find drugs that will either stimulate regrowth of the missing helper T cells or prevent the AIDS virus from multiplying. Some drugs are aimed at preventing the virus from making a DNA copy of its RNA genes. Other drugs are designed to prevent new viral parts from assembling inside the cell. All of these drugs, when mixed with the virus in laboratory culture, prevent the growth of the virus. Some of these have actually been tried on patients. Although they do decrease the amount of virus in the blood, they have not caused any permanent improvement.

Meanwhile, other teams of scientists are trying to develop a vaccine against AIDS. One question they must resolve is whether the virus's antigens frequently mutate to disguise the virus from the immune system. If these changes do not happen very frequently, scientists might be able to create a vaccine based on the virus's outer protein coat or inner protein core. They might also be able to create a vaccine containing antigens from several strains of the AIDS virus or from a related, but harmless, virus.

No one has ever made a retrovirus vaccine for human beings. One was developed in the early 1980's against an AIDS-like disease that afflicts cats, and this encourages scientists working on an AIDS-virus vaccine for human beings. An AIDS vaccine will most likely be made using genetic engineering techniques. Scientists would remove the gene that codes for the protein coat, for example, and splice it into the genes of bacteria, yeast, or mammalian "host" cells. The cells would grow and multiply, and the AIDS virus gene would direct the production of large quantities of protein coat for use in a vaccine. Any vaccine made by these methods would have to be tried in chimpanzees before being tested in human beings. Making and testing the vaccine would take at least five years.

Meanwhile, efforts to halt the spread of AIDS center on educating people in high-risk groups and encouraging them to alter their behavior. Recommendations for preventing transmission of the AIDS virus from one person to the next focus on sexual behavior, since sexual contact is the most common mode of transmission. All public health officials and AIDS researchers caution individuals against having sexual relations with multiple partners or with members of an AIDS high-risk group. They also warn drug users not to share needles. With the prospects for a vaccine or cure not likely before the 1990's, our best hope for stopping or slowing the spread of AIDS may be through these behavior-modification methods.

Space probes and planetary geologists
have been giving us an increasingly
better picture of the planet Mars.

Changing Visions of Mars

BY STEVEN W. SQUYRES

For centuries, people have been fascinated by the planet Mars. In ancient times, Mars—named after the Roman god of war—inspired religious myths. In the early 1900's, reports of "canals" on Mars fired the imaginations of science-fiction writers. Today, Mars attracts scientific scrutiny by a breed of scientists known as planetary geologists, who study the surfaces of planets in our solar system.

Our current knowledge of Mars was a long time in coming. The scientific study of Mars did not begin until the late 1500's, when Danish astronomer Tycho Brahe made precise measurements of the planet's movements in relation to the stars. In the early 1600's, the

Opposite page:
The age of space exploration is bringing Mars into clearer focus. A model of the planet, assembled from photos taken by orbiting spacecraft, reveals towering volcanoes and huge canyons that provide clues to how the red planet evolved. *Viking Lander 2* (inset photo) returned a close-up view of an apparently lifeless, boulder-strewn plain.

German astronomer Johannes Kepler used these as well as other measurements to arrive at his laws of planetary motion, which describe how the planets orbit the sun. The use of telescopes to study Mars began in the early 1600's with Italian astronomer Galileo Galilei and continued in the mid-1600's with Dutch astronomer Christian Huygens. But their telescopes were crude and simple instruments and were not powerful enough to reveal more than a few details of the planet's surface.

Scientific study of Mars through telescopes began in earnest with the discoveries of the English astronomer William Herschel. During observations in the late 1700's, Herschel determined the length of the Martian day and the tilt of Mars's rotational axis. Both are remarkably similar to Earth's. The Martian day lasts 24 hours and 37 minutes, compared with Earth's 23 hours and 56 minutes. The rotational *axis* of Mars—an imaginary line through its center—is tilted at an angle of about 25°, compared with 23½° for Earth. This tilt is responsible for the change of seasons on Earth, and Herschel correctly concluded that Mars must have seasons as well. Herschel, like others before him, noted bright caps at the north and south poles of Mars and concluded that they were thin ice deposits advancing and retreating with the seasons. He also noted and recorded a number of dark markings near Mars's equator, which he thought were large bodies of water.

Herschel's observations were followed by those of many other scientists, the most influential of whom was Italian astronomer Giovanni V. Schiaparelli, who in 1878 published a map of Mars showing the dark regions in much greater detail. His map also showed an intricate network of lines connecting many dark regions and crisscrossing the Martian surface like strands of a misshapen spider web. Schiaparelli saw these features only during nights of extreme atmospheric clarity—during "good seeing" to use the jargon of astronomers—and he called them *canali* (channels).

"Canals" on Mars?

What followed was one of the strangest episodes in the history of astronomy. When Schiaparelli's observations were published in English, the Italian word *canali* was translated as the English word *canals*, meaning human-made waterways, rather than as *channels*. The mistranslation may or may not have led to the popular misconception that canals existed on the surface of Mars, but nevertheless, the idea became firmly fixed in the minds of the public and in the minds of many scientists as well. The American astronomer Percival Lowell was fascinated by the reports of dark lines on the surface of Mars and particularly by the idea that such regular features might have been created by intelligent beings.

A wealthy man, Lowell established an observatory in Flagstaff, Ariz., in 1894 and dedicated it largely to observations of Mars. In three books that were widely read in the early 1900's, Lowell put

The author:
Steven W. Squyres is a research scientist at the Ames Research Center of the National Aeronautics and Space Administration at Moffett Field, Calif.

forth the details of his theory. Briefly stated, it was this: Mars was a dry planet, with most of its water locked up in the polar caps as ice. Mars was also the home of a civilization, advanced in its technology but dependent on the small and dwindling water supply. This civilization had built a network of irrigation canals connecting its agricultural areas and cities, drawing water from the edges of the polar caps. Believers in the theory were fascinated by the hypothetical Martians, sympathetic with their plight, and frightened of their technological prowess.

The theory had its disbelievers, however, including French astronomer Eugène M. Antoniadi and American astronomer Edward E. Barnard, who were unable to detect the canals with superb telescopes on exceptionally clear nights. Nevertheless, Lowell's theory dominated popular thought about Mars during the first half of the 1900's. Skepticism among scientists regarding the canals grew during the 1930's, 1940's, and 1950's, but the technological tools needed to put the matter to rest did not become available until the advent of space flight.

Space flights to Mars begin

The first United States spacecraft to be sent toward Mars was *Mariner 3*, launched from Cape Canaveral, Fla., on Nov. 5, 1964. The mission failed due to problems in the nose cone design, however, and the spacecraft went into orbit around the sun. Engineers worked around the clock to improve the design, and the launch of *Mariner 4* on Nov. 28, 1964, went off without a hitch. On July 14, 1965, the spacecraft flew by Mars, taking 22 pictures of the Martian surface.

The pictures failed to reveal any signs of a Martian civilization. Instead of smooth plains laced by a network of canals, they showed a rugged surface much like the moon's, pockmarked by craters and without any evidence of life. The preservation of the craters, which probably formed when meteorites bombarded the surface very early in the history of Mars, suggested to scientists that there had been little geologic activity on Mars for several billion years. Otherwise, such activity in the form of volcanic eruptions or water erosion would have changed the surface of the planet,

Facts About Mars

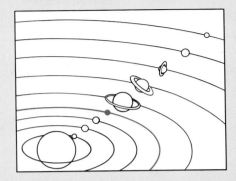

Distance from sun:
Shortest 128.5 million miles
Greatest 154.9 million miles
Average 141.7 million miles

Distance from Earth:
Shortest 48.7 million miles
Greatest 248 million miles

Length of year:
687 Earth days

Diameter at equator:
4,200 miles

Period of rotation:
24 hours, 37 minutes

Atmosphere:
98% carbon dioxide
1.7% nitrogen
Traces of oxygen, argon, and other gases

Number of satellites:
Two

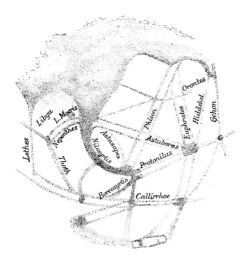

Italian astronomer Giovanni V. Schiaparelli in 1878 drew a map, *top,* of Mars after he observed what looked like channels on the planet's surface. But the Italian word for "channels" was mistranslated as "canals," suggesting the work of intelligent beings and inspiring science-fiction conceptions or creations of Martians like that *above.*

erasing many of the craters. But as later explorations showed, *Mariner 4*'s cameras obtained only a partial glimpse of the surface. *Mariner 4* virtually ended the speculation about canals, however. The canals had been optical illusions, existing only in the minds of some imaginative astronomers.

Mariner 6 and *Mariner 7* followed *Mariner 4* to Mars in 1969. (*Mariner 5* went to Venus.) Like *Mariner 4*, they were fly-by missions, making one swift pass by the planet, rather than going into orbit around it. Together, they produced 58 high-quality pictures of the Martian surface. Again, the vast majority of the pictures showed little but heavily cratered terrain, separated in some areas by featureless plains. By the end of 1969, the three fly-bys of Mars had photographed a small fraction of the Martian surface in detail. The photographs showed no evidence of life and revealed precious little evidence to suggest that life could ever have existed there or that the planet itself had ever been geologically active. The surface of Mars began to seem dull and uninteresting.

This view of Mars was also proved wrong, however, by the next—and far more ambitious—exploration of Mars. Two U.S. spacecraft—*Mariner 8* and *Mariner 9*—were to have gone into orbit around the planet, mapping its entire surface in detail. *Mariner 8* was launched on May 8, 1971, but an hour after launch, it lay at the bottom of the Atlantic Ocean. Engineers traced the problem to the rocket's guidance system. After they made the necessary corrections, *Mariner 9* was launched on May 30, 1971. It performed flawlessly.

Astounding geologic features

Although things went well with the spacecraft, in late September, astronomers noticed a problem on Mars. A small dust storm had developed in one region, and it spread swiftly across the planet's surface. When *Mariner 9* entered orbit around Mars on Nov. 13, 1971, the planet was completely obscured by swirling dust.

The *Mariner 9* mission was planned to last 90 days, but for the first 90 days that the spacecraft orbited Mars, the storm continued to rage. The only features visible were four dark spots—a spot called Nix Olympica that had been seen earlier with telescopes and three others to the southeast

North Pole

Olympus Mons

Tharsis bulge

Ascraeus Mons

Pavonis Mons

Valles Marineris

Arsia Mons

South Pole

that were dubbed "North Spot," "Middle Spot," and "South Spot." Then in early January 1972, to the immense relief of all involved, the winds began to die down, and the dust clouds began to settle. Gradually, the true nature of the "spots" became clear. They were the summits of enormous volcanoes, far larger than any mountains on Earth. As the dust continued to settle, an astounding variety of geologic features was slowly revealed. Scientists still saw impact craters. But they also saw volcanoes, a canyon system 3,000 miles long, vast plains of lava spewed out by volcanoes, enormous dry riverbeds, and regions of finely layered dust deposits—unlike anything seen on Earth—at the planet's poles. Mars was far more complicated than geologists had dreamed. The *Mariner 9* spacecraft functioned

The Surface of Mars
The first close-up views of the Martian surface became possible in 1971 when spacecraft began orbiting the planet. A photo of Mars's western hemisphere reveals volcanoes such as Olympus Mons, Arsia Mons, Pavonis Mons, and Ascraeus Mons; a huge upland region known as the Tharsis bulge; and a vast canyon system, Valles Marineris.

The Evolution of the Surface of Mars

By studying photos returned from spacecraft, geologists can determine the types of features found on Mars and can then theorize about how these features came into being during the planet's evolution.

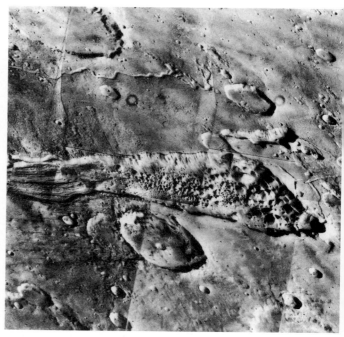

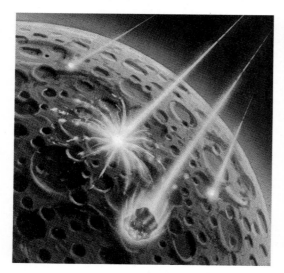

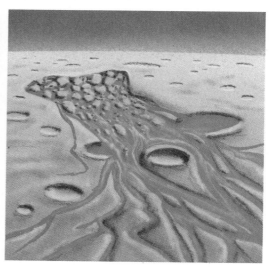

A photo showing huge craters, *top,* that have not been erased by wind erosion or by lava flows from volcanoes, provides evidence that a heavy bombardment of meteorites, *above,* struck the surface of Mars early in the planet's history, creating these impact craters.

A photo from *Viking 1, top,* shows a long depression that geologists believe is evidence that water once existed on the surface of Mars. Geologists theorize that the channel, which is several hundred miles long, was created by a massive flood, *above,* caused by melting permafrost.

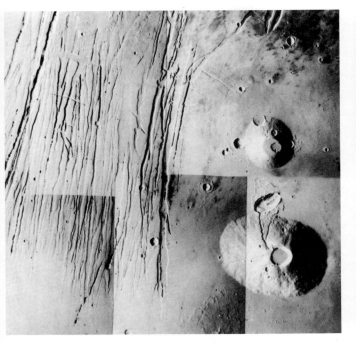

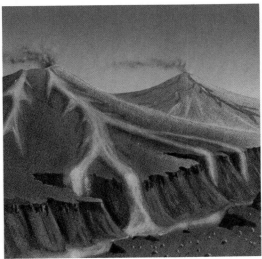

A mosaic of photos from space, *top,* shows two volcanoes (at right) and a series of faults, or major cracks in the ground. Geologists see this as evidence that the interior of Mars was once hot enough to melt rock and create the internal pressures that cause volcanoes and faults, *above.*

A cloud of dust about the size of Colorado, *top,* sweeping across the surface of Mars, was photographed by *Viking 2* in 1977. Water erosion and volcanic activity appear to have ended on Mars, leaving only the planet's dramatic dust storms, *above,* to carve changes on the surface.

nearly four times longer than its intended lifetime, and through the summer and autumn of 1972 it mapped the entire surface of Mars.

The next mission to Mars—and the last to date—consisted of *Viking 1* and *Viking 2*, launched in 1975. In June 1976, *Viking 1* entered orbit around Mars and began to photograph the surface. This time there was no dust storm to block the view. The cameras on board the *Viking* orbiters were much better than those on *Mariner 9* and revealed a wealth of surface detail that had not previously been visible. Like *Mariner 9*, the *Viking* orbiters lived far longer than expected. The primary objective of the *Viking* orbiters was to find safe landing sites for the two *Viking* landers that the orbiters carried with them. The landers were sophisticated laboratories designed to photograph the surface and sample the Martian soil for signs of primitive life. On July 20, 1976, the first *Viking* lander touched down safely in an area called Chryse Planitia. The second orbiter, *Viking 2*, arrived at Mars in August, and its lander came to rest in Utopia Planitia on Sept. 3, 1976.

The landers' close-up photographs revealed a dry Martian landscape strewn with reddish rocks and boulders. Tests of Martian soil samples aboard the landers failed to detect any evidence of life.

The *Viking* and *Mariner* missions returned a wealth of data that scientists are still analyzing. For geologists, the most important data were provided by the photographs these spacecraft returned to Earth. The techniques used to obtain and transmit these pictures are far different from those used to produce ordinary photographs. To begin with, the spacecraft cameras have little in common with the photographic cameras we are familiar with. Instead, they are similar in some ways to television cameras. Light entering a spacecraft's camera is converted into radio signals that are then transmitted to Earth, where a computer converts the signals into a photographic image that looks like a black-and-white television picture.

Analyzing the photographs

The interpretation of these photographs is not always a simple matter. Typically, a planetary geologist who examines photographs of another planet tries to determine two things: the events that formed the planet's landscape and how long ago these events occurred. To interpret the events, scientists often rely on what they know from studying Earth or other planets. For example, we know that Mars has volcanoes because the pictures of these features look very much like some volcanoes on Earth. But what makes planetary geology both frustrating and fascinating is that many features found on Mars are not comparable to anything on Earth or anywhere else in the solar system.

Even when we understand what formed a particular feature, we may not be able to pin down when it was formed. We can never accurately determine the true age of any feature on Mars from photographs alone, but we can often determine much about its relative age—that is, whether one feature is older or younger than another. One way we do this is by analyzing what geologists call *stratigraphy*. When a material forms on a planet's surface, it covers the materials already there. This creates a series of layers, or strata, with the oldest stratum at the bottom and the youngest stratum at the top. For example, if rocks thrown out when a meteorite created an impact crater are lying on top of a lava flow, we know that the lava flow formed first and the crater was made later. By closely examining a series of stratigraphic relationships, geologists can sometimes reconstruct a sequence of events in considerable detail.

Craters themselves provide another tool for determining relative ages. Throughout its history, Mars—like the moon and Earth—has been subjected to a continuous rain of meteorites. Some areas of Mars bear many impact scars, while other areas are relatively crater-free. Because heavy meteorite bombardment occurred early in Mars's history, geologists believe that the areas showing many impact craters date from this earliest period and, therefore, are probably the oldest unchanged regions on Mars. Elsewhere, however, other processes, such as lava flows or water erosion, have erased most of the impact craters. The areas that are somewhat crater-free are therefore younger than the heavily cratered regions. By counting and comparing the number of impact craters in different regions, the relative ages of the regions—that is, which is youngest and which is oldest—can be determined.

Age of geologic features still unknown

Geologists have also attempted to determine the absolute ages of regions on the surface of Mars—that is, precisely how old they are in years. The scientists do this by estimating the rate at which craters were made on the surface of Mars over a period of time. For example, they might calculate that one meteorite impact creating one crater could be expected to occur every million years. Then, by counting the number of craters in a given region, they try to calculate how many years were required, given the rate of impact, to produce that number of craters. The results have varied widely, however. We will not know the true age of Martian surface areas until spacecraft go to Mars and bring back Martian rocks for us to study.

From their study of photographs of Mars, however, geologists have determined that the planet's oldest regions are located in its southern hemisphere, a region that consists mostly of rugged, heavily cratered highlands. The youngest regions are located in the northern hemisphere, which consists largely of lowland plains. Scientists do not yet understand the reason for this difference.

The craters of the southern highlands not only preserve a record of the intense meteorite bombardment that formed Mars, but they also hold other clues about Mars's past. By studying photographs of these ancient southern highlands, geologists have gathered consid-

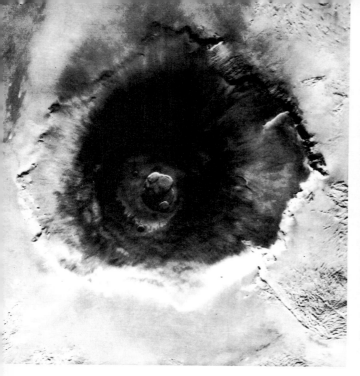

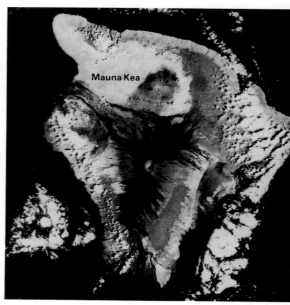

Mauna Kea

Scientists compare geologic features on Mars with similar features on Earth to learn more about the nature of the Martian landscape and how it formed. For example, Olympus Mons, *above left,* the largest volcano on Mars, resembles Hawaii's Mauna Kea, *above right,* a shield volcano, or conelike mountain, built up by layers of flowing lava.

erable evidence that liquid water once flowed on Mars. The *Viking* photographs, for example, revealed small valley systems in the ancient southern highlands that are similar to valleys on Earth that formed due to erosion from water in branching streams. Compared to Earth valleys, the valley systems in Mars's southern highlands are underdeveloped and stubby, as if water flowed in them for only a very short time. On Earth, valley systems result mainly from the runoff of rainfall. The valleys on Mars, however, are too poorly developed in most cases to have been formed by rainfall. Instead, they seem to have formed when large amounts of ice in the ground melted and seeped out of the ground in a process known as *sapping.*

This evidence that liquid water once flowed on Mars suggests to geologists that Mars once had a very different climate and atmosphere. The average temperature and the present atmospheric pressure on Mars are far too low to allow small streams of liquid water to flow across the surface. Surface temperatures rise above the freezing point of water rarely and in only a few locations. The valley systems in the ancient southern highlands thus provide strong evidence that the climate on Mars shortly after its formation 4½ billion years ago was much warmer and wetter than it is now. A thicker atmosphere in Mars's past would have trapped more of the sun's heat, causing surface temperatures to rise and thus allowing liquid water to flow.

The ancient southern highlands also have features indicating that huge floods once occurred on Mars. These enormous features—called *outflow channels*—extend for many hundreds of miles out onto the lowland plains. They are hundreds of feet deep, and some are more than 100 miles wide. Like the valley systems, they seem to have been formed by flowing water, but the similarity ends there. They have few branches but instead suddenly appear fully developed from hilly, rocky regions known as chaotic terrain. The beds of the outflow channels are deep, indicating that large amounts of rock and soil have been carried, perhaps by a vast, sudden flood of water.

The features in the outflow channels are strikingly similar to features in the central and southeastern region of Washington state known as the *channeled scablands*. The channeled scablands were created thousands of years ago during the most recent ice age by a large body of water trapped behind an ice dam on a river. When the ice dam broke, water from this glacial lake thundered across the plains of the Columbia River Valley. On Mars, similar floods apparently created the outflow channels, but the cause of the floods is not well understood. They may have occurred when ice in the ground melted due to heat released by molten rock beneath the surface. We believe that Mars—at least during certain periods—had molten rock inside because photographs show so many volcanoes.

Mars's volcanoes larger than Earth's

The most spectacular of these volcanoes are concentrated in two regions known as Elysium and Tharsis. The volcanoes are broad and gently sloping like those on the Hawaiian Islands. Such volcanoes on Earth are called *shield volcanoes* and are the least violent type of volcano. They are generally formed of very fluid lava, which rises from inside Earth and is released from several vents on the surface in a series of flows that spread like syrup and build up, layer by layer, into a dome-shaped mountain. The Martian shield volcanoes, however, are far larger than any on Earth. The three major Tharsis volcanoes—Arsia Mons, Pavonis Mons, and Ascraeus Mons—all rise more than 9 miles above their base. These were the "spots" that protruded through the dust during the *Mariner 9* mission.

Olympus Mons (renamed from Nix Olympica after the *Mariner* flights) is just northwest of the main Tharsis volcanoes and is even larger. It is some 400 miles in diameter—about the same size as the state of New Mexico—and rises 16 miles above the surrounding plains. This makes it almost three times as high as Mount Everest or the Hawaiian volcano Mauna Loa, Earth's largest volcano, which rises more than 5½ miles from the ocean floor. The volcanoes are apparently inactive, but because there are few impact craters on their slopes, they appear to be among the youngest volcanic features on the planet, indicating that they were active relatively recently in the long span of Martian history.

The Tharsis volcanoes stand atop the Tharsis bulge, a region that rises 4 miles high and covers a 1,500-mile-wide area. Radiating from Tharsis like the spokes of a wheel is a pattern of ruptures in the Martian crust that apparently formed when the bulge developed,

After studying a close-up view of a region near Mars's south pole, scientists determined that the alternating bands of dark and light areas contain layers of ice and dust, each from 30 to 150 feet thick. Each layer holds clues to how Mars's climate has changed over millions of years.

How the Canyons Formed on Mars

A photo reveals two sections of the vast Valles Marineris canyon system running parallel to each other. The entire canyon system is hundreds of miles wide and, in some places, four miles deep. If placed on Earth, the system would stretch from New York City to Los Angeles. How it may have formed is shown below the photo.

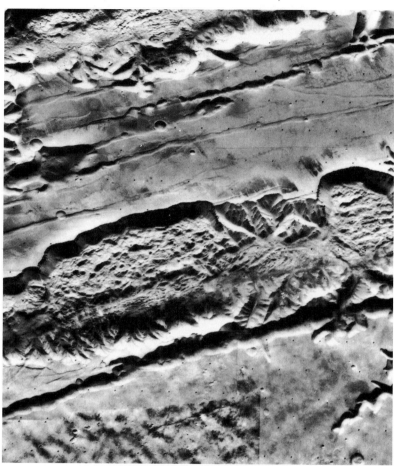

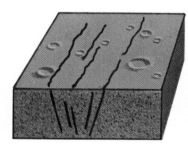

Stresses in Mars's crust, possibly caused by volcanic activity, created *faults,* or cracks, on the surface of the planet.

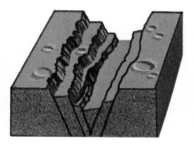

The faults widened as the stresses kept pulling the crust apart, creating vast canyons that dwarf our Grand Canyon.

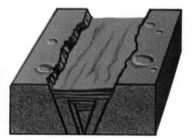

The canyons filled with sediment, which may have been deposited by lake water or from volcanic ash.

like cracks in a sidewalk forced upward by tree roots. This process is called *faulting*. Along the equator to the east of Tharsis, these ruptures or faults are spectacular. There, the crust of Mars has been torn apart, creating a vast canyon system called the Valles Marineris (named after the *Mariner* spacecraft). It is hundreds of miles wide, up to 4 miles deep, and—if placed on Earth—long enough to stretch from New York City to Los Angeles.

Soon after the canyons formed, scientists believe, they became partially filled with layered sediments. The scientists reached this conclusion after studying photographs showing features that resemble layered sediments found on Earth. Where the sediments came from is among the most puzzling questions about Mars. One possibility is that volcanic eruptions took place on the canyon floors, depositing layers of ash into the canyons. But it appears more likely that the sediments were once the beds of large lakes that formed in the canyons early in their history. The lake waters later drained or evaporated, leaving behind the sediments that now partially fill the canyons. No matter how they formed, the features of the Valles Marineris must be among the most spectacular in the solar system.

If the most spectacular scenery on Mars lies in the canyons, the most bizarre lies at the poles. From measurements taken during the *Viking* mission, scientists know that Mars has an atmosphere that is 98 per cent carbon dioxide and an atmospheric pressure that is less than 1 per cent that of Earth's. Each winter on Mars, temperatures become so cold near the poles that much of the carbon dioxide in the atmosphere freezes. The freezing takes place on the surface, giving the poles a seasonal coating of solid carbon dioxide—also called dry ice. This seasonal coating falls upon the permanent polar caps, which scientists believe are made of water ice. As the atmosphere at the poles condenses onto the planet's surface, winds are drawn from warmer areas of the planet to the poles. These winds carry dust blown into the atmosphere by windstorms. At the poles, this dust falls along with ice condensation onto the surface. When

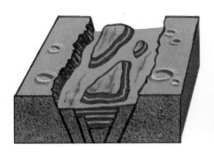

Erosion carved away the layers of sediment, leaving mesas along the canyon floor like those in the Western U.S.

Landslides, possibly triggered by Marsquakes, seem to have created the most recent changes in the canyons.

Although scientists have learned much about Mars from careful study of photographs and other data returned by spacecraft, future advances in understanding Mars will likely come from laboratory analysis of Martian rocks and soil. Future missions to Mars may send robot landers to travel on the surface, picking up small rocks and dropping them into a capsule, which will be rocketed back to Earth.

the carbon dioxide ice evaporates with the coming of summer, some of the dust is left behind.

Over the ages, this process has built up dust deposits several miles deep at the poles. The dust has become intermingled with water ice, cementing the two together in a mass that can partially resist the intense winds that blast the poles. In photographs, the deposits show a complex pattern of gently sloping depressions apparently carved by the wind. The deposits are composed of many layers, each 30 to 150 feet thick.

The most widely accepted theory for the origin of these polar layered deposits is that they are related to long-term changes in the climate of Mars. We know that the amount of sunlight that shines on Mars varies because in its annual journey around the sun, Mars is acted upon by the gravity of all the other bodies in the solar system, most notably its neighbor, the immense planet Jupiter. The combined gravitational effects on Mars cause a number of changes in Mars's orbit and rotation. The most important of these is that the tilt of its axis of rotation is altered and changes slowly from as little as 15° to as much as 35°. When the tilt is low at 15°, only a small amount of sunlight can reach a pole, while a high tilt of 35° exposes a pole to large amounts of sunlight.

Cold and warm periods alternate

These extreme periods of dark and light, cold and warm, alternate every 100,000 years. But how these changes in sunlight and temperature affect the Martian climate is very complex and poorly understood. Scientists believe that at times of extremely low polar temperature, when the tilt of Mars's axis is low at 15°, a great amount of the gases that make up the atmosphere become stored in the Martian soil, making the atmospheric pressure even lower and the winds gentler. This may reduce the frequency of dust storms and, therefore, the amount of dust placed in the atmosphere and transported to the poles. At the same time, lower temperatures may increase the amount of water ice at the poles, either by freezing liquid water or by the condensation of water vapor in the atmosphere. But when the poles are warm, caused by a change in the tilt of Mars's axis so that the poles receive more sunlight, the reverse is true. There is more dust and less water ice at the poles.

These layered deposits at the poles may record millions of years of changes in the Martian climate, perhaps akin to the ice ages that have left their mark on Earth. One day, by obtaining core samples of these layered deposits and measuring the amount of dust in each layer, geologists may be able to reconstruct a history of the climate on Mars.

Even with the many discoveries of the *Mariner 9* and *Viking* spacecraft, Mars still holds mysteries. We know little about the interior of the planet, for example. Geologists believe that Earth's interior consists of a solid metal inner core, a liquid metal outer core, a mantle of dense rock that is mostly solid, and a thin outer crust of lighter solid rock. The outer crust of Earth's surface is made up of rigid "plates" that move slowly about, apparently driven by motions in the mantle. These plates spread apart, collide together, and inch past one another to produce Earth's geologic features in a process called *plate tectonics*.

Nothing like plate tectonics seems to have taken place on Mars. Because Mars is smaller than Earth, it contains less of the natural radioactive material that heats the interior of the Earth. Therefore, Mars is probably cooler inside than Earth. Cooler temperatures should make the outer crust of Mars thicker and stronger than Earth's because there is less molten rock and more solid rock.

Beyond these conclusions, however, scientists know little about the interior of Mars. We do not know how thick the crust is, or whether molten rock still lies beneath the surface. We do not know why the northern hemisphere is younger, smoother, and lower than the southern hemisphere, or why the Tharsis region bulged. And we do not know what kind of rocks make up Mars's surface.

Space flights to probe mysteries

The National Aeronautics and Space Administration hopes to launch the *Mars Observer* spacecraft in the 1990's to help solve a few of the mysteries. Its instruments will be able to detect many of the chemical elements on the surface. To learn what the rocks are made of and to discover whether primitive life ever existed on Mars, however, we must either bring samples of rocks back to Earth or send astronauts to Mars. Sometime in the 1990's, the United States may send a robot lander to Mars that will be able to trundle about the surface, picking up small rocks and dropping them into a capsule that will be rocketed back to Earth.

Many scientists are urging a manned mission to Mars to set up a base that might become permanent. Ultimately, real exploration of the planet can be done best only by people. The people who will do it are children today, and to succeed, they will require technological breakthroughs, international cooperation, and considerable determination and courage. They will be the ones to answer the most important question about Mars—whether we can ever call it home.

A peculiar light ray invented 30 years ago
for no particular purpose has come to play
major roles in research, medicine, and industry.

The Fabulous Laser

BY ARTHUR FISHER

"Slowly a humped shape rose out of the pit, and the ghost of a beam of light seemed to flicker out from it . . . . As the unseen shaft of heat passed over them, pine trees burst into fire . . . . I saw the flashes of trees and hedges and wooden buildings suddenly set alight . . . . Whatever is combustible flashes into flame at [the beam's] touch, lead runs like water, it softens iron, cracks and melts glass, and when it falls upon water, incontinently that explodes into steam."

That passage is science fiction, an excerpt from *The War of the Worlds* (1898) by British novelist and historian H. G. Wells. But the following is science fact: In one of the most powerful nations on Earth, a general in charge of a top-secret military research program announced that a beam of intense energy had shattered a fuel tank removed from an intercontinental missile. The general was James A. Abrahamson, Jr., of the United States Air Force. Abrahamson is director of the U.S. government's Strategic Defense Initiative, also known as "Star Wars," and he made that announcement in September 1985.

Wells's prophetic book and Abrahamson's announcement described essentially the same device—the laser. This device produces a very narrow and intense beam of light of only one color, with all the light rays traveling in exactly the same direction.

Opposite page: A technician adjusts a laser beam used to draw intricate electronic circuits with great precision on a light-sensitive film.

143

Glossary

Coherent light: Light whose waves are identical in wavelength and direction, and are "in step" with one another.

Electromagnetic radiation: Radiant energy ranging from long-wave radio waves down through microwaves, infrared rays, visible light, ultraviolet rays, and X rays, to very-short-wave gamma rays.

Electron: A subatomic particle that absorbs and emits photons.

Excited atom: In a laser, an atom with one or more electrons boosted to a higher energy level.

Incoherent light: Light composed of different wavelengths, moving in different directions, or whose waves are not "in step" with one another.

Laser: A device that produces a narrow, intense beam of coherent light.

Photon: A packet of electromagnetic radiation.

Wavelength: The distance between successive identical peaks or troughs of a wave.

The real laser can be every bit as destructive as the imaginary beam described by Wells. But this is only one measure of the stunning progress made by an invention that is only some 30 years old. For a brief time after it was invented, the laser was merely a tabletop laboratory curiosity. Now, however, lasers perform vital jobs in every area of modern life. For example, laser beams are used to:

- Perform eye surgery, close bleeding ulcers, remove once-inoperable brain tumors, and unclog coronary arteries
- Read price codes on cans, bottles, and boxes at supermarket checkout counters
- Clean paintings, sculptures, and architectural ornaments
- Measure the incredibly slow movement of continents
- Play videodiscs and compact audio disks
- Send telephone and other messages over cables made from hair-thin strands of glass
- Analyze very rapid physical movements and chemical reactions
- Cut materials ranging from fabric to sheet steel

Remarkably, these are all current applications. Specialists in every branch of science, engineering, and medicine are happily predicting dozens more. Perhaps the most exciting of these would be laser fusion—a process that would tap the tremendous energy of the atomic nucleus in a new way to provide an unlimited and nonpolluting source of electric power.

Clearly, the laser must have very special properties to permit it to be the jack of all trades of modern technology. To understand the details of what lasers do—from vaporizing metals to pinpointing a satellite 3,600 miles high—it is necessary to understand just what a laser is and how it works.

The story of the laser began in 1951 with physicist Charles H. Townes of Columbia University in New York City. Townes specialized in using radio waves and microwaves to analyze molecules. These waves are part of the *electromagnetic spectrum,* a family of radiation that goes from long-wavelength energy, such as radio waves, down through microwaves, infrared rays, visible light and ultraviolet rays to very-short-wavelength X rays and gamma rays.

Townes and his colleagues had been using vacuum tubes to generate radio waves in their work. But Townes wanted to obtain microwaves of shorter wavelength than was possible with vacuum tubes. For two years, he had led an unsuccessful investigation of an advanced device called a *resonator* designed to produce such waves.

One spring morning, while sitting on a park bench, Townes had a moment of insight "more vivid and complete than almost any other in my experience." A three-minute calculation on the back of an envelope, he recalls, showed him how to design the device he wanted. This device would use a remarkable atomic phenomenon known as *stimulated emission of radiation* to induce molecules of ammonia gas to emit microwaves.

The author:
Arthur Fisher is science and engineering editor of *Popular Science* magazine.

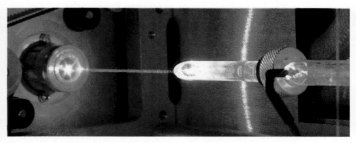

Laser beams are produced in a variety of materials, including solids, such as a ruby rod, *far left;* gases, such as argon in the test-tube-like chamber, *above;* and liquids, such as the yellow dye, *left,* flowing through the curved tubes.

The next step was to get it built. Townes turned the job over to two associates at Columbia, and in 1953 the device produced power. Townes and his colleagues christened it the *maser,* for *m*icrowave *a*mplification by *s*timulated *e*mission of *r*adiation.

In 1956, Townes realized that it might be possible to use the principle of the maser to produce the shorter wavelengths of visible or infrared light. In 1958, he and physicist Arthur Schawlow, then of Bell Telephone Laboratories in Murray Hill, N.J., published a paper showing that a maser-type device could be made to produce a beam of visible light if the chamber containing the material that was to emit the light were built with mirrors at each end. The paper set off a race to build the first laser (*l*ight *a*mplification by *s*timulated *e*mission of *r*adiation).

The honors for demonstrating the first operating laser went in 1960 to physicist Theodore H. Maiman of Hughes Aircraft Company in Malibu, Calif. Instead of using a gas such as ammonia to emit the beam, he constructed his laser from a crystal of synthetic ruby. Polished ends served as mirrored surfaces.

The laser works by manipulating the energy levels of particles called *electrons* that orbit the nuclei of atoms. Such electrons can exist in any of several different orbits or energy levels. When an atom or a molecule absorbs energy—whether as light, heat, or chemical energy—its electrons can be *excited,* or boosted to a higher level.

An excited atom falls back to its original energy level, usually without any prompting. In doing so, it releases a tiny bundle of light energy called a *photon.* This release of energy is called *spontaneous emission.*

In spontaneous emission, excited atoms release light irregularly. As a result, the light has different wavelengths and, because color

Two Kinds of Light

The Production of Light
Light is produced after an atom absorbs energy, boosting one of the electrons orbiting its nucleus to a higher orbit, *right*. An atom in this higher energy state is called an *excited atom*. The electron soon drops back to a lower energy orbit, *far right*, emitting a bundle of energy called a *photon*. Light consists of streams of photons.

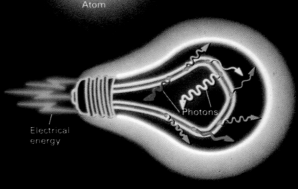

Atom

Photon

White Light
Ordinary light is produced when atoms in the filament of a light bulb absorb electrical energy, then emit photons with varying levels of energy, or wavelengths, traveling in all directions. Color depends upon wavelength, so the various wavelengths produce a mixture of colors, which the human eye interprets as white light.

Electrical energy

Photons

Laser Light
Laser light is produced in a laser medium, such as a rod made of artificial ruby, with a mirror and a partial mirror at its ends. Light from a powerful flash lamp provides energy to excite atoms in the rod.

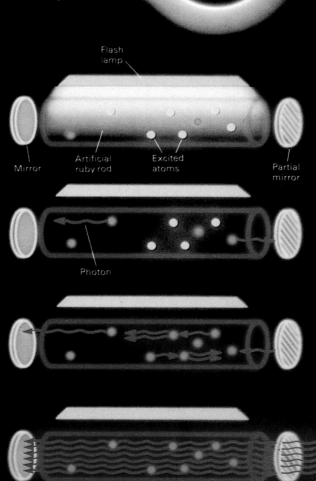

Flash lamp

Mirror

Artificial ruby rod

Excited atoms

Partial mirror

As excited atoms in the rod drop back to their normal energy state, they emit photons, mainly of a single color, red.

Photon

Laser light is created as the red photons bounce back and forth between the mirrors. These photons stimulate other excited atoms into emitting more photons that have the same wavelength and travel in the same direction, with their waves "in step" with one another.

As the red light bounces back and forth, it builds up in intensity until it shoots out through the partial mirror as a beam of laser light. The beam is narrow and intense *coherent light* that contains only one wavelength, with all the waves traveling in the same direction, and "in step" with one another.

Laser beam

depends upon wavelength, different colors. Our eyes interpret mixtures of many different colors of light as white light. Such light is produced by the sun and ordinary light bulbs.

Excited atoms may also release light systematically, by stimulated emission of radiation. In this process, a photon near an excited atom causes that atom to emit a duplicate photon. The duplicate travels in exactly the same direction as the original photon, with its waves precisely "in step" with those of the original.

Maiman's ruby laser provides a model for understanding the role of stimulated emission in a laser. The ruby laser consisted of an artificial ruby crystal rod surrounded by a powerful flash lamp. When the lamp flashed, a burst of light bathed the ruby, exciting a large number of its atoms. In an instant, some of these atoms dropped to a lower energy level, emitting photons. Many of these photons, in turn, caused other excited atoms in the rod to emit duplicate photons. Because the ends of the rod were mirrors, much of the light continued to bounce back and forth inside the crystal, triggering other atoms to emit photons, and building in power. Within one-millionth of a second after the flash, the light was clearly visible as a beam emerging from one of the ends.

Laser light is made up of photons of identical wavelength—and therefore color—and with all waves traveling in the same direction and in step. Such light is called *coherent light*.

To grasp the idea of coherence, imagine scattering a handful of pebbles onto the surface of a pond. At the point where each pebble hits the water, a ripple is created and starts moving outward in a circle. But these ripples are disorganized. They crisscross one another randomly; they are *incoherent*. This is the way the waves of ordinary light, such as the light of a flashlight beam, behave.

Now imagine taking a single pebble and dropping it into the pond. It starts a train of ripples moving evenly outward from the spot where you dropped the pebble. Then imagine dropping an identical pebble in exactly the same spot a moment later, timing the dropping of this pebble so that its ripples will be in step with those of the first pebble. If you kept dropping single pebbles in this way, you would generate continuous, coherent ripples.

The purity of wavelength and the coherence of their rays make laser beams the most intense, the most directional, and the most concentrated light ever seen on Earth. The consequences are remarkable. Aim a flashlight—even the most powerful ever devised—and its beam spreads out so quickly that the energy falling on a distant object fades to nothingness. But the light rays from a laser remain concentrated in a narrow beam to an incredible degree. For example, laser beams that traveled to the moon spread only about 500 yards during the trip.

Today, the maser and laser have many powerful offspring, operating with many kinds of materials. In fact, there are a variety of laser materials in all the states of matter—solids, liquids, gases, and *plasmas* (mixtures of free, or unattached, electrons and atomic nuclei that have been stripped of electrons). Taken as a whole, lasers and masers can emit virtually the entire gamut of the electromagnetic spectrum, from radio waves to X rays.

Physicists have built lasers with an amazing range of power. At one end of the scale are handheld lasers that emit a red ray of less than one-thousandth of a watt and are used as pointers by lecturers. At the other end are giant laser fusion devices capable of blasting targets with trillions of watts.

Laser beams have many unusual characteristics that fit them for a wide variety of tasks. Their straightness and purity of color, for example, make them a hit at a light show, *right*. Their narrow beam is vital to a device that reads prices and other encoded data at a supermarket checkout counter, *below*.

Many relatively low-powered lasers are used in medicine. Since the early 1970's, for example, doctors have used lasers in eye surgery to prevent *detached retina*, the pulling away of the light-sensitive surface in the back of the eye. A surgeon uses a laser beam of about 0.1 to 1 watt to burn the area where the retina has begun to pull away. The resulting growth of scar tissue strengthens the bond between the retina and the supporting tissue. This bloodless surgery is possible because the degree of heating can be precisely controlled, and because the beam can be focused on a tiny spot, perhaps only a few cells wide.

Tightly focused low-powered lasers also play important roles in the supermarket and the home. At supermarket checkout counters, beams from gas lasers scan the Universal Product Code—a series of narrow black and white stripes—printed on cans and other items. The laser light bouncing off the stripes is converted to electric impulses, which convey price and inventory information to the cash register.

A low-powered laser beam in a compact disk player reads an encoded message in much the same way. But instead of stripes, the laser scans billions of tiny pits etched onto the surface of an aluminum-and-plastic disk 4.7 inches in diameter to reproduce sound.

A photographic technique involving low-powered lasers produces pictures called *holograms*. When viewed in various ways, holograms give rise to three-dimensional images or create two quite different pictures. Holograms have a wide variety of decorative and practical applications in everything from candy wrappers to navigation aids in aircraft cockpits.

Lasers have ushered in a new era of precision measurement. The phenomenally straight and narrow laser beam is the answer to a tunnel-borer's prayer. Excavators used to have trouble keeping road and railway tunnels perfectly straight, especially when drilling

Laser light pulsed through hair-thin glass strands called optical fibers can carry voice and data transmissions. The laser light carrying these encoded messages travels through miles of glass fibers at rates of about 100 million flashes per second.

Laser beams have a tremendous range of power. An industrial laser, *above,* cuts saw blades out of a thick steel plate, while a surgical laser, *right,* is delicate enough even for eye operations.

through a mile or so of solid granite in a mountain. Now, however, an excavator simply aligns a boring machine along the beam of a laser, and bores a tunnel that is true to within a fraction of an inch.

Lasers can also measure length over long distances. In an astonishing experiment conducted in 1969, a laser device was used to determine the distance to the moon to an accuracy within 1 foot. Scientists bounced a pulse of laser light off a reflector left on the moon by astronauts, measured the time it took the pulse to make its trip, and then used this measurement to calculate the distance.

The same technique, called *laser ranging*, is now being used to monitor the exceedingly slow drift of continents. Earth's crust moves constantly, with great segments called tectonic plates sliding ponderously atop the planet's hot, semimolten interior. Where plates crunch together, earthquakes are a constant threat. So keeping track of a motion of even 3 or 4 inches per year may someday help geologists predict a disastrous earthquake.

Important as these uses are, they could be overshadowed by one single laser application—controlled nuclear fusion. This is the goal of massive research efforts in the United States, the Soviet Union, Western Europe, and Japan. Energy from a laser beam would make atomic nuclei *fuse* (combine) to form heavier nuclei. The energy released during fusion can be tremendous. Fusion, for example, provides the energy of both the sun and the hydrogen bomb.

For decades, physicists have dreamed of controlling fusion so that it could be used in electric power plants. Today's nuclear power plants get their energy from the opposite process—*fission*, in which a uranium nucleus breaks up to form two lighter nuclei, converting mass to energy. Physicists want to switch from fission to fusion because the radioactivity of uranium presents serious safety problems, and uranium supplies are limited.

A power plant fusing the nuclei of two forms of hydrogen would produce much less radioactive waste than does a fission plant. And, because the oceans contain a virtually inexhaustible amount of hydrogen, fusion would overcome the fuel-supply problem.

One way to fuse hydrogen nuclei would be to shine enormously powerful laser beams on a hollow glass ball—about one-fifth of an inch in diameter—filled with a mixture of the two forms of hydrogen. The beam would heat the mixture to 100,000,000°C—about six times the temperature at the center of the sun—and compress it to 20 times the density of lead. Energy released by the fusing nuclei

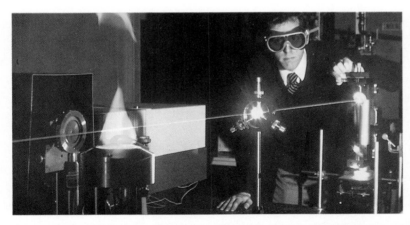

Lasers can perform a variety of industrial tasks. An automotive researcher, *left,* uses an argon gas laser to measure the amount of soot in a flame during a study of how cleanly fuels burn. Earth movers use a laser beam, *below* (multiple exposure), to guide them in precisely leveling fields so that land can be irrigated without wasting water.

The Laser in "Star Wars"

On March 23, 1983, United States President Ronald Reagan called for a study to determine whether "there is not a defensive weapon . . . that can . . . render a system of horrifying weapons obsolete." The "horrifying weapons" are missiles with nuclear warheads. The research program that resulted from this call was given the title of Strategic Defense Initiative (SDI), but it was almost instantly labeled "Star Wars."

Originally, the SDI concept consisted of a system using a number of advanced defensive weapons. The scenario would play something like this: Suppose an enemy power launched intercontinental missiles toward the United States. At the instant of attack, radar and laser ranging devices and other instruments mounted on U.S. satellites would detect the missiles and then transmit information to an enormous network of computers. Within seconds, the computers would calculate the enemy missiles' trajectories and flash the calculations to a variety of weapons, including a dazzling assortment of lasers.

Some weapons would intercept enemy missiles almost immediately. Others would destroy them in midflight. The remaining few missiles would be intercepted as they reentered the atmosphere to strike their targets.

The SDI has been controversial from the outset. Some political observers say that the program threatens to upset the delicate balance of power that keeps the United States and the Soviet Union at peace with each other. Many scientists say that a sufficiently reliable network of computers could not be built in the foreseeable future. Another scientific criticism is that even an extremely effective defensive system would not prevent all of an enemy's nuclear warheads from reaching their targets in the United States.

As originally contemplated, the SDI called for ground-based chemical, excimer, and free-electron lasers; space-based chemical and excimer lasers; and hard-X-ray lasers that would be launched in response to an attack. The hard-X-ray laser is highly controversial, because the energy for exciting the laser would come from a nuclear explosion. In all likelihood, researchers would have to test the device in space at some stage in its development, violating a U.S.-Soviet treaty.

All the weapon-type lasers are still in the early stages of development. As researchers continue to experiment with them, some concepts will come to the fore while others will fall by the wayside, causing the SDI strategy to shift.

A major shift has already occurred. In November 1985, SDI Director James A. Abrahamson, Jr., announced that the development of space-based chemical and excimer lasers would be shifted to the background. He said that experiments on free-electron lasers had made "incredible progress."

It is much too early to tell where all the research will lead—if the SDI continues to receive political support. The United States eventually may put an assortment of laser weapons in place, as originally proposed. Or perhaps there will be an SDI system based instead on *particle-beam* weapons designed to fire streams of highly energetic electrons at enemy missiles. Or perhaps—if much of the scientific criticism is correct—the SDI will never get off the ground.

[A. F.]

In one Strategic Defense Initiative proposal, *far left,* a ground-based laser would destroy enemy missiles in space. A 1985 test conducted on Earth, *left,* showed that lasers already have the power to destroy a rocket body.

would be used to boil a supply of water. This would produce steam to drive turbines connected to electric generators.

The latest in a long series of experimental laser fusion devices is Nova, located at Lawrence Livermore National Laboratory (LLNL) in Livermore, Calif. Nova—named after a class of star that suddenly becomes extremely bright—is the world's most powerful laser, a $176-million monster occupying four rooms. The largest room is the size of a football field; the tallest room soars to five stories. Laser beams travel down 10 arms, all converging on a single pellet. Nova is designed to produce—for one-billionth of a second—beams with a total of about 100 trillion watts of power, about 200 times the output of all the electric power stations in the United States.

On Jan. 9, 1986, Nova generated its first fusion reaction. An 18-trillion-watt pulse of laser light lasting one-billionth of a second blasted a hydrogen-filled glass sphere, causing a small amount of the hydrogen to fuse. But physicists are still a long way from developing lasers that are intense enough for a power plant.

Meanwhile, other laser scientists are working at the frontiers of physics, developing exotic devices that will make the laser even more versatile. Four leading examples are the femtosecond laser, the excimer laser, the free-electron laser, and the X-ray laser.

A *femtosecond laser* produces light pulses that last for periods of time measured in quadrillionths of a second. A femtosecond is an unimaginably short amount of time. There are as many femtoseconds in one second as there are seconds in 30 million years. The recordholder for the shortest pulse of light is a 12-femtosecond laser developed in 1984 by physicists Jean-Marc Halbout and Daniel Grischkowsky of International Business Machines Corporation (IBM) in Yorktown Heights, N.Y.

A femtosecond laser could act as a kind of strobe light for stop-action photographs of ultrafast processes involving molecules, atoms, and electrons, some of the most fundamental processes in chemistry, physics, and biology. To measure the speed of an extremely rapid chemical reaction, for example, researchers would shoot two laser pulses—one after the other—into a chemical mixture. Energy in the first pulse would initiate a chemical reaction, and the reacting chemicals then would absorb additional energy from the second pulse—the amount depending upon how far the reaction had progressed. The scientists would measure the amount

A free-electron laser (FEL), unlike an ordinary laser, does not use a laser medium. Instead, it converts some of the energy in an electron beam into coherent light. First, electrons stripped off a heated metal plate flow into a machine called a particle accelerator, which boosts them to tremendous speeds. Then, they enter the FEL, which bends their path with magnetic energy, causing them to emit light photons. The photons bounce between mirrors and finally emerge as a laser beam.

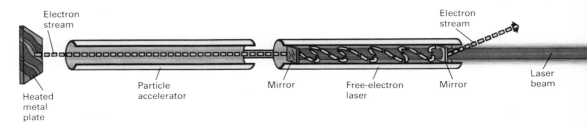

Electron stream · Heated metal plate · Particle accelerator · Mirror · Free-electron laser · Mirror · Electron stream · Laser beam

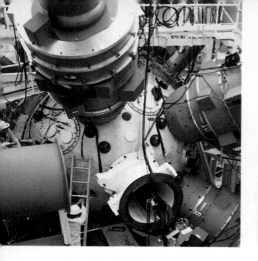

The world's largest laser is Lawrence Livermore National Laboratory's Nova laser in Livermore, Calif. Research at Nova may lead to the generation of electric power by nuclear fusion—the joining of atomic nuclei. In a January 1986 experiment, beams totaling 18 trillion watts of power streaked through 10 gigantic tubes, *top right,* and converged on a spherical chamber, *top left,* where they struck a tiny pellet, causing nuclei in the pellet to fuse, *above.*

of energy absorbed from the second pulse to determine the progress of the reaction. They could monitor the reaction from beginning to end by shooting several pairs of pulses into the chemicals and varying the time between the first and second pulses.

The *excimer laser*—a kind of gas laser—derives its importance not from its pulse length but from its wavelength. "Excimer lasers are the most intense source of ultraviolet energy available," according to the laser's developer, physicist Jeffrey I. Levatter of Acculase Incorporated in San Diego. Such energy would be useful in the manufacture of materials for electronic devices and the separation of rare radioactive elements from nuclear waste.

The U.S. Navy is interested in the excimer laser for a more pressing reason. Until now, it has been impossible to communicate with submarines while they are submerged in deep water. To communicate, a sub had to be in relatively shallow water so that it could tow a radio antenna near the surface. But communications signals carried by pulses of excimer laser light could penetrate to depths of hundreds of yards.

The *free-electron laser* (FEL) is a maverick among lasers because its laser material is not a solid, a liquid, a gas, or even a plasma. Rather, it consists of a high-speed beam of free electrons. Its main attraction is its potential to produce beams that can be tuned from microwaves through the colors of visible light through the ultraviolet.

The potential benefits of such tunability in chemistry alone are tremendous. An FEL would help chemists build new products by functioning as a versatile molecular "scissors." The electrical forces that hold molecules together depend on the energy levels of certain electrons. The amount of energy varies from place to place in a molecule. So, to cut a molecule apart at a certain place, a precisely tuned FEL would supply an electron or electrons at that place with exactly enough *additional* energy to break the molecule apart.

One drawback is that the FEL requires large, complex, and expensive equipment to speed up the free electrons that serve as the laser material. The first FEL, demonstrated in 1976 by physicist

John M. J. Madey of Stanford University in California, employed a 150-foot-long tubular machine called a linear accelerator. The electrons began their journey when an electric current heated a metal plate, exciting billions of electrons to such high energies that they left their orbits around atomic nuclei. The electrons rushed into the accelerator tube, where powerful electromagnetic devices boosted them to nearly the speed of light—186,282 miles per second.

The electrons then streaked out the other end of the tube and into the 50-foot-long FEL, essentially a series of magnets arranged to deflect the electrons to the left and right several times. Each time the electrons changed directions, they emitted photons. Many of these photons stimulated electrons to emit duplicate photons, eventually resulting in a laser beam.

Many new FEL's are much smaller. Madey now works with one that is 12 feet long, for example, and is connected to a 10-foot-long accelerator.

Well beyond the energy range of the FEL—or any other laser— is the newly developed *X-ray laser*. Researchers in this area are interested in two kinds of radiation—*soft* and *hard* X rays. In October 1984, physicists headed by Dennis L. Matthews at LLNL announced the first successful trial of a soft-X-ray laser. Because X rays have much higher energies than light, it takes a great deal of energy to excite atoms enough to give off X-ray photons. The experimenters used a powerful solid laser to vaporize a target made of selenium, creating a plasma with high-energy free electrons. When these free electrons collided with selenium atoms, the atoms became excited enough to give off soft X rays.

X-ray lasers could prove invaluable as microscopes for taking pictures of tiny details in living cells and viruses and for examining their biological processes. X-ray lasers could also help materials scientists understand corrosion, crystal growth, and other processes that take place at the surface of materials.

Hard X rays have more energy per photon and therefore penetrate materials more deeply than do soft X rays. The search for a hard-X-ray laser is intimately connected to the U.S. government's "Star Wars" research (see THE LASER IN "STAR WARS," page 152).

Proposed uses of these and future lasers are emerging very quickly. One promising area just beyond the frontiers of laser physics is the explosively developing discipline of molecular biology. Because a laser beam can be focused so precisely, it might be used to alter an individual's genetic makeup, eventually becoming an important instrument in the fight against inherited diseases.

The speed with which researchers are proposing new uses for lasers contrasts sharply with the slow pace of application in the early days of the device. The pace was so slow, in fact, that the laser was once called "a solution in search of a problem." The laser's future now seems as bright as its remarkable light.

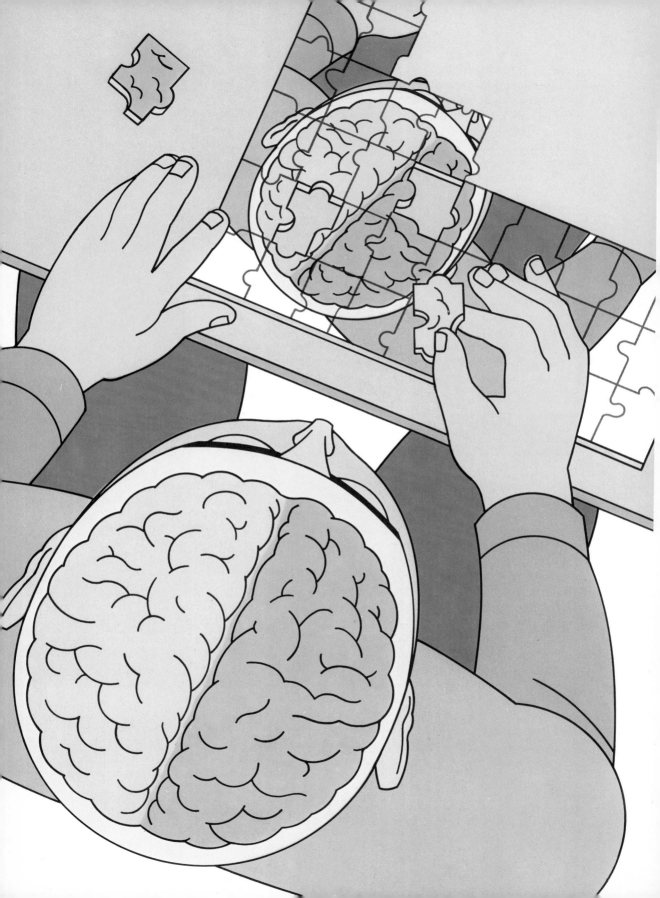

Research is solving the puzzle of
how mental functions are divided
between the brain's two halves.

Our "Two Brains":
Facts and Myths

BY MICHAEL S. GAZZANIGA

A number of articles have appeared in newspapers and magazines urging people to get in touch with their "creative brain." By that, the authors mean the right half of the brain, which supposedly contains nearly all of a person's artistic abilities. One best-selling book on learning to draw claimed that would-be Picassos can enhance their drawing skills by suppressing the verbal, analytical left brain and stimulating the right brain. Even some educators took up the cause in the 1980's, arguing that schools for too long have emphasized "left-brain learning," such as literature, science, and mathematics, over "right-brain learning," such as painting, dancing, and music appreciation. One education professor urged teachers to take their classes into the outdoors whenever possible. Interacting with nature, he asserted, will develop the students' right brains.

Such right-brain, left-brain claims are everywhere, and most of them are not true. Where did such ideas come from? The fact is that stories about "the artistic right brain" and "the analytical left brain" that show up in the popular press are based on actual scientific findings. Too often, however, those findings have been misunderstood or exaggerated—in some cases, by the researchers themselves. Thus, it is not surprising that misconceptions have arisen about the division of functions within the brain.

For centuries, physicians and scientists have studied the human brain in an effort to learn how it works. Beginning in the 1500's, anatomists, such as the Flemish physician Andreas Vesalius, made detailed *post-mortem* (after death) examinations of human brains. Vesalius' drawings show clearly the two hemispheres, or halves, of the brain, connected by the thick band of nerve fibers known as the *corpus callosum*. Knowing the brain's basic anatomy, however, did not help scientists understand its inner workings. Why the brain is divided into two equal parts remained a mystery. Many researchers were convinced that there was no difference between the hemispheres. Others held that because the brain is divided physically, its functions must also be divided.

In the late 1800's, the work of two European scientists—surgeon Pierre Paul Broca of France and neuropsychiatrist Carl Wernicke of Germany—provided the first evidence that there are indeed differences between the two hemispheres. Broca and Wernicke studied the brains of deceased persons who had suffered from severe speech disabilities. The two scientists noted that all the brains showed damage in the left hemisphere. From that finding, Broca and Wernicke concluded that human language ability is located in the left half of the brain.

By the early 1900's, scientists had learned how information moves to and from the brain. They discovered that sensory information from one side of the body goes primarily to the opposite side of the brain. Conversely, they learned that each half of the brain provides the major control over the opposite side of the body. Vision was found to be a bit more complicated. If you look straight ahead, images from the right visual field—the area on the right side of an imaginary line extending out from your nose—are focused on the left half of each *retina*, the light-sensitive tissue at the back of the eyeball. From there, the visual information is transmitted to the left hemisphere. Similarly, images from the left visual field are focused on the right side of each retina and sent to the right hemisphere.

The two halves of the brain are in constant communication by way of the corpus callosum, which consists of some 200 million nerve fibers. Thus, each hemisphere is immediately made aware of the information that has been sent to the opposite hemisphere. The function of the corpus callosum was not confirmed until the 1960's. Although scientists reasoned that such a large bundle of nerves must be of great importance, earlier experimental evidence suggested otherwise. In the 1940's, a group of doctors at the University of Rochester in New York severed the corpus callosum in 26 patients suffering from epilepsy. Epilepsy is a disease in which millions of the brain's *neurons*—nerve cells—discharge in an abnormal way, creating a sort of electrical storm within the brain. This "storm" moves back and forth from one hemisphere to the other, becoming increasingly severe. Eventually, the victim loses control of muscular

The author:
Michael S. Gazzaniga is a professor of psychology at Cornell Medical College in New York City.

The Two Halves of the Brain

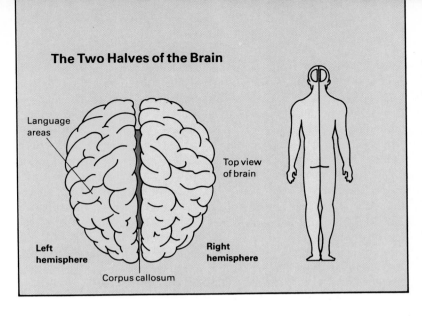

Language areas

Top view of brain

Left hemisphere

Right hemisphere

Corpus callosum

The brain is divided into left and right *hemispheres,* or halves. The hemispheres are connected by a thick band of nerve fibers called the *corpus callosum.* Each hemisphere receives information from, and controls, primarily the opposite side of the body. Scientists have long known that language skills are located in the left hemisphere. They have wondered whether other mental abilities, such as creativity or analytical ability, are also confined to a particular hemisphere.

activities such as speaking and walking and may even lapse into unconsciousness.

The Rochester researchers reasoned that cutting the corpus callosum would confine an epileptic seizure to the hemisphere in which it started and would thereby lessen its effect. Their main worry was whether cutting the corpus callosum would have an effect on the patient's personality and thought processes. Ordinarily, this uncertainty would have prevented the researchers from attempting such a radical new surgical technique. But the patients' epilepsy was so severe that it threatened their lives, so the operation was thought to be worth the risk.

The results of the surgery were puzzling. Although the severity of the patients' seizures was reportedly reduced, the patients themselves seemed otherwise unchanged by the operation. Many scientists concluded, therefore, that sensory information—as opposed to the electrical discharges that occur during epileptic seizures—can move from one side of the brain to the other without the aid of the corpus callosum.

That view, however, was soon called into question by animal studies conducted at the California Institute of Technology (Caltech) in Pasadena, under the direction of psychobiologist Roger W. Sperry, one of the world's foremost brain researchers. In the early 1950's, Sperry began a series of "split-brain" experiments on cats. After surgically severing a cat's corpus callosum, Sperry and graduate student Ronald E. Myers discovered that information learned by one half of the cat's brain was not known to the other half. For example, a split-brain cat might be taught to push a certain pedal with its left paw—controlled by the right hemisphere—to obtain a piece of liver or other reward. The cat would have no difficulty with this task as long as it could use its left paw, but it would be unable to perform the task with its right paw, controlled by the left hemisphere. Nor-

Vision and the Brain

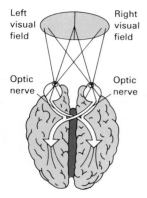

Left visual field

Right visual field

Optic nerve

Optic nerve

The Flow of Images
Information from the eyes is transmitted to the brain by the optic nerves. Images from the left or right visual field are relayed by each eye to the brain's opposite hemisphere.

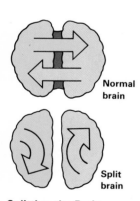

Normal brain

Split brain

Splitting the Brain
In a normal brain, *top,* all information received by one hemisphere, including visual images, is shared with the other hemisphere through the corpus callosum. When the corpus callosum is severed, *above,* the hemispheres can no longer communicate.

mal cats were able to transfer the knowledge from the right hemisphere to the left with no problem. These findings indicated that the corpus callosum is essential for the transmission of information between the hemispheres and that each hemisphere can operate independently of the other.

In 1961, when I was a graduate student in Sperry's laboratory, I had a chance to conduct split-brain experiments with Sperry on an epileptic patient whom we shall call W.J. The patient's epilepsy stemmed from a World War II brain injury suffered when he was clubbed in the head with a rifle butt. Over the years, his epilepsy grew worse. In searching for medical help, W.J. came under the care of neurosurgeon Joseph E. Bogen of White Memorial Hospital in Los Angeles. Bogen reviewed the epileptic surgery cases from the 1940's and decided that severing the corpus callosum might be the answer to W.J.'s problem. W.J. consented to the surgery, and Bogen then arranged for Sperry and me to test the patient both before and after the operation. The postoperative tests would try to determine whether information could be given to one half of a surgically divided human brain without the other half's knowing about it. If the tests showed that the information was indeed available to only one hemisphere, it would prove that in human beings—as in Sperry's cats—the corpus callosum is the route by which the two halves of the brain communicate. On the other hand, if information was still known to both sides of the brain, then other, less obvious brain pathways must connect the hemispheres.

In tests prior to the surgery, W.J. was directed to stare at one point on a screen while pictures or words were flashed onto the screen to either the left or right of the point. Because of the way the visual system works in normal people, images flashed to the right side of the screen were relayed to W.J.'s left brain, while images projected to the left side of the screen went to his right brain. But regardless of which side of his brain first received a word or picture, W.J. could tell us what he had seen. This result showed that the language centers in the left brain always had access to the information received by either hemisphere. In addition, W.J. could name objects that we placed in either of his hands, but which he could not see, indicating that touch information was also being shared in his brain. The outcome of these tests was exactly what we expected with a person whose corpus callosum was intact, and they showed that W.J., except for his epilepsy, had a normally functioning brain.

About a month after his corpus callosum had been severed, W.J. was again brought to Caltech for testing. Once more, he sat in front of the screen, and pictures and words were flashed to either side of the screen. W.J. easily named images appearing on the right half of the screen, which were transmitted directly to his left hemisphere. But when images were flashed to the left side of the screen—and thus to his right hemisphere—the result was dramatically different.

The Split Brain—Two Brains in One

Research has shown that in split-brain patients—persons whose corpus callosum has been severed to control epilepsy—the brain's two hemispheres take on separate identities.

How the Experiment Is Conducted
The patient sits in front of a screen onto which pictures can be projected from the opposite side. The patient stares fixedly at the center of the screen while the experimenter flashes pictures to the right or left half of the screen.

What the Intact Brain Sees
A person with an intact brain can identify pictures flashed to either the right or the left side of the screen—and thus to the brain's left or right hemisphere, respectively—because information is being shared between the hemispheres.

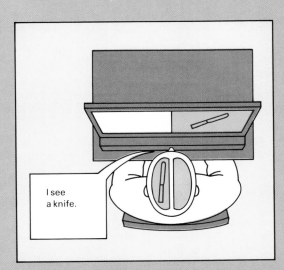

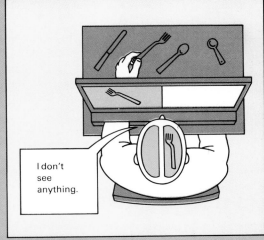

The Verbal Left Brain
A person whose corpus callosum has been cut can verbally identify pictures flashed to the right side of the screen because those pictures are transmitted to the left hemisphere, which controls speech.

The Mute Right Brain
The same patient denies seeing anything when the mute right hemisphere receives an image. But the right brain can direct the left hand to find, by touch, a matching object behind the screen.

161

A Right-Brain, Left-Brain Myth Emerges

Split-brain experiments in the 1970's seemed to show that the right hemisphere is superior to the left hemisphere at tasks involving visual perception. These studies, though conducted with only a small number of patients, led some researchers to conclude that the right brain contains almost all of a person's artistic ability and creativity and that the left brain is suited mainly for tasks involving language and logic.

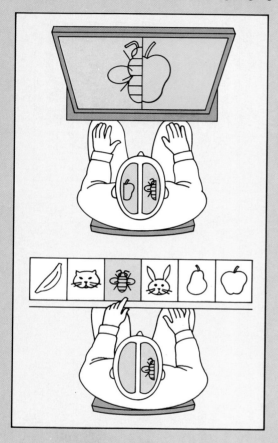 

Remembering Visual Images

A split-brain patient sits at a screen, *top,* while a pair of images—half of an apple next to half of a bee—are flashed onto the two sides of the screen. Then the patient is shown pictures of a number of objects, *above,* including an apple and a bee, and asked to point to the one he remembers. In this instance, he chooses the bee. Like other split-brain persons who are given the test, the patient usually chooses the object that was seen by his right hemisphere.

Matching a Pattern

A split-brain patient is asked to arrange red-and-white blocks to match designs on printed cards. The patient may take as much time as he likes but may use only one hand at a time. In most cases, the patient performs better at this task with his left hand (right brain) than with his right hand (left brain). Again, the experimental results indicated that the right hemisphere has greater visual aptitude than the left hemisphere.

W.J. would respond, "I didn't see anything." The outcome was the same for touch information. W.J. could name unseen objects placed in his right hand but not those placed in his left hand. Clearly, W.J.'s surgery had interrupted the pathway by which the left half of the brain—the talking half—learns about right-brain activity.

The experiments we conducted that afternoon were the first modern, controlled observations of the human split-brain phenomenon. But they were just the beginning. Having learned that W.J.'s right brain no longer communicated with his left brain, our next task was to see whether the mute right hemisphere possessed conscious awareness. The right brain couldn't talk about what it saw, but could it perhaps direct the left hand to point to a matching picture? With another series of experiments using pictures flashed on a testing screen, we learned that the answer to that question was yes. If, for example, we flashed a picture of a spoon to W.J.'s right hemisphere, he could use his left hand to point to a matching picture placed in front of him. He could also reach under the screen with his left hand and pick out a spoon, using touch alone, from a group of objects behind the screen. All the while, W.J., speaking from his left hemisphere, insisted that he had seen nothing on the screen and felt nothing with his hand. These results provided clear evidence that the right hemisphere, despite its inability to express itself through language, does have its own thought processes. Normally, the right hemisphere's consciousness is merged with that of the left hemisphere. But when the corpus callosum is severed, the right brain takes on a separate identity.

We next wanted to gain a better understanding of how the two hemispheres function. Are they basically the same except for the left hemisphere's language abilities, or does each hemisphere have its own unique skills and ways of perceiving the world? To shed some light on that mystery, we gave W.J. another battery of tests, including several in which he was required to arrange objects to match patterns. In one such test, W.J. was asked to arrange four small red-and-white blocks to correspond with designs on printed cards. Each face of the blocks was either all red, all white, or divided diagonally into two triangles, one red and the other white. W.J. was able to arrange the blocks in the desired pattern with his left hand but not with his right. In other words, W.J.'s left hemisphere was stumped by this task, but his right hemisphere could do it easily.

Starting in the early 1970's, other students of Sperry's, notably Jerre Levy and Colwyn Trevarthen, did further studies of patients who had undergone split-brain surgery. The experimenters again used the pictures-on-a-screen technique. But this time, the pictures they flashed—faces, geometric shapes, and other images—were designed so that one hemisphere saw half of one picture while the other hemisphere saw half of another picture. Thus, the patients might be shown half of a bee next to half of an apple, the bee visible

Revealing the Left Brain's Visual Skills

Recent studies indicate that the reason the left hemisphere seems to lack visual skills is that it often tries to do too much with the information it receives. By complicating what should be a simple perceptual task, the left brain slows itself down. If the left hemisphere is forced to work faster, however, its visual perception is shown to be equal to that of the right hemisphere.

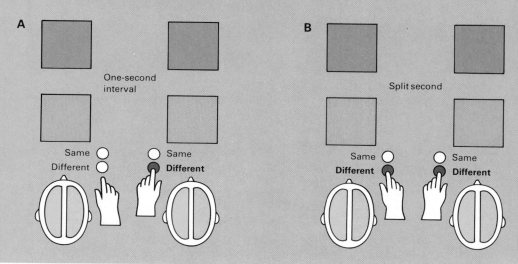

A — One-second interval — Same / Different — Same / Different

B — Split second — Same / Different — Same / Different

Two colors are flashed 1 second apart to a split-brain patient's left or right hemisphere (**A**). The patient, by pressing one of two buttons, indicates whether the colors are the same or different. In a series of such trials, the left brain takes longer than the right brain to make a decision and seems inferior at this task. But when the interval between the flashes of color is reduced to a fraction of a second (**B**), the left brain's performance matches that of the right brain. This result suggests that when it is given more time than it really needs (1 second), the left brain gets bogged down in trying to name the colors.

to the right brain and the apple to the left brain. They were then shown a group of cards printed with various illustrations, including one of a bee and one of an apple, and were asked to point to the picture they remembered seeing on the screen. The patients more often chose the image that had been seen by the right brain.

From this test, the block test, and other experiments, many investigators concluded that the right brain is dominant for visually oriented tasks. Soon, a number of researchers began to assert that the two halves of the brain are vastly different—that the left brain is strictly verbal and analytical and that the right brain contains all of a person's visual and creative abilities. As it turned out, that claim, based as it was on such limited data, was about half wrong. Nonetheless, journalists picked up the story, and soon articles on the supposed differences between the two halves of the brain were appearing everywhere. References to "the analytical left brain" and "the creative right brain" became so common that most people assumed those labels were an established scientific fact. Further research, however, showed that the brain's functions cannot be divided so neatly.

In the mid-1970's, surgical treatment of epilepsy became more common. Neurosurgeons at several major medical centers began treating epilepsy by severing the corpus callosum. By 1986, more than 200 people in the United States had undergone the operation,

The Left Brain as "Interpreter"

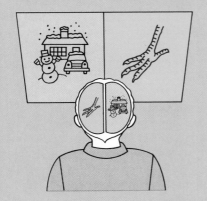

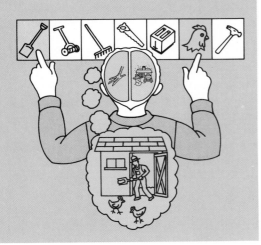

As a split-brain patient looks at a screen, *top,* a picture of a chicken claw is flashed to his left hemisphere and a snow scene is flashed to his right hemisphere. The patient must then look at a group of illustrations, *above,* and choose two that relate in some way to the pictures he saw on the screen. The patient selects the correct pictures, pointing to a chicken with his right hand and to a shovel with his left hand. The left brain knows why the right hand has chosen the chicken. Having no knowledge of the snow scene, however, it does not know why the left hand—controlled by the right brain—is pointing to the shovel. So, when asked, it makes up a logical, but incorrect, explanation: "You need a shovel to clean out the chicken shed." This experiment indicates that the left brain is constantly analyzing and trying to explain what it sees and will make up theories to cover gaps in its knowledge.

and many of these patients have taken part in split-brain studies. This greatly enlarged pool of experimental subjects has enabled researchers, myself included, to obtain a clearer view of how the hemispheres of the brain work together. One striking fact has emerged from these later investigations: So-called right-brain processes, such as visual skills, are rarely confined to the right hemisphere. The left brain, in fact, seems just as adept as the right brain at most perceptual tasks. In other words, the fanciful, creative right brain and the no-nonsense, analytical left brain are largely a myth.

This conclusion is based in part on research with split-brain patients conducted at my laboratory at Cornell Medical College in New York City. In one experiment, my associates and I flashed two similar or identical colors, presented with a one-second delay between them, to one or the other hemisphere of a split-brain patient. The patient had to decide, by pressing one of two buttons, only whether the two colors were the same or slightly different. In a series of such trials, the left brain, though it always came up with the correct answer, was slower than the right brain and seemed inferior at distinguishing colors. When we reduced the time lag between the presentation of the two colors to a fraction of a second, however, the left hemisphere's performance matched that of the right.

The results of this and other experiments suggest that the left hemisphere's language processes tend to mask many left-brain skills. The left brain apparently tries to name and categorize all the information it receives—in this instance, colors—with the result that it often gets bogged down in irrelevant details. The right brain, unencumbered by language, carries out most perceptual tasks in a more direct manner. But if the left hemisphere is not given enough time to activate its language processes, it can solve a perceptual problem—such as discerning differences among colors—just as well as the right brain can.

As we see, then, it is language more than anything else that distinguishes the left brain from the right. Every waking moment of our lives, the language centers of the left hemisphere are analyzing and interpreting the information that pours into the brain. Because the left brain has this great responsibility, it is usually content to let the right brain handle simpler perceptual chores that do not require language. But, as our studies have shown, that does not mean that the right brain is more specialized for such tasks.

My colleagues and I designed a split-brain experiment to test the left hemisphere's role as analyst and interpreter. Using the same sort of setup as in previous experiments, we flashed two pictures simultaneously on the screen. The patient's left hemisphere saw a picture of a chicken claw, and the right hemisphere saw a snow scene. We then showed the patient a series of cards with various illustrations and asked the patient to point to the cards that related in some way to the pictures that were flashed on the screen. The correct answer for the left hemisphere was a chicken; for the right, a shovel. The patients had no trouble picking the correct illustrations, pointing to the chicken with their right hand and to the shovel with their left. But when asked why they had made those selections, they gave answers that revealed much about the brain's nature.

A typical response was, "The chicken claw goes with the chicken, and you need a shovel to clean out the chicken shed." This explanation was concocted by the left hemisphere because it did not know why the left hand was pointing to the shovel. The right hemisphere, in control of that hand, knew that the shovel was related to the snow scene. But the left hemisphere had no knowledge of the snow scene, so it had to make up a reason for the left hand's choice—that the shovel was needed to clean out the chicken shed.

The experiment shows not only that the language centers of the left hemisphere feel compelled to explain behavior, but also that this left-brain "interpreter" constructs theories to cover information unavailable to it. In the experiment, of course, the reason the left brain knew nothing about the snow scene was that the severed corpus callosum prevented the left hemisphere from receiving that information. What about normal brains—is the left-hemisphere interpreter sometimes denied access to the activities of other parts of the brain? My ongoing research indicates that it is.

I have conducted a revealing experiment with patients who are undergoing a neurosurgical procedure called the Wada test. In this test, given to patients who are scheduled for brain surgery, an anesthetic is fed to just the left side of the brain. The anesthetic causes the left hemisphere to lose consciousness while leaving the right hemisphere awake. The purpose of this procedure is to confirm that the patient's language areas are located in the left brain. In about 4 per cent of the general population, the functions of the hemispheres are exactly reversed.

While the patient is in the bizarre state of semiconsciousness produced by the Wada test, I place an object such as a spoon in the patient's left hand, which is controlled by the alert right hemisphere. After about 30 seconds, I take the spoon away and several minutes later the anesthetic wears off. I then tell the fully awake patient, "I placed something in your left hand while you were asleep. Can you tell me what it was?" The patient looks puzzled and denies any knowledge of what I am talking about. But if I then show the patient a group of objects, including a spoon, the patient points to the correct object and adds, "Oh yes, the spoon."

Here again, despite an intact corpus callosum, the right hemisphere knows something that the left hemisphere does not. The right hemisphere directs the finger to point to the spoon, and the left brain—trying to cover its ignorance—falsely claims to remember the spoon as the object that had been placed in the left hand. A key question raised by this experiment is, why doesn't the right hemisphere tell the left hemisphere about the spoon once the anesthetic has worn off? The answer, I think, is that during the crucial two or three minutes when the left brain is still asleep, the right brain encodes the information about the spoon in a form that cannot be understood by the language centers of the left hemisphere.

This experiment, as well as others, suggests that the brain is organized into what I call *modules*, independent systems capable of producing actions and emotions. The language areas of the left brain constitute one module. But there may be hundreds of other modules in both hemispheres, many of them inaccessible to the left-brain interpreter. This notion raises profound questions about the concept of self—the idea that the conscious mind is one indivisible "me." Early split-brain research indicated that the brain contains two selves, one in each hemisphere. But the modular view of the brain raises the possibility that the brain has any number of mental units, each of which has its own memories, values, and emotions. Each such unit would be, in a very real sense, a self.

Testing the theory of mental modules is one of the next goals of my research on the brain. I, like many other investigators, am moving away from studying the right brain versus the left brain and concentrating on the brain as a whole. The two hemispheres may yet be found to differ in some fundamental ways besides language abilities. There is, for example, some evidence that the right hemisphere adds emotional "color" to our speech and thoughts. Despite that possibility, it can be said with certainty that human beings are neither "left-brained" nor "right-brained." The normal human brain is essentially a single, beautifully integrated system. Understanding how the many parts within that system interact to produce thoughts, actions, and emotions is the challenge of the future.

For further reading:

Gazzaniga, Michael S. *The Social Brain*. Basic Books, 1985.
Levy, Jerre. "Right Brain, Left Brain: Fact and Fiction," *Psychology Today*, May 1985.
Restak, Richard. *The Brain*. Bantam Books, 1984.

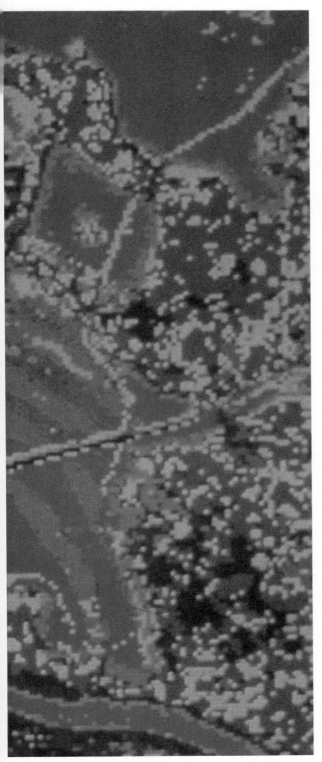

Airborne sensing devices that "see" beyond the range of human vision are guiding archaeologists to ancient sites.

Archaeology's New Eyes in the Sky

BY THOMAS L. SEVER

The workers looked surprised. "Dig here," we had said, pointing to a gully running down the side of a steep hill. The gully looked like all the other gullies scoring the jungle landscape in northwestern Costa Rica. In our hands, however, we held photographic evidence that this gully was in fact a special place. The photos, taken from the air, showed an ancient roadway buried beneath the surface of the gully.

The buried roadway was only one of several running from an ancient graveyard on the hilltop above us. In the graveyard were the remains of a previously unknown people who had lived here nearly 4,000 years ago. The site had been discovered in 1983 by archaeologist Payson Sheets of the University of Colorado in Boulder. For nearly a year since then, Sheets and his team of workers had been excavating the cemetery and other sites along the shore of nearby Lake Arenal.

I became involved in the project in early 1984, when the National Aeronautics and Space Administration (NASA) and the National Science Foundation decided to investigate the usefulness of remote sensing devices in archaeological exploration.

An archaeologist by training, I had spent several years learning how to use remote sensing instruments. Sheets's dig in Costa Rica was one of the places where we were experimenting with the devices.

Remote sensing is the science of detecting and recording information from a distance. In the past, instruments such as binoculars, optical telescopes, and camera lenses have enabled us to extend the range of our built-in remote sensors—our eyes. Modern remote sensors, carried by satellites, the space shuttle, and high-flying aircraft, have taken us even further by recording information that lies beyond the range of human vision.

For several days, I had flown over this part of Costa Rica in a specially equipped NASA aircraft, while sophisticated radar instruments on board recorded information about Earth's surface below. Then, using a computer, I had converted this radar information into the photographic images we held in our hands. Although Sheets and I were fairly sure that certain lines in the photos represented prehistoric roadways beneath the surface, there was really only one way to find out for sure—dig.

The photos seemed to show that one roadway ran down the hillside, split at the bottom, then headed off in two directions. So Sheets decided that we needed four trenches—one at the top of the hill, one in the middle of the slope, and two at the bottom—to prove that the roadway actually existed.

The skeptical workers began to dig, slowly and carefully removing the soil. When they were about 4 feet down, they stopped. Sheets disappeared into the trench. Moments later he yelled, "Congratulations. We've got it. It's a roadway."

In the layers of soil lining the sides of the trench, Sheets had seen an irregularly shaped, partially eroded layer characteristic of dirt roadways. The roadway had been preserved by a covering layer of volcanic ash from one of the 11 volcanic eruptions that have rocked nearby Mount Arenal during the past 4,000 years.

Evidence in the three other trenches confirmed our finding. Now we could be fairly sure that similar lines in the NASA photos also represented roadways. Space age technology had provided us with an exciting new way to discover the remains of an ancient society. Instead of hiking around the Costa Rican jungle looking for the lost villages and cities of the people of Arenal, Sheets and his team could follow the roadways.

Traditionally, archaeologists looking for places where people lived in the past have spent a lot of time walking. Sometimes, of course, the ruins of buildings, tombs, and other archaeological sites are clearly visible. Often, however, they are buried below the surface. Scattered artifacts, such as pots and tools, sometimes provide archaeologists with clues to the location of a site. Sometimes archaeologists look for areas where people are likely to have lived, such as along lakesides or at the point where rivers meet.

The author:
Thomas L. Sever is an archaeologist and remote sensing specialist with the National Aeronautics and Space Administration.

But more often, archaeologists must look for subtle differences in soil and vegetation. For example, the soil at an archaeological site usually has high levels of phosphates, chemical compounds present in decayed garbage and human waste. In addition, constructing a building or a roadway, like tilling a garden, enriches the soil by mixing soil layers, adding air, and making it easier for water to circulate. Consequently, the soil at abandoned sites not only looks different from the surrounding soil but also is richer and more fertile, and the vegetation at the site is often unusually lush and thick.

Once archaeologists suspect they have found a site, they dig exploratory trenches, as we did to locate the roadways in Costa Rica. But trenches cover only a small area, and unless archaeologists dig in just the right spot, they could miss a site completely. Finding even one site is a slow and costly process. Finding and studying the remains of an entire society—its settlements, farmlands, travel routes, and mines—can take several lifetimes and cost a fortune.

Remote sensing offers archaeologists a faster, cheaper, and more efficient way to locate, map, and study sites. For many archaeologists, remote sensing represents a scientific breakthrough as significant as the development of radiocarbon dating. (Radiocarbon dating allowed archaeologists for the first time to accurately determine the age of ancient objects.)

The first remote sensing instrument used to study archaeological sites was a camera attached to an unmanned balloon. It was used in 1891 by a British archaeologist who photographed ancient ruins near Agra, India, from the air. These photos, however, went largely unnoticed.

Then, in 1907, a British engineer named J. E. Clapper presented to the British Society of Antiquarians a photograph of Stonehenge taken from an unmanned balloon. Stonehenge, probably built between 2800 and 2000 B.C., is a ring of huge stones in southern England that many scientists believe was an ancient astronomical observatory. It's hard for us today, accustomed as we are to seeing photos of Earth taken from airplanes and spacecraft, to appreciate what an exciting moment that was. For the first time, the scholars could see all of Stonehenge, which covers about 2 acres, at once. Aerial photography had provided an exciting new way of looking at objects and features on Earth's surface.

By 1914, British archaeologists were taking photographs from airplanes and had discovered that aerial photos could reveal the patterns of archaeological features that are either invisible or easily overlooked at ground level. Study of an aerial photo could determine, for example, that what looked like an ordinary ditch from the ground was actually an ancient roadway or the remains of an ancient wall.

American archaeologists became interested in aerial photography in 1929, when Charles A. Lindbergh, who in 1927 made the first solo nonstop flight across the Atlantic Ocean, and archaeologist A. V. Kidder photographed Chaco Canyon in New Mexico from the air. The photos revealed a number of previously unknown *pueblos*—multistory cliff dwellings—built into the walls of the canyon by the Anasazi Indians, who abandoned the area about A.D. 1300.

Since the 1930's, aerial photographs have been used by archaeologists all over the world. With them, they have found ancient Indian villages and cities in the tropical rain forests and highland deserts of South America, prehistoric Eskimo campsites in the Arctic, and buried towns and villages from the Middle Ages in England.

Although valuable, aerial photography has several major limitations. For one, aerial photos must be taken in daylight under clear skies. For another, they record only what the human eye can see. Color infrared photography, developed in the 1940's, for the first time extended the range of human vision by recording information beyond the visible light portion of the electromagnetic spectrum.

The electromagnetic spectrum is the range of radiant energies from very short-wave gamma rays, which are fractions of an inch long, to radio waves, which can be hundreds of miles long. The spectrum also includes X rays, ultraviolet waves, visible light, infrared waves, and microwaves. All of these, with the exception of visible light, are invisible to the human eye.

Visible light makes up only a tiny portion of the spectrum. If the entire electromagnetic spectrum were wrapped around Earth's equator, visible light would represent a portion less than the diameter of a pencil. In short, human beings can see very little of the universe around them.

Remote sensing instruments extend human vision by, in a way, seeing the invisible. Infrared cameras, for example, can detect the infrared rays, or heat energy, given off by all objects, no matter how cool their temperatures. Therefore, sensitive infrared detectors are useful in revealing temperature differences on Earth's surface. Archaeologists have found infrared photos particularly helpful in finding areas of unusually lush vegetation that might mark an archaeological site. (Areas of thick vegetation are warmer and give off more infrared radiation than areas of sparse vegetation.)

Ordinary images, whether taken in the X-ray, visible, or infrared range, are chemically processed and developed in much the same way as photographs. In contrast, the newest remote sensing instruments create their images in an entirely different way—by numbers. The numbers are processed by a computer, which produces an image that looks very much like a photograph.

These remote sensing devices may be carried by satellites, airplanes, or the space shuttle, and they may "see" in any part of the known electromagnetic spectrum. As the remote sensing system passes above Earth, a special camera *scans* the surface. That is, it collects electromagnetic waves given off by objects and features on

Electromagnetic Spectrum

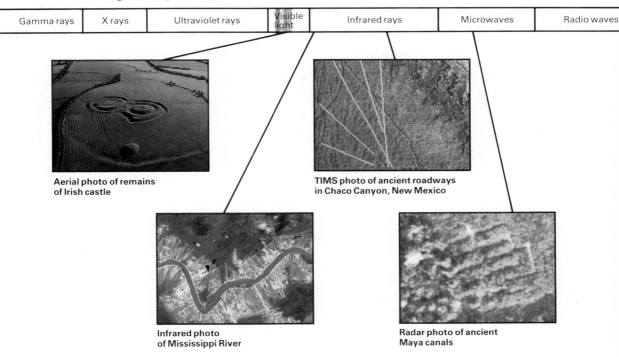

| Gamma rays | X rays | Ultraviolet rays | Visible light | Infrared rays | Microwaves | Radio waves |

**Aerial photo of remains
of Irish castle**

**TIMS photo of ancient roadways
in Chaco Canyon, New Mexico**

**Infrared photo
of Mississippi River**

**Radar photo of ancient
Maya canals**

the ground. The system scans one strip or *line* at a time. The width of the line can vary from 100 miles to ½ mile, depending chiefly on how high the system is above Earth.

Each line is made up of individual parts called *pixels* (picture elements). A pixel is the smallest area a sensor can see. Pixels vary in size from 1½ miles wide to only 1 foot wide. Each sensor in the scanning system assigns each pixel a number from 0 to 255, depending on the strength of the waves given off by the objects in the pixel. The darkest objects—those reflecting few or no waves—receive a 0 rating.

Together, the various numbers make up a pixel's signature. Similar objects have similar signatures. As a result, scientists using a computer can separate pixels into different categories. For example, they can find all the pixels representing water or forest. In fact, they can analyze pixels even more closely and determine whether the water is in a pond, a river, or a lake and identify some kinds of trees in the forest. Scientists also can locate human-made objects, such as buildings and roadways. As a result, scientists can make extremely detailed maps of Earth's surface. In the past, it took scientists several months to produce surface maps of an archaeological site using aerial photography and ground surveys. Today, remote sensing technology has cut that time to one day.

In my work, I have relied chiefly on two remote sensing instru-

Remote sensing devices used to find and study archaeological sites "see" in different sections of the electromagnetic spectrum. Aerial photos, like the human eye, depend on the visible light portion of the spectrum. Infrared photos and TIMS images are both made by detecting infrared, or heat, radiation. TIMS images are made by detecting differences in the rate at which objects, such as vegetation, give off heat. Unlike infrared images, TIMS images can reveal objects beneath the ground. Radar images are created by microwave beams reflected off objects. Some radars can penetrate jungle treetops to reveal hidden objects, such as canals.

Ancient Costa Rican Roads

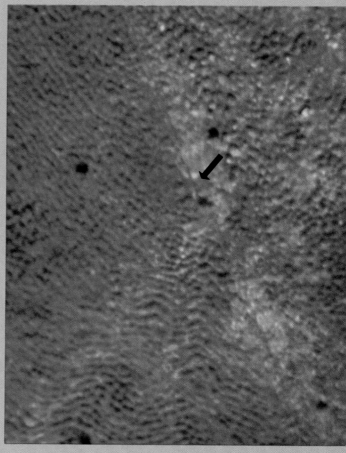

Slight dips in the ground on either side of a fence, *above* (foreground), are the only signs of two ancient roadways in Costa Rica, now buried. But a high-altitude image of the site taken by ground-penetrating radar, *right,* shows the location of one of the roadways (arrow).

ments—the specially designed radar I used in Costa Rica to see below Earth's surface and an infrared system called TIMS that records the rate at which objects and features on the surface give off heat. Both of these instruments have been carried aboard NASA's specially equipped jet.

Conventional radar sends out microwaves that are reflected by objects. The type of radar that I and other scientists use in archaeological exploration originally was designed to penetrate clouds and vapors on other planets. In 1977, archaeologist Richard E. W. Adams of the University of Texas in San Antonio and anthropologist T. Patrick Culbert of the University of Arizona in Tucson first used this specially designed radar to penetrate the thick jungle of northern Guatemala. They made an aerial survey of Maya sites there to find out whether the radar could see through the leaves to the land below. The experiment was a great success. When Adams

Workers dig an exploratory trench, *above,* to confirm that the Costa Rican roadways exist where the radar images indicated. In a graveyard where the roadways began, archaeologists found stone slabs framing the entrance to a tomb, which contained a human skull heavily encrusted with soil, *left.*

examined radar images of the area, he discovered a network of lines forming grids. Expeditions to the sites revealed that the grids were the remains of a vast system of canals and raised farm fields used by the Maya thousands of years ago.

Different kinds of radar reveal different features. For example, the radar that I used to find the Costa Rican roadways and the radar used to find the Maya canals transmit long microwaves that are not reflected strongly by moisture and so can penetrate damp jungle foliage. A radar that transmits even longer microwaves that penetrate farther below the surface was used in the Libyan Desert to find something even more ancient.

Infrared photos of the Libyan Desert in southern Egypt and northern Sudan taken by satellite early in 1981 had revealed only differences in the type of sand. But when specialists aboard the space shuttle *Columbia* photographed the area using a radar that

Roads in Chaco Canyon

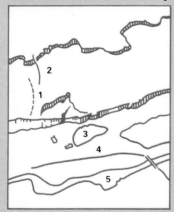

An aerial photograph of Chaco Canyon in New Mexico taken by Charles A. Lindbergh in 1929 shows a small section (1) of one of the roadways built by the Anasazi Indians nearly 1,000 years ago. Lindbergh's photos of the canyon were the first aerial photos of an archaeological site taken in the United States. The photo also shows a modern footpath (2), the ruins of an Anasazi pueblo (3), a modern road (4), and Chaco Wash, a dry stream bed (5).

penetrated about 4½ feet below the surface of what is one of the driest regions on Earth, they found ancient riverbeds. The riverbeds were visible because the sand above and around them was smooth and appeared dark in the pictures. In contrast, the buried riverbeds were rough and appeared bright in the pictures.

In 1982, a team of Egyptian archaeologists acting on this information excavated an area of the riverbeds and found a number of artifacts, including ostrich shells that once had been used as containers. Some of the other artifacts dated back 200,000 years. The scientists also discovered the fossils of land snails, which live only in moist tropical environments. The age of the fossils indicated that at times in the past, this part of Africa was a hospitable place.

The other remote sensing instrument that I've used to help make several exciting discoveries is the thermal infrared multispectral scanner, called TIMS for short. TIMS records waves in the infrared

A TIMS photo of the northern edge of Chaco Canyon, *left*, reveals buried ancient roadways (white lines) invisible in aerial photos. TIMS pinpointed the roadways by detecting differences in the rates at which the soil and vegetation along the roadways and that of the surrounding areas gave off heat.

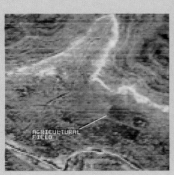

Because different types of soil and vegetation give off heat at different rates, the time of day at which a TIMS photo is taken may affect the visibility of features on the surface. For example, a TIMS photo of a section of Chaco Canyon taken at night, *far left,* reveals an ancient agricultural field not visible in a TIMS photo of the area taken at noon, *left*.

portion of the electromagnetic spectrum. Like infrared photography, TIMS can record the temperature of objects and features on Earth's surface. Unlike infrared photography, however, TIMS also measures the rate at which these objects or features cool off, or release the heat they have absorbed from the sun. For instance, a block of wood and a block of concrete both might be 150°F. But the two blocks give off their heat at different rates. The TIMS system consists of sensors that can detect these differences by recording variations in the infrared rays given off by the blocks.

NASA built TIMS in the early 1980's for geologic research, to map soil variations and rock formations. At the time, no one realized what a versatile instrument it was. I got a chance to find out after talking to archaeologists working in Chaco Canyon in New Mexico.

Chaco Canyon is one of the most important archaeological sites in

Ancient Louisiana Settlement

A TIMS photo of Poverty Point, La., *right,* an ancient Indian settlement abandoned by the 600's B.C., clearly reveals the location of six ridges, barely visible in an aerial photo, *above*. The ridges surrounded a large plaza, and archaeologists believe the inhabitants built houses on the ridges.

North America, because it has the largest number of pueblos. The Anasazi, who built the pueblos, then abandoned them about A.D. 1300, were a highly developed farming people. The makers of artistic pottery and fine stone tools, they also traded with their neighbors in what are now Mexico and the central United States.

In 1971, archaeologists working in Chaco Canyon took a second look at the aerial photographs taken by Lindbergh in 1929. In these photographs, archaeologists saw signs of what appeared to be a network of roads running along the floor of the canyon and across the tops of the surrounding *mesas* (flat-topped hills). In the photos, the roadways appeared as strips of unusually thick vegetation. In the 1940's, however, Indians in the area began grazing their sheep in the canyon; so by 1971, most of the vegetation had disappeared.

Other aerial photographs taken over the years also showed what seemed to be small sections of the roadways. In addition, excavations turned up some physical evidence of the roadways, such as

To confirm the accuracy of the TIMS images of Poverty Point, fieldworkers, *left,* dig for evidence of pathways leading across the ridges to the central plaza. In addition to evidence of pathways, excavations turned up many small figurines, *above.*

ramps, curbs, and stairways. But these remains, like the lines in the photos, extended only short distances.

In 1976, archaeologists began trying to piece the photographic and archaeological evidence together in order to map the roadways, but it was a difficult job. After talking with several of the Chaco archaeologists, I decided to see if TIMS could locate the mysterious roadways. So in August 1982, I photographed the area with a TIMS system aboard the NASA jet.

When I began analyzing the data, I was disappointed. I could see lines in the pictures, but they were very faint. The lines indicated that the soil and vegetation in these areas was different from that of the surrounding areas, but there was no way of knowing what the lines were. Luckily, a co-worker, geologist Douglas Rickman, happened to be working on a computer technique to make features in TIMS photographs more visible. To do this, he was screening out characteristics shared by adjacent areas and magnifying the differences. We began working together to make the lines more visible. In two weeks, we had completed our study, had decided that the lines did indeed represent prehistoric roadways, and had mapped all the roadways on the mesa lying on the northern edge of Chaco Canyon. Excavations confirmed that the TIMS data were correct.

Over the next few months, I used TIMS data to find other archaeological features in Chaco Canyon. The photos revealed not only more roadways but also the buried walls of pueblos, prehistoric garbage dumps, and ancient agricultural fields.

Archaeologists are especially intrigued by the purpose of the roads, which seem to connect with the sites of small villages outside the canyon. The roads are surprisingly wide—usually about 30 feet—and very straight, unlike the modern roads that wind and curve through the area. But the Anasazi had no knowledge of the wheel, nor did they use animals as beasts of burden. So the purpose of these wide straight roads remains a mystery.

Remote sensing promises to play a growing role in archaeology, revealing important but hidden archaeological sites. Among the sites that may be explored with ground-penetrating radar is Herodium, *above,* an ancient fortress in Palestine (now Israel) believed to be the site of Herod the Great's tomb. The tomb may contain some of the world's richest archaeological treasures.

Buoyed by our success at Chaco Canyon, I offered to use TIMS to photograph Poverty Point, an ancient Indian settlement in northeastern Louisiana. This massive 400-acre site, which dates back to 1500 B.C., had been abandoned by 600 B.C.

The site consists of a large central plaza surrounded by six concentric ridges. The ridges, once mounds of earth now flattened by erosion, are 165 feet wide and 115 feet apart. Archaeologists think the Indians who lived at Poverty Point built their houses on the ridges. Outside the ridges to the west is a large mound that from the air resembles a bird in flight.

Archaeologist Jon Gibson of the University of Southwestern Louisiana in Lafayette had been digging at Poverty Point since the early 1970's. As a guide for his excavations, he was using a map made in 1950 by archaeologists who had conducted a ground survey of the site and had dug a number of exploratory trenches. Gibson also had an aerial photograph taken in 1930 that seemed to show several features not indicated on the map.

Gibson was particularly interested in pathways shown on the map and in the aerial photo. The map showed four pathways, each from about 100 to 165 feet wide, leading from the central plaza across the ridges. The aerial photo showed what seemed to be two more pathways—one running to the plaza from the southwestern corner of the site and a second running to the plaza from the mound.

To determine whether the pathways really existed, Gibson selected five test areas. At these areas, TIMS data indicated the presence of a pathway, but there was no surface evidence to confirm this. In the summer of 1985, Gibson and his team began excavating. Gibson's decision to use the TIMS data showed considerable courage. Time and money are always limited in archaeological excavations, and had the data been inaccurate, he would have wasted both. But the TIMS data were correct—at all five areas.

We discovered that the 1930 aerial photo was right. There was a pathway running to the plaza from the mound and another running from the southwestern corner of the site. In this corner, Gibson's team found evidence of some sort of storage area.

We also found that one of the apparent pathways on the 1950 map was actually an ancient stream bed. We discovered that another pathway shown on the map did not exist at all. And finally, we confirmed TIMS data showing a small area in the central plaza where the soil was completely different from the surrounding soil. Gibson speculated that this area might not be a prehistoric site but the site of a plantation house built at Poverty Point in the 1840's. The house had collapsed and disappeared about the time of the Civil War, and its exact whereabouts are unknown. In the summer of 1986, Sheets planned to test about 30 more sites where TIMS photos indicate the presence of a pathway or other archaeological feature.

In just a short time, remote sensing devices have taken their place alongside the trowel and the brush as essential archaeological tools. And the sophistication and number of remote sensing instruments being used by archaeologists continues to grow rapidly. For example, in Costa Rica, Sheets and his colleagues are using *lidar* to look for roadways and other sites. Lidar, a radar that sends out laser light beams instead of microwaves, is more accurate than radar in mapping the hills, valleys, and other surface features of an area.

Lidar also promises to be especially useful in helping archaeologists identify sites that may once have been inhabited. For instance, if most of the known settlements of an ancient culture are located on hills of a certain elevation and within a certain distance from a stream, archaeologists can use lidar maps of the surface to find other sites with these geologic characteristics. Scientists are also using this technique to find sites in Africa where early human beings or human ancestors may have lived.

New radars have also been developed to penetrate even farther into the ground. In Connecticut, for example, archaeologists are using radar that can "see" 10 feet below the surface to search for the buried walls and stockade lines of a Revolutionary War battlefield.

In the summer of 1986, I planned to work with a team of scientists looking for cities that are mentioned in the Bible but whose locations are now unknown. Using radar, we intended to search for buried walls and buildings. Radar should also prove helpful in archaeological explorations in Jerusalem, where scientists have been looking for the walls of the ancient city of David, and where some Jews and Muslims oppose excavation for religious reasons. Radar will enable the archaeologists to explore without digging.

What an exciting time it is to stand on the threshold of so much discovery. Five years ago, remote sensing provided little help to archaeologists. Today, the capabilities are spectacular. Five years from now, they will be unbelievable.

New theories about the universe intrigue
our imagination with concepts such as
shadow matter and a 10-dimensional world.

Mind-Boggling
Mysteries
of Matter

BY ROBERT H. MARCH

The author:
Robert H. March is a professor of physics at the University of Wisconsin and the author of the Special Report THE NEW ATOM SMASHERS in the 1985 edition of *Science Year*.

Imagine that we share our universe with unseen worlds of *shadow matter*—shadow stars that shine with light to which our eyes and our scientific instruments are blind and shadow rocks that could plunge right through our solid Earth without leaving so much as a ripple. Imagine also that, in addition to the familiar three dimensions of space—width, height, and depth—and the one dimension of time, the universe has six *invisible* dimensions. And imagine that the tiniest particles of matter are incredibly short strings.

These are wild speculations, to be sure. But they are not the musings of a science-fiction writer. Instead, they represent the best guess of a few of our more creative theoretical physicists as to what our universe might really be like.

Ironically, the physicists came up with these mind-boggling notions in an attempt to simplify and combine previously developed descriptions of the universe. In conceiving of such ideas, they carried on a tradition that dates back to the early 1900's.

Before that time, scientists viewed space according to principles developed by the Greek mathematician Euclid in about 300 B.C. Space had the three dimensions that are familiar to us today. But, by itself, space was nothing at all—a bare stage on which the drama of existence was played out by matter.

Gravity and the fourth dimension

Scientists based their view of matter largely on theories published by British scientist, astronomer, and mathematician Sir Isaac Newton in 1687. Newton said that all material objects attract one another by means of the *force of gravity*. The amount of the force depends upon how massive the objects are. The extremely massive Earth, for example, exerts much more gravitational force than does an apple. The mutual attraction between extremely massive objects is quite apparent. The force of gravity between Earth and the sun, for example, keeps Earth in orbit.

How does the force of gravity travel from object to object? Newton did not say. Objects seemed to reach out mysteriously across empty space and pull each other.

Physicist Albert Einstein found Newton's force of gravity altogether too mysterious, and in 1916 he proposed his own revolutionary theory of gravitation, the general theory of relativity. Einstein said that the three dimensions of space and the one dimension of time are really parts of a four-dimensional structure called *space-time* and that matter distorts space-time by creating smooth curves in it. We can imagine this by picturing a bowling ball causing a depression in a soft mattress. The amount by which an object distorts space-time depends upon the mass of the object—the larger the mass, the deeper the depression and curvature. Earth moves in its orbit, according to Einstein's theory, because a distortion in space-time created by the extremely massive sun causes Earth to follow a curved path along the "wall" of the depression. So, with Einstein's theory, our view of space changed. It was not an empty stage; gravity was built into the structure of space. And, as a result, Einstein concluded that gravity is not a force.

How could Einstein's theory be proved superior to Newton's? By measuring how gravity could bend light. Einstein's theory stated that curved space-time always has some effect on every object, even a ray of light. Einstein predicted that the sun's powerful gravity would distort space enough to bend light passing close by the sun by an angle of about 0.0005 degree from its normal path through the sky. Newton's theory predicted a deflection caused by the influence of the force of gravity on light, but one only half as great. The chance to find out which theory was correct came during a total eclipse of the sun in 1919.

British astronomer Sir Arthur S. Eddington performed the measurement during the eclipse. He needed photographs of stars whose light had passed near the sun. Ordinarily, this starlight would be invisible on Earth because of the sun's brilliant glare.

The test was a supreme challenge to an astronomer's skill. In a photograph the size of this page, with the sun's blanked-out image barely fitting between the margins, a star would appear out of position by about 0.004 inch—considerably less than the radius of the dot on an *i*. Eddington succeeded in finding this tiny variation.

Eddington had a flair for publicity and arranged to have the results of his measurements announced before an audience of Britain's greatest scientists. In solemn tones, he proclaimed the confirmation of Einstein's theory. The world press got caught up in the excitement, and to everyone's surprise Einstein became a genuine international celebrity, the only scientist in Western history to know the adulation of crowds and ticker-tape parades. In one stroke, he had dethroned both Euclid and Newton. This modest man in rumpled clothing was hailed as the greatest genius of all time. Einstein shook his head in disbelief at all the fuss, which only made the crowds love him more.

The electromagnetic stumbling block

Einstein was never one to rest on his laurels. If gravity is an effect of curved space-time, might not electromagnetism—another force known to science—be the same kind of effect?

The theory of electromagnetic force had been proposed by British scientist James Clerk Maxwell in 1873. Maxwell worked out a force theory for magnetism, electricity, and light. Maxwell's task was more complicated than Newton's had been. Maxwell had to explain not only a force of attraction, as Newton had, but also a *force of repulsion*—a pushing force.

People had known since ancient times that two magnets either attract or repel each other. Opposite poles—the north pole of one magnet and the south pole of another—attract, while like poles repel. Similarly, two objects carrying opposite electric charge—positive

Glossary

Electromagnetic force: The force responsible for magnetism, light and other types of electromagnetic radiation, and the behavior of electrons orbiting an atomic nucleus.

Force of gravity: The force through which objects attract one another in proportion to their masses.

Messenger particles: Pointlike subatomic particles that transmit the fundamental forces of nature—gravity, the electromagnetic force, the strong force, and the weak force.

Shadow matter: Material unlike anything known. It cannot be seen or felt but might be detected through the force of its gravity.

Space-time: A geometrical concept that consists of the three dimensions of space (length, depth, and height) and one dimension of time.

String: In certain theories attempting to unify the forces, any particle of matter or messenger particle.

Strong force: The force that holds the atomic nucleus together.

Weak force: The force responsible for certain kinds of radioactivity.

and negative—attract each other, while objects of like charge repel each other.

According to Maxwell, the magnetic and electrical forces of attraction and repulsion are all forms of one and the same force—the *electromagnetic force*. In this theory, light consists of electromagnetic waves with *wavelengths*—distances between successive wave crests—ranging from 0.4 to 0.7 millionths of a meter. Infrared rays are longer electromagnetic waves; ultraviolet rays, shorter. Later, scientists discovered X rays, with even shorter wavelengths; and radio waves, with wavelengths longer than those of infrared rays.

After his success with a geometric explanation of gravity, Einstein hoped that Maxwell's force could also be shown to be a consequence of the geometry of space. For 30 years, until his death in 1955, he searched in vain for a geometric theory of electromagnetism similar to his geometric theory of gravity. Through geometry, Einstein sought to unify the forces.

The difficulty lay in the fact that, unlike gravity, electromagnetism includes forces of both attraction and repulsion. Consider the atom, which is made up of one or more negatively charged electrons orbiting a positively charged nucleus, much as the planets orbit the sun. Each electron and the nucleus, having opposite charges, are attracted to each other electrically, as Earth and the sun are attracted to each other gravitationally. In a theory of electromagnetism comparable to Einstein's gravitational theory, a depression in space-time caused by the nucleus would keep the electron in orbit. This would explain attraction, but what about repulsion? A downward slope in space-time toward the nucleus could not also account for repulsion. If a positive charge moves in one direction, a negative one starting in the same place will move in the opposite direction, and a neutral object won't move at all. These contrasting responses could not be explained by the geometry of space-time.

The idea of a fifth dimension

One possible way out of this dilemma was proposed in 1921 by Theodor Kaluza, a man as obscure as Einstein was famous. After 20 years of teaching mathematics at the engineering college in Königsberg (then part of Germany but now in the Soviet Union and renamed Kaliningrad), he was still on the lowest rung of the academic ladder. Kaluza proposed that positive and negative objects seem to respond differently because they are not really in the same place. He theorized that electric charge is actually an effect of an object's location in a hidden *fifth* dimension of space-time.

To imagine how the Kaluza theory works, suppose that human beings were limited to seeing only what was on the ground. We would see in only two dimensions, with no inkling that there was a third dimension called *height*. All we would know of clouds, for example, would come from watching their shadows move across the ground. We would notice that the shadows usually move in the same direction, but not always. Occasionally, we would even see two shadows cross each other.

Our two-dimensional physicists would make up theories to account for the various cloud motions. They might well imagine some mysterious distinction between shadows, similar to the distinction between positive and negative electric charges. But suppose the third dimension of height were suddenly revealed to these two-dimensional scientists. They would then see that the shadows on the ground were merely projections of clouds blowing in various directions at different heights in the previously unseen third dimension. Similarly, Kaluza said essentially that charged objects are projections of as-yet-unknown bodies located at various places in an unseen fifth dimension.

A fifth dimension would account for the forces of both attraction and repulsion with curves and depressions similar to Einstein's gravity curvature. A fifth-dimension attraction curvature would be like a depression in an otherwise flat surface. An object rolling along the surface would veer toward the center of the depression. A repulsion curvature would be like a hill in an otherwise flat surface. An object rolling along the surface would veer away from the center of the hill.

Where's the proof?

Kaluza realized that such a peculiar idea, coming from an obscure individual like him, was unlikely to be taken seriously, so he wrote to Einstein for an opinion. At first, Einstein was taken aback. Kaluza's theory seemed to be stretching the notion of dimension too far. But after a while, Einstein took to the idea. He encouraged Kaluza to publish his theory, and he helped him land a better job.

Others joined the bandwagon. Swedish mathematician Oskar Klein suggested how the fifth dimension might differ from the other four. It might be incredibly small—much "lower in altitude" than an atom is small in diameter. If this were so, we would never see the fifth dimension as an extension of space.

The ideas of Kaluza and Klein enjoyed a brief vogue in the 1920's and 1930's but then dropped out of fashion. The reason they dropped out was simple enough: The theories predicted every-

The Three Dimensions of Space

The world we perceive has three dimensions. The first is a simple extension, like a line with no height or depth. The second is perpendicular to the first, as in a plane with only length and depth. The third adds the dimension of height.

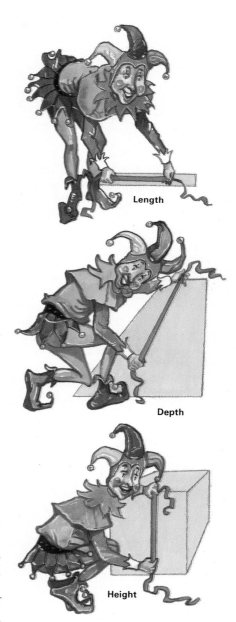

Length

Depth

Height

SUN

EARTH

The First Force

Sir Isaac Newton in the 1680's proposed the first theory of force to explain what holds the planets in orbit around the sun and holds us down on Earth. He said that there was a mysterious force called *gravity,* which somehow reaches across the empty three-dimensional space separating two objects.

thing you would get if the prevailing theory of the electromagnetic force were true. They left no room for the kind of unique test that scientists demand before they will embrace a radically new theory. So they remained on the shelf for nearly 50 years.

From the 1950's on, the central focus of research into the fundamental forces of nature turned to subatomic particles. By that time, physicists had discovered two additional forces, the *strong* and *weak* forces, and by 1975, they believed they understood these forces quite well. The strong force is a force of attraction that binds together particles called *quarks* in sets of three to form *protons* and *neutrons,* which make up atomic nuclei. The weak force is responsible for certain kinds of *radioactive decay* in which one particle changes into another—a neutron into a proton, for example.

A subatomic view of force

The understanding of the strong and weak forces as well as the electromagnetic and gravitational forces rested on a new way of visualizing a force—quantum field theory. The new theory, developed and refined by a number of particle physicists, departed from the ideas of both Newton and Einstein.

Quantum field theory paints a starkly simple picture of the subatomic world and the forces that operate there. Subatomic particles seem to have no size at all. They are like mathematical *points*, defined as having a position in space, but no width, height, or depth. The four forces are transported across the space between particles by pointlike *quanta*, or bundles of energy, which serve as *messenger particles*. Thus, on the subatomic level, matter is a swarm of rapidly moving particles, none of which has any significant size.

The messenger particle responsible for electromagnetism is the *photon*. Two electrons repel each other, for example, when one electron absorbs a photon that the other has radiated. The absorbing electron is "pushed" away from the radiating electron.

The *gluon* is responsible for the strong force. The quarks that make up protons and neutrons attract one another by tossing gluons back and forth in a three-way "game of catch."

The particle relationship to the weak force is more complicated. In one weak reaction, a neutron changes into a proton by emitting a messenger particle called a *weakon*, or W particle, which in turn is quickly transformed into an electron and an electrically neutral counterpart of the electron called a *neutrino*.

But what about gravity? According to quantum theory, a messenger particle called a *graviton* transmits the force of gravity between objects that have mass.

Most physicists had accepted the existence of the electromagnetic photon by the 1920's. Experimenters used *particle accelerators* (atom smashers) to discover evidence of gluons and weakons in the late 1970's and early 1980's. Experimental physicists have not, however, found evidence for gravitons, because gravity has no significant role in the particle reactions that can be studied with accelerators.

Meanwhile, theoretical physicists were trying to come up with a

The Fourth Dimension
Albert Einstein in 1916 proposed a new theory to explain gravity, which eliminated the concept of a force reaching across empty space. According to Einstein, Earth remains in orbit because of a curve in *space-time,* a combination of three-dimensional space and the fourth dimension—time. Just as a body might press into a soft mattress, the sun pushes against the "fabric" of space-time, creating a vast sloping depression from which Earth and the other planets cannot escape.

SUN

EARTH

FOUR DIMENSIONAL SPACE-TIME

formula that would explain all the forces in terms of a single master force that must have existed at the moment the universe began. These physicists constructed compelling mathematical combinations of the electromagnetic, weak, and strong forces. With these three forces combined, at least in theory, physicists set their sights on Einstein's goal of unifying electromagnetism and gravity.

Searching for a master force

The goal remained elusive. The theorists faced an obstacle that seemed insurmountable—a fundamental contradiction between quantum particles and curved space-time. In quantum theory, matter behaves in "jumps" or "steps" by radiating and absorbing the bundles of energy called quanta. In Einstein's theory, matter interacts evenly and smoothly, following the curving distortions of space-time.

Because quantum theory and curvature theories start from radically different ideas of what a force is, it was not clear that they could ever be combined into a single theory. Could "a swarm of messenger particles" and "curvature of space-time" really be two ways of saying the same thing? Many scientists had their doubts, and many still do.

But a few brave theorists kept struggling to combine the theories. Some of them dusted off the Kaluza-Klein ideas, realizing that with more forces to accommodate, the answer might lie in many more dimensions of space-time than five. The theories that came out of their studies came to be known as *supergravity theories*.

Mathematical bugs infested the first supergravity theories. Calculations of seemingly straightforward quantities, such as the strength of the gravitational attraction between two subatomic particles, gave answers that were infinitely large. Furthermore, some equations indicated the existence of particles that remained undiscovered, even when experimenters focused their atom-smashing "microscopes" where theorists said the particles should be. Most physicists concluded that supergravity theories were doomed to failure.

Then, in 1982, two young theoretical physicists—Michael Green of the University of London and John Schwarz of the California Institute of Technology in Pasadena—hit upon a way to exterminate the mathematical bugs. Most of the problems, they found, came from treating particles mathematically as *points*. If instead they were regarded as tiny one-dimensional *strings*, infinite forces and unwanted particles vanished from the equations. Supergravity theories thus gave way to *superstring theories*.

According to superstring theories, the strings are unimaginably short. The most likely length is about 10^{-35} meter—a decimal point followed by 34 zeros and a 1. Strings come in three basic shapes. The graviton is a closed string—its ends joined to form a loop. All other messenger particles are open strings. A particle of matter, such as an electron or a quark, is somewhat like a long, narrow strip

Three More Forces

In addition to gravity, modern scientists uncovered three other fundamental forces of nature—forces that give an atom, *below*, its form. A theory first proposed in the 1930's says that "messenger particles" carry these forces among subatomic objects moving in three-dimensional space.

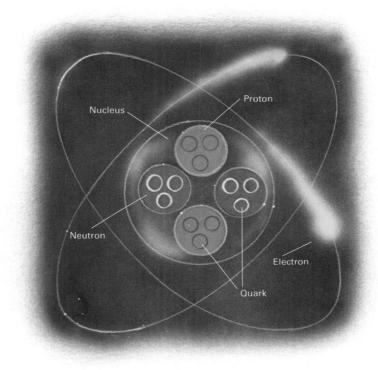

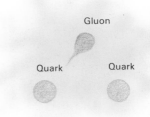

The electromagnetic force, which is responsible for electricity and magnetism and which holds electrons in orbit around the nucleus, is carried by tiny bundles of light called photons.

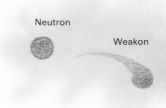

The strong force, which binds quarks together to form protons and neutrons, is carried by packets of energy called gluons.

of paper that has been given a half twist and then had its ends taped together. As in quantum theory, matter particles interact by tossing messenger particles back and forth.

The simplest superstring theory proposed by Green and Schwarz calls for 10 dimensions, including the familiar four dimensions of Einstein's space-time. The other six dimensions are very small, as in Kaluza-Klein theories. They are just wide enough to allow a superstring to turn.

At first glance, superstring theories seem to suffer from the same kind of flaw that condemned Kaluza-Klein theories to their long oblivion. They seem to predict almost everything you would get if previously held theories of quantum fields and curved space-time were true. To verify the few predictions that differ from those of Einstein's theory and quantum theory would require accelerators more powerful than any likely to be built on Earth.

There is, however, one possible test that does not require an accelerator. According to the Green-Schwarz theory, there may exist

The weak force—responsible for certain types of radioactivity—is carried by subatomic particles called weakons.

Exploring the World in Other Dimensions

Scientists, in trying to explain the four forces of nature in terms of one master force, have come up with mathematical solutions that indicate there are many more dimensions than we can perceive, perhaps as few as 5 or as many as 10. Explaining what the world is like in other dimensions requires a leap of imagination.

Discovering the Third Dimension
First, imagine what it would be like to see the world in only two dimensions, *below.* How might we explain the dark, mysterious objects approaching each other on the ground? Our imagination might create a theory stating that messenger particles carry a force of attraction between dark objects. But, by looking up, *right,* the third dimension is revealed, and the dark objects turn out to be created by clouds blowing overhead at different altitudes in the third dimension of height.

Imagining a Fifth Dimension
Tied to a world of three dimensions of space and one of time, we must use our imagination to explain the curved tracks left by electrically charged particles during a physics experiment, *below.* We note that oppositely charged particles seem to attract each other, while objects of like charge repel each other, so we theorize that messenger particles carry forces of attraction and repulsion between charged objects. But if we could "see" into a fifth dimension, *right,* we might discover that the tracks are merely projections of objects moving along at different "heights" in this dimension. As in Einstein's space-time, smooth curves account for apparent forces.

something called *shadow matter*, a substance that interacts with ordinary matter through the force of gravity, but not through the electromagnetic, strong, or weak forces. (Do not confuse shadow matter with *antimatter*, whose existence was established decades ago. Antimatter and matter interact all too well—they annihilate each other.) Finding some shadow matter would prove the Green-Schwarz theory. But this curious stuff may be extremely difficult to identify. Our universe could well be full of shadow matter, without our being aware of it. We see mainly by means of electromagnetism, not gravity, so we could not see shadow matter. And we could not feel shadow matter the way we feel solid objects that we touch, because shadow matter could pass freely through ordinary matter.

Elusive as shadow matter is, however, there is one way we could detect it. Gravity can indicate the presence of shadow matter. In fact, gravitational effects hint that certain galaxies may contain large amounts of invisible matter. These galaxies exert stronger gravitational forces than would be expected from the amount of matter

Superstrings
A new theory attempting to unify the four forces of nature blends the concept of smoothly curved space-time with the concept of messenger particles transmitting forces in tiny jumps. In this *superstring* theory, all subatomic particles are incredibly tiny strings moving about in a 10-dimensional universe. The strings' shapes determine their roles in shaping our world.

visible in their stars, gas, and dust. In the Special Reports section, see GALAXIES—ISLANDS IN THE UNIVERSE.

Astronomers might one day detect shadow matter by observing the effects of a shadow star in our galaxy, the Milky Way. Such an invisible star would reveal itself by the visible pull that its gravitational force exerts on an ordinary companion star.

A shadow world and us

A shadow matter star might even play a role in a fantastic drama on Earth—the mass extinctions of species that seem to take place every 30 million years or so. Such a mass extinction may have wiped out the dinosaurs. To support the idea that the extinctions occur at regular intervals, astrophysicist Marc Davis and physicist Richard A. Muller of the University of California, Berkeley, and astronomer Piet Hut of the Institute for Advanced Study in Princeton, N.J., have suggested that our sun might have an invisible companion, for which they propose the ominous-sounding name Nemesis.

According to this theory, Nemesis makes a vast elongated orbit around our sun, spending most of its time more than 5 trillion miles away. On its periodic sweeps near the sun, it disturbs comets that normally orbit safely beyond Pluto, sending them plunging into the inner solar system to wreak havoc. About 65 million years ago, for example, a large comet may have struck Earth, kicking tremendous clouds of dust into the atmosphere. The clouds could have blocked out a great deal of sunlight for many years. As a result, the environment may have become too cold for the dinosaurs.

There are many possible holes in this theory. Some scientists doubt the extinctions were caused by impacts, and others challenge the 30-million-year cycle. And even if Nemesis exists, it need not be made of shadow matter to have remained undiscovered.

Many mysteries remain

Superstrings too may prove no more than a lovely flight of fancy, destined to fade into obscurity. But fanciful theories are the engine that drives much of scientific progress, reawakening the curiosity that leads scientists to search where no one had thought to look before. Usually, they lead to nothing. Occasionally, something important turns up, but not always what the theory predicted.

If the superstring theory proves to be correct, there will be no need to burn the old geometry books. We already know that on the vast scale of the cosmos, a nearly imperceptible curvature rules the universe. If strings of matter coil and join in 10 dimensions at the infinitesimal end of the scale, the old rules of three-dimensional space laid down by Euclid will still have their place in our everyday world. But the problems confronted and the theories proposed by modern physics make us realize that there are many mysteries yet to be uncovered about the true nature of the universe we live in.

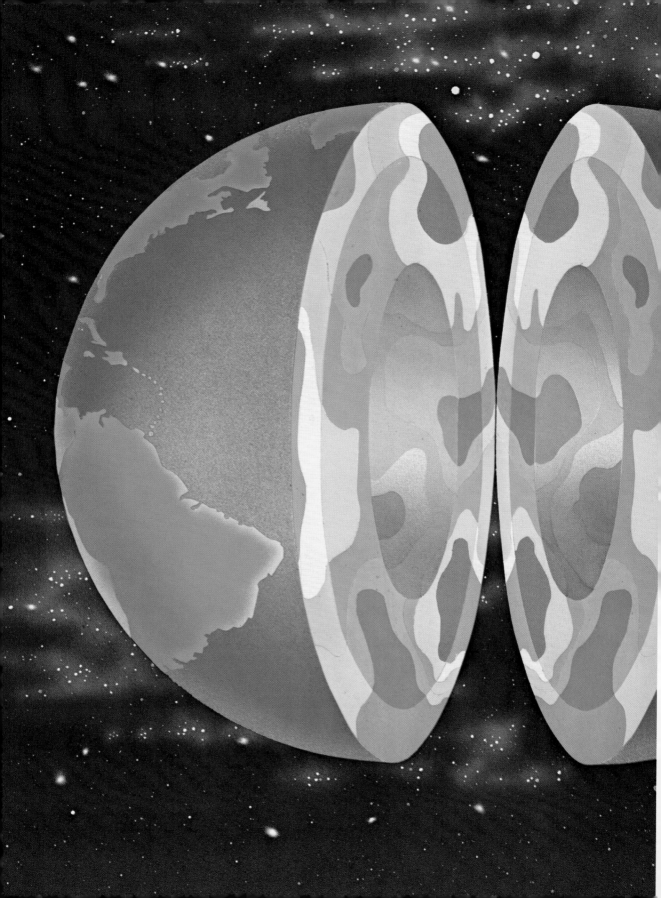

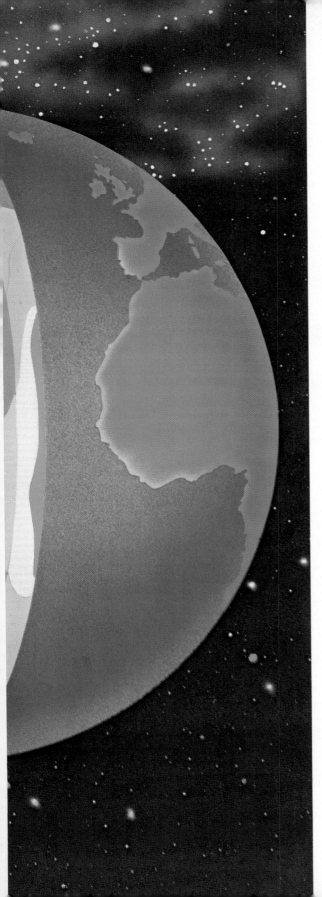

The first 3-D maps of Earth's interior and the world's deepest well are opening new windows into inner Earth.

Exploring Earth's Inner Space

BY DON L. ANDERSON

Giant apes, a vast subterranean sea, and enormous sea monsters were only a few of the remarkable sights witnessed by Professor Von Hardwigg and his nephew, Harry, as they descended to Earth's core in Jules Verne's adventure tale *A Journey to the Center of the Earth* (1864). In his later stories, Verne, who died in 1905, wrote about airplanes, space travel, submarines, and Earth satellites many years before they were developed. Most of Verne's wild ideas are no longer science fiction but technological fact. Yet we are no closer to journeying into Earth's interior than we were in Verne's time.

Nor are we ever likely to make such a journey, considering the interior's crushing pressures and searing temperatures. Even the deepest caves, mines, and wells barely scratch Earth's surface. In fact, we can travel to the moon easier than we can penetrate 10 miles beneath our feet.

This inability to see directly into Earth is one of

the main reasons we are so remarkably ignorant of the inner workings of the planet we live on. Until recently, scientists had only a very crude picture of the interior. But two developments—a new way of analyzing earthquake waves that has enabled scientists to create the first three-dimensional maps of the interior, and the deepest well ever drilled—are opening new windows into inner Earth.

The findings from these projects—some of them startling—have given geologists a much clearer picture of the interior and raised questions about some long-held geologic theories. They also have provided new insights into the processes deep within Earth that control mountain building, the movement of the continents, the formation of new ocean floor, and the eruption of volcanoes. Equally exciting, these projects may help scientists find valuable mineral deposits and even predict earthquakes.

Early "looks" inside Earth

The idea that Earth is hollow and riddled with cavities, as Verne imagined, is very old. The ancient Greeks, for example, believed that the underworld was a place of vast caverns where hot sulfurous winds blew fiercely, creating violent earthquakes.

Well before Verne's time, however, scientists—using studies of the moon—had concluded that Earth was not hollow but solid. This conclusion followed soon after English astronomer and mathematician Isaac Newton published his theories of gravitation in 1687. Newton determined that the gravitational attraction between two heavenly bodies, such as Earth and the moon, depends on the *mass* (amount of matter) of the bodies and the distance between them. By turning the equation around a bit—using calculations of Earth's gravitational effect on the moon and the moon's distance from Earth—scientists were able to determine Earth's mass.

When scientists compared Earth's mass with its volume to determine its density, however, they got a surprise. They found that Earth's average density is twice the average density of rocks near the surface. This indicated that surface rocks are much lighter than those in the interior.

For several reasons, scientists soon settled on the presence of iron inside Earth to explain this puzzle. Not only is iron dense enough to account for the difference between Earth's average density and the density of surface rocks, but it also is the most abundant heavy metal in the solar system. Many meteorites consist chiefly of iron and represent material left over from the formation of the solar system or from broken-up planets. As such, they provide clues about the material that makes up Earth and other planets. Scientists concluded that as Earth cooled from its early *molten* (partially liquid) phase, iron and other heavy metals sank to the center of the planet.

In the mid-1800's, scientists began using instruments called seismographs to measure and record *seismic waves* (vibrations generated by earthquakes). Then in 1889, Baron E. von Rebeur Paschwitz, a

The author:
Don L. Anderson is professor of geophysics and the director of the Seismological Laboratory at the California Institute of Technology in Pasadena.

German geologist, made a discovery that revolutionized geology. He found that his seismographs in Germany had picked up seismic signals only minutes after an earthquake struck Tokyo. His readings provided the first recorded evidence that seismic waves travel through Earth's interior. Geologists soon began using seismic waves to study Earth's interior in much the same way as doctors use X rays to see inside their patients.

There are two main types of seismic waves—body waves and surface waves. Body waves travel through Earth. The body waves called primary (P) or compressional waves are very similar to sound waves and cause rock to vibrate back and forth. Secondary (S) or shear waves, another type of body wave, cause rock to move from side to side and up and down. It is S waves that cause most of the damage at the site of an earthquake. Surface waves, so named because they travel along Earth's outer layers, cause the ground to rise and fall like the waves on the surface of the ocean. The waves weaken with depth. Although surface waves, like other seismic waves, grow weaker the farther they travel from the site of an earthquake, they can cause great destruction at considerable distances from the quake. Surface waves from very large earthquakes may travel around Earth many times and register on seismographs for several weeks.

Seismic waves are useful for studying the interior because they behave differently in different types of rock. For example, P waves and some surface waves can travel through both solid and molten rock. S waves, on the other hand, because of their side-to-side motion, cannot pass through liquids. In addition, the speed of seismic waves depends on the density of the material they are passing through. For instance, the waves slow down when passing through molten rock or rock that is not very dense. The waves speed up when passing through cold, dense rock.

Discovering Earth's layers

Scientists using seismic waves to study the interior quickly discovered that Earth consists of several separate layers. In 1906, the year of the great San Francisco earthquake, British geologist R. D. Oldham of the Geological Survey of India published the first evidence that Earth has a large distinct central core. He found that P waves slow down sharply at a certain depth. In addition, at this depth, S waves are either reflected back to the surface or disappear. Oldham concluded that this point marked the outer boundary of the core, and he theorized that the inability of S waves to pass across the boundary indicated that the core was fluid, probably molten iron.

Only three years later, in 1909, Yugoslavian seismologist Andrija Mohorovičic discovered a boundary about 20 miles below the surface where the speed of seismic waves increases sharply, suggesting a change in the density and, perhaps, the type of rock. Mohorovičic concluded that the boundary, now called the Moho or Mohorovičic

Jules Verne's characters in *A Journey to the Center of the Earth* (1864) walked to Earth's core along a series of subterranean passageways. In reality, the interior's searing temperatures and crushing pressures make traveling to the moon easier than penetrating 10 miles below Earth's surface.

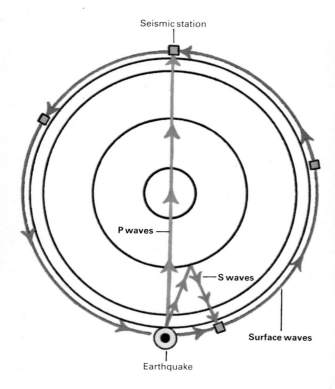

Seismic station

P waves

S waves

Surface waves

Earthquake

Clues to the Inner Earth

Seismic waves caused by earthquakes provide clues to what lies deep inside Earth by the way they travel through different materials. Primary (P) waves pass through solids and liquids (*above*). Secondary (S) waves cannot pass through liquids and are reflected back to the surface. Also, the speed of P, S, and surface waves, which travel along only Earth's outer layers, vary, depending on the type of rock through which they are passing.

discontinuity, separates Earth's outer skin, called the crust, from a middle layer, called the mantle.

Shortly after Mohorovičic's discovery, Danish seismologist Inge Lehmann found that the liquid core seems to have a solid center. She based her conclusions on seismic recordings indicating that although P waves slow down as they pass through the outer core, they travel more quickly than they would if the inner core were completely liquid. So by the early 1900's, geologists had concluded that Earth had a light crust, a denser middle layer called the mantle, and a liquid iron core with a solid center.

Since then, seismographs have become more numerous and more sensitive. These improvements have enabled scientists to map the interior in greater detail. We now know, for example, that the mantle has three layers—an upper layer that is semimolten in some places, a solid transition zone, and a solid, very dense lower layer. We also know that the crust is divided into at least an upper and lower layer.

Seismic studies have their limitations, however. Most seismic stations are concentrated in earthquake-prone regions on land. Very few are on the ocean floor, which covers 70 per cent of our planet. Moreover, most major earthquakes occur in several relatively narrow belts, such as around the Pacific Ocean, along the boundaries of several of the huge tectonic plates that make up Earth's outer

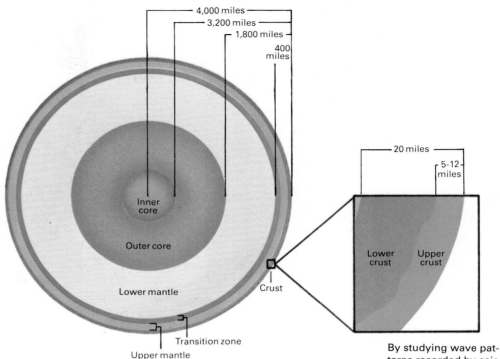

4,000 miles
3,200 miles
1,800 miles
400 miles

Inner core

Outer core

Lower mantle

Crust

Transition zone

Upper mantle

20 miles
5-12 miles

Lower crust

Upper crust

By studying wave patterns recorded by seismographs, *opposite page, right,* scientists have learned that Earth is made up of a solid crust; a mantle consisting of an upper layer that is semimolten in some places, a solid transition zone, and a solid lower layer; and a liquid outer core with a solid center.

layers. Seismologists can study Earth's outer layers by using explosives or powerful vibrating machines to create their own seismic waves. To probe deeper, however, they must rely on earthquakes and underground nuclear explosions. As a result, seismologists cannot easily look into Earth anywhere and anytime they please.

3-D maps of inner Earth

In the early 1980's, geologists developed a way to make better use of even limited seismic information. Several groups of scientists, including a group at the California Institute of Technology, began analyzing seismic waves using a technique similar to computerized tomography (CT) scanning, a medical procedure for examining the human body. The word *tomography* comes from a Greek word meaning a *cutting* or *section*. A CT scanner uses X rays to produce images of a patient's body and a computer to convert this information into "slices" or cross-sectional images of the body. Seismic tomography works the same way but uses seismic waves instead of X rays to create cross-sectional images of Earth's interior.

The three-dimensional maps of the interior produced by seismic tomography have created a revolution in earth sciences by giving geologists a much clearer picture of the inner Earth. The difference between conventional seismic studies and seismic tomography is the

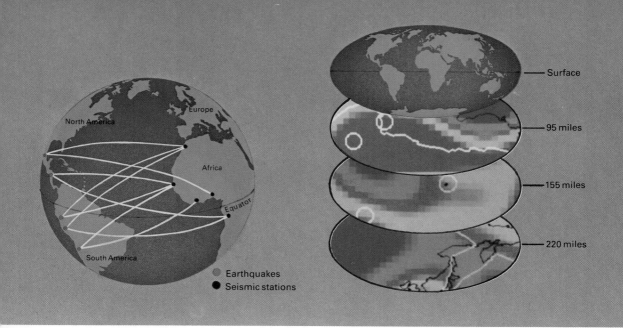

North America

Europe

Africa

Equator

South America

○ Earthquakes
● Seismic stations

Surface

95 miles

155 miles

220 miles

Mapping by the Slice
By comparing the speeds of waves from earthquakes, picked up at
many seismic stations and following crisscrossing paths at different
depths, *above left,* scientists can map horizontal "slices" of Earth's
interior, *above right.* Because seismic waves move faster through
colder, denser rock than they do through hotter, more fluid rock, scientists can deduce the temperature and other characteristics of the
rock through which the waves passed.

difference between looking at a dark, blurred photograph of a
room and being able to walk around and examine the room.

Like conventional seismic studies, seismic tomography is based on
the speed of seismic waves traveling from earthquakes to seismic
stations. Seismic stations have very accurate clocks that precisely record the arrival time of each wave generated by an earthquake.
From the information collected at a number of seismic stations, seismologists can calculate the waves' average speed. Knowing the average speed alone, however, doesn't tell scientists much about the
density and temperature of the rock through which the waves have
passed, just as knowing the average speed of cars traveling from
New York City to Los Angeles wouldn't tell you where the cars were
stuck in city traffic and where they were zipping along on highways.

But by comparing the average speeds of thousands of waves from
many earthquakes traveling along crisscrossing paths at different
depths, seismologists can find "fast" areas, where the rock is cool
and dense, and "slow" areas, where it is hot and less dense.

Seismic tomography has produced some exciting results. One of
the most significant things we have learned is that Earth's interior is
not like an onion with layers whose thickness is the same everywhere. We have known for some time that the thickness of the crust
varies from 5 miles under the ocean floor to 20 miles under the

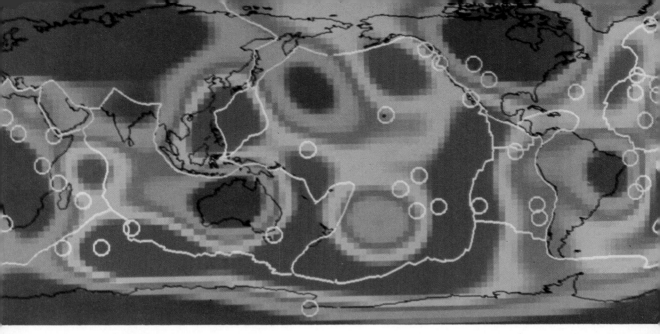

A Look Below the Surface

A color-coded map of one slice of Earth's interior about 95 miles down, *above,* based on computerized wave analysis, *right,* shows regions of cooler rock (blue) under the continents (black lines). Red and yellow indicate regions of hotter rock along the boundaries (white lines) of the tectonic plates on which the continents ride. There, the plates are moving apart where magma is rising from the mantle or creating volcanoes where one plate is plunging beneath another.

continents. Now, tomographic maps have revealed that this variation in thickness also occurs in the mantle and perhaps in the core.

We also have found that certain features on the surface extend much farther down into the mantle than we had expected. The maps show, for example, that the continents have deep cold "roots" that penetrate at least 125 miles into the mantle.

This connection between Earth's surface and its interior also holds true for the system of midocean ridges, chains of underwater mountains circling Earth, where magma wells up from the mantle to form new crust. Maps of the interior show vast areas of hot rock or magma underlying the ridges 100 miles down.

At a depth of 220 miles, however, the picture changes. The midocean ridges no longer form a continuous line but are instead broken up into segments. At this depth, the rock under some ridges, particularly the Southeast Indian Ocean Rise and the East Pacific Rise, is colder and denser than the rock above. This was the first evidence scientists had that the magma pushing out at the ridges does not always follow a vertical path from the mantle to the surface. Instead, the magma may flow horizontally through the mantle for great distances. Maps of the interior at greater depths show that the Indian Ocean Rise and the East Pacific Rise 10,000 miles away may be fed by a hot region under the South Pacific Ocean.

Tomographic maps have also offered an explanation for the bulges and depressions in Earth's surface. Our planet is not a perfect sphere. The Western United States, East Africa, and the central Pacific Ocean sit atop huge bulges in the planet, while Antarctica, parts of the Indian Ocean, and most of the continents are settled in low areas. The maps show that beneath the bulges are enormous pockets of hot rock that have caused Earth to swell. Beneath the depressions are areas of colder, denser rock that have caused the surface to sink.

Finding an ancient sea floor

Seismic tomography also has helped us find the floor of the ancient Pacific Ocean—right where we expected it to be. For the past 200 million years, the Pacific Ocean has been shrinking because of *subduction*. Subduction occurs when two tectonic plates collide and the edge of one plate is thrust under the edge of another. Friction and heat inside Earth cause the upper layers of the sinking plate to melt, fueling volcanoes on the surface. Farther down, however, the colder, unmelted layers of the sinking plate cool the mantle rock, just as putting ice cubes into warm tea makes iced tea.

Along its western edge, the tectonic plate on which the Pacific sits is being subducted beneath the plates on which eastern Asia, Australia, and some Pacific islands ride. Along its eastern edge, the Pacific Plate is being subducted under the plates on which North and South America sit. Scientists believed—but had little evidence—that the subducted Pacific floor lay beneath these plates. When we mapped the interior at a depth of 220 miles, we found huge areas of cold, dense rock under eastern Asia and Australia, as well as under South America and the central and southern Atlantic Ocean. These cold areas are what remains of the ancient Pacific sea floor.

Some of the most fascinating discoveries about the interior are those that have shed new light on the movement of the hot, soft rock that makes up the mantle. This rock can flow because of the high temperatures in the interior. Scientists believe mantle rock is constantly churning in a large-scale, slow-motion version of what happens

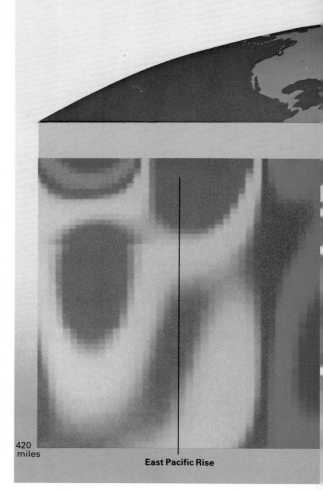

420 miles

East Pacific Rise

A Window into the Earth
Scientists use information from seismic wave analysis to produce vertical cross sections of the Earth's interior. A cross section of the interior at the equator to a depth of 420 miles shows areas of hot rock under the Mid-Atlantic Ridge and the East Pacific Rise, where molten rock rises from the mantle to form new ocean crust. The areas of blue under South America and Africa reveal that the "roots" of the continents extend far down into the mantle.

South America   **Mid-Atlantic Ridge**   **Africa**

to a pot of water on a hot stove. According to the theory of plate tectonics, hot mantle rock rises under the midocean ridges. The hot rock then moves along the top of the mantle cooling as it goes to subduction zones, where it sinks. Eventually, the rock flows back to the ridges at lower depths. We have found, however, that the currents in the mantle are a great deal more complicated than we thought. There may, in fact, be currents within currents. For example, tomographic maps and other geologic data indicate that under central North America the mantle rock is flowing from north to south. Under Siberia, however, mantle rock seems to be moving in the opposite direction.

We have also been able to determine where mantle rock is rising and where it is falling. For instance, our three-dimensional maps show upward movement under the midocean ridges and downward movement at subduction zones. But both hot and cold material rise and fall in other areas of the mantle. In addition, material seems to move between the midocean ridges and subduction zones at many depths.

The World's Deepest Well

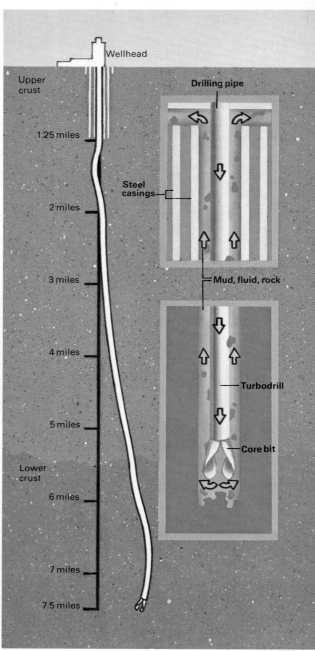

The Kola well, the first well to penetrate into Earth's lower crust, is being drilled on the Kola Peninsula, a barren region of the Soviet Union north of the Arctic Circle, *top and above middle.* Soviet scientists supervise the drilling from a control room, *above.* The turbodrill that drills the hole, *right,* is powered by fluid pumped from the surface through a drilling pipe. Mud, fluid, and rock are returned to the surface in the space around the pipe. The core bit of the drill has wandered about half a mile from the vertical as it bores into the crust.

The maps also show regions of hot soft rock and cold hard rock in the lower mantle, indicating that currents exist there, too. But the maps have not yet indicated whether the currents and the material in the upper and lower mantle remain separate or whether the currents and the material in the two layers mix freely. Tomographic evidence may eventually tell us whether subducted crust moves across the boundary between the upper and lower mantle, which lies 400 miles below the surface. Unfortunately, the boundary area is difficult to map because surface waves barely reach this far down. In addition, P waves and S waves become extremely difficult to interpret at this depth.

Seismologists are counting on the Incorporated Research Institutions for Seismology (IRIS) to help provide information that will answer this and other questions. IRIS is a nonprofit corporation formed in 1984 by some 50 universities and research centers to improve seismological research. Among IRIS's projects is a plan to set up at least 200 new seismic stations and position about 1,000 portable seismometers in regions where these instruments are scarce. The seismic data they provide should enable us to see even farther and more clearly into the interior.

Drilling into Earth's past

Of course the most direct way to study Earth's interior is to drill a hole. The only sure way to determine the pressure at a certain depth, for example, is to go down there and measure it. Drilling also opens a window into Earth's past, since in general, as one goes deeper into the crust, one encounters older rocks.

Drilling on the ocean floor has provided scientists with extremely valuable information about the composition of the crust and upper mantle—both now and in the past—ancient climates, and the history of the oceans. Ocean wells usually penetrate only several hundred yards below the surface, and few have gone below the layers of sediment that have gradually built up on the ocean floor. And these wells have revealed little about Earth's structure.

Nearly all wells on land in the United States and elsewhere have been drilled for the commercial

A Few Surprises from Kola

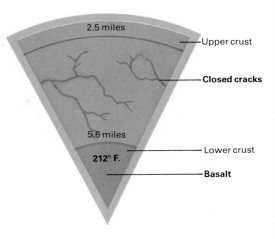

Seismic studies and findings at shallower drill sites had led Kola scientists to believe that there would be no open cracks in the rock below 2.5 miles and that temperatures would increase slowly with depth. They also believed that the lower crust, below 5.6 miles, consisted of basalt, a volcanic rock.

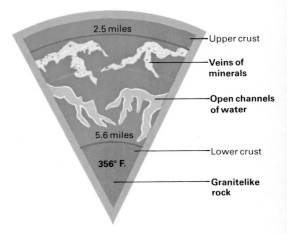

To their surprise, the scientists found large open channels filled with hot, mineral-rich water. They also found veins of minerals, and temperatures reaching 356°F., much hotter than the 212°F. temperature expected. In addition, instead of finding basalt in the lower crust, they found granitelike rock, like that in the upper crust.

exploration of petroleum, natural gas, and minerals. Most of these wells are fairly shallow, rarely going deeper than 4⅓ miles. In fact, the deepest U.S. well ever drilled was the Bertha Rogers natural gas well in Oklahoma, which extended down 6 miles.

Unfortunately, drilling has several limitations. As one goes deeper, rocks get harder and temperatures get higher. Consequently, drilling has been both difficult and expensive.

World's deepest well

Advances in drilling technology, however, are making deep wells easier and less expensive to drill and are spurring deep drilling projects in a number of countries, including the United States, the Soviet Union, West Germany, and Japan. These projects are still in the planning stages everywhere except the Soviet Union, where scientists have already bored more than 7.5 miles into the crust, farther than anyone else has ever drilled.

The Soviet Union's well is being dug on the barren and rocky Kola Peninsula, just east of Finland and 155 miles north of the Arctic Circle. Soviet scientists chose this site because from 3 to 9½ miles of granite that once covered this area have been worn away by erosion. As a result, the lower crust begins only about 5½ miles down, fairly close to the surface. The well, begun in 1970, passes through rock holding 1.4 billion years of geologic history. The drillers plan to dig down a total of 9.3 miles, about halfway through the crust in this area.

The Soviet scientists hoped the well would reveal new details about the structure and history of the deep parts of the crust and provide information that would help in detecting the presence of mineral deposits far below the surface. They have not been disappointed. The Kola well has uncovered a wealth of information about the crust, including a few surprises.

The Kola well is the first to bore into the lower crust. Seismic studies indicated that at this site, the boundary between the upper and lower crust is 5.6 miles down. At this point, the speed of seismic waves increases sharply. Scientists had believed that this increase in speed was the result of a change in the type of rock, from the granitelike rock that makes up the upper crust to basalt—a dense volcanic rock.

Instead, at a depth of 5.6 miles, the drillers found more granitelike rock. They also found that they had come to the bottom of a deep zone of cracked rock that began about 2½ miles below the surface. The Soviet scientists believe the increase in the speed of the seismic waves merely reflects the shift from cracked rock to uncracked rock. These findings suggest that perhaps both layers of the crust are made of the same material and that an increase in the speed of seismic waves may not necessarily mean a change in rock type.

In the zone of cracked rock, the drillers made the most surprising discovery of all. The rock was laced with large open cracks filled with mineral-rich water. Scientists had thought that the pressure at this depth would be so great that any cracks in the rock would be closed, like a sponge being squeezed. Perhaps rock is simply stronger than we supposed and can resist these great pressures. Perhaps the flowing water, which at that depth is also under great pressure, keeps the cracks open and even creates new cracks by dissolving the rock.

Scientists suspect these streams may be responsible for the higher-than-expected temperatures found in the well. Scientists had predicted that the temperatures would increase slowly with depth. Instead, at 1.8 miles down, temperatures began to rise $2\frac{1}{2}$ times faster than expected. At a depth of 6 miles, the rock was 356°F., rather than the 212°F. predicted. Scientists think the streams of water may be one of the means by which heat escapes from the interior.

In the well, scientists also found rich veins of many minerals, including gold, iron, cobalt, and zinc. These veins probably formed from minerals that had been transported through the crust by the streams of water.

Deep drilling in America

Scientists in the United States expect to begin drilling their own deep wells in 1986 or 1987. One site being considered is in the Appalachian Mountains near the Georgia–South Carolina border. There, scientists plan to drill down at least $6\frac{1}{2}$ miles to test the theory that the Appalachian Mountains formed because of the collision of Africa and North America between 500 million and 250 million years ago. Scientists think that when Africa crashed into North America, huge slabs of African crust several miles thick slid over the sedimentary rock on the surface of North America. According to the theory, these slabs were driven several hundred miles inland, buckling the rock and pushing up the Appalachian Mountains. Scientists hope a deep well will bring up samples of the African crust, now buried under new sedimentary rock, and the older sedimentary rock below the African crust. Such a discovery could have economic value in the future since petroleum and natural gas are found in sedimentary rock.

Another proposed site is in Creede, Colo., in the San Juan Mountains. There, scientists hope to find the paths taken by metal-bearing liquids that carried gold, lead, zinc, and copper to the surface 20 million years ago.

In just a short time, deep drilling and seismic tomography have opened exciting new windows into Earth's interior. Despite these advances, however, the picture we have of the interior is still fuzzy and incomplete, as if we were looking at it through dark and dirty glasses. But the science of seismic tomography is still young, and more deep holes will be dug. The picture will get sharper and come into clearer focus as time goes on.

Science File

Science Year contributors report on the year's major developments in their respective fields. The articles in this section are arranged alphabetically.

Agriculture	**Chemistry**
Anthropology	**Computer Hardware**
Archaeology, New World	**Computer Software**
Archaeology, Old World	**Deaths**
Astronomy, Extragalactic	**Dentistry**
Astronomy, Galactic	**Drugs**
Astronomy, Solar System	**Ecology**
Books of Science	**Electronics**
Botany	**Energy**

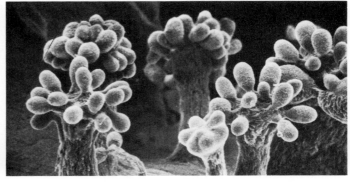

Agriculture

Agricultural experts meeting at a two-part international conference in late 1985 contended that farmers must raise productivity to remain profitable and that only science and technology will enable them to achieve that goal. The conference meetings, held in October in Harbor Springs, Mich., and in December in Airlie, Va., were sponsored by Michigan State University in East Lansing and the Charles F. Kettering Foundation of Dayton, Ohio.

Conference speakers emphasized that higher productivity does not necessarily mean larger harvests. Productivity can also be increased by achieving the same crop yield, or even a smaller yield, at a lower cost. Many of the recommendations emerging from the conference therefore focused on how farmers can improve their operations to increase profits. Farmers were urged, for example, to reduce soil erosion and ground-water contamination and use fertilizers more efficiently.

Making waste into food. Treating straw with a dilute solution of alkaline hydrogen peroxide makes it much more digestible, according to a report in November 1985 by animal scientists at the University of Illinois at Urbana-Champaign and the United States Department of Agriculture's (USDA) Northern Regional Laboratory in Peoria, Ill. The scientists said that after treatment with peroxide, straw and other agricultural wastes, such as corncobs and cornstalks, could become an economical feed for livestock.

The researchers conducted several experiments to determine the digestibility of peroxide-treated *wheat straw* (the stems of wheat plants). They fed the material to lambs and compared the animals' day-to-day body weight with that of lambs eating untreated wheat straw. The animals eating the treated straw gained weight, while the other animals lost weight.

By testing the urine and feces of mature sheep that ate the treated wheat straw, the scientists determined that the peroxide solution increased the digestibility of the *cellulose* (a substance forming the walls of plant cells) in the straw by up to 85 per cent. This re-

A plant researcher at Kansas State University in Manhattan, *below,* removes pollen from goat grass, a wild grass that is an ancestor of wheat. The pollen will be added to a stalk of wheat to produce hybrid seed. The research is aimed at developing wheat with increased resistance to the Hessian fly, *right, top,* which lays its eggs on wheat plants. The larvae, *right, bottom,* then feed on wheat seedlings.

An entomologist in Madison, Wis., slips a plastic cover over a beehive to create a solar heating system. The cover traps heat from the sun, keeping the hive warm. Such covers enable most bees in solar-heated hives to survive a hard winter.

search may lead to a nearly inexhaustible food supply for farm animals.

Conservation tillage — or methods of plowing that reduce soil erosion and water loss—is being practiced by a growing number of U.S. farmers, according to a November 1985 report by agricultural experts. USDA scientists, together with plant and soil researchers in Colorado, Minnesota, Missouri, and Wisconsin, reported that about 28 per cent of U.S. farmland was being cultivated with conservation tillage methods as of 1983, the latest date for which figures were available. This planting system offers several advantages over conventional plowing—it not only conserves water and soil but also requires less labor and fuel for farm equipment.

Conservation tillage takes several forms and may include plowing patterns, such as contour plowing, to reduce soil erosion by runoff. Another method of conservation tillage is called no-till planting. In this technique, the ground is broken up in strips just wide enough to provide enough loose soil to cover the planted seeds.

In most forms of conservation tillage, plant residues from the previous crop are left on the ground—rather than plowed under—to reduce erosion by wind and rain. This sometimes causes an increase in weeds, insects, and plant diseases. Soil scientists must find ways to reduce or eliminate these disadvantages of conservation tillage if farmers are to truly benefit from this approach to cultivation. Agriculture officials hope that conservation tillage will be used on more than 50 per cent of U.S. farmland by the year 2000.

Freeze on Frostban. Hopes for the use of genetically engineered organisms in agriculture received a setback in March 1986 when the Environmental Protection Agency (EPA) suspended the permit of a California company to field-test genetically altered bacteria. The EPA in November 1985 had authorized Advanced Genetic Sciences (AGS) of Oakland to test the bacteria—designed to reduce frost damage to crops—on a field of strawberry plants located in Monterey County, California.

That test, scheduled for spring 1986, was then delayed while the Mon-

"Killers" on the Loose

In an oil field near Lost Hills in Kern County, California—just north of Los Angeles—a worker unknowingly stopped his earthmoving vehicle near an underground nest of unusually ferocious wild bees. At once, thousands of these bees attacked the cab in which the man was—fortunately—safely enclosed. As he watched, the bees turned on a rabbit and promptly stung it to death.

This incident occurred on June 9, 1985. Two weeks later, Kern County authorities caught a few of the insects, which laboratory examination soon identified as Africanized honeybees, more commonly known as "killer" bees. The Lost Hills nest was the first established colony of killer bees found in the United States.

Killer bees are descendants of highly aggressive African honeybee queens that were taken to Brazil for experimental purposes in 1956. The next year, unfortunately, 26 of these aggressive African queens, along with swarms of their pure African offspring, escaped from the experimental hives where they were being studied. In the wild, the African bees mated with European honeybees, the type of bee used in commercial honey operations. This interbreeding produced a strain of "Africanized" bees closely resembling the pure African strain in behavior. Since 1957, these Africanized bees have spread steadily northward, reaching Honduras in 1985.

Africanized bees are called killer bees because they pour out of their hive by the thousands to attack any person or animal who disturbs them. They have been known to kill animals as large as a horse and have probably killed hundreds of people in Central and South America. This aggressive behavior evolved over millions of years as a way for the bees to defend themselves and survive in Africa's harsh environment.

California agricultural officials theorized that the bees had arrived in a shipment of oil-drilling equipment from Central or South America. Analysis of the underground nest indicated the bees had been living there at least two years. The task then facing officials was to find out how far the bees had spread and how many nests they had made.

The state authorities established a 1,200-square-kilometer (460-square-mile) quarantine zone around Lost Hills and prohibited the movement of commercial beehives into or out of the zone. Crews collected bees from each hive in the area, and from every wild nest they could find, and sent them to laboratories for identification. Identifying killer bees is complicated and time-consuming because the bees look very similar to European bees.

During the next six months, 12 killer-bee colonies were found and destroyed, mostly in or near the quarantine zone. Significantly, none of the 12 colonies contained "pure" Africanized bees because the Africanized queens apparently had mated primarily with pure European bees. This process of "genetic dilution" would probably have caused the Africanized bees to disappear eventually.

Although California's killer-bee crisis ended in early December 1985, when authorities declared that the Africanized bees in the state had been eradicated, the final chapter of the drama has yet to be written. Massive numbers of Africanized bees are expected to enter Texas from Mexico by the end of the 1980's. They will then spread east and west across the Southern United States, where the weather is warm enough for their survival. It is doubtful that anything can be done to stop this migration. And because the number of killer bees will be so large, we will not be able to depend on genetic dilution to rid us of them. Killer bees will be a threat not only to human life and to the honey industry, but also to agriculture as a whole. Widespread quarantines undoubtedly will interfere with farmers' and growers' operations throughout the Southern United States, where honeybees are needed to pollinate crops.

Science will be our best defense against killer bees. In the three or four years remaining before the bees arrive, geneticists and other experts will be searching for a way to blunt the invasion.   [Norman E. Gary]

Agricultural inspectors collect bees from a hive near Lost Hills, Calif., during efforts to track down "killer" bees.

Agriculture

Continued

With the push of a few buttons, a soil scientist in California, *above,* records *salinity* (salt content) readings being taken by a co-worker with an electromagnetic monitor. Data from various areas are used to create a computer-generated map, *above right,* showing places with potential salinity problems. Such maps tell farmers and growers where corrective action is most needed.

terey County Board of Supervisors sought proof from AGS that its Frostban bacteria were safe. Meanwhile, the EPA learned that the company had earlier conducted secret outdoor tests of the bacteria. The EPA then withdrew its permission to test Frostban and fined AGS $20,000 (later reduced to $13,000).

In May, the EPA issued a permit to plant pathologists Steven E. Lindow and Nickolas Panopoulos of the University of California at Berkeley to field-test engineered bacteria that are nearly identical to those developed by AGS. Lindow and Panopoulos, who did most of the pioneering work on antifrost bacteria, planned to conduct a test on two potato fields near Tulelake, Calif., close to the Oregon border. Hundreds of Tulelake residents, however, signed petitions to block the proposed test.

Ice-resistant bacteria are derived from strains of *Pseudomonas syringae*, which are common in nature. Normally, the bacteria secrete a protein that acts as a "seed" around which ice

crystals form. AGS and the University of California scientists deleted the gene that *codes for* (specifies the production of) the "seed" protein, resulting in bacteria that cannot promote frost formation. If sprayed on crops in large numbers, the altered bacteria would, researchers think, overwhelm the naturally occurring *P. syringae* and protect the crops from frost down to temperatures of about −4°C (25°F.).

Opponents of outdoor tests say the engineered bacteria might spread into the atmosphere and alter weather patterns. But scientists say that is very unlikely because up to 5 per cent of the naturally occurring *P. syringae* lack the ice-protein gene, and those bacteria have never posed any danger to the environment.

Anticutworm bacteria. Scientists at Monsanto Company in St. Louis, Mo., in early 1986 sought EPA approval for a field test of genetically altered bacteria to protect corn plants from cutworms, a type of caterpillar. The Monsanto researchers first isolated a bacterial gene that codes for a *toxin*

Agriculture

Continued

(poison) lethal to cutworms. They then spliced this gene into the genes of *Pseudomonas fluorescens*, bacteria that live in the roots of corn plants.

The scientists planned to spray altered bacteria on a 0.4-hectare (1-acre) cornfield near St. Charles, Mo., and thus establish the altered bacteria on the roots of the plants. Cutworms attacking the corn roots would eat the bacteria and die from the toxin.

Agricultural disasters. In July 1985, agricultural officials in California discovered that thousands of watermelons in the state had been contaminated with the pesticide aldicarb. Some 180 cases of tremors, dizziness, and nausea reported in California, Oregon, Washington, and British Columbia, Canada, were traced to the tainted melons. All 10 million watermelons already in the state's food markets were destroyed.

The citrus canker, first identified in Florida in August 1984, had by January 1986 spread to 18 nurseries. The spread of the disease, which causes *cankers* (ulcerlike patches) on leaves, twigs, and fruit, resulted in a total quarantine on all Florida citrus nurseries for at least a year. The bacterial disease is harmless to humans but is capable of destroying full-grown citrus trees. There is no cure for citrus canker, and it can be controlled only by burning the plants affected with it.

"Chemigation"— or the irrigation of crops with chemicals such as fertilizers and pesticides—is growing rapidly, according to a November 1985 report by irrigation engineer Inge Bisconer of El Cajon, Calif. Chemigation is usually done with so-called microsystems, which use special piping to drip small amounts of chemicals at the base of plants.

Because of its pinpoint accuracy, microsystem irrigation uses much smaller amounts of chemicals to treat a field than are required in conventional irrigation techniques. This system saves farmers money while at the same time reducing the possibility of environmental damage and hazards to human health.　　　　[Sylvan H. Wittwer]

In WORLD BOOK, see AGRICULTURE.

Anthropology

The discovery in northwestern Wyoming of fossil teeth and pieces of jawbone from what may be the oldest known ancestor of modern primates was reported in January 1986 by paleontologist Philip D. Gingerich of the University of Michigan in Ann Arbor. The fossils, found in 1984 by Victor Torres, a graduate student at Michigan, were identified as belonging to the genus *Cantius*, an extinct group of *prosimians* (lower primates) about the size of a squirrel. They were dated at 53 million years old, making them about 1 million years older than the oldest previously known *Cantius* fossils, which were found in Europe.

The fossils challenge current theories about the migration of early primates, according to Gingerich. Most scientists believe that primates spread out from Africa, where they originated, to Europe and then to North America. Gingerich speculated that, instead, early primates migrated from Africa to Asia and then to North America across the Bering Strait. From North America, they could have crossed to Europe over a land bridge that once spanned what is now the North Atlantic Ocean.

Burmese fossil primate. A lower jaw, newly reconstructed from fossils found in Burma and dated at 40 million to 44 million years old, may represent the earliest known *anthropoid* (higher primate). It could be the ancestor of modern monkeys, apes, and human beings, according to a report published in August 1985 by a team of scientists headed by Russell L. Ciochon of the State University of New York in Stony Brook. The animal, named *Amphipithecus mogaungensis*, weighed from 6.8 to 9 kilograms (15 to 20 pounds), was about 76 to 91 centimeters (2½ to 3 feet) long, and lived in the trees.

Ciochon and his colleagues contended that the jaw, reconstructed from fossils found in Burma in 1923 and 1978, suggests that anthropoids originated in Asia rather than Africa as most scientists believe. Other scientists, however, argue that the fossil evidence is too limited to classify the creature as an anthropoid.

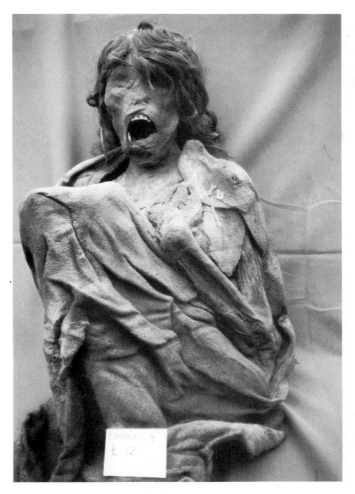

Calculating age at death. The layers of enamel in fossil teeth may provide scientists with a more reliable method of calculating the age at death of fossil *hominid* children, according to research published in October 1985 by anthropologist Timothy G. Bromage and anatomist M. Christopher Dean of University College in London. (Hominids include human beings and our closest human and prehuman ancestors.) In the past, scientists have estimated the biological age of fossil teeth of hominid children by comparing their time of eruption, maturation, and their wear patterns with those of the teeth of modern children.

For their research, Bromage and Dean used an electron microscope to examine coarse and fine growth lines in nine fossil teeth from hominids that lived between 1 million and 3.7 million years ago in Africa. Studies of the teeth of modern human beings and animals indicate that the finer lines represent layers of enamel that seem to form every 24 hours. Bromage and Dean reported finding seven or eight finer lines between each coarse line, indicating that the coarse lines represent weekly intervals. The researchers contended that by counting the number of coarse lines, scientists can determine the age of a fossil tooth and, therefore, the age of the individual when he or she died. The new technique can be used only with children's teeth, however, because the layers of enamel wear off with use.

The scientists' analysis indicated that the biological age of the fossil teeth, previously thought to be from 4½ to 7 years, was actually 3 to 5 years. The findings suggest that the growth pattern of teeth in early hominids was closer to the growth pattern of modern apes than that of human beings. This implies that the period of infancy in early hominids was short, as it is in apes, rather than prolonged, as it is in modern human beings.

World's oldest mummies. The discovery of the world's oldest mummies was reported in October 1985 by pathologist Marvin J. Allison at the University of Tarapacá, in Arica, Chile. Thirty-six mummies were found in an ancient cemetery near Arica that had been used by the Chinchorro, an ancient

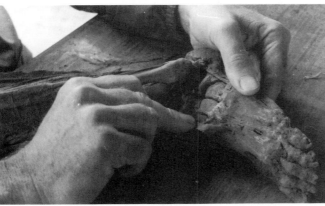

The mummy of a young woman, *top,* who may have died in childbirth, and a mummified human leg, *above,* are among the remains found in an ancient cemetery in Chile that contained the world's oldest mummies, up to 8,000 years old.

"Let's all get a good night's sleep. We've got
a big day tomorrow. It's the dawn of history."

Anthropology

Continued

hunting and gathering people who lived along the coast of northern Chile. The earliest Chinchorro mummies date from 7,810 years ago, about 3,000 years before the Egyptians began to embalm their dead.

Although their techniques varied over time, the Chinchorro generally followed the same procedure. They removed the skin, muscles, internal organs, and brain of the corpse and dried the body with hot charcoal or ashes. They then inserted a wooden framework into the body and stuffed the body cavity with vegetable fibers, ashes, llama skin, feathers, or earth. The skin was often replaced on the body, the face and genitals modeled in clay and attached to the body, and the finished mummy painted either black or red. The scientists speculated that the wooden framework was used to make the body rigid so that it could be displayed on important occasions.

Barbadian "belly-ake." The bones of slaves who worked on sugar plantations on the West Indies island of Barbados between 1620 and 1810 show high levels of lead. A possible explanation for this was proposed in April 1986 by a team headed by pathologist Arthur C. Aufderheide of the University of Minnesota in Duluth and anthropologist Jerome S. Handler of Southern Illinois University in Carbondale. The bones of the slaves have approximately 120 parts per million (ppm) of lead, compared with 25 to 30 ppm in modern Americans.

For their research into possible causes, the scientists relied primarily on the written reports of Barbadian planters and doctors of that period, which included references to "dry belly-ake"—abdominal pain without diarrhea—a primary symptom of lead poisoning. The researchers identified the source of the lead as rum, which was distilled in equipment made of lead. According to historical accounts, the slaves drank large quantities of the rum, and the researchers concluded this was the source of their lead poisoning.   [Charles F. Merbs]

In WORLD BOOK, see ANTHROPOLOGY; MUMMY.

Archaeology, New World

The discovery of one of the oldest examples of early Maya writing was announced in September 1985 by archaeologist Eric C. Gibson of Harvard University in Cambridge, Mass. The writing—seven delicately shaped Maya hieroglyphs—was carved on a 19-centimeter (7½-inch) rib found by Gibson in a grave at the Maya site of Kichpanha in northern Belize. The bone was found with pottery vessels dated to about A.D. 100 to 200, making the hieroglyphs from 50 to 100 years older than other examples of Maya writing.

Because so few examples of early Maya writing exist, interpreting the glyphs will be difficult. Peter Mathews of Harvard, an expert in ancient Maya script, suggested that one hieroglyph may represent the name of the person buried in the grave. He also recognized hieroglyphs that, later in Maya history, meant bloodletting and death. Gibson believes that the carved bone was probably used as a bloodletting tool, perhaps during the burial ritual. Such activities are depicted on Maya vases from 200 to 300 years later.

Mexican theft. More than 140 extremely valuable gold, jade, and carved stone artifacts from several ancient Mexican civilizations were stolen from the National Museum of Anthropology in Mexico City in December 1985. The stolen items included artifacts from the Zapotec, Mixtec, Maya, and Aztec civilizations. (In the Special Reports section, see THE GREAT TEMPLE OF THE AZTECS.) Mexican authorities quickly released descriptions of the artifacts in an effort to prevent the sale of the stolen items by the thieves.

Tourism threat to Machu Picchu. The tremendous influx of tourists at Machu Picchu, the site of an ancient Inca city near Cusco in southern Peru, is threatening the survival of the ruins, according to a report published in November 1985 by Lynn A. Meisch, an author and guide at the site. Spanish conquerors, who destroyed Mexican civilizations in the 1500's, never reached Machu Picchu, which is high in the Andes. Its location was unknown to the outside world until 1911. The walled city's imposing mountain

Scientists search for fossils at a 10,000-year-old site in a cave that was exposed when the ground above it collapsed. At the site, near Miami, Fla., archaeologists uncovered some of the oldest human fossils found in North America and the bones of at least 50 animal species.

A salvager in October 1985 chips corrosion from a bronze bell raised from a shipwreck off Cape Cod, Massachussetts, confirming that the wreck is that of the *Whydah,* a pirate ship that sank in 1717. The ship, found in July 1984, is believed to be the first pirate wreck identified and salvaged.

Archaeology, New World

Continued

location and impressive stone walls made it a popular tourist attraction.

More than 100,000 tourists each year take the four-hour train ride to the ruins from Cusco. Another 6,000 visitors hike to the site—a 3- to 5-day trek over an ancient Inca road. The road travels through a Peruvian national park that includes not only Machu Picchu, but also several other important Inca ruins that archaeologists have not yet adequately studied.

Current excavations and restoration work at Machu Picchu are often interrupted in order to repair damage caused by tourists, according to Meisch. Walls are being loosened by the pounding feet of the visitors as they travel along the main path through the site. When tourists wander off the paths and make new trails, they destroy ground vegetation and create channels along which rain water can run. This sometimes causes erosion that weakens the foundations of the stone structures, causing low walls to fall over. Some tourists carve their initials into the stone walls or chip off

pieces for souvenirs. Visitors also leave a great deal of trash at Machu Picchu and along the hiking trails.

This unexpected type of damage—caused by visitors, rather than looters or vandals—led Peruvian government officials, archaeologists, and travel agents to organize the Machu Picchu Sanctuary Project in 1986. The project is designed to inform visitors about the damage they can cause and to enlist their aid, as well as that of worldwide preservation agencies, in the effort to conserve the invaluable archaeological resources at Machu Picchu.

Early farming in New Mexico. The discovery of some of the earliest remains of cultivated plants in the Southwestern United States was reported in January 1986 by archaeologist Alan H. Simmons of the University of Nevada in Reno. For many years, archaeologists have sought to learn where and when agriculture began in the New World. This quest is particularly important in the Southwest, where the development of agriculture was closely tied to the evolu-

Archaeology, New World

Continued

tion of the distinctive Indian cultures of that region, such as the Basket Maker and the Anasazi, or Pueblo.

Simmons found the plant remains—charred squash seeds and *maize cobs* (corncobs)—at several sites in the San Juan Basin of northwestern New Mexico. These sites, which are called *Archaic* sites, were occupied by nomadic Indians who relied chiefly on hunting and gathering for their food. At a site called Sheep Camp Shelter, excavators found the remains of both maize and squash. The squash seeds were radiocarbon dated to between 950 and 270 B.C., making them the earliest squash remains ever found in the American Southwest. Maize found at other Southwestern Archaic sites studied by Simmons date back even further, spanning the period from 2000 to 1000 B.C.

The plant remains may mark the beginning of agriculture among the Archaic hunting and gathering people of this region, according to Simmons. He theorized that during the winter, the Indians camped in caves or under rock ledges, chiefly to gain protection from the weather. In the spring and summer, the Indians moved to the open grasslands and planted maize and squash, which were harvested before winter set in. Simmons suggested that maize may have been the Indians' "survival" food during the winter, when game and other food were scarce.

Simmons' excavations revealed that during the 2,000 years the Archaic groups practiced limited farming there were no major changes in any aspect of daily life, including the design of the stone tools used by the Indians. It was not until the development of the Basket Maker culture, in the first centuries A.D., that the nomadic Indians became farmers and settled in permanent villages. When, where, and why this transition occurred is still largely unknown.

Wet sites in Florida. In October 1985, archaeologists Barbara A. Purdy and LeeAnn Newsome of the University of Florida in Gainesville reported on the results of their excavations at a *wet site* on Hontoon Island in Florida's St. Johns River. A wet site is an archaeological site that has been covered by rising water levels. Such sites are found at lakesides or in areas that have become a marsh or bog. The site on Hontoon Island has been submerged for more than 1,500 years.

Using special techniques developed for excavating wet sites, Purdy and Newsome unearthed wooden artifacts, animal bones, and plant remains left by the Indians who lived on the island. The excavators found the remains of more than 60 species of plants and more than 50 species of land and aquatic animals. These findings indicate that 1,500 years ago marshy Hontoon Island had a somewhat different environment, characterized by hardwood forests, freshwater marshes, and open areas crossed by flowing rivers.

The evidence of the island's wide range of plant and animal resources led Purdy and Newsome to suggest that fairly large Indian populations lived there year-round without relying on cultivated plant crops. This way of life seems to have continued up to the early 1500's, when Spanish explorers first made contact with the Indians of this area. At that time, the Indians began farming.

The archaeologists also found a significant increase in the number of Indian artifacts after the Spaniards arrived. This may reflect a population increase at the site, perhaps as the island became a refuge for other Indian groups fleeing the Spaniards.

Evidence of the value of wet sites came from a comparison of items recovered from the wet site with items found at a nearby "dry" site. The dry site was a shell *midden*, a refuse pile containing shells and remains of clams and other shellfish eaten by the Indians. Over the years, wood, plant remains, and other fragile materials fell or were thrown onto the midden. Subjected to the effects of weather, erosion, animal scavenging, and human trampling, many fragile materials in the midden were destroyed. In contrast, a greater number of fragile materials were found at the wet site, which was preserved by water. As a result, the archaeologists were able to learn much more about life on the island. [Thomas R. Hester]

In WORLD BOOK, see ARCHAEOLOGY; INCA; INDIAN, AMERICAN; MAYA.

Archaeology, Old World

Findings that challenge accepted ideas about how prehistoric human beings made and used stone tools were reported in September 1985 by archaeologist Nicholas Toth of the University of California and the Institute of Human Origins in Berkeley. Toth argued that many stones identified as tools are really waste products from the toolmaking process.

Many archaeologists believe that the first tools were fist-sized sharpened stones, called core tools, that were used chiefly to butcher animal carcasses. Prehistoric toolmakers created these tools by knocking sharp chips called *flakes* from stones.

To learn more about how these tools were produced, Toth made hundreds of his own stone tools out of the same kinds of stones and in the same shapes as those produced by prehistoric toolmakers up to 2 million years ago in East Africa. He found that the final shape of the core tool seemed to depend chiefly on the shape of the stone before flaking. As a result, Toth concluded that early toolmakers did not set out to fashion the stone in a particular shape.

He also examined the edges of 54 core tools and flakes up to 2 million years old found near Lake Turkana in northern Kenya for microscopic marks indicating that the tools had been used to cut meat or plants or scrape skins. Toth discovered that while many of the ancient flakes had microscopic scratches, none of the core tools showed traces of use. Toth argued that this evidence suggests the object of early toolmakers was to create flakes to be used as tools. The core tools were simply by-products of flaking.

While making his stone tools, Toth also discovered differences in the shape of flakes produced by right-handed people and those produced by left-handed people. About 90 per cent of modern human beings are right-handed. In contrast, apes and other primate species are either able to use both hands equally well or are fairly evenly divided between left-handed and right-handed. When Toth examined flakes dating from 1.5 million to

Israeli archaeologists display some of the artifacts recovered from one of 60 ancient shipwrecks discovered in the Mediterranean Sea in an area 16 kilometers (10 miles) long and 180 meters (200 yards) wide off the coast of Haifa in northern Israel.

Archaeology, Old World

Continued

2 million years ago, he found evidence indicating that, by this time, most human beings were right-handed.

Life on Jersey. Archaeologist Paul Callow of Cambridge University in England reported in January 1986 on studies of life on the island of Jersey in the English Channel 250,000 years ago. For many years, scientists have been analyzing stone tools and bones from La Cotte de St. Brelade, an archaeological site on the island. Often during the last Ice Age, the sea level dropped, because much of the world's water was locked up in glaciers and snow. During these periods, the area that is now the English Channel was a rich woodland inhabited by many people and animals. When Earth's climate warmed and the sea level rose, however, people and animals were trapped on what became Jersey and other islands in the channel.

The studies reported by Callow suggest that the people who lived on Jersey beginning about 250,000 years ago had adapted to the changes in sea level and climate. For example, most of the flint used to make stone tools came from beach pebbles. When the sea level rose and covered the beaches, less flint was available, and the island's inhabitants had to conserve their tool-making material. At archaeological sites dating from periods when the seas were high, excavators found many flint tools that had been resharpened frequently.

Findings on Jersey have also provided clues about the kinds of animals the people on the island hunted and how they killed them. In two places at La Cotte, archaeologists found large piles of animal bones neatly stacked against the wall of a ravine. The older stack contained the remains of at least 9 mammoths and 2 rhinoceroses. The other stack included 11 mammoths and 3 rhinos. Callow suggests that the people on Jersey may have hunted by stampeding groups of mammoths and rhinos into the ravine.

Ancient Middle East settlement. In late 1985, archaeologist Gary O. Rollefson of San Diego State University in California reported on his excavations at one of the earliest known farming communities, Ain Ghazal, near Amman, Jordan. The people who lived at Ain Ghazal, about 8,000 to 9,000 years ago, harvested wheat and barley with stone sickles, lived in substantial stone and plaster houses, and apparently had a rich religious and social life.

One of Rollefson's finds was a cache of 12 clay statues representing human beings. The statues, each about 90 centimeters (3 feet) tall, have featureless torsos, long necks, and oversized heads. Excavators also found numerous smaller clay figurines, many with the exaggerated female characteristics associated with fertility rituals.

At Ain Ghazal, Rollefson also discovered the remains of 67 people. Most were found in graves dug in the floors of houses, near the hearths. One-third of these individuals were children. Many others were young women who may have died in childbirth.

Sheba and Solomon. Findings in southwestern Arabia that may shed light on the empire of the Biblical Queen of Sheba were reported in early 1986 by archaeologist James A. Sauer of the University of Pennsylvania in Philadelphia. The Bible records that the Queen of Sheba visited King Solomon of Israel in Jerusalem, presented him with gifts, and asked him "hard questions" to test his wisdom.

Many scholars doubt that such a meeting took place—even if the queen existed—because Solomon ruled Israel in the 900's B.C. and the oldest remains found in Sheba were 300 years younger. While excavating near the ruins of Sheba's capital, however, Sauer found evidence that Sheba may be older than scholars had believed.

Sauer excavated Hajar at-Tamrah, an ancient mound in present-day Yemen (Sana). Near the bottom of the mound, Sauer found a piece of wood that was radiocarbon dated to the 1200's B.C. Proving that a queen from Sheba actually visited Solomon would be very difficult. But Sauer's work and other excavations suggest that a rich trading nation existed in southwestern Arabia in Solomon's time.

Blueprints on the wall. West German archaeologist Lothar Haselberger reported in December 1985 that he may have solved one of the most interesting questions of Greek archaeology: How did the ancient Greeks build their temples? His studies were funded by the

Archaeology, Old World

Continued

The ruins of a 10,000-year-old building found near Diyarbakir, Turkey, and reported in June 1985, represent one of the earliest known examples of a structure built for reasons other than housing. In the building, one of three found at the site, excavators discovered the burned tops of 50 human skulls, probably the result of a death rite.

German Archaeological Institute and the German Research Society.

Scholars had thought that no descriptions of ancient Greek construction methods had survived. But at the Temple of Apollo at Didyma in southwestern Turkey, begun in 334 B.C., Haselberger found the blueprints for the temple on the walls of the temple itself.

He noticed that 200 square meters (240 square yards) of the temple walls were covered with lines. The lines, about the width of a pencil mark, were etched to a depth of about one-half millimeter (0.02 inch) into the marble surface. The lines trace out the exact design of various temple structures.

Some of the drawings show how the Greeks achieved the architectural effect of *entasis* (tension), which causes a building to appear to gently curve upward. To produce this effect at Didyma, the Greeks carved the column shafts so that they curved slightly inward and built the center of the temple about 11 centimeters (43 inches) higher than the corners.

Roman London. John Maloney, excavations officer of the City of London, reported in February 1986 on excavations that have revealed portions of the first great public building erected by the Romans in England after their invasion in A.D. 43. This building, called the basilica by the Romans, was about 152 meters (166 yards) long and included a great hall supported by massive columns. It was flanked by law courts, administrative offices, and probably some storerooms and shops. The basilica and an open plaza enclosed by more shops and offices made up a complex that covered more than 3 hectares (8 acres).

In 1985, excavators digging at the east end of the basilica discovered the remains of three Roman buildings below the basilica. These buildings were buried 7.5 meters (25 feet) below the street level of modern London. The findings suggest that the basilica was rebuilt and perhaps modified several times.   [Robert J. Wenke]

In WORLD BOOK, see ARCHAEOLOGY; PREHISTORIC PEOPLE.

Astronomy, Extragalactic

A new type of *supernova* (the violent explosion of a dying star) was discovered in 1985 by astronomers using the 508-centimeter (200-inch) Hale telescope at the Palomar Observatory in southwestern California. A picture taken in early 1985, *below left,* about nine months after the explosion, reveals the supernova as a bright dot (arrow) in the galaxy NGC 4618. By December 1985, the supernova was beginning to fade, *below right*.

The discovery of the most distant galaxy ever observed was announced in December 1985 by astronomers Stanislaus Djorgovski, Hyron Spinrad, Patrick McCarthy, and Michael Strauss of the University of California, Berkeley. The galaxy is so far away that its light has taken more than 10 billion *light-years* to reach us. (A light-year is the distance light travels in one year at a speed of 299,792 kilometers [186,282 miles] per second.) The light reaching Earth now represents the galaxy as it was 10 billion years ago.

This newly discovered galaxy will give astronomers more information about the early universe. By comparing distant, and therefore young galaxies with nearer, older galaxies, scientists hope to better understand how the universe evolved.

New observational technique. One of the most remarkable features of the discovery of the most distant galaxy is that it is based on a new observational technique that may allow astronomers to find many other distant galaxies. Previously, the most distant galaxies

known were discovered with radio telescopes that identified powerful radio sources. Djorgovski and his colleagues, however, used a special filter attached to an electronic camera on an optical telescope—the 305-centimeter (120-inch) Lick Observatory telescope on Mount Hamilton in California.

They began their search for distant galaxies by looking near the positions of known *quasars*—very distant objects that give off enormous quantities of radiant energy. Quasars may be located at the centers of very distant galaxies. Knowing that galaxies tend to group together, the scientists used distant quasars as signposts or indicators for equally distant galaxies. Galaxies at such great distances, however, are very faint, so that observing them is not easy. In fact, ordinary galaxies such as our Milky Way, which is about 85,000 light-years across, would be almost impossible to detect at those distances. So the Berkeley astronomers looked for galaxies that give off large amounts of light at wavelengths corresponding to light given off by elements such as *ion-*

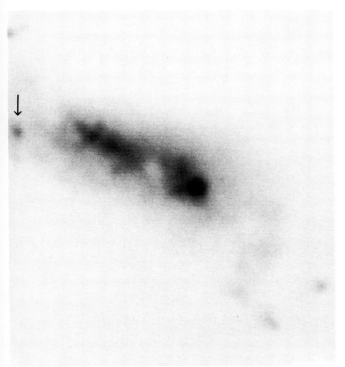 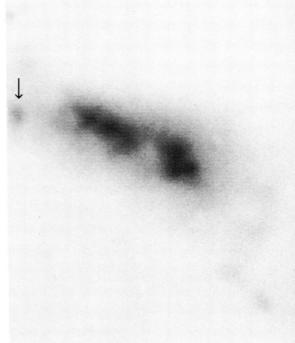

ized (electrically charged) hydrogen. Astronomers believe that galaxies that formed early in the history of the universe contain large amounts of both ionized hydrogen and ionized carbon.

Djorgovski took electronic pictures of regions of the sky near several distant quasars using a filter that is especially sensitive to light produced by ionized hydrogen. Near a quasar known as PKS 1614+051, Djorgovski found a galaxy whose *spectrum* (color pattern) showed the expected ionized hydrogen and ionized carbon.

Using the red shift. In determining the galaxy's distance, the astronomers noted that its light was shifted toward the red, or longer, wavelength end of the *electromagnetic spectrum*. (The electromagnetic spectrum is the range of radiant energies from short-wave gamma rays to very long radio waves and includes visible light.) This *red shift* is an indication that an object is moving away from Earth, and the velocity of this movement is proportional to the distance of the object. The astronomers found that the light from this galaxy had a red shift comparable to that of the quasar—10 billion light-years—making it the most distant galaxy known.

The researchers pointed out that the electronic image they obtained of this galaxy does not resemble images of nearby galaxies, which appear spread out. Instead, it looks pointlike, just like a star. The outer regions of a galaxy at such an enormous distance, however, are not expected to be visible. At such distances, it is likely that only the bright nucleus of the galaxy will be seen. But the spectrum from this galaxy is similar to other, less distant galaxies, lending support to the astronomers' assumption that the object they found is indeed a galaxy.

How did galaxies form? The discovery of a 10-billion-year-old galaxy close to a quasar supports a theory of galaxy formation called the *fragmentation theory*, because it suggests that *clustering* occurred early in the universe's history. Galaxies tend to clump together in clusters, and clusters clump together in larger structures called superclusters. The fragmentation theory of galaxy formation proposes that the large structures existed very early in the history of the universe. Material fragmented from these structures to form galaxies. An opposing view, known as the *hierarchical* theory, proposes that galaxies formed first and later were bound together by gravity to form clusters, a process that would take much more time and therefore could not have occurred as early as 10 billion years ago. This particular galaxy-quasar connection may or may not be a rare occurrence. If astronomers find more very distant galaxies in the vicinity of quasars, this will give the fragmentation theory substantial support. Astronomers will continue to look for more of these very distant galaxies and for so-called *primeval* galaxies that are still forming.

Intergalactic bubbles. A startling discovery about "bubbles" in space was announced at an American Astronomical Society meeting in Houston in January 1986. During a five-year-long study, astronomers Valérie de Lapparent, Margaret Geller, and John P. Huchra of the Harvard-Smithsonian Center for Astrophysics in Cambridge, Mass., measured red shifts to calculate the distances from Earth of hundreds of galaxies in a relatively small, narrow strip of the sky that contains the Coma Cluster of galaxies.

Using the distances to plot a three-dimensional map of the area, the Harvard astronomers found that the galaxies in this region appear to be on the surfaces of bubblelike structures in intergalactic space. The typical bubble is about 75 million light-years in diameter. The researchers detected large voids inside these bubbles that contain almost no galaxies, similar to the void in the constellation Boötes that was discovered in 1982 by astronomer Robert P. Kirshner of the University of Michigan in Ann Arbor.

The Harvard-Smithsonian astronomers compared their observations with theories that predict how the universe evolved and how it should look now. Many theories cannot account for the astronomers' discovery of an abrupt transition from regions where galaxies are very dense to regions where galaxies are very sparse. The bubbles seem to imply that powerful explosions must have occurred to move so much galactic matter together.

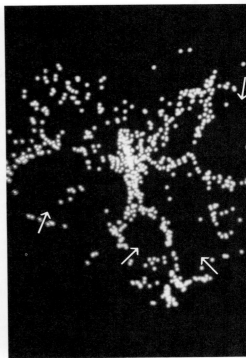

Astronomy, Extragalactic

Continued

Astronomer Margaret Geller, *above left,* of the Harvard-Smithsonian Center for Astrophysics in Cambridge, Mass., displays a computer-generated map showing the positions of about 1,100 galaxies in a relatively narrow strip of the sky. The large empty spaces in the map, *above right,* may represent bubblelike structures in intergalactic space that may have been formed by shock waves from explosions very early in the history of the universe.

A theory that does fit with this observation of bubbles, however, was proposed in 1981 by astrophysicists Jeremiah P. Ostriker of Princeton University in New Jersey and Lennox L. Cowie of the Space Telescope Science Institute in Baltimore. They suggested that galaxy formation in the early universe was triggered by explosions of very massive stars that were the first objects to be formed after the *big bang*—the explosion of energy that created the universe. According to Ostriker and Cowie, energetic blasts swept up gas that filled the early universe, forming it into "shells" at a density high enough for the shells eventually to fragment and form galaxies. This would explain the bubbles and voids, but the enormous size of these shell structures and the explosive energy needed to pile up so much material in them appear much greater than can be explained by the theory.

The Harvard-Smithsonian astronomers cautioned that the size of the bubbles and voids observed so far are limited by the scope of their survey.

Surveys extending to greater distances may find even larger structures, requiring new theories to explain them and how they were formed. The search for large-scale structures in the universe promises to extend our knowledge about how galaxies formed and how the universe evolved.

Massive halos of galaxies. An analysis of X-ray images has shown massive "halos" surrounding many bright elliptical galaxies. The finding was reported in June 1985 by astronomers William Forman, Christine Jones, and Wallace Tucker of the Smithsonian Astrophysical Observatory. These halos may be regions containing the so-called *missing mass,* or dark matter, of the universe.

X rays from objects in outer space cannot penetrate Earth's atmosphere, so the X-ray images were taken with the *Einstein* Observatory, an X-ray telescope that observed the sky from Earth orbit between 1979 and 1981.

The X rays of the halos were radiated from hot gas, and the astronomers believe the gas is held in place around the galaxies by the gravitational force of dark matter. The hot gas that gives off X rays makes up only a small amount of the total galaxy mass, but because it can be seen with X-ray telescopes, it could be useful as a tracer of the unseen dark matter that may hold it in place.

Astronomers came to suspect the existence of dark matter because studies show that the orbiting speed of stars in outlying regions of a galaxy is the same as the orbiting speed of stars near the center of the galaxy, where there is more visible mass. Because outlying stars are farther from this central mass, the force of gravity should be less and their orbiting speed, therefore, should be slower. Since this is not the case, scientists believe that there must be more unseen matter exerting gravitational forces in outlying regions of galaxies.

The X-ray halos may provide clues to the amount of dark matter that may exist around these galaxies. The Smithsonian astronomers showed that calculations—based on the expansion pressure of a hot gas and the force of gravity needed to slow that expansion—can provide an estimate of how much dark matter exists in the halo regions. They found that there is up to 10 times more mass associated with these galaxies than was previously known.

These observations may also help astronomers solve the problem of missing mass in clusters of galaxies. Astronomers have not observed enough mass to account for the gravitational attraction that binds galaxies together in clusters. The discovery that many galaxies are much more massive than was previously thought may help to resolve this problem. The Smithsonian astronomers suggested that halos of dark matter may be stripped from individual galaxies within a cluster due to various interactions between the galaxies. The material is then distributed throughout the cluster, making up the missing mass.   [Stephen S. Murray]

In the Special Reports section, see GALAXIES—ISLANDS IN THE UNIVERSE. In WORLD BOOK, see ASTRONOMY.

Astronomy,
Galactic

The International Astronomical Union (IAU), meeting in New Delhi, India, announced in November 1985 that our Galaxy, the Milky Way, is about 15 per cent smaller than was previously thought. This conclusion was based on the work of a committee that reviewed research carried out over the last 20 years by dozens of astronomers. The committee sought to make the best estimate of the size of the Galaxy and the motion of our sun. Based on this review, the IAU recommended that astronomers adopt new standards for the size of the Galaxy and the orbital speed of the sun as it travels around the center of the Galaxy.

Since 1963, astronomers have calculated that the diameter of our Galaxy is about 100,000 *light-years* and that our sun is located about 30,000 light-years from the center of the Galaxy. (A light-year is the distance that light travels in one year, about 9.5 trillion kilometers [5.9 trillion miles].) The new calculations estimate that the distance between our sun and the center of the Galaxy is 27,700 light-years and that the Galaxy is about 85,000 light-years in diameter.

The IAU also agreed to adopt 220 kilometers (137 miles) per second as the speed of the sun as it orbits the center of the Galaxy. This means that the sun takes almost 240 million years to complete one orbit around the Galaxy, compared with the previous estimate of 250 million years. Having internationally recognized standards such as these is valuable to astronomers when they compare the Milky Way with other galaxies.

New interstellar molecules. During 1985 and 1986, radio astronomers reported discoveries of several new chemical compounds in interstellar gas clouds that may yield clues to how new stars form. The discoveries brought the total number of molecules identified in these clouds to more than 60.

Interstellar gas clouds are interesting to astronomers because they are sites where new stars form. Using optical, infrared, and radio telescopes, astronomers have detected about 3,000 large interstellar gas clouds in the

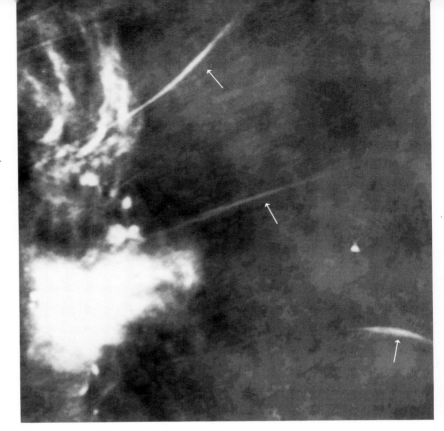

Radio astronomers reported in December 1985 that they had detected unusual threadlike structures (arrows) unlike anything seen before. The giant threads, which lie near the center of the Milky Way galaxy, are about one light-year (the distance light travels in a year) across and more than 100 light-years long. One astronomer speculated that they might be cosmic strings, defects in space left over from the big bang, the explosion from which the universe is believed to have evolved.

Astronomy, Galactic

Continued

Milky Way. The types of molecules identified give astronomers clues about a gas cloud's density, temperature, and magnetic forces.

The first of the recent discoveries came in July 1985, when a team of radio astronomers led by Thomas G. Phillips of the California Institute of Technology in Pasadena announced the detection of a molecule called H_2D^+. The H_2D^+ molecule consists of two hydrogen (H) atoms and one atom of deuterium (D), an *isotope*, or form, of hydrogen. The plus sign means that one of the atoms in the molecule has lost an electron, so the molecule as a whole has a positive electric charge. The astronomers recognized this molecule through the *characteristic radiation* that it produces at a wavelength of 0.8 millimeter (0.032 inch) of the electromagnetic spectrum.

All elements in nature either give off or absorb radiation at characteristic wavelengths of the *electromagnetic spectrum* (the range of radiant energies, including visible light). The spectrum ranges from the extremely short wavelengths of gamma rays to the long wavelengths of radio waves. The radio band of the electromagnetic spectrum includes wavelengths as small as 1 millimeter (0.0394 inch) and as long as 10,000 kilometers (6,200 miles). The wavelength of the newly discovered H_2D^+ molecule lies in the submillimeter band of extremely high radio frequencies. Astronomers have been able to detect radiation at these wavelengths only since the early 1980's, when new and more sensitive detectors that could be attached to telescopes were developed.

For the first observations of H_2D^+, Phillips and his colleagues used a special receiver attached to the telescope of the Kuiper Airborne Observatory, a high-altitude airplane equipped with telescopes and operated by the National Aeronautics and Space Administration (NASA). The aircraft flies above most of the water vapor in Earth's atmosphere; water vapor interferes with some submillimeter radiation from space.

In 1973, astronomers predicted the

Astronomy,
Galactic
Continued

An X-ray telescope designed to search for a massive black hole at the center of the Milky Way orbits above Earth. It was released into space in June 1985 from the space shuttle *Discovery,* which later retrieved it and returned it to Earth so astronomers could analyze the data that the telescope gathered.

existence in interstellar clouds of H_2D^+ and a related molecule, H_3^+, which has three atoms of hydrogen and carries a positive charge. Their predictions were based on various theories of interstellar chemistry, which generally agreed that these two molecules played a central role in much of the chemical activity in interstellar clouds.

Because Phillips and his co-workers proved the H_2D^+ molecule can be directly observed at high radio frequencies, it will be possible to examine many basic ideas about interstellar chemistry. For example, hydrogen, the most common element in interstellar clouds, exists mostly in the form of *neutral* (uncharged) hydrogen atoms (H) and hydrogen molecules (H_2). Subatomic particles, called cosmic rays, speeding throughout interstellar space sometimes collide with H_2, knocking out electrons and leading to the formation of H_3^+ and H_2D^+. Astronomers think that H_3^+ can react with carbon and oxygen, setting off complicated chains of chemical reactions that build up larger and larger molecules. Astronomers also think that the electrically charged H_3^+ and H_2D^+ molecules control magnetic forces that affect the formation of new stars in interstellar clouds.

More complex molecules. In November 1985, radio astronomers Henry A. Matthews of the Herzberg Institute of Astrophysics in Ottawa, Canada, and William M. Irvine of the Five College Radio Observatory at the University of Massachusetts in Amherst reported their observation of strong radiation at a microwave wavelength of 1.6 centimeters (0.63 inch) in a large number of interstellar clouds. Matthews and Irvine identified this interstellar radiation as the characteristic wavelength of a molecule known by the chemical formula C_3H_2—because it has three atoms of carbon (C) and two atoms of hydrogen.

Finding this molecule in interstellar space is significant because it has a more complicated chemical structure than most molecules found in interstellar space. It is the first ring-type carbon compound to be found outside the solar system or the atmosphere of a star. Most molecules in interstellar

clouds are chainlike structures, open at both ends. A ring-type molecule, however, is a closed loop, or ring.

Strange star. Astronomer Robert E. Stencel of NASA's Office of Space Science and Applications in Washington, D.C., in September 1985 issued a report on research devoted to an unusual star known as Epsilon Aurigae. The report represented the completion of a major study by hundreds of astronomers of the total eclipse that this star undergoes once every 27.1 years. Epsilon Aurigae's most recent eclipse lasted from July 1982 through May 1984.

Most stars that undergo total eclipses are members of *binary systems*—two stars that orbit each other. The eclipses occur when one of the two stars comes between Earth and the other star, blotting out the light of the other. Eclipses in binary star systems normally occur at intervals ranging from a few days to a few months or a few years. With an interval of 27.1 years, Epsilon Aurigae has the longest period between eclipses known for any star in a binary system.

Astronomers found that the cause of the eclipse is a cold, dark companion that is not visible in optical telescopes. In December 1985, astronomers Dana E. Backman and Frederic C. Gillett of Kitt Peak National Observatory in Tucson, Ariz., reported direct measurements of infrared light from the dark companion disk. Based on these measurements, the two astronomers determined that the disk is too cold to be a star. They also found that it has a diameter of 10 *astronomical units* (AU), about the same as the radius of Epsilon Aurigae. (An AU is equal to the distance between Earth and the sun, about 150 million kilometers [93 million miles].) The evidence indicates that this companion is not a star at all but a rotating disk of gas and dust orbiting Epsilon Aurigae.

In January 1986, astronomer James C. Kemp of the University of Oregon in Eugene and his collaborators published a detailed study of the effects the dark companion exerts on the visible light that is emitted from Epsilon Aurigae. [John H. Black]

In WORLD BOOK, see ASTRONOMY; MILKY WAY.

Astronomy, Solar System

The *International Cometary Explorer* (*ICE*) on Sept. 11, 1985, became the first spacecraft to "visit" a comet. *ICE*—a National Aeronautics and Space Administration (NASA) spacecraft—flew by Comet Giacobini-Zinner, coming within 7,800 kilometers (4,850 miles) of its *nucleus* (solid core). The encounter lasted about three hours as the spacecraft traveled at a speed of 21 kilometers (13 miles) per second. The comet was about 71 million kilometers (44 million miles) from Earth at the time.

The major scientific findings from the spacecraft's mission concerned the interaction between the comet and the *solar wind* (a continuous flow of gases that streams out from the sun). Scientists had long known that this interaction gives rise to a comet's *ion tail*, consisting of electrically charged gas molecules and atoms, but the *ICE* encounter revealed many new facts about the interaction. *ICE* discovered that the solar wind slowed down as it interacted with the comet, that a shock wave produced by the interaction was not as sharp as expected, and that the predominant ionized gas in the comet's ion tail is ionized water vapor.

Astronomers Tycho T. von Rosenvinge, John C. Brandt, and Robert W. Farquhar of NASA's Goddard Space Flight Center in Greenbelt, Md., led a team of scientists who monitored *ICE*'s instruments as it flew by Comet Giacobini-Zinner.

As it passed the comet, *ICE* traveled through four distinct regions. The first was a region about 1 million kilometers (620,000 miles) from the nucleus where the solar wind first began to interact with ionized gases from the comet.

ICE's instruments monitored the temperature, speed, and magnetic field of the solar wind, which originates in the sun's outer atmosphere where temperatures average about 2,200,000°C (4,000,000°F.). This tremendous heat accelerates the gas atoms to a speed great enough to escape the sun's gravity—about 500 kilometers (310 miles) per second. The solar wind also carries a magnetic field produced in the sun's interior, creating a magnetic field throughout the solar system.

ICE's instruments showed that all of these characteristics of the solar wind—temperature, speed, and the intensity of the magnetic field—began to vary as *ICE* entered the second region, known as the *sheath*. The solar wind slowed dramatically in this region as it swept up ionized gases from the comet. When it entered the sheath, scientists expected the solar wind to create a shock wave, or bow wave, like the wave that appears at the bow of a boat as it travels through the water. But this wave was not as prominent as expected, and scientists are still debating what kind of wave they detected.

As *ICE* entered the third region, known as the comet's atmosphere, its instruments found mainly neutral gas molecules—with no electric charge—indicating that the solar wind does not penetrate this region. Instead, the solar wind and its magnetic field begin to drape around the comet at this point.

Finally, *ICE* penetrated the comet's ion tail, the fourth region, about 16,000 kilometers (10,000 miles) from the nucleus. *ICE* observed that this was a region of relatively cold ionized gases from the comet and that it was surrounded by a magnetic field. Scientists believe that as the magnetic field in the solar wind drapes around the comet, a magnetic tail forms. This magnetic tail surrounds the comet's ion tail.

Halley's Comet returns. It was the legendary Halley's Comet, however, which orbits the sun once every 76 years, that was the object of the most detailed studies ever of a comet. Thousands of astronomers around the world joined efforts to study Halley's during 1985 and 1986. In addition to ground-based and airborne telescopes, their efforts were aided by a fleet of spacecraft that made their closest approaches to the comet in March 1986.

In November 1985, at the comet's first close approach to Earth, when it was 92 million kilometers (57 million miles) away, the comet became visible with binoculars. That same month, two Japanese spacecraft that had been launched earlier in 1985 to observe the comet sent back data that showed regular variations in the amount of hydrogen gas released into the comet's atmosphere. Astronomers concluded that these variations were due to the

Voyager 2 Encounters Uranus

A wealth of new scientific data about Uranus, its rings, and its moons was sent back to Earth on Jan. 24, 1986, by the United States unmanned spacecraft *Voyager 2*, which flew within 81,560 kilometers (50,679 miles) of the seventh planet from the sun. *Voyager 2* was launched by the National Aeronautics and Space Administration (NASA) in 1977 to explore the cold, dark environs of the outer solar system. Its close encounter with Uranus lasted only a day, but in that time, scientists learned more about this planet than they had since it was discovered in 1781.

Uranus came into view of the *Voyager 2* cameras in December 1985 and revealed itself to be a world unlike any we have ever known. All of the other planets in the solar system spin more or less upright like tops, but Uranus rotates on its side as if it were "rolling" through the solar system. Uranus has a thick atmosphere consisting of about 75 per cent hydrogen gas, about 25 per cent helium gas, and trace amounts of methane gas. The methane gas gives Uranus a greenish-blue color. The atmosphere hovers above a deep hot ocean that may consist of water from comets that collided with the planet and could be 8,000 kilometers (5,000 miles) deep. The planetwide ocean, in turn, surrounds a rocky core that is the size of Earth.

Among its many revelations, *Voyager 2* discovered two rings, bringing the total of known rings encircling Uranus to 11—9 of them originally discovered from Earth. These 11 rings are composed mostly of chunks of dark-colored material about 1 meter (3 feet) wide.

Prior to the *Voyager 2* encounter, Uranus was known to have five large moons. *Voyager 2* discovered an additional 10 smaller moons, ranging from 40 to 170 kilometers (25 to 43 miles) in diameter. Two of these small moons orbit just inside and outside the Epsilon ring, the outermost ring. Astronomers believe the two moons keep the chunks of dark material confined to that ring—in effect, acting like shepherds.

Astronomers believe that the five major moons of Uranus—Ariel, Miranda, Oberon, Titania, and Umbriel—are composed of about 60 per cent water ice and 40 per cent rock, along with small amounts of ammonia, methane, carbon, and other carbon-rich compounds. Ammonia and methane can form fluids inside these extremely cold moons, where the surface temperatures are about −201°C (−330°F.). Such fluids allow geologic processes similar to those associated with volcanic eruptions on Earth. For example, *Voyager 2*'s images of Titania show giant faults, or cracks, that have broken the surface. Some of these faults extend across the entire visible surface and show bright snowlike deposits along their steep slopes, suggesting that some kind of fluid erupted out of the crack and then froze. Ariel is laced by a network of giant faults even more extensive than those on Titania. *Voyager 2* revealed that Oberon and Umbriel have cratered surfaces resembling some of the most heavily cratered areas on our moon and on Mars.

Of all the moons, however, Miranda is the strangest. Miranda has enormous chasms with walls as steep as 20 kilometers (12 miles), more than 10 times steeper than the Grand Canyon's walls. Miranda also has a series of rectangular or oval regions about 200 to 300 kilometers (124 to 186 miles) across. Each of these *ovoids* is surrounded by ridges and cliffs that form patterns resembling giant race tracks.

Scientists think that Miranda may provide a glimpse of a geologic process that they believe occurred on all of the planets and on most of the moons in the solar system soon after they formed. In this process, the heaviest elements sink to form the interior core, and the lighter elements rise to the surface. Miranda looks as if it never completed this process. Some astronomers theorize that because Miranda is relatively small—only 470 kilometers (290 miles) in diameter—it lost its internal heat soon after it formed, and without heat currents, the heavier elements stopped sinking and the lighter elements stopped rising. According to this theory, the ovoids represent columns of lighter material that rose to the surface but were still surrounded by heavier material as Miranda's development was frozen in time.

Voyager 2 also discovered that Uranus has a unique magnetic field in which the north and south magnetic poles are oriented at 30° north and 30° south of its equator. The magnetic field of nearly every other planet is closely aligned with its axis of rotation. For example, Earth's north and south magnetic fields are at about 70° north and south of the equator. The orientation of the poles on Uranus causes the magnetic field to oscillate wildly as the planet spins on its axis of rotation.

The *Voyager 2* probe of Uranus provided scientists with some answers and many questions—mysteries that will occupy them for years to come. Meanwhile, *Voyager 2* ventures on to its 1989 encounter with the even more distant planet Neptune.   [Laurence A. Soderblom]

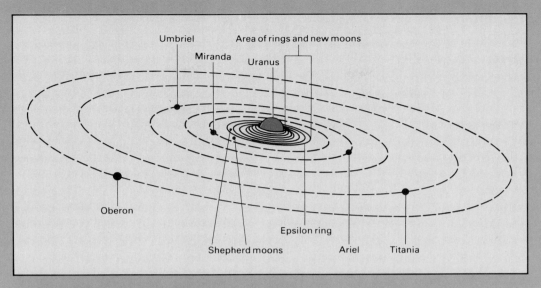

Umbriel

Area of rings and new moons

Miranda

Uranus

Oberon

Epsilon ring

Shepherd moons

Ariel   Titania

A system of moons and rings surrounds the distant planet Uranus, *above*. Astronomers knew of five moons and nine rings before *Voyager 2* flew by Uranus on Jan. 24, 1986. *Voyager 2* discovered two more rings and 10 small moons orbiting in the area of the rings, including two "shepherd moons," whose gravity keeps the Epsilon ring in place.

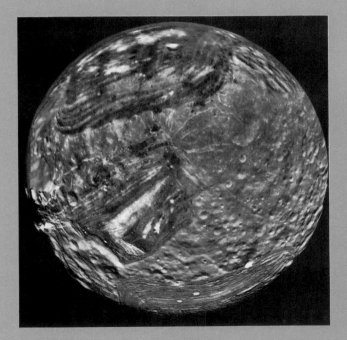

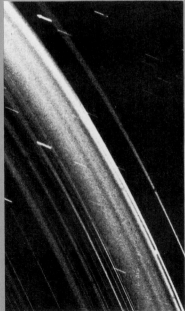

Analysis of *Voyager 2* photos revealed that Uranus' rings are made of boulder-sized chunks of dark material, along with fine particles of dust, *above right*. But *Voyager*'s most amazing discovery may be the rectangular and circular features on the moon Miranda, *above left*. Scientists think Miranda may provide a view of how other moons and planets looked billions of years ago.

Astronomy, Solar System

Continued

Halley's Comet streaks across the sky as it nears its closest approach to Earth in March 1986. The image was captured by a 46-centimeter (18-inch) telescope at the Palomar Observatory in southwestern California.

rotation of the comet's nucleus once every 2.2 days.

An infrared telescope on NASA's Kuiper Airborne Observatory, a high-altitude airplane, in January 1986 yielded the first direct observations of the major chemical component of a comet—water. Since the 1950's, astronomers have believed that comets are "dirty snowballs," mixtures of frozen gases and dust, including water-ice. The infrared observations by astronomers Michael J. Mumma of NASA's Goddard Space Flight Center and Harold P. Larson of the University of Arizona in Tucson confirmed the water content of Halley's Comet. Mumma and Larson also calculated that the temperature of the water-ice at the time the comet formed 4½ billion years ago was about −245°C (−409°F.).

Six spacecraft made direct observations of the comet and its immediate environment in March 1986. *ICE* monitored the properties of the solar wind as it was about to envelop the comet. The two Japanese spacecraft, both

about 150,000 kilometers (93,200 miles) from the comet, monitored the outer boundary of the sheath, where the solar wind encounters gases from the comet. The Soviet Union's *Vega 1* and *Vega 2* spacecraft in early March penetrated the comet's atmosphere, came to within 8,600 kilometers (5,344 miles) of the nucleus, and returned the first images of the nucleus that clearly showed its shape and size.

Finally, on March 14, the European Space Agency's *Giotto* probe flew to within 600 kilometers (373 miles) of the nucleus before the bombardment of cometary dust particles destroyed about half of the spacecraft's instruments and stopped transmission of data for 34 minutes.

The knowledge gained from these missions has been enormous. *Giotto*'s images of Halley's nucleus show an extremely dark, irregular-shaped object with three areas where cometary gases spew jets of fine dust. The shape has been compared to a potato or a peanut. The size of the nucleus was two to three times larger than expected. The

Astronomy, Solar System

Continued

nucleus is about 15 kilometers (9 miles) long and between 7 to 10 kilometers (4 to 6 miles) wide. Astronomers cannot be certain of the width because the dust jets obscure the view.

Scientists also found that about 90 per cent of the comet's dust appears to be made of *carbonaceous* (carbon-containing) materials. Earth-based observations had indicated that silicates were the chief components.

Exploring Venus by balloon. In June 1985, the Soviet Union's *Vega 1* and *Vega 2* spacecraft flew by the planet Venus en route to their encounter with Halley's Comet. While passing by Venus, the spacecraft dropped two landing craft onto the planet's surface and for the first time released weather balloons into Venus' atmosphere.

The dynamics of Venus' atmosphere have long puzzled astronomers. The motion of clouds in the boundary between Venus' troposphere and stratosphere—about 54 kilometers (34 miles) above the planet's surface—indicate that this region of the atmosphere rotates about 60 times faster than the planet's surface, a phenomenon known as *superrotation*.

To better understand the nature of Venus' atmosphere, the spacecraft released two weather balloons, which floated 53 kilometers (33 miles) above the surface, one just north and the other just south of Venus' equator. The balloons gave out radio signals and were tracked by 20 radio antennas on Earth.

The balloon data showed very large updrafts and downdrafts at 1 to 3 meters (3 to 10 feet) per second, in the atmosphere. During part of its flight, the balloon from *Vega 2* encountered a downdraft, lasting about five hours, that caused the balloon to drop some 3 or 4 kilometers (2 or 3 miles) below its normal float level. Since this drop occurred while the balloon was over a mountain, astronomers speculated that a turbulent atmospheric wave like those that form over large mountains on Earth may have caused the downdraft.   [Michael J. S. Belton]

In WORLD BOOK, see ASTRONOMY; COMET; HALLEY'S COMET.

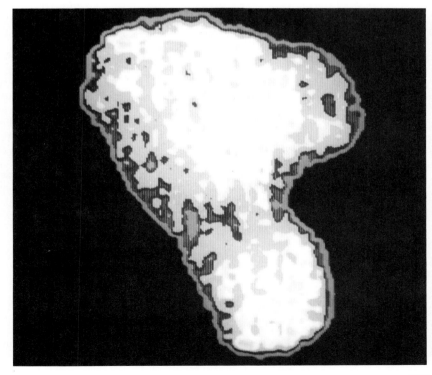

A computer-enhanced image of the *nucleus* (solid core) of Halley's Comet, taken by the European Space Agency's *Giotto* probe on March 14, 1986, revealed that the nucleus is shaped like a peanut or a potato. Until *Giotto* and the Soviet Union's *Vega 1* and *Vega 2* spacecraft intercepted Halley's Comet in March, astronomers had never seen a comet's nucleus.

Books
of Science

Here are 25 outstanding new science books suitable for the general reader. They have been selected from books published in 1985 and 1986.

Archaeology. *Huánuco Pampa: An Inca City and Its Hinterland* by Craig Morris and Donald E. Thompson uses archaeological evidence and historical records to describe the architecture, economy, and administration of Huánuco Pampa, a provincial city of the ancient Inca Empire. (Thames & Hudson, 1985. 181 pp. illus. $29.95)

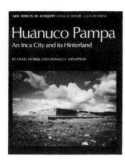

Astronomy. *Perfect Symmetry: The Search for the Beginning of Time* by Heinz R. Pagels is the story of the universe from its possible beginning to its possible end and the physical laws that govern it. The book describes the observable universe, current theories about its evolution, and the author's own personal views. (Simon & Schuster, 1985. 390 pp. illus. $18.95)

Space, Time, Infinity: The Smithsonian Views the Universe by James S. Trefil is a history of astronomy and the evolution of the universe. The book concludes with comments on unsolved problems in astronomy. (Pantheon Bks., 1985. 255 pp. illus. $29.95)

The X-Ray Universe by Wallace Tucker and Riccardo Giacconi is the authors' personal account of the development of X-ray astronomy, which studies the X rays emitted by the stars and other celestial objects. The book explains how artificial satellites have made such observations possible and tells of the discoveries that have been made. (Harvard Univ. Press, 1985. 201 pp. illus. $20)

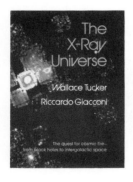

Biology. *In Self-Defense* by Steven B. Mizel and Peter Jaret explains how the human body combats disease, and describes recent dramatic breakthroughs in our knowledge of the disease-fighting process. (Harcourt Brace Jovanovich, 1985. 240 pp. $15.95)

Seven Clues to the Origin of Life: A Scientific Detective Story by A. G. Cairns-Smith argues that life originated on Earth 3 billion or 4 billion years ago in a primitive form based on clay crystals. (Cambridge Univ. Press, 1985. 123 pp. $17.95)

Time Frames: The Rethinking of Darwinian Evolution and the Theory of Punctuated Equilibria by Niles Eldredge, a paleontologist, tells how he and his colleague Stephen Jay Gould developed the theory that evolutionary development is not gradual but comes in bursts. (Simon & Schuster, 1985. 240 pp. illus. $17.95)

The Transforming Principle: Discovering That Genes Are Made of DNA by Maclyn McCarty, a bacteriologist, is a personal account of McCarty and Colin McLeod's 1944 discovery that genes are made of a chemical called *DNA* (deoxyribonucleic acid), which led to the recognition of DNA as the messenger of genetic information. (Norton, 1985. 252 pp. $14.95)

The Woods Hole Cantata: Essays on Science and Society by Gerald Weissmann, a physician and marine biologist, explores issues in medicine and biology, acknowledging the achievements of biology but lamenting how little has been done about social problems. (Dodd, Mead, 1985. 230 pp. $14.95)

Earth Sciences. *The Burgess Shale* by Harry B. Whittington describes the discovery of fossils of flattened but complete animals from the Cambrian Period, 600 million years ago, when animals lived only in the seas. The author explains how the fossils were created and how they contribute to our understanding of evolution. (Yale Univ. Press, 1985. 151 pp. illus. $25)

The Dark Side of the Earth: The Battle for the Earth Sciences, 1800-1980 by Robert Muir Wood is a history of theories of Earth from 1800 to the present. Drawing on such disciplines as seismology and marine science, Wood interprets the significance of plate tectonics and other revolutionary discoveries in the earth sciences during the 1960's. (Allen & Unwin, 1985. 246 pp. illus. $19.95)

General Science. *From Quark to Quasar: Notes on the Scale of the Universe* by Peter H. Cadogan is a pictorial survey of objects in the universe from tiny subatomic particles to huge astronomical structures, along with a descriptive text and a discussion of the methods used to measure distances. (Cambridge Univ. Press, 1985. 183 pp. illus. $24.95)

Metamagical Themas: Questing for the Essence of Mind and Pattern by Douglas R. Hofstadter is a collection of essays from the author's column in *Scientific American*. They include reflections on

Books
of Science

Continued

the strangeness of language, on patterns in the music of Frédéric Chopin, and on the human obsession with self-extinction. (Basic Bks., 1985. 852 pp. illus. $24.95)

Reflections on Gender and Science by Evelyn Fox Keller discusses the role of women in science from several perspectives, including historical and psychoanalytical ones. Keller disputes the perceptions that scientific objectivity and rationality are masculine attributes and that emotions and feelings are feminine. (Yale Univ. Press, 1985. 193 pp. $17.95)

Solid Clues: Quantum Physics, Molecular Biology, and the Future of Science by Gerald Feinberg surveys two relatively new areas of science—quantum physics, which deals with atomic and subatomic particles, and molecular biology, which studies the chemical processes of life at the molecular level. Feinberg argues that we are on the threshold of a new understanding of life and the universe. (Simon & Schuster, 1985. 287 pp. illus. $17.95)

Mathematics. *Enigmas of Chance* by Mark Kac is the autobiography of a Polish-born mathematician who was one of the founders of probability theory. Kac tells how he became a mathematician, what inspired and motivated him, and of his work with other well-known mathematicians. (Harper & Row, 1985. 163 pp. $16.95)

Mathematics and the Search for Knowledge by Morris Kline argues that mathematics has been the only means of providing us with much of what we know about the natural world, sometimes offering insights that contradict what our senses perceive. (Oxford Univ. Press, 1985. 257 pp. $19.95)

Natural History. *Bird Behavior* by Robert Burton is an illustrated survey of current information and ideas about bird behavior. The book discusses such basic life functions as caring for feathers and keeping warm or cool, as well as such complicated activities as rearing families and migration. (Knopf, 1985. 224 pp. illus. $18.95)

Insects and Flowers: The Biology of a Partnership by Friedrich G. Barth shows that we cannot understand flowers without understanding something about the insects that visit them in a 100-million-year-old interaction that

has altered both insects and flowers. (Princeton Univ. Press, 1985. 297 pp. illus. $35)

Insects in Camera: A Photographic Essay on Behaviour by Christopher O'Toole contains 287 color photographs by Ken Preston-Mafham grouped around major themes in the lives of insects such as feeding, mating, and defense. (Oxford Univ. Press, 1985. 154 pp. illus. $29.95)

Of Plants and People by Charles B. Heiser, Jr., describes a number of American plants, including gourds and peppers, their origins, and their interactions with people. (University of Okla. Press, 1985. 237 pp. illus. $24.95)

Physics. *Bird of Passage: Recollections of a Physicist* by Rudolf Peierls is the author's own recollection from memory of the role he played in the development of modern physics and of the famous physicists he has known, including his work with American physicist J. Robert Oppenheimer on building the first atomic bomb. (Princeton Univ. Press, 1985. 350 pp. illus. $29.50)

Quantum Reality: Beyond the New Physics by Nick Herbert recounts the history of quantum theory, which says that radiant energy is composed of tiny bundles of energy called *quanta*, and explains the predictions that the theory generates. Herbert also discusses the possibility of our gaining a deeper understanding of reality through quantum theory. (Anchor Press/Doubleday, 1985. 268 pp. illus. $16.95)

The Second Creation: Makers of the Revolution in Twentieth Century Physics by Robert B. Crease and Charles C. Mann is based on interviews with scientists and summarizes current knowledge in physics about waves, particles, and forces. (Macmillan, 1986. 480 pp. $25)

Technology. *Mechanical Metamorphosis: Technological Change in Revolutionary America* by Neil Longley York is a scholarly account of the creation of America's technologically oriented society during the 1700's. York shows how the Revolutionary War in America affected inventors and weapon production. (Greenwood Press, 1985. 240 pp. illus. $35)   [William G. Jones]

Botany

Botanists reported in October 1985 that a genetically altered pea plant may allow researchers to study *hydrotropism*, the tendency of plant roots to grow toward areas of higher moisture. Previous studies of hydrotropism had been hindered by gravity and light, which also influence root growth.

The investigators—at Wake Forest University in Winston-Salem, N.C., and the Bionetics Corporation at the John F. Kennedy Space Center in Cape Canaveral, Fla.—studied a pea plant named *Ageotropum*. The cells of *Ageotropum* contain a naturally *mutated* (changed) gene that makes the plant's roots immune to the effects of gravity and light. This characteristic enabled the researchers to study the response of the roots to moisture alone.

In their study, the investigators varied the humidity above the soil in which *Ageotropum* plants were growing, causing the roots of these plants to grow in all directions. Some even poked upward through the soil surface. If the relative humidity was higher than 90 per cent, the roots continued to grow upward. The scientists found, however, that if the air had a low relative humidity—indicating it contained less moisture than did the soil—those roots soon grew back into the soil. This result demonstrated that the plants' roots could sense areas of greater moisture.

Toxic metals in plants. Researchers at the University of Munich in West Germany reported in November 1985 that they had discovered the compounds in plants that *detoxify* (make harmless) the heavy metal *ions* that plants absorb from the soil. Ions are atoms that have gained or lost one or more electrons. Ions of such heavy metals as cadmium, copper, mercury, lead, and zinc can harm cells, including plant cells, by reacting with and altering protein molecules in the cells.

All plants, however—and all animals—have developed ways to detoxify low concentrations of heavy-metal ions—though high ion concentrations can overwhelm these protective systems. The detoxifying plant compounds discovered by the Munich researchers are simple protein molecules. But these protein molecules, known as *phytochelatins,* are rich in sul-

A branched colony of carnivorous lake algae "dines" on fluorescent latex beads (tiny bright spots) about the size of the bacteria the algae usually ingest. Scientists at McGill University in Montreal, Canada, in 1985 found six species of lake algae that feed on bacteria, the first algae known to eat other organisms. The scientists "fed" the algae glowing beads to track how much bacteria the algae consume.

fur. The sulfur forms chemical bonds with heavy-metal ions, attaching to them so that the ions cannot affect other proteins in the cell.

The investigators could not detect phytochelatins in plant cells that were free of heavy metals. But when the researchers exposed plant cells to heavy metals, large numbers of phytochelatin molecules appeared in the cells. The molecules attached to the metal ions, thus protecting other cell proteins.

Blue light and leaf pores. A new insight into *photosynthesis*, the process by which plants use the energy of sunlight to produce food from carbon dioxide and water, was reported by California scientists in January 1986. The researchers—at Stanford University and the Stanford branch of the Carnegie Institution of Washington, D.C.—studied the effects of different wavelengths of light on leaf surfaces. Wavelength determines the color of light. They learned how blue light causes leaves to absorb carbon dioxide.

Carbon dioxide enters a leaf through tiny pores called *stomata.* Each stoma is surrounded by two guard cells that control the opening and closing of the stoma. When these guard cells take up potassium ions from the leaf, they absorb water and swell, which causes the stomata to open. This process occurs when a plant is exposed to light. Botanists have long known that it is predominantly the blue wavelengths of light that cause stomata to open, but they were not sure why blue light causes guard cells to attract potassium ions.

The Stanford researchers isolated guard cells from the broad bean plant, a member of the pea family. They removed the cell walls, leaving the *protoplasts* (cells surrounded with membranes but not walls). They then placed the protoplasts under a red light and found that red light did not cause the protoplasts to swell, though it did cause photosynthesis. But when blue light was added to the red light, the protoplasts swelled.

The researchers found that the blue light caused the guard cell protoplasts to emit hydrogen ions. Potassium ions then moved in to take the place of the hydrogen ions. The hydrogen ions were originally part of other molecules

A Living Library of Endangered Plants

A group of scientists from 18 of the most important botanical gardens and arboretums in the United States met at the Smithsonian Institution in Washington, D.C., in April 1985 to plan an unprecedented conservation program. The 10-year project is designed to save all of the estimated 3,000 native American plant species in danger of extinction.

The effort is being coordinated by the newly formed Center for Plant Conservation, headquartered at Harvard University's Arnold Arboretum in Boston. Under the center's direction, botanical gardens and arboretums have begun building a living library of endangered plants in greenhouses or on well-tended land at 18 sites across the nation. By the end of 1985, botanists had collected specimens of 92 wild plant species in danger of immediate extinction, including the pygmy fringe tree, found in Florida, and Gray's lily, found in Tennessee, Virginia, and North Carolina. The scientists planned to gather specimens of 100 more species in 1986. The effort is expected to cost about $5,000 per species.

The chief threat to the endangered plants is the destruction of natural habitats by human beings. Conservationists believe that by the year 2000, the plant extinction rate could be 800 times the rate at which plant species normally become extinct.

For many years, conservationists have attempted to preserve endangered plant species by setting aside large tracts of wilderness as nature preserves. While efforts of this kind have not been abandoned, many ecologists are so alarmed by the threat to some plant species that they believe additional action is needed. By removing specimens of endangered plants from threatened habitats and placing them in "protective custody," conservationists not only ensure the continued existence of the species but also increase plant stocks for possible reintroduction into the wild.

In addition to collecting plant specimens, the center plans to stockpile seeds of some endangered species at U.S. Department of Agriculture long-term seed-storage facilities. Should disease or any other disaster strike the endangered species in greenhouses and gardens, seeds would be available to grow more.

Why is the survival of endangered plants important to us? Why should we preserve the frostweed, for example, or the northern monkshood, or the California lady's-slipper? Many of these plants simply are lovely to look at, a delight in gardens or along wilderness paths. But wild plants can also be tremendously useful.

Donald Falk, director of administration at the new center, points out that "well over a quarter of all prescription medicines in the United States are based on plant products. This makes plants an $8-billion business in this country every year." Childhood leukemia and Hodgkin's disease, for example, are treated with antitumor chemicals found in the Madagascar periwinkle. Who can say that researchers will not find another important drug in one of America's endangered plants?

In agriculture, wild plants have long been used to breed improved varieties of rice, wheat, corn, soybeans, and many vegetables. New gene-splicing techniques—in which genes from one organism are transferred to another—may make wild plants even more useful. For example, scientists may be able to use genes from wild plants to make food crops more resistant to disease and drought. But with every plant extinction, the pool of available plant genes gets shallower.

In addition, although a plant may seem useless today, it would be reckless to conclude that it will never be valuable. Rubber, for example, was considered a mere curiosity until the invention of the automobile and automobile tires.

We have hardly begun to consider the possible uses of plants, says Frank Thibodeau, director of science at the Harvard center. Allowing 3,000 plants to perish before we have had a chance to study their biochemistry, according to Thibodeau, is like destroying a library before you've opened the books.   [Christopher Reed]

Endangered plants find protection at the North Carolina Botanical Garden in Chapel Hill, one of 18 institutions affiliated with the Center for Plant Conservation.

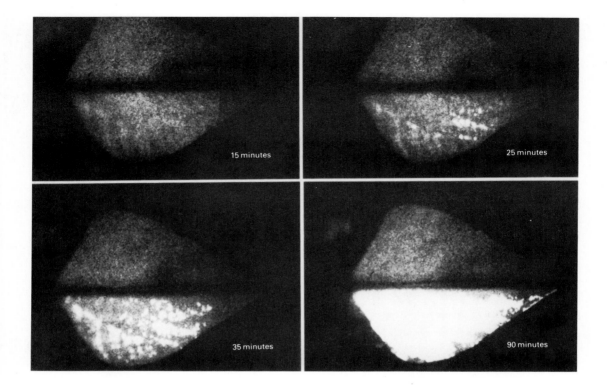

15 minutes

25 minutes

35 minutes

90 minutes

Botany

Continued

A series of images recorded with an ultrasensitive video system developed by scientists at Cornell University in Ithaca, N.Y., reveals a leaf giving off light in response to stress. A herbicide applied to half of the leaf caused the leaf's photosynthetic machinery to run in reverse and emit rather than absorb light. This reaction, which can be caused by many poisons and environmental stresses, had never before been directly observed.

in the protoplasts, but the potassium ions did not combine with anything when they replaced the hydrogen ions. Thus, the number of dissolved particles within the protoplasts increased, and that drew water into the protoplasts through the cell membrane.

Only 30 seconds of blue light were required to produce hydrogen emissions lasting for about 10 minutes. The scientists concluded, therefore, that the blue light was acting as a trigger and was not itself providing the energy that produced the hydrogen ions.

Simplified photosynthesis. A scientist at Oak Ridge National Laboratory in Tennessee also announced an important development in the study of photosynthesis—one that may have commercial applications. Chemist Elias Greenbaum reported in December 1985 that he had developed a simple system for splitting water molecules into hydrogen and oxygen.

Plants use light to split water into hydrogen and oxygen. The hydrogen combines with carbon dioxide to make various compounds; the oxygen is re-

leased into the air. Scientists have not been able to duplicate this plant process in the laboratory. The system developed at Oak Ridge might be called "semiartificial" because it still relies partly on plant leaves.

Greenbaum first removed *chloroplasts* from leaves. Chloroplasts are small bodies that contain the "machinery" for photosynthesis. The scientist put the chloroplasts in water, which caused the structures to swell and burst, releasing internal membranes called *thylakoids*. He then coated the thylakoids with particles of platinum.

When Greenbaum shone a light on the platinum-coated thylakoids, the chlorophyll absorbed the light and released hydrogen and oxygen simultaneously. The platinum served as a *catalyst*, a substance that causes a chemical reaction to occur without taking part in the reaction. Greenbaum's system might someday be used to produce commercial quantities of hydrogen and oxygen.   [Frank B. Salisbury]

In WORLD BOOK, see BOTANY; PHOTOSYNTHESIS; TROPISM.

Chemistry

A chemical technique that dramatically improves the ability of red blood cells to deliver oxygen to body tissues was announced in April 1986 by physician Murray Weiner of the University of Cincinnati Medical Center in Ohio. Weiner said that the new technique probably will benefit victims of strokes, heart attacks, and other illnesses involving reduced blood flow to tissues.

The technique, developed by Weiner and biochemical engineer Robert S. Franco, puts *phytic acid*, a natural compound derived from plants, into blood cells. Phytic acid weakens the ability of the blood protein hemoglobin to hold onto oxygen; therefore, the oxygen is more easily released to tissues.

Phytic acid normally does not pass through a red blood cell's *membrane*, or outer protective envelope. To get the phytic acid inside cells, the scientists used dimethyl sulfoxide (DMSO), a small molecule that easily enters blood cells. Then they added a solution containing phytic acid to a DMSO solution containing red blood cells. The cells swelled quickly, making them temporarily absorbent. The phytic acid then slipped inside the cells, and finally the cells shrank, trapping the acid inside.

Using this chemical technique can improve blood stored in blood banks—which loses its ability to deliver oxygen as it ages—and blood circulating in a patient's body. Treating blood in a patient's body may cost less than a transfusion and take only minutes to complete. Clinical testing of the new technique may begin in late 1987.

Soccer-ball molecule. Scientists at Rice University in Houston reported in November 1985 that they had made highly stable hollow carbon molecules that look like soccer balls. The surface of each molecule consists of 60 carbon atoms arranged as interlocking pentagons and hexagons. Because the new molecules also resemble the *geodesic dome*, an architectural structure developed by designer Buckminster Fuller, the scientists named them *buckminsterfullerene*. Chemist Richard E. Smalley and his colleagues made the molecules in an attempt to determine how long,

A worker removes a baseball bat made of graphite-reinforced resin from a mold at the Worth Bat Company plant in Tullahoma, Tenn. The materials were selected to make the bat last longer than a wooden bat yet still feel like wood in the hand and sound like wood when it connects with a ball.

Chemistry

chainlike carbon molecules form in the space between the stars.

The scientists used a laser to vaporize graphite, the most common form of pure carbon found on Earth. In ordinary graphite, the atoms are arranged in flat sheets of hexagons stacked on top of one another. During vaporization, the sheets apparently pull off the stack and curl to form the soccer-ball shapes.

The soccer molecules may be a common component of interstellar dust, produced by explosions of carbon-rich stars. They also may form the cores of ordinary soot particles on Earth.

Scientists suspect that buckminsterfullerene has unusual properties that could lead to the development of new lubricants and *catalysts*, molecules that speed up chemical reactions.

Memory drug. Experimental psychologist Victor J. DeNoble announced in April 1986 that a new drug called *vinpocetine* speeds up the rate at which rats learn by about 40 per cent. DeNoble and his colleagues at Ayerst Research, Incorporated, in Princeton, N.J., also found that certain chemicals or a lack of oxygen disrupted the memories of rats not receiving vinpocetine. But the chemicals or lack of oxygen did not affect memories of rats receiving the drug. Ayerst planned to file for United States Food and Drug Administration approval in February 1987 to test vinpocetine on people who have memory problems.

Scientists do not know how the new drug works. DeNoble says other research on the drug has shown that it truly enhances memory. It does not simply increase alertness, as does a stimulant such as caffeine. Vinpocetine may help brain cells to use sugars and other nutrients more efficiently.

The first people in the United States to benefit from the drug probably will be patients suffering dementia and mental deterioration because of a cutoff of blood to many small areas of the brain. Later, physicians may use vinpocetine to treat victims of Alzheimer's disease, and perhaps to treat people who have learning disorders such as *dyslexia*, marked by the inability to read and write letters and words in their proper order. In Hungary, where the drug was discovered, physicians already use it to treat a wide variety of ailments.

Communications breakthrough. In April 1986, scientists at GTE Laboratories in Waltham, Mass., announced development of a plastic crystal that may help improve fiber-optic communications. In a *fiber-optic system*, telephone conversations and data travel as flashes of laser light through hair-thin strands of glass. A laser used with an optical fiber typically flashes about 100 million times per second, sending from 1,500 to 8,000 simultaneous telephone calls over a single fiber. The laser can flash much more rapidly than this, however, and fiber-optic systems could handle much more information if the *switchers*, the devices that sort out the flashes that belong to the various calls, could keep up with the lasers.

Today's switchers consist of electronic circuits built into *chips*—pieces of silicon about the size of a fingernail. Polymer physicist Mrinal K. Thakur and his colleagues at GTE Laboratories reported making a plastic crystal that—if used as a switcher material—might enable lasers to transmit at least 1,000 times more calls than at present. The crystal also might enable computers to communicate with one another more rapidly by fiber optics.

The GTE scientists developed a new technique called *shear growth* to make the crystal. First, they put melted or dissolved crystals of plastics called polydiacetylenes under high pressure and gave them a sideways push—a *shear force*. In moving sideways, the crystals formed *thin films* (structures about as thin as a contact lens) that had fewer defects than any similar thin-film plastic crystal ever produced.

The new crystals sort out light signals faster than any other material. Switchers made from the crystals may be demonstrated in about two years.

Growing nerves. Polymer scientist Ioannis V. Yannas reported in September 1985 that he and his colleagues at the Massachusetts Institute of Technology (MIT) in Cambridge had caused severed nerves in the legs of mice to reconnect across gaps of about 19 millimeters (0.75 inch). The research offers hope that scientists eventually will develop a way to repair damaged human nerves.

Research on substances present in outer space led to the creation of a gigantic, hollow molecule made up entirely of carbon atoms. The molecule, which looks somewhat like a soccer ball, was named buckminsterfullerene after the eminent designer Buckminster Fuller, developer of the geodesic dome, which it also resembles.

"We laughed at first, but now it seems NASA is terribly interested."

Chemistry

Continued

The MIT scientists first packed silicon tubes with a *polymer* (a chainlike molecule) taken from cowhide or shark cartilage. Next, they anesthetized mice and cut through nerves in their legs. Finally, they connected the nerve endings to opposite ends of the tubes. The nerves grew together in six weeks, breaking down the polymer as they grew. The new nerve tissue looked normal and contained blood vessels.

To evaluate the polymer's effectiveness, the scientists also caused nerves to grow through unpacked tubes. This nerve tissue was 40 to 110 times narrower than the tissue that grew through the tubes with the polymer, and did not develop blood vessels.

The nerves studied in the experiment belong to the *peripheral nervous system,* made up of the nerves that branch out from the *central nervous system*—the brain and spinal cord. The researchers hope their work will lead to similar success with the more complex tissues of the central nervous system, especially those in the spine, and thus someday provide a cure for many paralysis victims.

Imitation of life. University of Pittsburgh chemist Julius Rebek, Jr., reported in December 1985 that he and his associates had produced small molecules called *diacids* that mimic the ability of biological molecules to "recognize" other substances. A major challenge for biochemists is to learn how various proteins that defend the body identify foreign bacteria and how plant and animal catalysts called *enzymes* pick out chemicals with which to react from a soup of similar substances. Such recognition processes are essential to life.

Molecular recognition is based largely on shape. One molecule recognizes another because the two have surface features called *recognition sites* that fit together as a key fits into a lock. Learning the shapes of various recognition sites would help scientists design new drugs, discover causes of diseases, and improve their control of *gene splicing*—the linking together of genes much as one splices a segment

Chemistry
Continued

of frames into a motion-picture film.

Unfortunately, research into molecular recognition has been difficult because many of the biological molecules involved are very large and complex. Scientists can learn a great deal about such a molecule's atomic structure, but it has often been difficult or impossible to study surface features in detail. The small molecules produced by the Pittsburgh researchers simplify such study.

Scientists may modify the new artificial recognition molecules so they can help the bloodstream deliver drugs to specific tissues. Rebek is also investigating the molecules' ability to function as catalysts.

Marking criminals. Research chemist Bruce Budowle of the Federal Bureau of Investigation (FBI) National Academy in Quantico, Va., reported in September 1985 that FBI scientists had developed a new way to help identify criminals—through analysis of their blood. The new technique is called *ultra-thin gel isoelectric focusing*, and with it investigators can do 5 to 10 tests on a single drop of blood. Each test identifies at least three blood proteins called *markers* that vary from individual to individual.

To determine what markers are present in the blood of a suspect, investigators place a drop of his or her blood on a special gelatin film and then apply an electric current. Differences in the gelatin's acidity, along with the electrical forces, separate the various marker proteins from one another. The proteins move to different places on the gelatin. Each specific location where they stop is characteristic of a certain marker. So investigators can "read" the gel to determine whether an individual's blood contains particular markers.

The new method is up to 10 times faster than conventional chemical methods of blood analysis, and it is much more precise. For example, the gel method revealed 10 variations of one marker, compared with only 3 variations of that marker revealed by other methods. [Peter J. Andrews]

In WORLD BOOK, see BIOCHEMISTRY; BLOOD; CHEMISTRY.

Computer Hardware

Sales of small business computers and personal computers dropped sharply in 1985, forcing a number of small manufacturers to close their doors. Firms that managed to survive offered discounts to reduce inventories.

Activity in the marketplace centered around scores of machines built to operate like the International Business Machines Corporation (IBM) PC personal computers. These so-called clones, both assembled and in kits, sold for 50 per cent of IBM list prices and sometimes for even less.

Japanese manufacturers were particularly active in producing IBM-compatible computers. At the Computer Dealers Exposition in Las Vegas, Nev., in November 1985, IBM-compatible models were displayed by Panasonic Industrial Company, Toshiba America Incorporated, Sharp Electronics Corporation, NEC Information Services, and Epson America Incorporated. Another exhibitor eager for U.S. business was Great Wall Computers, run by a government agency of the People's Republic of China.

New machines. Two major manufacturers introduced new personal computer models in mid-1985. Commodore Business Machines Incorporated of West Chester, Pa., announced the Amiga; and Atari Corporation of Sunnyvale, Calif., unveiled its ST Series. Both of the new models can make their screens show *windows*—simultaneous displays of two or more pictures or sets of data. Both computers use *icons* (on-screen illustrations that represent computer tasks) and *menus* (on-screen lists of tasks the computer can perform). The user can select from the menu using either the computer keyboard or a *mouse*, a handheld device that moves the screen's cursor.

The Amiga can store 262,144 bytes (256K) in its *random-access*, or temporary, memory (RAM), and its built-in disk drive, which uses 3½-inch (8.9-centimeter) disks, holds an additional 880K. (One byte is one letter, numeral, or other single symbol.) Impressive features of the Amiga are its ability to show simultaneously 50 *active windows*—displays of pictures or data that

Computer Hardware

Continued

the computer is actually working on—and its ability to run programs designed for IBM PC's without extra *processing chips*. (A chip is a piece of material—usually silicon—about the size of a fingernail and containing thousands of built-in electronic circuits. A processing chip performs arithmetic and logic operations.)

Atari's 520ST includes 512K of RAM. A separate 3½-inch disk drive provides an additional 400K. In early 1986, Atari extended the line to include the 1040ST with 1,024K of RAM.

"Star Wars" computers. U.S. President Ronald Reagan's Strategic Defense Initiative plan, also known as "Star Wars," calls for computers that are much faster and more reliable than today's machines. Computers in spaceborne scanners designed to detect rockets launched against the United States must be capable of processing 10 billion bytes per second. By contrast, today's spaceborne computers can process only 10 million bytes per second.

In the fall of 1985, Cray Research Incorporated of Minneapolis, Minn., delivered the Cray-2 supercomputer to the National Aeronautics and Space Administration's (NASA) Ames Research Center in Moffett Field, Calif. This machine contains four high-speed processors. Each second, it can perform more than 1 billion *floating-point operations*, computations in which the location of the decimal point may vary from number to number. The Cray-2 packs an enormous memory capacity—2 billion bytes or 256 million 64-*bit* words. (A bit is a 0 or a 1 in the binary system of numbers that computers use.)

In late 1985, Thinking Machines Corporation of Cambridge, Mass., delivered another advanced computer, the Connection Machine, to the U.S. government's Defense Advanced Research Projects Agency. The Connection Machine uses 64,000 processors and can execute 1 billion operations per second.   [Howard Bierman]

In WORLD BOOK, see COMPUTER; COMPUTER, PERSONAL.

An experimental speech-recognition system was developed in 1986 for the IBM Personal Computer AT. The monitor displays a printed message almost as rapidly as the words are dictated. The speaker also can use the system, which recognizes 5,000 words, to edit, store, or print the message, or to transmit it by electronic mail.

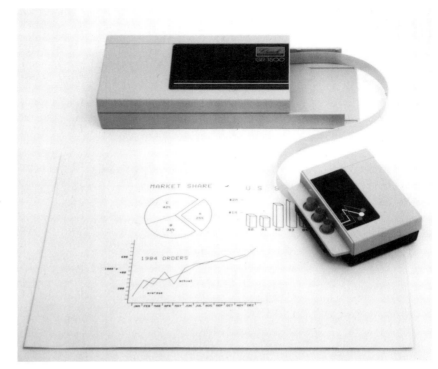

The self-propelled Penman draws computer-generated pictures, charts, graphs, and symbols in three colors on paper up to 3 feet (91 centimeters) long and 3 feet wide. The plotter also functions as a conventional mouse-type computer control, according to its manufacturer, Axiom Corporation of San Fernando, Calif.

Computer Software

A new breed of software called expert, or knowledge-based, systems, designed for personal computers appeared in 1985 and 1986. When they are presented with a series of facts, expert systems can diagnose problems and recommend courses of action to be taken. In effect, the new expert systems make the personal computer capable of offering advice on specific problems.

Expert system software has three main parts: an *interface* program that enables the user to communicate with the computer; an *inference engine*, which draws conclusions and recommends actions; and a *knowledge base*, which contains information supplied by a human expert. Most expert system software packages made for personal computers are *shells* or *tools*, so called because they contain only the interface and the inference engine. A human expert must program in his or her expertise.

In a typical expert-system procedure, the computer first asks questions about the problem. To answer, the user selects a number from a list displayed on the computer screen or types Y (yes), N (no), or ? (uncertain). After each response, the computer's questions become more specific. The step-by-step logic process is called *chaining. Forward chaining* begins with a series of facts and arrives at a conclusion, while *backward chaining* uses a known conclusion to arrive at the facts leading to this conclusion.

In the spring of 1985, research cardiologist Evlin Kinney of Miami Beach, Fla., developed an expert program called Chest Pain to help doctors diagnose patients' complaints about chest pains. The program prompts a physician to ask the patient questions about such matters as the duration and the location of the pain. The computer then offers a diagnosis of heart attack, acute angina, or neither of the two; or it tells the physician that it does not have enough information to reach a conclusion.

Another personal-computer expert system introduced in 1985 is Performance Mentor, from AI Mentor of Palo Alto, Calif. AI designed this system to

Computer Software

Continued

help managers evaluate employees and make certain other business-related decisions.

Educational software. Software developers in 1985 introduced a wide variety of programs for teaching various skills. Micro Cookbook, for example, is a cooking program available on a single disk from Virtual Combinations, Incorporated, of Oakland, Calif. The disk contains 120 recipes and has room for the user to add others. On a computer screen, the program lists the required ingredients and calculates the portions needed for a given number of guests so that even unskilled cooks can whip up an edible meal.

For people who like to grow their own vegetables, Plantin' Pals, a $29.95 program available from Home and Hobby Software Incorporated of Minneapolis, Minn., provides gardening information on 40 vegetables. The program tells when to plant the vegetables, how long they take to mature, the best type of soil for them, how to water and fertilize them, and what diseases and pests may destroy them.

Camera program. An inexperienced camera operator can slip the Camera Simulator program into an Apple II and quickly become adept at using a nonautomatic 35-millimeter camera. The $50 program, introduced in early 1985 by Brain Builders Incorporated of Hauppauge, N.Y., shows how to adjust aperture, focus, and shutter speed. It cleverly makes the Apple II imitate a camera so that the operator can use the computer keyboard to simulate focusing the camera, setting shutter speed, and even squeezing the shutter button. It even "processes the film" so that the operator can see how the pictures would have turned out if a real camera and film had been used. The computer screen displays a sharp picture if the user performs all the steps properly. If the user sets the camera improperly, the computer shows a blurry, overexposed, or underexposed picture. [Howard Bierman]

In the Special Reports section, see CREATING IMAGES WITH COMPUTERS. In WORLD BOOK, see COMPUTER; COMPUTER, PERSONAL.

The Puma RS Computer Shoe contains sensors that gather information about a runner's time, distance, and calorie expenditure. When the right shoe is hooked up to a computer, these data are displayed on the screen and can be stored in the computer's memory. The computer can also help a runner keep track of preset goals by displaying the total distance run and the distance still required to reach the goal.

Deaths of Scientists

Notable scientists and engineers who died between June 1, 1985, and June 1, 1986, are listed below. Those listed were Americans unless otherwise indicated. An asterisk (*) indicates that a biography appears in THE WORLD BOOK ENCYCLOPEDIA.

Browne, Secor D. (1916-March 23, 1986), aeronautical engineer who served as chairman of the United States Civil Aeronautics Board from 1969 to 1973.

***Burnet, Sir Macfarlane** (1899-Aug. 31, 1985), Australian physician and virologist, co-winner of the 1960 Nobel Prize for physiology or medicine along with Peter B. Medawar. The two scientists were cited for their discovery of acquired immunological tolerance, which led to major advances in organ transplantation. Burnet was also noted for his contribution to the theory that viruses could be cancer-causing agents.

Cooper, Irving S. (1922-Oct. 30, 1985), neurosurgeon who pioneered in the development of cryogenic surgery and other surgical techniques used to treat crippling disorders of the nervous system.

***Enders, John F.** (1897-Sept. 8, 1985), bacteriologist who shared the 1954 Nobel Prize for physiology or medicine with fellow Harvard Medical School researchers Thomas H. Weller and Frederick C. Robbins. The three scientists were recognized for their development of a simple method of growing polio virus in test tubes. Their research paved the way for vaccines against polio, measles, and mumps.

Flory, Paul J. (1910-Sept. 9, 1985), chemist who won the 1974 Nobel Prize for chemistry for his research on *polymers* (long chains of molecules or atoms). Flory found a systematic way of comparing various polymers. Previously, chemists had struggled with a chaotic jumble of unrelated measurements. After his retirement from Stanford University, where he taught from 1961 to 1975, Flory was active in the struggle for human rights.

Fossey, Dian (1932-Dec. 26, 1985), zoologist who studied the rare mountain gorilla in the rain forest of Rwanda in central Africa for 18 years. She also campaigned vigorously to prevent the gorilla's extinction. Her book *Gorillas in the Mist* (1983) describes the close-knit family structure of these endangered animals.

Gruentzig, Andreas R. (1939-Oct. 27, 1985), German-born physician who in 1977 developed the balloon catheter technique for cleaning arteries of fatty deposits.

Hanfmann, George M. A. (1911-March 13, 1986), Russian-born archaeologist best known for his work at Sardis, Turkey, from 1958 to 1978. He led excavations of the ancient city of Sardis, which reached its peak in the 500's B.C. under the rule of King Croesus, noted for his legendary riches.

Hynek, J. Allen (1910-April 27, 1986), astronomer and educator whose interest in unidentified flying objects (UFO's) legitimized scientific inquiry into the subject. He served as consultant to the U.S. Air Force on UFO's from 1952 to 1972.

Lehninger, Albert C. (1917-March 4, 1986), biochemist credited with developing the field of bioenergetics, which deals with how foods are converted into biochemically usable forms. His book *Biochemistry* (1970) became a classic textbook on the subject.

Menard, H. William (1920-Feb. 9, 1986), geologist whose discoveries in the Pacific Ocean floor helped set the stage for the revolutionary geological theory known as *plate tectonics*. This theory holds that Earth's crust is composed of more than 20 plates that slide around atop the hot soft mantle.

Morgan, Russell H. (1911-Feb. 24, 1986), Canadian-born radiologist who applied television technology to fluoroscopy, leading the way to such imaging developments as angiography, a technique for examining the condition of blood vessels.

Nyswander, Marie (1919-April 20, 1986), psychiatrist who in 1964 helped develop the methadone treatment for heroin addiction.

Polya, George (1887-Sept. 7, 1985), Hungarian-born mathematician who elaborated on the concept of "random walk" in probability theory and formulated the Polya enumeration theorem that is crucial to a mathematical process called combinatorial analysis. His book *How to Solve It* (1945) was an all-time mathematical best seller.

Porter, Rodney R. (1918-Sept. 7, 1985), British biochemist who shared

John F. Enders

Dian Fossey

Charles F. Richter

Deaths of Scientists

Continued

the 1972 Nobel Prize for physiology or medicine with American scientist Gerald Edelman. The two were cited for their discovery of the chemical structure of antibodies, important components of the immune system.

Rainwater, L. James (1917-May 31, 1986), physicist who shared the 1975 Nobel Prize for physics with Danish physicists Aage N. Bohr and Ben R. Mottelson. They were recognized for their work in showing how and why some atomic nuclei take different asymmetrical shapes.

Richter, Charles F. (1900-Sept. 30, 1985), pioneering seismologist who in 1935 devised the Richter scale, a method of measuring the strength of earthquakes by using information from a *seismograph* (an instrument that records ground motion caused by an earthquake). Richter worked at the California Institute of Technology's Seismological Laboratory for more than 40 years.

Robinson, Julia B. (1919-July 30, 1985), mathematician who in 1976 became the first woman mathematician elected to the National Academy of Sciences. She won a MacArthur fellowship in 1983.

Rose, William (1887-Sept. 25, 1985), biochemist who discovered and identified the amino acid threonine in the early 1930's, laying the foundation for modern nutritional research on proteins and amino acids, the building blocks of proteins.

Taussig, Helen B. (1898-May 20, 1986), the founder of pediatric cardiology and co-developer in 1944 with surgeon Alfred Blalock of a surgical operation used to open the constricted arteries of so-called blue babies. She was also noted for her role in warning the U.S. public of the dangers of thalidomide, a sedative that was given to thousands of pregnant women in Europe in the 1960's, causing major birth defects.

[Irene B. Keller]

Challenger's Crew

All seven crew members died when the space shuttle *Challenger* exploded 73 seconds after take-off on Jan. 28, 1986. Aboard was high-school teacher Sharon Christa McAuliffe, the first citizen observer to ride the space shuttle.

Mission specialist Ellison S. Onizuka

Schoolteacher Christa McAuliffe

Mission commander Francis R. Scobee

Mission specialist Judith A. Resnik

Payload specialist Gregory B. Jarvis

Mission specialist Ronald E. McNair

Shuttle pilot Michael J. Smith

Dentistry

An artificial mouth developed at the University of Minnesota School of Dentistry greatly speeds up the testing of new dental materials and techniques by producing the equivalent of five years' wear in just a few weeks. Jets circulate artificial saliva representing the different chemical conditions and temperatures that exist in the human mouth.

A new technique for quickly detecting the presence in the mouth of bacteria that cause *periodontal disease*—an infection of the gums and jawbone—was described in May 1985 by researchers at the State University of New York (SUNY) School of Dentistry in Buffalo. The conventional method for detecting these organisms involves taking a sample of bacteria from the plaque under a patient's gums and growing it in a laboratory culture. This method is difficult, slow, and impractical for routine use.

The SUNY researchers used a technique called *indirect immunofluorescence microscopy*. This technique involves the use of fluorescent dyes attached to specific *antibodies* (proteins that neutralize or destroy foreign substances in the body called antigens) to indicate the presence of specific antigens, such as a particular type of bacteria.

The Buffalo researchers used this technique to search for *Actinobacillus actinomycetemcomitans*, a bacterium suspected of causing *juvenile periodontitis*—a rare disease that causes rapid de-struction of bone around the teeth of teen-agers. The researchers treated plaque samples with antibodies to *A. actinomycetemcomitans* that had been combined with a fluorescent dye. When seen through a microscope, plaque containing the bacteria showed a fluorescent glow.

This method revealed *A. actinomycetemcomitans* in 98 per cent of the samples that were proved to contain the bacteria by growing them in culture. The new technique may help dentists diagnose and treat periodontal disease before obvious symptoms appear.

Testing for bone destruction. Dental researchers at the Harvard School of Dental Medicine in Boston in May 1985, reported a new technique that may quickly determine whether bone is being destroyed around the teeth of patients suffering from periodontal disease. In order to detect such bone loss, dentists must now compare X rays taken six months to a year apart.

The new technique involves the use of a radioactive chemical that concentrates in bone. The Harvard research-

Dentistry
Continued

ers injected the chemical in four beagle dogs with periodontal disease and then measured the level of radioactivity in the bone around the dogs' teeth. High concentrations of the radioactivity indicated bone loss—as confirmed by X rays taken six months later. Low concentrations of the chemical indicated that no bone loss was occurring. This new technique may someday enable dentists to detect bone destruction from periodontal disease in humans long before it can be seen by means of X-ray examinations.

Moving teeth magnetically. A growing number of orthodontists in the United States and Europe in 1986 began offering their patients an alternative to conventional braces for repositioning improperly aligned teeth. The technique uses small magnets—rather than the elastics and springs used in conventional braces—to create the forces needed to move teeth. Orthodontist Abraham M. Blechman of the School of Dental and Oral Surgery at Columbia University in New York City had reported on the new technique at

the Northeastern Regional Orthodontic Society meeting in September 1985.

Blechman treated two patients by attaching magnets to wires connected to their teeth. The magnets were aligned either to attract or repel each other, depending on the direction of force required to move the teeth into the correct position.

The success of treatment with conventional braces depends upon the cooperation of the patient in repeatedly adjusting the elastics and springs. The new technique does not require patients to remove and reapply the magnets. It applies force continuously, thus decreasing treatment time.

The total treatment time was approximately one year for each case, compared with more than two years of treatment with conventional braces for similar cases. The patients reported no discomfort during the treatment. The use of magnets also allowed better control of the direction in which force was applied than was possible with conventional braces.   [Paul Goldhaber]

In WORLD BOOK, see DENTISTRY.

Drugs

After more than 10 years of intense research, several new and highly sophisticated antibiotics became available in the United States during 1985. The United States Food and Drug Administration (FDA) approved the sale of ceftriaxone sodium (sold under the brand name Rocephin) in March 1985, ceftazidime (marketed under the brand names Fortaz and Tazicef) in July 1985, and imipenam-cilastatin (marketed under the brand name Cilastin) in November 1985. These new antibiotics are effective in treating a wide variety of infections including pneumonia and meningitis.

The new drugs are extremely expensive, however, costing hospitals an average of about $100 per day to treat a patient. By contrast, treatment with the older, simpler antibiotics costs about $10 to $30 per day.

In April 1986, however, infectious disease specialists at the University of Connecticut at Storrs proposed in an editorial in the *Journal of Infectious Diseases* that the cost of these new antibiotics has been overemphasized. The

doctors said that one of these new antibiotics often can be substituted for a combination of two or three of the older drugs. The cost of such a combination of drugs might total more than the cost of a new drug. They concluded that hospitals may be able to save money by using these new drugs more frequently.

Widespread and frequent use of these new drugs may present another problem, however. As newer and more powerful antibiotics come into use, bacteria often develop resistance to them. Many antibiotics that were effective 10 years ago are much less useful today because bacteria have become resistant to them.

In April 1986, infectious disease specialists James J. Rahal, Jr., of the Veterans Administration Medical Center in Manhattan, a section of New York City, and Robert H. Alford of the Veterans Administration Medical Center in Nashville, Tenn., suggested that if the new antibiotics are used widely and frequently we will soon be faced with bacteria that have become resistant to the new drugs. Rahal and Alford argued that the wisest course would be to use the new antibiotics only when absolutely necessary.

In 1985 and 1986, there were reports that some bacteria had already begun to develop resistance to these new antibiotics. Because of concerns about high cost and bacterial resistance, most U.S. hospitals restricted the use of the new antibiotics.

Tylenol troubles. On Feb. 8, 1986, a young woman in Peekskill, N.Y., died after taking a Tylenol capsule that had been contaminated with potassium cyanide. In 1982, seven people had died after taking Tylenol capsules containing cyanide. In response to this latest death, Johnson & Johnson, the manufacturer of Tylenol, on February 17 stopped making all nonprescription capsule drugs. Johnson & Johnson replaced Tylenol capsules with "caplets"—oval-shaped tablets that are more difficult to tamper with.

The popular acceptance of Tylenol as an aspirin substitute has been largely due to the enthusiasm of physicians for acetaminophen—the active ingredient in Tylenol and several other aspirin substitutes. Many physicians consider acetaminophen to be a relatively hazard-free alternative to aspirin. Aspirin can irritate the lining of the stomach and cause internal bleeding. Aspirin also causes changes in the ability of blood to clot and can cause asthma attacks in some people. In addition, the use of aspirin to treat children suffering from such mild viral illnesses as chicken pox and influenza has been associated with the development of *Reye's syndrome*—a serious disease of the liver and central nervous system. Acetaminophen, however, has been thought to be hazardous only when taken in very large doses.

In March 1986, however, hepatologist Leonard B. Seeff and his colleagues at Georgetown University School of Medicine and the George Washington University School of Medicine and Health Sciences in Washington, D.C., reported that people with a history of alcoholism might suffer serious liver damage from even moderate doses of acetaminophen. Seeff suggested that many cases of liver damage caused by acetaminophen may be overlooked or misdiagnosed by physicians who assume that a patient's liver damage is due to the poisonous effects of alcohol. Seeff concluded that patients suffering from alcoholism should be informed of the possible dangers of acetaminophen and that, if they must use the drug, they should take smaller-than-normal doses.

Drugs in the brain. For many years, pharmacologists have been conducting research aimed at understanding how drugs act in the human body. They have found that many drugs act by binding to special molecular structures called *receptors* on the surface of, or inside, living cells. These receptors control many of the activities of cells. By binding to the receptors, such drugs change the message that these receptors send to the rest of the cell. For example, dopamine-blockers—a type of tranquilizer used to relieve the symptoms of schizophrenia—work by binding to the brain's receptors for a substance called *dopamine*.

In the past, scientists could study these drug receptors effectively only by using animal tissues or human tissue obtained at autopsy. Attempts to study drug receptors in the brains of living human beings have had only limited success. But in January 1986, neuropsychiatrist Lars Farde and co-workers at the Karolinska Institute in Stockholm, Sweden, reported on a new technique for studying a particular type of brain receptor for dopamine in living human beings. The researchers injected four healthy male volunteers with a radioactive form of a substance that binds to dopamine receptors. Using a technique called positron emission tomography (PET) scanning, they produced images of the volunteers' brains based on the radiation emitted from the receptors. These images enabled the researchers to locate and analyze these dopamine receptors and describe how the receptors are affected by dopamine-blockers.

The technique offers a new method of investigating how drugs work in the body. In addition, it may help scientists understand how changes in cell receptors cause a wide variety of diseases.   [B. Robert Meyer]

In WORLD BOOK, see ANTIBIOTIC; DRUG.

Ecology

The ability to resist the damaging effects of drought and to actually benefit from fire has helped big bluestem grass become the most common species of grass on the tallgrass prairie, according to research published in August 1985. Ecologist Alan K. Knapp of Kansas State University of Agriculture and Applied Science in Manhattan, Kans., did the research at the Konza Prairie Research Natural Area in northeast Kansas.

Knapp focused on two of the major prairie grass species—big bluestem, which grows in fairly moist areas, and switchgrass, which is less common and grows in very moist areas. To compare the effects of fire and drought on these grasses, Knapp marked off two adjacent areas of prairie where both species grew. Both plots were about ½ hectare (1 acre) in size. One area was burned in the early spring before new grass shoots began to appear. The other plot was left unburned.

During the spring and summer, Knapp measured the ability of the two grasses in the plots to retain moisture in their leaves; their rates of *photosynthesis* (the process by which plants convert carbon dioxide, water, and sunlight to food) and *transpiration* (the process by which plants give off water); and the moisture level in the soil.

Knapp found that fire had a striking effect on big bluestem. Shoots of this species in the burned area grew faster, produced more nutrients more efficiently, and grew greener, thicker, and more abundant leaves than big bluestem in the unburned plot and switchgrass in both plots. Knapp concluded that the big bluestem thrived because the fire removed the dead leaves and stems remaining from the previous year's growth, allowing more sunlight to reach the new shoots.

Big bluestem also exhibited characteristics that helped protect it against drought. When drought occurred, the grasses in both the burned and unburned plots took in less water. As the soil got even drier during the spring and summer, however, the leaves of the big bluestem plants began to curl up. This action reduced the amount of

Large numbers of batstar, *below,* and other starfish species in waters off the coast of southern California are dying of a mysterious disease that damages the tissue on the animals' backs and arms, *below right,* exposing the inner organs and causing their bodies to fall apart.

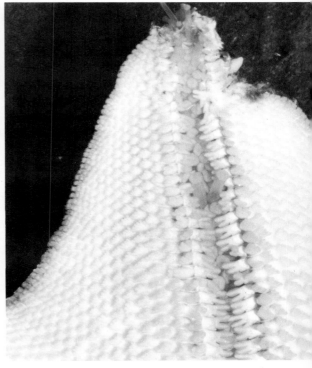

Ecology

Continued

A lightweight ultrasonic transmitter attached to the shell of an Atlantic blue crab, *above,* enables a scientist to track the crab's movements, *above right,* in Maryland's Rhode River, which flows into Chesapeake Bay. A device in the transmitter also reveals when the crab is eating. The study is the first to record the movements and foraging habits of the blue crab, one of the most commercially important shellfish in the bay.

sunlight and heat striking the leaves, thus reducing the amount of water lost through transpiration.

Knapp also found that big bluestem leaves were able to grow in a greater range of temperatures than switchgrass leaves. In addition, big bluestem, using less water, was able to produce the same level of nutrients as switchgrass. Knapp concluded that these are the main reasons why big bluestem became the dominant grass on the tallgrass prairie.

Grass and moisture. A study of the relationship between the amount of moisture in the soil and the type of prairie grass growing in an area of prairie was reported in December 1985 by ecologist Paul W. Barnes, then at the University of Nebraska in Lincoln. Barnes compared the growth patterns of big bluestem and sand bluestem in the Sand Hill Region of Nebraska, an area of sand dunes and meadows on the Great Plains. Big bluestem normally grows in the meadows of the area, and sand bluestem grows on the dunes.

Barnes chose two outdoor sites for his research—a meadow and an area of dunes. In each area, he planted 20 seedlings of each type of grass. In his laboratory, Barnes also planted seedlings of both types of grass. Special measurements of water use by the laboratory enabled Barnes to better interpret his findings with the outdoor plants. As the seedlings grew, Barnes measured their rates of transpiration and photosynthesis, the water they took in, and other growth processes.

The results of Barnes's experiments reflected the growth pattern of the two grass species found in nature. Equal numbers of seedlings in the meadow and in the dunes area survived until the first dry period when the soil at the dunes became extremely dry. At that point, many of the big bluestem plants in the dunes area died rapidly. In contrast, most of the sand bluestem plants survived.

Observations and measurements of the plants' growth processes revealed characteristics that protected the sand bluestem plants during drought. For

Ecology

example, the leaves of the sand blue-stem plants in the dunes area contained more moisture at midday, when sunlight and heat are most intense, than did those of the big bluestem plants. In addition, the sand bluestem leaves curled up faster and tighter and secreted more wax, which coated the leaves and reduced water loss.

In the meadow, where soil was more moist, many more big bluestem plants than sand bluestem plants survived, apparently because the sand bluestem plants are not as well adapted to moist conditions as big bluestem and so were not able to compete as well.

Barnes concluded that moisture levels in the soil play a major role in determining where various species of prairie grass grow. Big bluestem requires a fairly moist environment. But species such as sand bluestem survive in dry areas because they are better able to withstand the effect of drought.

Predators and birds. Predators are a major cause of the disappearance of many songbirds from the forest areas of the Eastern United States, according to research reported in August 1985 by ecologist David S. Wilcove of Princeton University in New Jersey. Scientists have known for some time that the number of migratory songbirds has declined in the *wood lots* (small tracts of forest) that are a characteristic feature of the landscape in the Eastern United States. To explain the decline, scientists have proposed a number of theories, including predators and the loss of forestland to human development. But there was little evidence to support these scientific theories.

For his study, Wilcove selected 11 sites—10 suburban and rural wood lots in central Maryland, ranging in size from 3.8 to 905 hectares (9½ to 2,240 acres), and 1 site in Great Smoky Mountains National Park in southeastern Tennessee. Because the park contains many species of songbirds that have long been extinct in central Maryland, it served as a control site.

Wilcove placed a number of artificial birds' nests containing three fresh quail eggs at each site in June 1983. The nests, straw-colored wicker baskets shaped like an open cup, were more conspicuous than the actual nests of migratory songbirds. Some of the nests were placed on the ground. Others were set 1 to 2 meters (3 to 6 feet) above the ground in bushes or on tree branches. Wilcove checked the nests periodically for two months and replaced any missing or damaged eggs.

To learn which type of nest was most vulnerable to predators, Wilcove also placed 22 tree nests in a 4-hectare (10-acre) wood lot in a suburban area of Maryland. These nests were made by hollowing out sections of small tree trunks.

Wilcove found that while only 2 per cent of the control nests in the Great Smoky Mountains National Park were attacked by predators, 70.5 per cent of the nests in the suburban wood lots and 47.5 per cent of the nests in the rural wood lots were raided. Wilcove attributed the high predation rate in the wood lots to the larger number of potential predators in these areas. These predators include blue jays, gray squirrels, and raccoons, as well as dogs, cats, and rats, which are more numerous in populated areas.

In general, Wilcove found that the smaller the tract, the greater number of damaged or missing eggs. Larger areas seemed to provide some protection. Nests in the largest wood lot in Maryland suffered the least damage. Nevertheless, 18 per cent of the nests there were raided, suggesting that even large tracts may experience declines in the number of songbirds.

Wilcove also found that open-cup nests were more vulnerable to predators than tree nests. Open-cup nests placed aboveground, however, were only half as vulnerable as those on the ground.

Ivory-bill sighting. At least two ivory-billed woodpeckers, members of a North American species believed to be extinct, were sighted in Cuba in March and April 1986. The last undisputed sighting of an ivory-bill in the United States occurred in 1941. The bird was later sighted in Cuba in the 1970's. The ivory-bill, the largest North American woodpecker, has shiny black feathers with white stripes down the back. [Stanley I. Auerbach]

In WORLD BOOK, see ECOLOGY; PRAIRIE.

Electronics

For manufacturers of *semiconductor chips* and for makers of personal computers, which use large quantities of chips, 1985 was a disastrous year. In the United States, chip sales dropped almost 30 per cent compared with sales in 1984. (A semiconductor chip is a piece of material—usually silicon—into which are built electronic circuits. A typical chip is about the size of a fingernail.) Japan continued to wrest a significant share of the worldwide chip market from U.S. manufacturers.

Major manufacturers in 1985 increased the memory capacity of their most powerful chips from approximately 256,000 *bits* to 1 *megabit*. (Bits are the 0's and 1's of digital computer language. A megabit is 1 million bits.) International Business Machines Corporation (IBM), Texas Instruments, and American Telephone and Telegraph Company introduced 1-megabit chips.

Electronic lock. To prevent unauthorized individuals from breaking into a large computer electronically, Intel Corporation of Santa Clara,

Calif., unveiled a *key-address chip* in the fall of 1985. A main computer and the remote computer terminals authorized to use it would contain such chips. When a user at an authorized terminal contacted the main computer, he or she would instruct the terminal's key-address chip to send a message to the main computer's key-address chip. The main computer's chip would recognize the message and allow the user at the terminal to operate the main computer.

Faster chips. U.S. Air Force fighter planes and Navy torpedo boats were scheduled in 1986 to benefit from the Department of Defense's ambitious Very High-Speed Integrated Circuits (VHSIC) program, initiated in 1981 to develop extremely fast, reliable integrated circuit chips. This kind of chip contains several kinds of electronic components and performs complex tasks.

Among 50 weapons systems scheduled to use such chips in 1986 was an electronic countermeasure pod designed to enable fighter aircraft to baf-

A two-way wrist radio made by Sawafuji Corporation of Japan weighs only 57 grams (2 ounces), yet has a range of 150 meters (500 feet). The Space Shuttle Wristalkie radio runs on a 9-volt battery and sells for about $40.

Electronics

Continued

fle enemy radar and confuse the guidance systems of enemy missiles. The VHSIC chips, built by TRW Incorporated's Electronic Systems Group in Redondo Beach, Calif., will cut the pod's power requirement in half and will make the pod 60 times as reliable as it is now.

Another series of chips was developed and built by IBM's Federal Systems Division in Manassas, Va., as part of a sophisticated antisubmarine warfare system. Martin Marietta Corporation's aerospace division in Orlando, Fla., worked on VHSIC chips for the Copperhead guided cannon shell. Honeywell Incorporated's Signal Processing Technologies group in Colorado Springs, Colo., designed and built VHSIC *processing units* that can perform 100 million arithmetical or logic operations per second.

Sound and sight. Sony Corporation of Japan in mid-1985 unveiled an 8-millimeter (mm) *camcorder* (video camera and recorder) that weighs 0.9 kilogram (2 pounds) and is only slightly larger than a paperback book. The camcorder has a digital sound system similar to that used in a compact disk player, rather than an analog system like those of Beta and VHS camcorders. Another advantage of the new camcorder is that the user can dub in sound such as a voice narration or a musical background. Dubbing is impossible with Beta and VHS.

Also new in the 8-mm format is the use of the tape to record six tracks of sound only. Sony introduced a video recorder and playback unit that converts to an audio player with the flick of a switch. In the Science You Can Use section, see VIDEO SYSTEMS: NEW CHOICES FOR HOME MOVIEMAKERS.

In an effort to increase sales, manufacturers of television sets in 1985 and 1986 replaced the traditional 12-, 19-, and 25-inch (30-, 48-, and 66-centimeter) screen sizes with 13-, 20-, 26-, and 28-inch (33-, 51-, 66-, and 71-centimeter) screens that have square corners and flat front surfaces. Mitsubishi Electric Sales America unveiled the first 35-inch (89-centimeter) direct-view color-TV receiver. Its screen is about the size of a projection-type TV screen but is much brighter and can be viewed comfortably from a much wider angle. The set was priced at about $3,000.

A "smart" pacemaker introduced at a conference of the American Association of Cardiologists in March 1986 contains a microcomputer and various sensing devices that enable the device to make the heart beat at a rate suitable for a patient who is exercising. The Activitrax pacemaker, made by Medtronic Incorporated of Minneapolis, Minn., is about as big as a pocket watch and weighs about 40 grams (1.5 ounces). The device senses physical movement in the body and adjusts the heartbeat within a range of 60 to 150 beats per minute. An ordinary pacemaker, by contrast, maintains a rate of 70 beats per minute. Even light exercise may tire a patient wearing a conventional pacemaker, because 70 beats per minute cannot supply enough oxygen to fuel his or her muscles.

Robots. Automation can help to maintain the vitality of certain U.S. industries, such as the automobile, steel, and home appliance industries. Industrial robots are excellent automation devices, but only about 16,000 of them are in use in the United States today, according to the Robotics Industries Association (RIA), a group of robot manufacturers and users. By contrast, Japan produced more than 50,000 industrial robots in 1985.

Most industrial robots are limited to such jobs as painting, welding, and moving heavy machinery because the robots do not have a delicate touch, their arms are not very flexible, and they have crude "vision" systems at best. But a new breed of robots became available in 1985, mainly in Japanese automobile assembly plants, which use 40 per cent of the industrial robots produced in Japan. Fujitsu Limited makes the new breed, known as Farot M6 robots. These machines have two highly flexible arms that can work together under computer control. The M6 can lift more than 450 kilograms (1,000 pounds). It can position a part within 0.03 millimeter (0.001 inch) of a selected location while the arm holding the part is moving at speeds of up to 2 meters (6.6 feet) per second.   [Howard Bierman]

In WORLD BOOK, see AUTOMATION; ELECTRONICS; VIDEOTAPE RECORDER.

Energy

The worst accident in the history of nuclear power occurred on April 26, 1986, at the Chernobyl nuclear power station about 110 kilometers (70 miles) north of Kiev in the Soviet Union. A large nuclear power plant exploded and began to burn, spewing radioactive substances into the open air. Soviet officials said the fire was extinguished on April 29.

Like almost all nuclear power plants, the Chernobyl plant produced energy from the *fission*, or splitting, of nuclei of uranium atoms. At Chernobyl, the uranium was contained in fuel rods that were surrounded by bricks made of *graphite*, a form of carbon. In normal operation, heat energy generated by the uranium boiled water, producing steam that powered a turbine connected to an electric generator. By removing heat energy from the rods, the water prevented the rods from overheating.

Apparently the water supply was cut off accidentally. As a result, the rods became dangerously hot. Water remaining in the reactor turned to steam. The steam reacted chemically with the overheated graphite and with material in the fuel rods, producing an explosive mixture of gases. The gases exploded, destroying the reactor, blowing the top off the building that housed it, and igniting the graphite.

According to Soviet reports, about 300 people were hospitalized as a result of the accident, and more than 20 had died by June 1.

The natural circulation of air in Earth's atmosphere eventually dispersed radioactive particles from the fire throughout the world. According to Western sources, however, they did not pose a major health risk to individuals outside the Soviet Union. See ENVIRONMENT.

Laser enrichment. The United States Department of Energy (DOE) announced on June 5, 1985, that it would continue to develop the Atomic Vapor Laser Isotope Separation (AVLIS) process to enrich uranium for nuclear reactors.

Uranium is a mineral that consists of two main *isotopes*, or forms. About 0.7

The reactor and surrounding buildings lie in ruins after the Chernobyl nuclear power plant near Kiev in the Soviet Union exploded and burned on April 26, 1986. In the worst accident in the history of nuclear power, radioactive substances spewed into the air and spread throughout the world.

per cent is fissionable U-235, and 99.3 per cent is heavier, nonfissionable U-238. For use in the type of reactors built in the United States, the U-235 content must be enriched to 3 per cent. A typical 1,000-*megawatt* (million-watt) reactor requires about 100 metric tons (110 short tons) of enriched uranium for initial loading and an additional 30 metric tons (33 short tons) per year of replacement uranium.

The DOE presently enriches uranium in *gaseous diffusion plants*. In these plants, molecules of a gas containing uranium are pumped through barrierlike structures that have millions of microscopic holes in them. Gas molecules that contain U-235 pass through the structures more rapidly than do molecules containing the heavier U-238, so pumping the gas through the structures increases the U-235 concentration.

These plants consume a great deal of energy, however, so since the early 1970's, the DOE has supported research on more efficient processes. The most promising methods were the AVLIS process and the *Advanced Gas Centrifuge* (AGC) process, in which a gaseous uranium compound is spun in a rotating cylinder. Centrifugal force concentrates U-238 at the cylinder wall, allowing the lighter U-235 to be skimmed away. The DOE called a halt to AGC research on June 5, 1985, after selecting the AVLIS process for continued development.

The AVLIS process is based on the fact that different isotopes of uranium absorb different colors of laser light. When a U-235 atom absorbs a certain combination of colors, it emits an electron. This changes the atom's electrical charge from neutral to positive.

U-238 atoms exposed to the same color combination do not emit electrons and therefore remain electrically neutral. This difference in charge between U-235 and U-238 atoms enables the AVLIS device to separate the two isotopes.

The AVLIS device heats metallic uranium to a temperature of 2200°C (4000°F.), driving off a stream of vaporized U-235 and U-238 atoms. Beams of red-orange laser light pass through the vapor stream, giving U-235 atoms a positive charge. These at-oms then flow to and are collected on negatively charged metal plates. The U-238 atoms, which have no charge, pass by the negatively charged plates and condense on an uncharged plate. The AVLIS process has been under development at Lawrence Livermore National Laboratory in Livermore, Calif., since 1973.

Powerful pulse. The Particle Beam Fusion Accelerator II (PBFA II), a device designed to produce energy by fusion—the merging of two atomic nuclei—fired its first pulse of electric current on Dec. 11, 1985, at Sandia National Laboratories in Albuquerque, N. Mex. In this process, two atomic nuclei *fuse*, or join, to form a larger nucleus. During fusion, mass is converted to energy.

The power of the first pulse was 70 trillion watts. Plans call for PBFA II eventually to produce pulses of 100 trillion watts.

The accelerator looks like a lot of electrical equipment submerged in a round swimming pool. It is 33 meters (108 feet) in diameter and 6 meters (20 feet) deep. Thirty-six submerged metal rods converge on the accelerator's target area like spokes on a wheel.

The PBFA II stores up to 3.5 million *joules* of electrical energy, and concentrates it into pulses of electric current that last fifty-billionths of a second. (One joule is the amount of energy expended by a one-watt device in one second.) The pulses travel down the arms to the target area, where they energize a device that generates a beam of electrically charged lithium atoms.

The first experiments will analyze and measure the beam's energy. When fusion experiments begin—probably in 1988—the beam will strike a target about the size of a pencil eraser and containing two isotopes of hydrogen. The impact of the atoms in the beam will compress the target, heating it to 100,000,000°C, some six times the temperature at the center of the sun. Hydrogen nuclei will fuse, giving off energy. Sandia researchers hope that the nuclei will give off more energy than needed to initiate fusion.

Sulfur removal from coal. Coal-burning plants generate more than half the electricity consumed in the United States. Sulfur dioxide and nitrogen oxides emitted from the smokestacks of these plants are the major cause of acid rain in the United States. During the winter of 1985, researchers in the DOE's Cool Water Gasification Program conducted the first test of a full-scale experimental plant using a technology that may reduce such emissions drastically.

The experimental plant, located in Daggett, Calif., produces 100 megawatts of electricity for the Southern California Edison Company. The plant emits a maximum of 3.5 metric tons (4 short tons) of sulfur dioxide per year for each megawatt of electricity produced. By contrast, plants burning *pulverized* (powdered) coal with only *electrostatic precipitators* to clean the gases in the smokestacks emit 130 metric tons (140 short tons) of sulfur dioxide per megawatt per year. (An electrostatic precipitator removes soot particles by giving them a positive electric charge and then attracting them to negatively charged metal plates.)

In the experimental plant, pulverized coal is mixed with oxygen and water, and burned at a high temperature and pressure in a device called a gasifier. The burning produces a synthetic fuel made up of hot carbon dioxide, carbon monoxide, hydrogen, and hydrogen sulfide gases.

The hot gases then heat water flowing through tubes; the water turns to steam. The steam drives a turbine-generator that produces 55 megawatts of electricity.

After the gases cool, they flow through a chamber in which a solvent absorbs 97 per cent of the sulfur compounds. Water is then added to the gas mixture to reduce the amount of nitrogen oxides produced during the next stage of the process—the burning of the mixture. The hot gases that result from this burning mixture drive another turbine-generator, supplying 65 megawatts of electricity. The heat in this machine's exhaust increases the temperature of the steam previously produced.   [Marian Visich, Jr.]

In WORLD BOOK, see ELECTRIC POWER; ENERGY; NUCLEAR ENERGY; URANIUM.

Environment

An explosion at the Chernobyl nuclear power station near Kiev in the Soviet Union on April 26, 1986, quickly became an international environmental issue as radioactive particles from the damaged plant were carried by atmospheric winds throughout the world. The accident was the worst in the history of nuclear power. See ENERGY.

On May 12, the European Community (EC or Common Market) banned the import of vegetables, fruit, dairy products, and other fresh food from the Soviet Union and six other Eastern European nations most affected by the radioactive fallout from the plant.

Radiation levels outside Europe, however, posed little danger, according to United States government officials. Radioactive fallout from the accident reached the United States on May 5. First detected in the Northwest, the radiation was barely above normal.

In early June, Soviet authorities reported that although radiation levels around the plant had dropped sharply, they were still quite far above normal. They said extensive decon-tamination measures would be needed to make the area around Chernobyl habitable again.

Chesapeake cleanup. High levels of pollution in Chesapeake Bay continued to be a focus of environmental concern in 1985 and 1986. But in September 1985, the U.S. government, three states, and the District of Columbia announced a comprehensive plan to clean up the bay.

Human sewage and industrial wastes from Pennsylvania, Maryland, Virginia, and Washington, D.C., drain into the bay, endangering the blue crabs, oysters, and other wildlife found there. In addition, livestock wastes, fertilizers, and topsoil from farmland in the bay's 166,000-square-kilometer (64,000-square-mile) drainage basin flow into the bay, dramatically increasing the level of nutrients, especially nitrogen, in the water. This enrichment process stimulates the growth of algae and other aquatic plants that use up dissolved oxygen in the water, causing the death of other aquatic plants and animals in the bay.

Environment

Continued

West German trash collectors wearing protective clothing dump a load of radioactively contaminated vegetables at a garbage dump in West Berlin. The vegetables were contaminated by fallout from an accident at the Chernobyl nuclear power station in the Soviet Union on April 26, 1986.

The completion of a plan to deal with pollution in the bay was announced on September 20. The Chesapeake Bay Restoration and Protection Plan called for reduction in the levels of nitrogen, phosphorus, and toxic substances, including heavy metals and pesticides, that enter the bay. The plan also called for improved sewage treatment in the region, the reduction of fertilizer and other agricultural runoff into the bay, and restrictions on the discharge of industrial wastes into streams that run into the bay.

Clues in seawater. The proportions of molybdate and sulfate in seawater can help explain why algae grow rapidly when nitrogen is added to coastal waters and estuaries, according to research reported in August 1985 by ecologists Robert W. Howarth of Cornell University in Ithaca and Jonathan J. Cole of the Institute for Ecosystem Studies in Millbrook, both in New York.

Molybdate is the dissolved form of molybdenum, a trace element essential to plant growth. Molybdenum is needed in larger quantities by certain species of *nitrogen-fixing algae*. Nitrogen-fixing algae take nitrogen from the air and convert it into a form that can be used by other algae. Although all plants need nitrogen for growth, most cannot use the nitrogen directly from the atmosphere.

Howarth and Cole found that sulfate, which is abundant in seawater, inhibits nitrogen-fixing algae from absorbing molybdate. As a result, their rate of nitrogen fixation is low. Nitrogen flowing into the water with sewage and farm runoff, however, supplies the needed nitrogen, stimulating algal growth.

In laboratory tests on water and algae from the Baltic Sea, Howarth and Cole showed that by adding molybdate to the water sample they increased the nitrogen-fixation rate of the algae. But, when they increased the ratio of sulfate to molybdate in the water sample to twice that of seawater, nitrogen fixation by algae dropped by 25 per cent. These findings may help scientists understand the chemical processes

Environment

Continued

Floating booms surrounding the oil tanker *Grand Eagle* contain some of the 1.6 million liters (435,000 gallons) of crude oil that spilled from the tanker into the Delaware River in September 1985. The booms limited the damage in what may have been the worst oil spill in the river's history.

that lead to algal growth in Chesapeake Bay and other estuaries.

Tracking oil pollutants. Tracking the source of airborne pollutants emitted by oil-burning power plants and oil refineries may be easier because of research reported in September 1985 by chemists Ilhan Olmez and Glen E. Gordon of the University of Maryland in College Park. Pinpointing the major sources of airborne pollutants has been difficult because the pollutants can be carried by the wind for hundreds of miles before falling in rain, snow, dust, or fog. Olmez and Gordon, however, found that oil pollutants contain telltale chemical "signatures" that can help scientists identify their point of origin.

The two chemists reported that the ratios of certain rare earth elements in oil pollutants differ sharply from the ratio of these elements in ordinary dust. The rare earth elements are useful as tracers because their ratios are not affected by cleansing processes in the atmosphere and so remain stable over long distances.

Acid rain study. The level of sulfate in the rain and snow falling in the Rocky Mountain States is directly related to the amount of sulfur dioxide emitted by metal smelters in Arizona, New Mexico, Nevada, and Utah, more than 1,000 kilometers (620 miles) upwind. This finding, reported in August 1985 by atmospheric scientists Michael Oppenheimer, Charles B. Epstein, and Robert E. Yuhnke of the Environmental Defense Fund in East Setauket, N.Y., is one of the first studies to directly link sulfur dioxide emissions and the sulfates in acid rain.

Scientists have been able to combine sulfur dioxide and oxygen in the laboratory to create sulfates, one of the main ingredients in acid rain. They have found it more difficult, however, to show that the same process accounts for the formation of sulfates in the atmosphere, because the atmosphere also contains many other chemicals.

Oppenheimer and his colleagues measured the level of sulfates in rain and snow in the Rocky Mountain States from 1980 through 1983. They then compared these measurements with sulfur dioxide emissions from the smelters. The researchers found that the level of smelter emissions was directly related to the level of sulfates in the acid precipitation.

Acidic droplets. An important new discovery about how and why acid rain forms from sulfur dioxide emissions was reported by environmental engineers J. William Munger, Christine Tiller, and Michael R. Hoffmann of the California Institute of Technology in Pasadena in January 1986. The scientists found that hydroxymethanesulfonate (HMSA), a strong acid containing sulfur, may be a key compound.

The researchers discovered that HMSA can form in fog or cloud droplets in areas with sulfur dioxide pollution, such as southern California. Once in the polluted water droplets, HMSA promotes the conversion of sulfur dioxide gas to sulfate—one of the main ingredients needed to form acid rain. The HMSA also increases the amount of sulfate a water droplet can hold. The researchers suggest that HMSA-laden water droplets may play a major role in transporting acid forms of sulfur through the atmosphere.

Space junk. *Science* magazine reported in October 1985 that so many pieces of debris are now orbiting Earth that they have collided with and damaged—or sometimes even destroyed—Earth satellites. This garbage includes 4,000 large objects, such as rocket parts; 40,000 marble-sized pieces of debris, the remains of broken-up satellites; and billions of paint flecks believed to have chipped off rockets.

Lead reduction. In October 1985, a team of oceanographers headed by John H. Trefry of Florida Institute of Technology in Melbourne reported on their study of the level of lead in the Mississippi River and sediments in the Mississippi Delta. They found that curbs on lead in gasoline in the United States, in effect since 1975, have resulted in a 40 per cent decrease in the amount of lead flowing into the Gulf of Mexico.   [Walter E. Westman]

In WORLD BOOK, see ALGAE; ENVIRONMENTAL POLLUTION.

Genetic Engineering

A new method for inserting deoxyribonucleic acid (DNA) into corn cells was reported in February 1986 by geneticists at Stanford University in California. DNA is the molecule genes are made of. The Stanford scientists' method involved using strong electric pulses to open holes in the cell membrane and allow the gene to enter.

Geneticists had earlier succeeded in adding new genes to the cells of some plants using the common soil bacterium *Agrobacterium tumefaciens*. The DNA of this bacterium contains a *transposable element* (jumping gene) that jumps into the chromosomes of plant cells that the bacterium has infected. *Agrobacterium* cannot, however, infect the cells of many crop plants.

The Stanford researchers used genetic-engineering methods to splice a bacterial gene—coding for a protein that confers resistance to a particular antibiotic—into a circular *Agrobacterium* DNA molecule. They mixed many of the genetically engineered *agrobacterium* molecules with corn cells and applied a pulsating electric field.

They then exposed the corn cells to the antibiotic, which can kill plant cells as well as bacteria. Only cells that had taken up the engineered DNA, with the protective gene, would be able to survive. Out of approximately 2 million corn cells, 161 had taken up the new DNA and survived.

Although still experimental, the method developed by the Stanford group may have important commercial applications in the creation of improved varieties of corn and other crops.

DNA "fingerprints." A new test that makes it possible to identify individuals from their DNA was reported in July 1985 by British geneticist Alec J. Jeffreys and his colleagues at the University of Leicester in England. The test is certain to have important applications, particularly in aiding criminal investigations.

The method uses DNA that has been extracted from cells and cut into many pieces with chemicals called *enzymes*. The pieces are placed on a gel and subjected to an electric field,

"What a humiliation! The home economics
department beat us in the race to create life!"

Genetic Engineering

Continued

which causes them to separate from one another in a distinctive pattern, much like the parallel lines of the bar codes on products in stores. The separated pieces are identified by the way they attach to genetic "probes"—radioactively tagged DNA molecules. When photographic film is placed over the pieces of DNA that have combined with the probes, radioactivity in the probes produces a series of black bands on the developed film.

Every human being's genes contain more than 50 pieces of DNA that combine with the probes, resulting in more than 50 bands on the film. Each individual's DNA, however, yields a unique pattern in the exact number of bands and the relative spacing between them.

This DNA "fingerprint" is inherited. Each segment of a person's DNA that creates a band on the photographic film comes from that person's mother or father. Only the DNA of identical twins will produce the same pattern of DNA bands. The chance of two unrelated people having the same genetic fingerprint is about 1 in 100 billion.

The first practical use of DNA fingerprinting was reported by Jeffreys and his colleagues in October 1985. They used the technique to identify a boy whose mother lived in England and whose father lived in Ghana. The boy, born in England, had gone to Ghana to join his father, then later returned to England. British authorities, doubting the boy's identity, refused to let him remain in England.

Jeffreys' team obtained blood samples from the boy and the mother and compared their DNA. The two were found to have 40 DNA bands in common, proving that they were closely related. The boy was then permitted to stay in England.

An important application of this technique will be the identification of blood and tissue samples in police investigations. The scientists reported that they were able to produce DNA fingerprints from dried bloodstains up to four years old.   [Daniel L. Hartl]

In WORLD BOOK, see CELL; GENETIC ENGINEERING; GENETICS.

Genetics

Scientists at the University of Georgia are studying myxobacteria, one-celled organisms found in soil, to learn how genes cause cells to assume specialized roles. Colonies of myxobacteria form tiny treelike structures called fruiting bodies, *below right*. Fruiting bodies with chemically caused *mutations* (genetic changes) grow in a Petri dish, *below left*. The mutations reveal which genes are responsible for converting individual cells into particular parts of a fruiting body.

Geneticists at the University of California at Berkeley reported in January 1986 that they had discovered how a gene that functions only in *germ cells* (egg cells or sperm) is controlled. The researchers—Frank A. Laski, Donald C. Rio, and Gerald M. Rubin—studied a *transposable element*, or jumping gene, called the P element, which occurs in the fruit fly. Transposable elements are genes that can change their position on chromosomes.

Movement of the P element is made possible by a protein called *transposase*. The genetic blueprint for making transposase is contained within the P element itself, encoded in the gene's deoxyribonucleic acid (DNA). DNA is composed of a long string of building blocks called *nucleotides*.

The P element contains just one gene—the one coding for transposase. Like most genes, the transposase gene is split into several segments. The protein-coding segments of the gene are called *exons*. Between the exons are parts with no known function, called *introns*.

When a gene's protein is to be manufactured in a cell, all the nucleotides in the gene's DNA are copied into a similar molecule called ribonucleic acid (RNA). Certain chemicals in the cell, called *enzymes*, then cut the introns out of the RNA copy and join the exons to form a continuous coding sequence that can be read by special protein-assembling molecules. This process is called *splicing*.

Because the P element is able to move around only in germ cells, geneticists had thought that the gene's DNA is not copied into RNA in *somatic cells* (all the other cells of the body). The Berkeley scientists, however, found that RNA made from the P element is present in somatic cells.

The researchers discovered that P-element RNA in somatic cells was about 200 nucleotides longer than RNA in germ cells. Since one P element intron is almost exactly 200 nucleotides in length, the researchers suspected that the gene's RNA is incorrectly spliced in somatic cells, leaving that intron in place. This

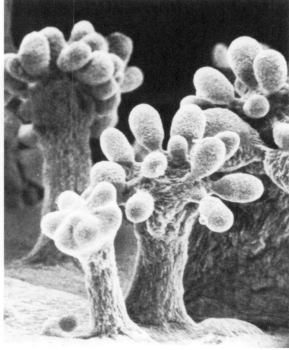

would make the RNA incapable of producing the transposase that allows the P element to move around.

To test their theory, the investigators created a P element in which the 200-nucleotide intron was eliminated. They injected multiple copies of the altered P element into a strain of fruit flies whose chromosomes contained a *mutant* (genetically changed) gene for eye color. In the presence of transposase in somatic cells, the mutant gene produces white eyes instead of the normal red eyes. As the scientists expected, the experiment resulted in flies with white eyes, showing that the flies' somatic cells were able to use the correctly spliced P element gene to produce transposase.

The Berkeley research indicates that RNA splicing for genes is carried out differently in germ cells than in somatic cells. Geneticists must now determine whether that is true.

Cystic fibrosis marker. The discovery of a *genetic marker*—a particular DNA variation—linked with the gene for cystic fibrosis (CF) was reported in No-

vember 1985 by a team of scientists in Canada, Denmark, and the United States, directed by geneticist Robert G. Knowlton of Collaborative Research Incorporated in Lexington, Mass.

CF is a serious genetic disorder of the lungs and pancreas caused by a defect in a single gene, which has not yet been identified. The newly discovered genetic marker for CF is a DNA segment of a particular length produced by enzymes that cut DNA apart at specific points. In searching for the CF marker, the investigators used DNA from 39 families in which two or more children had cystic fibrosis. Of the more than 200 DNA segments studied, only one of them proved to be from the general region of DNA where earlier research had indicated the CF gene is located.

The genetic marker should help scientists pinpoint the exact location of the CF gene. The marker will also enable physicians to identify persons who carry the gene.   [Daniel L. Hartl]

In WORLD BOOK, see CELL; GENETIC ENGINEERING; GENETICS.

Geology

The first comprehensive survey of the geology of the terranes that make up western North America was published in June 1985 by a team of geologists at the United States Geological Survey (USGS) in Menlo Park, Calif. Terranes are blocks of Earth's crust that have been transported from one place to another on the tectonic plates that form Earth's solid outer shell. The North American terranes, which formed thousands of kilometers from North America and journeyed across the Pacific Ocean, range from mountain-sized blocks to blocks the size of Delaware.

Some North American terranes were originally islands or underwater mountains created by underwater volcanoes. They became attached to North America when the tectonic plates of which they were a part *subducted* (plunged) under the North American Plate. The thicker areas of the plates would not fit into the subduction zone, so they were scraped off their underlying plates and added to the edge of the continent.

Some terranes were fragments of other continents. These fragments split off when a *spreading center* (a crack in the crust on the ocean floor where molten rock wells up) penetrated the crust beneath the continent. As the spreading center continued to extend beneath the continent, it stretched the continental crust above, eventually causing slivers of land to break away from the continent. These slivers were carried by tectonic plates across the Pacific Ocean on a journey that may have lasted 100 million years or longer. Finally the slivers collided with and became attached to North America.

Fossils and the record of magnetism in the rocks of terranes offer some of the best clues to the paths taken by the drifting blocks of crust. (A rock's magnetic orientation depends on the latitude at which it was formed.)

One of the terranes whose history was charted by the USGS geologists is the Wrangellia terrane, which makes up Vancouver Island, Canada, and part of the coast of British Columbia. Originally a volcanic island in the Pa-

Geology

cific Ocean somewhere north of the equator, the terrane began moving toward North America about 250 million years ago. It first drifted south, reaching a point 30° south of the equator, about 180 million years ago. It then started its northward journey, first colliding with the southern part of North America about 120 million years ago, then continuing northward and finally becoming attached at its present location about 80 million years ago.

The geologists noted that nearly all the land masses that border the Pacific Ocean are made up of terranes. The gradual addition of these blocks of crust has changed the shapes of North and South America, Asia, and Australia over time, like a geologic jigsaw puzzle.

Oldest meteorite evidence? The discovery of what may be the oldest debris from meteorite impacts on Earth was reported in January 1986 by sedimentologist Donald R. Lowe and igneous petrologist Gary R. Byerly, both of Louisiana State University in Baton Rouge. The researchers found the debris—layers of silicate spheres about the size of grains of sand—in rocks 3.2 billion to 3.5 billion years old in South Africa and Australia. Lowe and Byerly contend that the spheres represent droplets that were formed early in Earth's history when rocks struck by comets or meteorites were instantly melted. If Lowe and Byerly are correct and if similar spheres can be found in other ancient rocks, scientists may be able to estimate the rate at which meteorites bombarded the early Earth. Other scientists dispute Lowe and Byerly's theory, arguing that the silicate spheres formed during volcanic eruptions.

Rock layers and monsoons. The unusual repeating pattern of thick and thin or hard and soft layers often found in sedimentary rock formed from 100 million to 65 million years ago may be the result of periodic changes in the intensity of *monsoons* (seasonal winds) blowing over Earth. This theory, proposed by a team of geologists headed by Eric J. Barron of the University of Miami in Florida, was

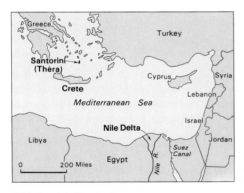

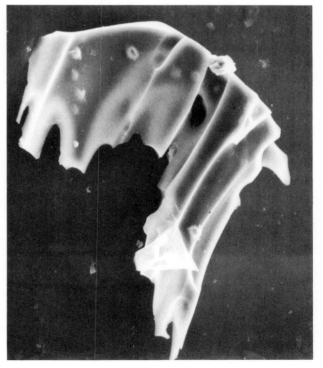

A Link with Exodus?

A microscopic grain of volcanic ash, *right,* one of 12 discovered in silt from the Nile Delta in Egypt, is chemically similar to ash from the eruption of a volcano on the Greek island of Santorini, *above,* in about 1450 B.C. Some scholars believe clouds of volcanic ash from the eruption account for the Biblical description of darkness that covered Egypt at the time of the Exodus, when the Israelites departed from Egypt.

discussed extensively at a conference held in Denver in December 1985. Patterned rock of this type is found in the United States along the Gulf of Mexico and in the plains east of the Rocky Mountains.

The scientists based their theory in part on the work of climatologist John Kutzbach of the University of Wisconsin in Madison, who used a computer model to study the relationship between Earth's orbit, the amount of solar radiation reaching Earth, and climate changes on Earth.

In 1984, Kutzbach suggested that Earth's orbit has changed every 9,000 years and that these shifts affect the amount of solar radiation reaching Earth. In the present era, Earth is closest to the sun on January 3. In January, the Northern Hemisphere is experiencing winter because it is tilted away from the sun and receives less sunlight. But because Earth is nearest the sun during this time, the difference between average winter and summer temperatures is relatively small.

About 9,000 years ago, however, Earth was closest to the sun on June 21, when the Northern Hemisphere was tilted toward the sun and experiencing summer. As a result, the Northern Hemisphere received much more heat from the sun during the summer than during the winter and the difference between average summer and winter temperatures in the Northern Hemisphere was much greater.

Kutzbach calculated that during such periods, the Northern Hemisphere would receive about 7 per cent more solar radiation in summer and 7 per cent less in winter than it does today. He also found that while the increased contrast between average summer and winter temperatures affected all weather patterns in the Northern Hemisphere, the contrast significantly increased the intensity of monsoons. Monsoons occur because of seasonal differences in the temperature of the air over the ocean and land. The summer monsoons produce torrential rains.

Barron and his colleagues suggested that this cycle explains the pattern of thick and thin or hard and soft layers often found in 100-million-year-old sedimentary rock. At that time, a global ocean called the Tethys Sea formed a belt of water around Earth north of the equator. The researchers concluded that North America and Eurasia experienced monsoons that waxed and waned in their intensity every 9,000 years.

During the periods when monsoons were more intense, more rain fell, rivers flooded, and more sediment was carried into the sea. As a result, the layers of sedimentary rock that formed at this time on the ocean floor and along the edges of continents bordering the ocean were thick.

During periods when the monsoons were less intense, less rain fell and the layers in the sedimentary rock were thinner. In some areas of North America, the sedimentary rock formed during these 9,000-year cycles is alternately hard and soft, but scientists are unsure about how the monsoon cycle caused this effect.

Ocean trough details. In March 1986, marine geologists John A. Madsen and Paul J. Fox of the University of Rhode Island in Kingston and Ken C. MacDonald of the University of California at Santa Barbara reported on the first detailed study of the Orozco Trough. The Orozco Trough, a valley running east and west on the floor of the Pacific Ocean off the coast of southern Mexico, connects two segments of the East Pacific Rise, a spreading center running north and south where new ocean crust is being created.

To map the trough, the scientists used the Sea Beam sonar system recently installed on oceanographic research vessels. Sonar creates underwater images by recording data from echoes of sound waves. The system's sound transmitters and receivers, mounted on the ship, feed data to an on-board computer, which maps the sea floor as the research ship cruises along. The system, which can map 1,200 square kilometers (460 square miles) of sea floor per day, creates charts with much greater detail than those created by any other sonar system.

In addition, because the system's receivers transmit the data in *digital* form (0's and 1's of computer language), the computer can interpret the data to cre-

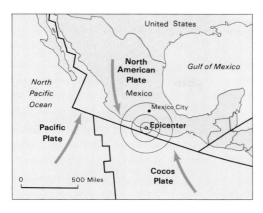

Mexican Devastation

Piles of rubble, *right,* testify to the destructive power of the two earthquakes that struck Mexico City on Sept. 19 and 20, 1985. The earthquakes, which were centered 360 kilometers (224 miles) southwest of the city, were caused by the edge of the Cocos Plate, one of the huge tectonic plates that make up Earth's crust, sliding under the North American Plate, of which Mexico is a part, *above.*

Geology

Continued

ate maps of the sea floor from different angles. For example, the computer can produce maps that show the sea floor from above and maps that show the sea floor from the side.

Madsen and his colleagues found that at the west end of the trough, a segment of the East Pacific Rise extends to the north. At the east end of the trough, a segment of the rise extends south. As new crust is created in the rise segments, the sea floor on either side is pushed away. The scientists found that the sea floor to the north of the trough is moving east while the sea floor to the south is moving west. The two sections of ocean crust are slipping past each other at the rate of about 9 centimeters (3.5 inches) per year—a relatively fast speed, geologically speaking.

The maps revealed that instead of being of a uniform width, the trough is wider and deeper on the east end than it is on the west end. The scientists believe this has occurred because the trough is being pulled apart at one end by the new ocean crust.

Mexico City earthquake. On Sept. 19 and 20, 1985, Mexico City was devastated by two powerful earthquakes measuring 8.1 and 7.3 on the Richter scale. The earthquakes were centered about 360 kilometers (224 miles) from the city in a region known as the Michoacan *seismic gap.* Seismic gaps are areas along the boundary between two tectonic plates where an earthquake has not occurred for a long time.

The quakes damaged thousands of buildings and killed at least 7,000 people in Mexico City. Some geologists think that the damage was so severe because the rock between the Michoacan gap and Mexico City is structured in such a way that it concentrated the energy from the earthquake into the area of the city, the way a magnifying glass focuses light. Also, Mexico City is built on an ancient lake bed and bog, which tend to shake like jelly during earthquakes.   [William W. Hay]

In the Special Reports section, see EXPLORING EARTH'S INNER SPACE. In WORLD BOOK, see GEOLOGY; METEOR; MONSOON; SONAR.

269

Immunology

Techniques that allowed an entire leg to be transplanted on a rat might lead to a revolution in transplant surgery for humans. Scientists at the University of California at Irvine in July 1985 reported their success in transplanting rat legs—bones and complexes of tissue made up of nerves, blood vessels, skin, and muscle. They used cyclosporin, a drug that suppresses immunity, to prevent the rat's immune system from rejecting the transplanted leg. Cyclosporin, along with sophisticated surgical techniques, might make the transplantation of human limbs possible.

The number of cases of acquired immune deficiency syndrome (AIDS) continued to rise in the United States during 1986, reaching a total of 21,302 by June 2. Doctors remained helpless to treat this devastating viral disease, which destroys the immune system. Researchers, however, were making progress in understanding the disease and the nature of the virus that causes it. In the Special Reports section, see Unraveling the Secrets of AIDS.

Protection against colds. Two teams of scientists, one in Australia and the other in Virginia, reported in January 1986 that nasally administered interferon, a natural antivirus substance, is effective in preventing colds caused by rhinoviruses. The investigators—at the Institute of Medical and Veterinary Science in Adelaide, Australia, the University of Adelaide, and the University of Virginia School of Medicine in Charlottesville—said interferon prevented colds in many volunteers who had been exposed to the virus.

Prevention of the common cold has been difficult because there are many different strains of rhinoviruses, the group of viruses that cause as many as half of all colds. Moreover, strains of rhinoviruses change slightly from year to year, making prevention even more difficult. Complicating the problem still further is the temporary nature of the body's immunity to these viruses. Within a few years after being infected by a particular rhinovirus, the body's natural immunity has fallen to levels that make it susceptible to reinfection from the same strain.

No effective treatment is available for the common cold, and researchers have been unable to develop a vaccine against it. But in the 1980's, many immunologists have become enthusiastic about the possibility of using interferon to ward off colds. Interferon is a protein produced by virus-infected cells that help other cells resist invasion by the virus.

The Australian investigators tested interferon in 97 families. Family members used a nasal spray containing either a *placebo* (an inactive substance) or

Immunology

Continued

interferon at the first sign of a cold in another family member. Participants were not told which kind of spray they were using. The virus that was causing each person's cold was determined by laboratory analysis of nasal and throat secretions.

Persons receiving interferon came down with approximately 41 per cent fewer colds of all types than those who received the placebo. Almost all of the interferon spray's protective effect, however, was against rhinovirus infections; the interferon users had almost 86 per cent fewer rhinovirus colds than the placebo group.

The Virginia researchers conducted similar tests, giving a nasal spray containing interferon or a placebo to members of 60 families, and they obtained nearly identical results. Volunteers receiving interferon came down with 39 per cent fewer colds of all types, and 88 per cent fewer rhinovirus colds, than persons using the placebo spray.

The only side effects of the interferon nasal spray were mild nosebleeds reported by a few of the volunteers. The investigators said that although their tests found interferon to be effective mainly against rhinoviruses, different dosages or application methods of interferon might protect against other cold viruses and influenza. See MEDICAL RESEARCH.

New treatment for herpes. A possible breakthrough in the treatment of *herpes simplex* infections was reported in April 1986 by investigators at the University of Oregon at Portland. The researchers said an antiviral ointment, intervir-A, decreased the severity and frequency of herpes eruptions in a group of infected patients.

There are two forms of the herpes simplex virus that cause human infections. Type 1 usually causes lip sores known as fever blisters or cold sores. Type 2 infections usually involve the genital area and are transmitted through sexual contact. Part of the problem with herpes infections is that the virus evades destruction by the immune system and thus can cause recurring symptoms.

The researchers treated 35 patients suffering from herpes symptoms with intervir-A. All the patients said the drug quickly eased their discomfort, and 70 per cent noted a considerably longer-than-normal interval before the recurrence of symptoms.

Cancer-fighting blood cells. A natural tumor-fighting substance called interleukin-2 (IL-2) may be an effective weapon against some advanced cancers. Oncologist Steven A. Rosenberg and his colleagues at the National Cancer Institute (NCI) in Bethesda, Md., reported in December 1985 that white blood cells treated with this substance greatly reduced tumors in patients with several forms of cancer.

Medical researchers had known for some time that certain white blood cells can destroy cancer cells and that substances called lymphokines, produced by white blood cells, can increase this cancer-fighting ability. One type of lymphokine, IL-2, was found to be particularly effective at boosting white blood cells' ability to destroy tumor cells, at least in the laboratory. White blood cells treated with IL-2 are known as *lymphokine-activated killer* (LAK) cells.

In studies in the early 1980's, Rosenberg and his colleagues found that neither LAK cells nor IL-2, when used alone, had much effect on cancers in the body. They wondered, however, whether a combination of LAK cells and IL-2 might benefit cancer patients.

The researchers removed large numbers of white blood cells from 25 patients with advanced cancers that had spread to other parts of their bodies. They treated the cells with IL-2 to create LAK cells, which were then given to the patients in an intravenous solution. The patients also received IL-2 intravenously.

The tumors of 10 of the patients decreased in size, and the tumors of 1 patient with malignant melanoma, a deadly form of skin cancer, disappeared completely. The other 14 patients were not helped.

The NCI research, though far from being a complete success, opens the door for other approaches to cancer therapy that capitalize on the natural ability of the immune system to fight cancers.   [Paul Katz]

In WORLD BOOK, see COLD, COMMON; HERPES; IMMUNITY; INFLUENZA; INTERFERON.

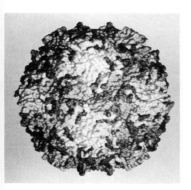

A three-dimensional picture of the poliovirus, generated by a computer from more than 1 million pieces of X-ray crystallography data, was published in September 1985 by researchers at the Massachusetts Institute of Technology in Cambridge and the Scripps Clinic in La Jolla, Calif. The detailed image of the virus's surface should help scientists study the relationship between the virus's form and its ability to cause disease.

Medical Research

Two groups of medical researchers—one in Australia, the other in the United States—reported in January 1986 that they may have found a way to prevent the common cold. Both studies were aimed at determining whether people using the antiviral protein interferon for only short periods when they knew they were being exposed to the cold virus could avoid nasal irritation and still ward off colds. Earlier studies had indicated that the long-term use of nasal sprays containing interferon helped to thwart the spread of infections caused by *rhinovirus*—the microbe responsible for up to 50 per cent of colds. But many people using interferon in these studies developed nosebleeds and sore nostrils.

The Australian researchers, at the University of Adelaide, provided 48 families with nasal spray containing interferon and 49 families with a *placebo* nasal spray (containing no medically active ingredients). For six months, every family member more than 14 years old used the spray for seven days if any member of that family suffered cold symptoms. All the people with cold symptoms took swabs of their nasal secretions. The researchers then determined what viruses, if any, the secretions contained.

The researchers found that the families who used the interferon spray had 41 per cent fewer respiratory illnesses and 86 per cent fewer rhinovirus infections than did the families using the placebo. Minor nosebleeds occurred in 12 per cent of the interferon users and 3 per cent of the placebo users.

The U.S. team, at the University of Virginia Medical Center in Charlottesville, provided 30 families with interferon spray and 30 with placebo spray. The people using the interferon spray had 39 per cent fewer episodes of respiratory illness and 88 per cent fewer rhinovirus colds than did those using the placebo. Nosebleeds occurred in 12 per cent of interferon users and 9 per cent of placebo users.

Both teams of researchers concluded that the short-term use of interferon sprays causes few side effects and might prevent people who have

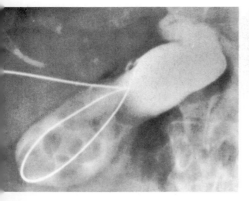

An experimental technique developed at the Mayo Clinic in Rochester, Minn., may eliminate the need for major surgery for many patients with gallstones, *above*. Doctors insert a tube into the gall bladder and inject a chemical that dissolves cholesterol gallstones, *right*. In less than three days, the stones dissolve and are flushed out through the common bile duct into the small intestine.

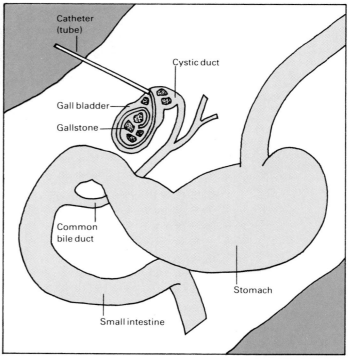

Catheter (tube)

Cystic duct

Gall bladder

Gallstone

Common bile duct

Stomach

Small intestine

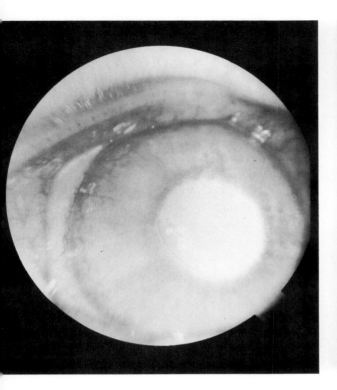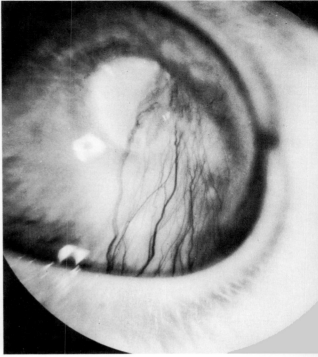

Medical Research

Continued

A rabbit's eye injected with *angiogenin*—a protein that stimulates blood vessel growth—shows a network of small blood vessels, *above right,* that do not ordinarily grow in an eye, *above*. Angiogenin, discovered by researchers at Harvard Medical School in Boston, may someday be used to prevent heart attacks and strokes by stimulating the development of new blood vessels around clogged arteries. Further research may help scientists understand how tumors generate their own blood vessels.

been exposed to rhinoviruses from developing colds. They noted that more research is necessary to determine whether interferon sprays can be used safely by children and whether repeated short-term use of such sprays is harmful to adults.

Growing new blood vessels. Biochemist Bert L. Vallee and colleagues at Harvard Medical School in Boston in September 1985 announced that they had isolated and determined the chemical structure of a protein that can cause blood vessels to grow. For some time, scientists have known that tumors produce substances that aid their growth. One such substance triggers the development of blood vessels that feed the tumors. The Harvard team found that protein, called *angiogenin,* after a 10-year search.

The researchers isolated the protein from fluid in which they had grown colon cancer cells. They then added the protein to two tissues that do not normally have blood vessels—a membrane from a *chick embryo* (the form of a chick before it hatches) and a rabbit

cornea (the membrane covering the eyeball). In both cases, tiny blood vessels appeared within a few days.

The researchers next analyzed the chemical composition of the protein using a device that determines the order in which the protein's building blocks—amino acids—are assembled. Based on this knowledge, they were able to predict the composition of the gene that directs the production of angiogenin. With the help of biochemists from the University of Washington in Seattle, the researchers located such a gene in healthy human liver cells.

The identification of the angiogenin gene will enable scientists to use genetic engineering techniques to produce angiogenin in quantities large enough for use in medical research. The Harvard team plans to use angiogenin to investigate how tumor cells and normal cells generate the blood supplies necessary for their survival. Because the system of blood vessels is considered an organ, studying angiogenin's activity may provide clues as to how other organs are formed.

273

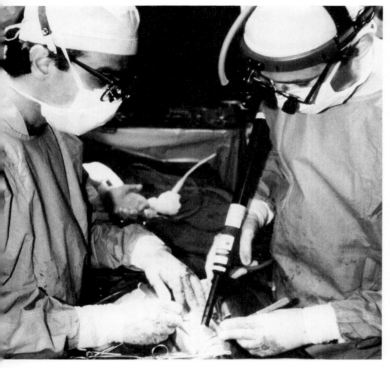

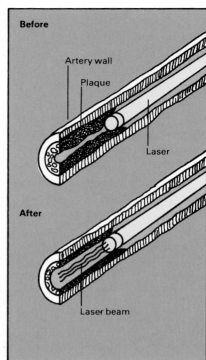

Before
Artery wall
Plaque
Laser

After
Laser beam

Medical Research

Continued

Surgeons at the Texas Heart Institute in Houston, *above,* use a laser to remove plaque blocking a patient's coronary arteries. The U.S. Food and Drug Administration in 1985 approved a two-year test program for the experimental operation. The surgeons thread a tube containing the laser through the artery to the area of obstruction. There the laser beam vaporizes the plaque, *above right,* restoring blood flow through the artery to the heart.

Angiogenin may also become a valuable therapeutic agent. Some scientists speculate that angiogenin may be used to prevent heart attacks and strokes by stimulating the growth of new blood vessels around arteries that are becoming blocked.

New cancer therapy. Researchers at the National Cancer Institute (NCI) in Bethesda, Md., announced in December 1985 that they had used a new treatment to shrink tumors in patients with several types of cancer. The new therapy involved the use of the antiviral protein interleukin-2 (IL-2), which is produced by white blood cells. In the body, a special type of white blood cell called a *natural killer* (NK) *cell* attacks and destroys certain developing tumor cells. By exposing NK cells outside the body to IL-2, scientists get them to reproduce rapidly. Cells produced in this way are called *lymphokine activated killer* (LAK) *cells.* Previous studies had shown that using either IL-2 or LAK cells separately in patients with advanced cancers was only partially effective. But animal studies suggested that treatment with a combination of the two might produce a better result.

The researchers, under the direction of oncologist Steven A. Rosenberg, took blood samples from 25 patients with advanced cancers. They used IL-2 to produce LAK cells and returned these cells to the patients intravenously. At the same time, they also gave the patients IL-2 intravenously.

In 11 patients, tumors shrank to less than half their original size. In one patient who had many tumor nodules from *melanoma* (a form of skin cancer), the disease disappeared entirely. And in another patient, three of five lung tumors that had spread from a rectal tumor disappeared and the other two became small enough to be removed surgically. The treatment caused fluid retention in several of the patients, but these patients lost the excess fluid after their therapy ended.

Because this study involved only a few patients who were followed for less than a year after treatment, the investigators cautioned that further studies were needed to determine the ultimate value of the therapy.

Artificial blood cells. A team of pharmacologists and chemists led by C. Anthony Hunt of the University of California in San Francisco reported in December 1985 that they had developed an oxygen-carrying artificial blood cell. Because the use of human blood products for transfusions involves the risk of virus transmission and the need for matching blood types, many researchers have been trying to develop artificial blood cells.

Hunt and his co-workers call their creation a *neohemocyte*. It is a microscopic pellet consisting of *hemoglobin* (the blood's oxygen-carrying molecule) encased in a double membrane. It can transport the same amount of oxygen as a natural red blood cell, does not trigger clot formation, and can pass through the narrowest capillaries.

To determine how long neohemocytes can last in the body, researchers replaced 50 per cent of the blood of five rats with a solution containing 25 per cent neohemocytes. They also added pellets that had the neohemocyte's membrane but contained radioactive *sucrose* (a form of sugar) instead of hemoglobin. Periodic measurements of the amount of radioactivity in the rats' blood showed that 60 per cent of the pellets were broken down within eight hours. Other studies had shown that the same proportion of *free hemoglobin*—another proposed red blood cell substitute containing hemoglobin that is not encapsulated—disappears from the blood in only four hours.

The researchers then replaced 95 per cent of the blood of 15 rats with free hemoglobin or a solution containing 25 per cent neohemocytes. The rats given free hemoglobin survived an average of only 10 hours, but those receiving neohemocytes lived at least 18 hours, and two survived more than six days. The researchers speculated that neohemocytes may someday be useful as a red-cell substitute in treating people who have lost a great deal of blood or are in shock. [Beverly Merz]

In WORLD BOOK, see BLOOD; CANCER; COLD, COMMON; MEDICINE.

Medicine

The problem of finding an effective means of diagnosing and treating victims of acquired immune deficiency syndrome (AIDS) remained unsolved during 1985 and 1986 as the number of people suffering from this fatal illness continued to mount. Researchers, however, made progress in unraveling the structure and behavior of the AIDS virus. Such information might eventually lead to a vaccine or better drugs for treating AIDS. In the Special Reports section, see UNRAVELING THE SECRETS OF AIDS.

Brain by-pass reconsidered. In November 1985, researchers reported the results of a study of the benefits of an operation called the extracranial-intracranial (EC-IC) by-pass. The researchers found that the operation was no more effective than aspirin and high blood pressure medication in reducing the risk of stroke for people with obstruction of the middle cerebral artery, a major blood vessel leading to the brain. The by-pass has been used to treat patients in whom plaque deposits of cholesterol, white blood cells, and smooth muscle cells have severely narrowed or blocked the artery.

In the procedure, developed in 1967, neurosurgeons separate a segment of an artery in the patient's scalp. Then they drill a small hole in the patient's skull, thread the scalp artery through the hole, and sew it into an opening cut in the middle cerebral artery. This by-pass is beyond the blocked section of the cerebral artery, so the rerouted scalp artery increases blood flow in the middle cerebral artery. The blood is eventually channeled into the capillaries of the brain.

Angiograms (arterial X rays) taken before and after surgery had shown that EC-IC by-passes improved blood flow to the brain. But no one knew whether patients who had undergone the by-pass operation had fewer strokes thereafter than patients who received only the standard stroke-prevention medication—four aspirins per day and high blood pressure medicine.

To find out whether the by-pass operation reduced the rate of strokes, the National Institutes of Health (NIH) in

Medicine

Continued

A "conveyer belt" operating room at the Moscow Eye Surgery Research Institute in the Soviet Union enables surgeons to perform about 100 operations per day. At each of five operating stations, a surgeon performs one step in an operation to correct near-sightedness by reshaping the patient's *cornea*—the bulge of clear tissue covering the eye's lens.

Bethesda, Md., funded a study to compare both forms of treatment at 70 medical centers in the United States, Canada, Japan, and several European countries. The study was coordinated by a team of physicians at the University of Western Ontario in London, Canada. The study included 1,377 people who had narrowed arteries. A computer randomly assigned 714 people to receive drug treatment and 663 people to undergo by-pass surgery in addition to drug treatment.

The operation was successful in nearly all the by-pass patients. Angiograms taken a month after surgery showed improved blood flow in 96 per cent of these surgical patients.

During the month after by-pass surgery or the beginning of drug treatment, 4 (0.6 per cent) of the surgical patients died from a stroke and 16 (2.5 per cent) had nonfatal strokes. But only 9 (1.3 per cent) of the patients receiving drugs had a stroke—none of which was fatal.

By the end of the study in 1985, 20 per cent of the surgical patients and 17

per cent of the medical patients had died. Among the surgical patients, 20 per cent had one stroke and 11 per cent had two or more strokes. Among the patients treated with drugs, 18 per cent had one stroke and 10 per cent had two or more.

At the end of the study, the physicians also evaluated the patients' ability to care for themselves, walk, communicate, understand written material, and swallow. The researchers found no substantial difference between the two groups in ability to function. The investigators concluded that, although the EC-IC by-pass operation improves blood flow to the brain, it does not reduce the risk of stroke or improve the patient's ability to function.

Coronary by-pass study. The results of another large surgical study, reported in January 1986, indicate that the standard procedure for performing coronary artery by-pass grafts is not necessarily the best approach.

Surgeons perform the coronary by-pass operation to relieve chest pain and to prevent heart attacks that can

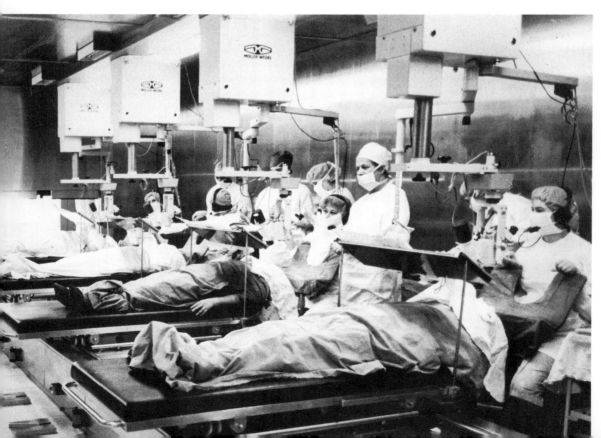

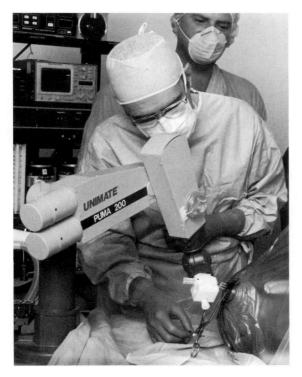

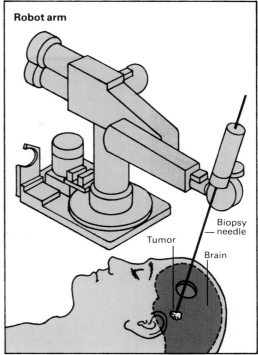

Robot arm

Tumor

Biopsy —needle

Brain

Medicine

Continued

Surgeons at Long Beach (Calif.) Memorial Medical Center use a robot arm during brain surgery, *above*. The computer controlled robot arm, *above right*, accurately positions a needle that surgeons then insert in the patient's brain to perform a *biopsy*, removing a tissue sample from a tumor for analysis. The robot can position the needle more accurately than even a skilled surgeon's hand, thus causing less damage to the patient's brain.

result when the blood supply to a person's heart is reduced by an accumulation of plaque in the coronary arteries—the vessels that bring blood to the heart muscle. The by-pass operation increases the blood flow to the heart by rerouting it around the blocked section of coronary artery.

In performing this operation, surgeons usually remove a section of vein—the saphenous vein—from the patient's leg. They sew one end of the vein segment to a major artery called the aorta and the other end to the coronary artery beyond the blockage, rerouting blood around the blocked region of the coronary artery.

Most surgeons have used the saphenous vein for the graft because it is relatively easy to remove from the leg and sew to the aorta and coronary artery. Like the coronary arteries, however, the saphenous vein graft often becomes blocked by plaque, sometimes only a few months after surgery.

For more than 15 years, some cardiovascular surgeons have used an artery in the chest for the by-pass graft instead of the saphenous vein. Because some studies have indicated that artery grafts do not become blocked with plaque as quickly as vein grafts do, physicians at the Cleveland Clinic in Cleveland, Ohio, designed a study to compare the results of the two types of by-pass grafts. The researchers, led by cardiovascular surgeon Floyd D. Loop, compared the survival rate for 3,625 patients who had received the vein graft with that for 2,306 patients who had received the artery graft. All of the patients in the study had a narrowing of at least 50 per cent inside a coronary artery.

The researchers recorded deaths among these patients for periods ranging from 8 to 15 years after surgery and used these data to calculate the average survival rates for both groups. Their calculations indicate that 86.6 per cent of patients who have a chest artery graft would be alive 10 years after the operation, compared with only 75.9 per cent of patients who had vein grafts. Moreover, the investigators calculated that 14 per cent of the patients with artery grafts would have heart attacks, compared with 18 per cent of those with vein grafts.

The researchers concluded that the artery graft is preferable to the saphenous vein graft for treating patients with severely blocked coronary arteries.

Breast cancer chemotherapy. An NIH panel of experts issued a report in December 1985 outlining their recommendations for the use of drugs in the treatment of breast cancer. The report was based on the results of using chemotherapy to treat patients suffering from breast cancer who had already undergone surgery or radiation therapy, or both.

The standard treatment for breast cancer includes surgery to remove the tumor and some of the lymph nodes in the patient's armpit. Pathologists then examine the lymph nodes and the tumor to determine whether there are cancer cells in the lymph nodes or molecules called *receptors* for the female hormones estrogen and progesterone on the tumor cells. If these hormone receptors are present, they will bring the hormones, which are necessary for the growth of these tumors, inside the cancer cells.

The NIH panel advised physicians to use the information provided by the pathologists in planning any further therapy for a patient. The panel also recommended that physicians consider whether or not the patient has reached *menopause* (the time in a woman's life when she stops menstruating). Based on these considerations, the panel suggested several therapeutic approaches.

For premenopausal women with breast cancer whose lymph nodes contain cancer cells, the panel advised treatment with one of several combinations of anticancer drugs, regardless of whether the tumor contained hormone receptors. Patients undergoing this form of therapy are given a series of two or three drugs, each of which attacks a different type of fast-growing tumor cell. Because these anticancer drugs also affect such rapidly growing normal cells as those in hair, blood, and the lining of the gastrointestinal tract, patients taking these drugs may lose hair, develop infections easily, and feel nauseated.

For most premenopausal women with breast cancer whose lymph nodes were free of cancer cells, the panel did not recommend drug therapy in addition to surgery and radiation. The experts did note, however, that physicians might want to consider using chemotherapy if such a patient had a very large tumor.

For postmenopausal women with both cancerous lymph nodes and tumors with hormone receptors, the panel recommended therapy with *tamoxifen*, a drug that removes estrogen from circulation instead of killing cells. Tamoxifen fights tumors by depriving any remaining tumor cells of estrogen—their most important requirement for growth. Because tamoxifen does not kill normal cells, it causes few side effects.

The NIH panel had no firm recommendation regarding drug treatment for postmenopausal women with cancerous lymph nodes and tumor cells without hormone receptors. Studies have shown that chemotherapy adds only slightly to the life span of such patients. For this reason, the panel members advised physicians to discuss the advantages and disadvantages of chemotherapy with such patients.

The panel recommended no chemotherapy for most postmenopausal women with breast cancer whose lymph nodes were free of cancer cells.

In their report, the panelists cautioned that their recommendations were not meant to imply that there is an ideal form of therapy for any particular group of patients suffering from breast cancer. They emphasized that much more study is needed and that their recommendations probably will be revised when results from other studies become available in a few years.

The panelists also noted that most women being treated for breast cancer are eligible to join studies in which their progress will be compared with that of other patients who have similar tumors but are receiving different types of therapy. They urged all such women to ask their physicians about the possibility of taking part in these studies.　　　　[Beverly Merz]

In WORLD BOOK, see CANCER; HEART; MEDICINE; STROKE.

An implantable electronic defibrillator that automatically senses and corrects potentially fatal rapid heart rhythms was approved by the U.S. Food and Drug Administration in October 1985. The unit is implanted beneath the patient's skin, and wires leading to the heart sense when a dangerously rapid heart rate develops. The device then automatically delivers a shock to correct the rhythm.

Meteorology

Research that may shed light on what causes the violent force of *downslope winds* that descend from mountains to low-lying areas was reported in March 1986 by meteorologists Dale R. Durran of the University of Utah in Salt Lake City and Joseph B. Klemp of the National Center for Atmospheric Research in Boulder, Colo. In Colorado, the often-destructive winds that blow down the slopes of the Rocky Mountains in winter and spring are called *chinooks.* Similar powerful downslope winds from the Alps in Europe are called *foehns,* while on the mountainous Adriatic coast of Yugoslavia they are called *boras.*

Scientists have long wondered why these downslope winds become so violent. They can reach speeds as high as 200 kilometers (120 miles) per hour, tearing roofs from houses and overturning mobile homes.

Durran and Klemp used a computer to simulate the behavior of these winds. They found that the winds gather speed going up a mountain due to changes in air pressure. At the base of the mountain, where the wind begins, the air pressure is high. As the air "parcel" carried by the wind rises, it encounters lower air pressure the higher it goes. The change from high to low pressure gives energy to the wind, and it picks up speed. This phenomenon is known as *mechanical acceleration,* and the two researchers compared it to the way water speeds up as it flows over a rock.

The researchers noted that once this wind reaches the crest of the mountain, it has become colder than the surrounding air. Since cold air is heavier and denser than warm air, this cold heavy air begins to spill down the other side of the mountain and picks up even more speed. This *downslope acceleration* is similar to what happens to a car as it picks up speed coasting down a hill. Knowing why and how these downslope winds gather such force may someday enable meteorologists to predict and give warning of especially severe downslope winds.

"Greenhouse" gases. A research team led by atmospheric scientist Joel

In a special "dust" chamber, *right,* meteorologists at the University of Wisconsin in Madison studied how effective snowflakes are at removing pollutants from air. The researchers allowed snow to fall through particles injected into the chamber and reported in late 1985 that snowflakes with many branches, such as the 12-sided snowflake, *far right above,* and the more common six-sided snowflake, *far right below,* were both very efficient pollutant removers.

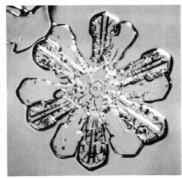

Meteorology

S. Levine of the National Aeronautics and Space Administration's (NASA) Langley Research Center in Hampton, Va., reported in November 1985 that they were able to reconstruct the concentration of methane and carbon monoxide gases that existed in the atmosphere in 1950.

The research team based its findings on an analysis of infrared radiation from the sun obtained by solar astronomers at the Jungfraujoch International Scientific Station in the Swiss Alps in 1950. The astronomers had found that some of the infrared radiation was absorbed by methane, carbon monoxide, and other gases in Earth's atmosphere.

By analyzing the portion and amount of infrared light absorbed, the researchers were able to calculate the amount of methane and carbon monoxide gas in the atmosphere. Since 1977, when a monitoring instrument known as a gas chromatograph was developed, atmospheric scientists have been able to make direct measurements of these gases.

The NASA studies show that the concentrations of these two gases in the atmosphere have been increasing at their present rates since at least 1950, and not just since 1977.

The concentration of atmospheric methane increased by 40 per cent between 1950 and 1985 and that of atmospheric carbon monoxide by as much as 70 per cent during the same period. By contrast, carbon dioxide has increased only 15 per cent over the past 100 years. The NASA findings are significant because they indicate that methane and carbon monoxide have been increasing over a longer period of time than was previously thought and at a faster rate than that of carbon dioxide.

The three gases—carbon dioxide, carbon monoxide, and methane—are known as "greenhouse" gases because they trap heat radiated up from Earth's surface, thus warming the atmosphere. In this sense, they act much like the windows in a greenhouse. Scientists are concerned about the possible adverse effect of the warming of Earth's climate resulting from a long-term build-up of such gases.

To study how the increasing concentrations of carbon monoxide and methane would affect other gases in the atmosphere, Levine developed a mathematical computer model that included interactions among 80 different gas compounds. His calculations showed that since 1950 increased methane and carbon monoxide have caused a 25 per cent decrease in the levels of the *hydroxyl radical.*

The hydroxyl radical cleans many pollutants from the lower atmosphere, including ozone, which is related to smog problems in urban areas. Consequently, Levine's findings could have important implications for a variety of environmental problems such as smog and acid rain.

El Niño prediction. The effects of an El Niño would be noticeable off the South American coast in May 1986, according to a March 1986 prediction. But the prediction—issued by oceanographers Mark A. Cane and Stephen E. Zebiak of Columbia University's Lamont-Doherty Geological Observatory in Palisades, N.Y.—failed to come true. The failure of the forecast, however, did not cause the researchers to abandon their basic approach, but to refine their method, which holds promise for future predictions.

El Niño (Spanish for *the child*) is unusually warm Pacific Ocean water that appears in place of the relatively cold water normally found off the coast of Peru. El Niño occurs every two to seven years, usually near Christmas, and brings abnormal levels of rainfall to South America. The warm water also sets off changes in wind and weather patterns across the tropical Pacific and in areas north and south of the equator.

Using a mathematical computer model that included the effect of surface winds on the upper layer of the tropical ocean, Cane and Zebiak forecast the occurrence of the next El Niño to begin in May 1986. By mid-June, however, the expected warming near Peru had not occurred, and a new El Niño was no longer expected.

Cane and Zebiak tested their model by using data about past weather conditions. They were able to "forecast" in retrospect past El Niños over the last 15 years by examining the conditions preceding the development of the

Meteorology

Continued

warm water. Each time the model "predicted" an El Niño, one had actually occurred.

The two meteorologists then began using the model to make real predictions. Every monthly forecast made with Cane and Zebiak's model after the summer of 1985 indicated that an El Niño would occur in the spring of 1986. This failed forecast will spark new research into El Niño models as meteorologists seek a breakthrough in long-range forecasting.

Acid rain received new attention in March 1986 in a report released by a committee of the National Research Council (NRC), part of the National Academy of Sciences. *Acid rain* is precipitation that has a high concentration of sulfuric and nitric acids. It has had adverse effects on lakes and streams, killing fish and plant life. In a comprehensive three-year study, the NRC committee found that a definite cause-and-effect relationship exists between industrial sulfur emissions produced by the burning of fossil fuels and the occurrence of acid rain. Committee

Chairman James H. Gibson, an ecologist at Colorado State University in Fort Collins, stressed, however, that the extent of damage to individual lakes varied widely due to differences in local conditions.

The NRC study reviewed data on trends in pollutant emission, precipitation chemistry, and surface water chemistry in streams and lakes of the Eastern United States and southeastern Canada. The researchers found that the pattern of environmental damage closely resembled the pattern of pollutant emission. For example, the Northeastern United States has had the highest levels of sulfur dioxide emissions from industrial plants and the highest proportion of acid rain and acidified lakes over the last 10 years. And in the Southeastern United States, increased amounts of acid rain and surface water acidity have also accompanied increases in local industrial emissions. [W. Lawrence Gates]

In the Special Reports section, see NATURE'S FIREWORKS. In WORLD BOOK, see METEOROLOGY; WEATHER.

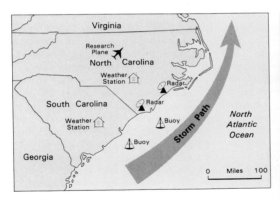

The GALE Project

During the winter of 1985-1986, meteorologists conducted the GALE project on the North and South Carolina coasts, *above,* in an effort to understand why storms known as *East Coast cyclones* develop in this region. The researchers used airplanes, weather balloons, ocean buoys, and sophisticated radar to look for ways of predicting weather conditions that can lead to sudden and crippling ice and snowstorms, *right.*

Molecular Biology

A major advance in the understanding of human color vision was reported by molecular biologists at Stanford University in California in April 1986. The scientists discovered the genes that *code for* (carry the genetic instructions for making) color-vision proteins in the eye. The pigmentlike proteins are responsible for absorbing each of the three primary colors of light—red, green, and blue. The different light-absorbing characteristics of the proteins enable the brain, which receives visual information from the eyes, to see in full color.

The structures of the proteins, found in the *retina* (light-sensitive tissue at the back of the eye), are nearly identical to one another. The proteins also closely resemble the structure of *rhodopsin*, the only protein associated with vision whose structure had been previously known. Rhodopsin is responsible for our ability to detect shades of gray in dim light but does not contribute to color vision.

Scientists have long been fascinated by color vision and have proposed many theories to explain how it might work. Modern thinking on the subject dates back to the late 1600's when British scientist Isaac Newton discovered that white light contains all the colors of the rainbow.

Building on Newton's work, two physicists of the 1800's—Thomas Young in England and Hermann von Helmholtz in Germany—advanced a theory of color vision that has now received final confirmation from the Stanford researchers. The Young-Helmholtz theory held that our ability to perceive the rich variety of colors that we see could be accounted for by three types of "fibers" in the eye that are sensitive to red, green, and blue light. The perception of other colors arises, according to their theory, from variations in the blending of the three primary colors.

Finding molecular evidence for the Young-Helmholtz theory has been exceptionally difficult because only a small fraction of the cells in the retina contribute to color vision. Most of the retina's light-receiving cells are called rod cells and are incapable of distinguishing colors because they contain only rhodopsin. Color vision is made possible by *cone cells*, which contain the color pigments.

Color-vision genes. The Stanford researchers theorized that the molecules responsible for color vision were similar to rhodopsin. To test their theory, they searched through human deoxyribonucleic acid (DNA) for genes that might code for previously unknown rhodopsinlike proteins. The scientists used a sophisticated technique called *hybridization*, which enabled them to "fish out" any genes that were similar to the rhodopsin gene. One advantage of looking for the genes in DNA instead of searching for the proteins themselves was that the genes are present in all the cells of the body. The visual pigments, on the other hand, can be extracted only from cone cells.

The Stanford researchers found three different genes that were similar to the rhodopsin gene. They determined the exact molecular makeup of these genes and confirmed that each coded for the production of a rhodopsinlike protein.

To determine whether the newly discovered proteins could be the red-, blue-, and green-light receptors predicted by the Young-Helmholtz theory, the scientists tested DNA taken from 25 color-blind men. They wanted to learn whether particular forms of color blindness are associated with changes in any of the three genes.

The researchers found that nearly everyone whose color blindness was marked by an inability to see the color red had an altered structure in one of the genes. Persons who were unable to see green had an altered structure in another of the genes.

Defects in the color-pigment genes are inherited. The color blindness that has run for generations in some families originated with a genetic change in the *germ cells* (egg cells or sperm) of one or more ancestors. The investigators concluded that such changes happen during the division of germ cells, when *chromosomes* (structures that carry the genes) sometimes exchange pieces of DNA.

The scientists discovered that the genes for the red and green visual pigments are located next to each other on the X chromosome, one of the two chromosomes that determine an indi-

The world's smallest thermometer, *top,* is far smaller than a human hair, *above* (both shown greatly magnified). The thermometer measures temperature changes in single cells. It can detect temperature changes as tiny as one ten-millionth of 1 Celsius degree in one ten-thousandth of a second. It was developed at the State University of New York at Buffalo.

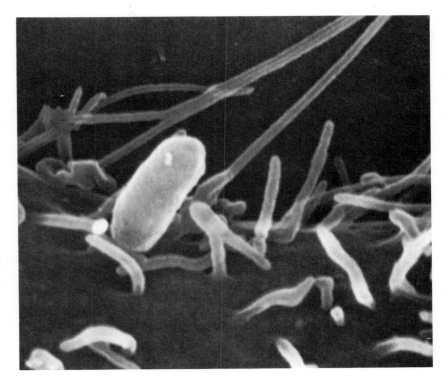

An *Escherichia coli* bacterium—the large, oblong structure—invades a human lung cell. Ordinarily, *E. coli* cannot enter human cells, but this bacterium has been given an extra gene, taken from a disease-causing bacterium. With its new gene, the *E. coli* produces a protein that enables it to invade cells just as the disease-causing bacterium does. The identification of this "invasion gene" may help scientists learn more about how bacteria cause disease.

Molecular Biology

Continued

vidual's sex. The location of the genes on the X chromosome explains why red and green color blindness is much more common among males than among females. Because males have just one copy of the X chromosome, a fault in one of the two pigment genes will result in color blindness. Females have two X chromosomes, so a properly constructed color gene on one of the chromosomes will "overrule" a faulty gene on the other chromosome.

Because inherited defects in the ability to see the color blue are extremely rare, the reseachers have not yet been able to determine whether this form of color blindness is associated with altered structures in the third type of rhodopsinlike gene.

Blood vessel protein. The discovery of a protein secreted by malignant tumors that causes surrounding tissues to develop new blood vessels was reported in September 1985 by a group of researchers at the Harvard Medical School and Brigham and Women's Hospital, both in Boston. The scientists called the protein *angiogenin*, from

the Greek words for *vessel* and *produce*. This finding may lead toward the development of new drugs to treat cancer and heart disease.

Tumors are unable to grow and spread without the development of new blood vessels, which bring oxygen and nutrients to the tumor cells and remove wastes from them. Scientists have long known that tumor cells must secrete a substance that stimulates the growth of blood vessels in nearby tissues, but they were unable to find it.

Isolating angiogenin required finding solutions to a series of technical problems that seemed insurmountable just a few years ago. To begin with, the protein is secreted from tumor cells in tiny quantities, and its detection requires complex biological experiments. In addition, tumor cells are difficult to grow in the laboratory.

The Harvard researchers purified angiogenin from a *culture medium* (a liquid bath of nutrients) in which human tumor cells had been grown for several days. Because of the extremely small amounts of angiogenin secreted

Molecular Biology

Continued

into the culture medium, it was necessary to grow the cell culture on a huge scale. The scientists used industrial techniques developed at the Monsanto Company in St. Louis, Mo.

Using sophisticated purification techniques, the Boston researchers finally obtained several millionths of a gram of pure angiogenin and succeeded in determining its exact chemical structure. Like all proteins, angiogenin is a chainlike molecule made up of amino acids. The scientists determined that angiogenin contains a sequence of 123 amino acids, and they worked out the exact amino acid sequence throughout the chain.

By using techniques similar to those employed by the Stanford researchers in their color-vision research, the Boston scientists located the gene that codes for angiogenin, and they reproduced the gene in the laboratory. Genetic-engineering techniques will enable the researchers to produce larger quantities of angiogenin.

Molecular biologists hope that further research on angiogenin will lead to new treatments for many kinds of cancer. Because tumors evidently need angiogenin to establish a blood supply, interfering with the action of this vital protein might starve a tumor and cause it to wither. Angiogenin might also be of benefit to victims of heart disease by causing new blood vessels to grow in the heart.

The development of anticancer drugs targeted on blocking angiogenin is sure to be an area of intense research in coming years. Up to now, most useful drugs have resulted from trial-and-error testing. Biologists hope, however, that as we learn what molecules are involved in the basic processes of human cells, it will be possible to design new drugs that act against those molecules to block precise steps in the development of diseases. A compound that defeats the cancer-promoting effects of angiogenin would be a major triumph of this new approach to pharmacology.   [Maynard V. Olson]

In WORLD BOOK, see BIOCHEMISTRY; CELL; COLOR BLINDNESS; MOLECULAR BIOLOGY.

Neuroscience

Neuroscientists at the Marine Biology Laboratory in Woods Hole, Mass., and the National Institutes of Health in Bethesda, Md., reported in October 1985 and January 1986 that they had discovered a protein in *neurons* (nerve cells) that is responsible for the movement of other proteins through the cell fibers. Researchers had known for some years that proteins produced in the body of a neuron move along the *axon*—the cell's fiber through which nerve impulses are transmitted—packaged in tiny membrane-enclosed *vesicles*, or packets. The study revealed the mechanism that causes vesicles to move.

The investigators examined the neurons of squids, octupuslike sea animals. Squid neurons are easy to study because they have axons that are from 100 to 1,000 times larger than the axons of most *vertebrates* (animals with backbones).

A newly developed technique called video microscopy enabled the scientists to tape moving images of the squid axons. The videotaped pictures showed that the vesicles moved along tiny filaments, called *microtubules*, within the axon. Biochemical analysis showed that the vesicles traveled only in the presence of a particular protein, which the researchers called *kinesin*. The microtubules and the kinesin molecules thus work together as a kind of "molecular motor" to move the vesicles.

Kinesin was later found in other kinds of cells, where it appears to have the same function as in nerve cells.

Handedness and the brain. Psychologist Sandra F. Witelson of McMaster University in Hamilton, Canada, reported in August 1985 that there is a physical difference between the brains of left-handed people and those of right-handed people. Witelson spent several years studying the *corpus callosum*, a bundle of nerve fibers connecting the right and left hemispheres, or halves, of the brain. She reported that people who are left-handed or *ambidextrous* (using both hands equally well) have a corpus callosum that is larger than that of right-handers.

Witelson did her research with the

Neuroscience

cooperation of seriously ill cancer patients who agreed to donate their brains for study after their death. During the course of the study, 42 patients died, and autopsies revealed that the left-handed and ambidextrous patients had a corpus callosum about 11 per cent larger than the corpus callosum of the right-handers.

Witelson speculated that the division of functions in the brain may account for why left-handed and ambidextrous people have a larger corpus callosum. Language, for example, is centered primarily in the brain's left hemisphere, while many spatial tasks are handled mainly by the right hemisphere. But Witelson speculated that left-handed and ambidextrous people may have a more even distribution of functions in their brains, involving more communication between the hemispheres. That, she said, would require a larger corpus callosum. See PSYCHOLOGY.

Is alcoholism inherited? The sons of alcoholic men show the same kind of brain activity that their fathers do, re-

searchers in New York reported in September 1985. The discovery—made by neurophysiologists Henri Begleiter and Bernice Porjesz and their colleagues at the State University of New York Health Science Center in New York City—provided further evidence that some people have an inherited tendency to become alcoholics.

Alcoholics, including those who no longer drink, produce a particular pattern of brain waves that researchers had thought was a result of chronic alcoholism. But the New York investigators found the same kind of pattern in the young sons of alcoholics. Because the boys had never used alcohol, the finding demonstrated that the brain-wave pattern precedes alcoholism rather than being caused by it.

The scientists studied 25 boys between the ages of 7 and 13 whose fathers had been diagnosed as alcoholics. The boys were given tests in which they were asked to identify various pictures while their brain waves were recorded through electrodes pasted to their heads. The boys produced brain-

The brain of an ambidextrous person, bottom, has a larger corpus callosum (blue) than the brain of a right-handed person, top. The corpus callosum connects the two halves of the brain and enables them to communicate with each other. A study reported in August 1985 revealed that the corpus callosum is consistently larger in left-handed and ambidextrous people than in right-handers.

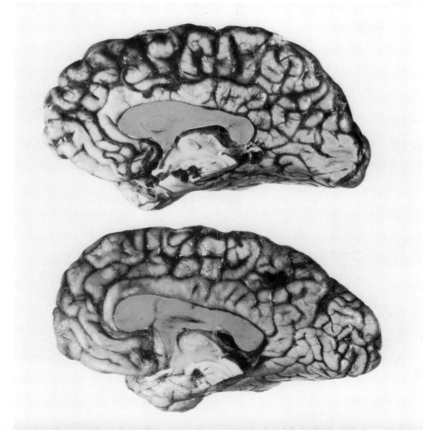

wave patterns similar to those produced by alcoholics. The researchers also tested 25 boys whose fathers were not alcoholics. Those boys' brain patterns were significantly different from the patterns of the alcoholics' sons. Scientists must now learn what part genes play in the production of the brain activity characteristic of alcoholism and how that brain activity may be involved with this disease.

New stroke therapy. Neuroscientists at the University of Massachusetts Medical Center in Worcester reported in October 1985 that their experiments with rabbits may point the way to a new treatment for stroke. Stroke is the third leading cause of death in the United States, after heart disease and cancer. In the most common form of stroke, a clot forms in an artery of the neck or the brain and obstructs blood flow. The obstruction damages the part of the brain served by that blood vessel and often results in death.

Physicians have tried to treat many stroke victims by giving them *anticoagulants*—medicines that hinder the clotting of blood. Most of these treatments, however, have been unsuccessful because anticoagulants often cause heavy bleeding or fail to dissolve the clot that caused the stroke.

The University of Massachusetts neuroscientists tested a new drug called tissue plasminogen activator (t-PA), which has proved effective in dissolving clots in the coronary arteries of heart attack victims. To test t-PA on stroke, the scientists injected small blood clots into the brain circulation system of 23 rabbits. One minute later, the researchers fed t-PA into the veins of 11 of the rabbits for 30 minutes.

Ten of the 11 rabbits acted normally a day later. Among the remaining 12 rabbits who were injected with the clots but not given t-PA, 7 either died or suffered severe brain damage. These results suggest that t-PA may be useful in preventing brain damage in human stroke patients if it is given quickly after the first symptoms of stroke appear. [George Adelman]

In WORLD BOOK, see BRAIN; NERVOUS SYSTEM; STROKE.

Nobel Prizes

Nobel Prizes in chemistry, physics, and physiology or medicine in 1985 went to five scientists—four from the United States and one from West Germany. The awards, each valued at $225,000, were presented in Sweden in December 1985.

Chemistry. The Nobel Prize for chemistry was shared by Herbert A. Hauptman, research director and vice president of the Medical Foundation of Buffalo, N.Y., and Jerome Karle, a chief scientist at the United States Naval Laboratory in Washington, D.C. The two men, experts in X-ray crystallography, were recognized for their development of a mathematical method of determining the three-dimensional structure of complex biological molecules.

Hauptman and Karle, who were classmates at City College in New York City in the 1930's, developed their method at the Naval Research Laboratory in the 1950's. With the advent of computers, their formula enabled scientists to analyze a molecule in crystal form in days rather than years.

As a result, the structure of thousands of biological molecules have been analyzed, including hormones, antibiotics, vitamins, and brain chemicals called enkephalins, which are the body's natural painkillers.

Hauptman was born in New York City in 1917. He received his Ph.D. degree from the University of Maryland in 1955. He worked at the Naval Research Laboratory with Karle, then became a professor of biophysics in 1970 at the State University of New York in Buffalo. In 1972, he became research director and vice president of the Medical Foundation.

Karle was born in New York City in 1918. He received his Ph.D. degree in 1943 from the University of Michigan. He joined the Naval Research Laboratory soon after graduation and now works on the structure of matter.

Physics. The Nobel Prize for physics went to Klaus von Klitzing of the Max Planck Institute for Solid State Research in Stuttgart, West Germany. Von Klitzing was cited for his 1980 discovery of the *quantized Hall effect*, in

Nobel Prizes

Continued

Molecular geneticists Michael S. Brown, left, and Joseph L. Goldstein, co-winners of the Nobel Prize for physiology or medicine, congratulate each other. The two scientists were cited in 1985 for their work on blood cholesterol.

which electrical voltage changes in extremely precise jumps, rather than gradually. He used the theory of quantum mechanics to measure with great accuracy how voltage changes when a magnetic field is applied perpendicularly to the flow of an electric current. His work was based on research done by physicist Edwin H. Hall in 1879.

Von Klitzing's work has been important in studying the properties of materials used in electronic components. It has enabled physicists to determine with greater accuracy the *fine structure constant*, a ratio involving speed of an electron to the speed of light.

Von Klitzing was born in Schroda (now in Poland) in 1943, and received his Ph.D. degree at the University of Würzburg in West Germany in 1972. He became director of the Max Planck Institute in Stuttgart in 1985. In the People in Science section, see THE MAX PLANCK SOCIETY AT 75.

Physiology or medicine. The Nobel Prize for physiology or medicine was shared by molecular geneticists Michael S. Brown and Joseph L. Gold-stein of the University of Texas Health Science Center in Dallas.

In 1973, Brown and Goldstein discovered that human cells have on their surface molecules called receptors for a fatty substance called low-density lipoprotein (LDL), which transports cholesterol. If a person does not have any—or enough—LDL receptors to bring these molecules into the cells, blood cholesterol rises to high levels.

Brown was born in New York City in 1941 and received his M.D. degree at the University of Pennsylvania Medical School in Philadelphia. In 1968, he became a clinical associate at the National Institutes of Health in Bethesda, Md. In 1971, he became a research fellow at Southwestern Medical School of the University of Texas.

Goldstein was born in Sumter, N.C., in 1940. He received his M.D. degree from Southwestern Medical School in 1966, did research at the National Heart Institute and the University of Washington, then returned to Dallas in 1972.   [Irene B. Keller]

In WORLD BOOK, see NOBEL PRIZES.

Nutrition

A study of calcium supplements published in mid-1985 has shown that one form of calcium may be more effective than another in preventing osteoporosis—a disease that causes bones to become brittle and fracture easily. Osteoporosis affects large numbers of women who are past *menopause* (the time in a woman's life when she stops menstruating). Adequate calcium intake is an essential factor in maintaining the mineral content of bone and decreasing a person's risk of developing this disorder. But the diet of the average American does not include adequate amounts of calcium, and the absorption of calcium by the body is often depressed in postmenopausal women. Several calcium supplements are available, but there is little scientific evidence about how much of the calcium they contain actually becomes available for the body's use.

In May 1985, Michael J. Nicar and Charles Y. C. Pak of Southwestern Medical School of the University of Texas Health Science Center in Dallas reported the results of a study in which they compared the amount of calcium available to the body from calcium citrate with that from calcium carbonate. Fourteen normal, healthy adults participated in each of three phases of the study. In each phase, they took either calcium carbonate, calcium citrate, or water. Then the amount of calcium absorbed was calculated from the concentration of calcium in their urine. The concentration of calcium was 20 to 66 per cent higher following a dose of calcium citrate than it was following a dose of calcium carbonate.

This greater absorbability of calcium from calcium citrate may be due to its greater capacity to dissolve. This property is important for people who need extra calcium but are likely to develop kidney stones that form due to high concentrations of undissolved calcium. Because calcium citrate dissolves so readily, people taking this form of calcium rather than calcium carbonate may reduce the risk of kidney stone formation.

Fluoridation and bone strength. Fluoridation of public water supplies may help prevent osteoporosis, according to a study published in August 1985. Researchers at the National Board of Health of Finland and at Kivelä Hospital in Helsinki, Finland, reported on bone fragility as indicated by the number of thighbone fractures in people aged 50 and older in two Finnish towns. The town of Kuopio has fluoridated its water supply since 1959, but the town of Jyväskylä has not and has only tiny amounts of natural fluoride in its drinking water. The incidence of fractures was greater in Jyväskylä than in Kuopio. The number of thighbone fractures per 1,000 men in five years was 7.0 in Jyväskylä and 2.5 in Kuopio. The number of such fractures per 1,000 women in five years was 9.0 in Jyväskylä and 6.0 in Kuopio. These results suggest that the significantly lower number of fractures among the population in Kuopio was associated with the fluoridation of the town's water supply.

Obesity and health. Obesity has numerous causes, and there are probably several types of obesity, according to participants in a conference held at the National Institutes of Health (NIH) in Bethesda, Md., to review recent studies and assess the impact of obesity on health. The conference findings were published in December 1985.

In the past, obesity was considered to be primarily the result of consuming too many calories. Recent studies of obesity, however, suggest that the condition is much more complex than was previously thought.

A recent report from researchers studying a large population over a long period of time in Framingham, Mass., has shown that increasing levels of obesity are associated with increasing risk of coronary artery disease. Another study has shown that the incidence of *hypertension* (high blood pressure) is 2.9 times higher among overweight people than among people who are not overweight, and among obese adults between 20 and 44 years of age, it is 5.6 times higher. The occurrence of abnormally high concentrations of cholesterol in the blood is 2.1 times greater in young overweight adults than in those who are not overweight. In addition to these findings, researchers have noted that the incidence of *insulin-independent* or *adult-type* diabetes mellitus—the most com-

Preserving Food with Radiation

Decisions made by the United States Food and Drug Administration (FDA) during 1985 and 1986 have cleared the way for increased use of irradiation as a means of preserving food. Since the 1960's, the FDA has allowed the use of irradiation on wheat and wheat flour to control insects and on potatoes to prevent sprouting. And in 1983, the agency approved the irradiation of spices to reduce microorganisms. In 1985, the FDA decided to permit irradiation of pork to kill *Trichinella spiralis* (the organism that causes trichinosis), and in April 1986, the agency approved irradiation of fruits and vegetables to control insects. The FDA is currently considering the use of irradiation on chicken and seafood.

Irradiation involves exposing food to *ionizing radiation*—high-energy gamma rays, X rays, or electrons. Ionizing radiation damages *genes*—structures that guide the biochemical processes of living cells. Genetic damage caused by exposure to radiation can kill molds, bacteria, and other organisms that cause food spoilage or make such organisms unable to reproduce. At low doses, however, radiation does not greatly damage the molecular structure of the food itself. Irradiation does cause biochemical changes that slow the ripening of fruit. It also affects cell division, keeping onions, garlic, and potatoes from sprouting.

The most common type of radiation used to treat food is gamma rays. The FDA approved treating foods with gamma rays in doses of up to 100 kilorads and spices with up to 3,000 kilorads. (Radiation is measured in units called rads; one kilorad equals 1,000 rads.)

Irradiation was first used to preserve food in France in 1930. Research in the United States during the 1940's indicated that military rations could be preserved by exposing them to ionizing radiation. Since the 1950's, many government agencies, universities, and food industry groups have conducted food irradiation research programs. Irradiation is currently used to preserve food in about 30 nations.

Approval of food irradiation for use in the United States has been slow, due in part to concerns about its safety. In 1958, Congress classified irradiation as a food additive, thus requiring extensive testing for toxic effects before the FDA could approve the use of irradiation on a particular food.

A large collection of scientific evidence suggests that properly applied doses of irradiation are no more harmful than more conventional food-processing or cooking techniques. In more than 30 years of animal feeding studies, there has been no confirmed evidence of any harmful effects of food that has been treated with the radiation levels needed to control insect pests and bacteria.

In November 1980, the Joint Expert Committee on the Wholesomeness of Irradiated Food, sponsored by three United Nations agencies—the Food and Agricultural Organization, the International Atomic Energy Agency, and the World Health Organization—concluded that irradiation of any food with average doses of up to 1,000 kilorads presents no toxic hazard to people who eat it. The use of irradiation to preserve food has also been endorsed by the American Medical Association and a number of food industry organizations.

In December 1985, former Secretary of Health and Human Services Margaret M. Heckler said that, "Unlike chemical pesticides, some of which are now under attack, irradiation leaves no residue in food. It does not make food radioactive, nor does it pose any radioactive danger to the consumer."

Despite such assurances, food irradiation has its critics. Opponents argue that not enough is known about the chemical changes that irradiation causes in food. They also point to the risk involved in having to transport radioactive materials needed for irradiation.

The final verdict on food irradiation, however, will be made in the meat and produce aisles of United States supermarkets when consumers find food items labeled "Treated with radiation." [Joseph A. Liuzzo]

NON - IRRADIATED -   IRRADIATED - (0.2 M RAD)

Irradiated strawberries, right, are free of mold, unlike untreated berries, left, after both were stored for 15 days at 38°F. (4°C).

Drawing by W. Miller; © 1985 The New Yorker Magazine, Inc.

"That's bass with broccoli and mushrooms. Stop calling it animal, vegetable, and fungus."

Nutrition

Continued

mon type of diabetes—is 2.9 times higher among overweight people than among those who are not overweight.

An American Cancer Society study showed a higher death rate among obese men from cancer of the colon, rectum, and prostate than among men who were not obese. Obese women had a higher rate of mortality from cancer of the gall bladder, breast, bile ducts, uterus, and ovaries than women who were not obese. Longevity studies have shown that the more obese people are, the higher their mortality rate will be. Participants at the NIH conference emphasized the importance of preventing obesity in order to lessen the risk of other diseases.

Obesity and heredity. In January 1986, psychiatrist Albert J. Stunkard of the University of Pennsylvania in Philadelphia and his colleagues reported the results of a study that assessed the relative importance of hereditary factors and childhood family environment in the development of obesity. They studied 540 Danish adults who had been adopted as chil-

dren as well as their natural and adoptive parents. The adoptees were divided into four weight classifications—thin, middle-range weight, overweight, and obese. The investigators also obtained information about the height and weight of both the natural and adoptive parents of the adoptees.

This study revealed that the adoptees closely matched the natural parents across the entire weight range from thin to obese. But there was no relationship between the adoptees' weight classification and the degree of obesity of the adoptive parents. These findings suggest that genetic factors play an important role in determining amounts of body fat. The investigators pointed out, however, that a genetic tendency to obesity does not necessarily mean that a person is destined to be obese. New knowledge about the causes of obesity provided by this study will help physicians to identify people at risk for developing obesity and to plan programs to prevent this condition.   [Eleanor A. Young]

In WORLD BOOK, see NUTRITION.

Oceanography

The British luxury liner, *Titanic,* unseen since it sank in 1912, was discovered on Sept. 1, 1985, by a team of United States and French scientists using a remote-controlled submarine known as *Argo.* See Close-Up.

Sea-floor research. Scientists aboard the 143-meter (469-foot) research drill ship *JOIDES Resolution* found new evidence during the summer of 1985 of the movement of Earth's crust in the Arctic regions of the Atlantic Ocean. The scientists were led by oceanographers Shiri Srivastava of the Bedford Institute of Oceanography in Dartmouth, Canada, and Mike Arthur of the University of Rhode Island in Kingston.

Their work confirmed a geological theory that Greenland, Canada, and Western Europe once formed a single land mass. Then, about 85 million years ago, Greenland and Europe began to break away from the North American continent to form the Labrador Sea. A theory known as *plate tectonics* maintains that Earth's crust—the outer covering of rock that includes the ocean floor—consists of about 20 huge plates, or segments, that drift on a subsurface layer of molten rock. The movement of these plates over millions of years has formed the continents we know today.

The oceanographers based their conclusions on an analysis of sediment and rocks contained in core samples drilled out of three locations in the floor of the Labrador Sea.

By comparing cores from different depths—and therefore, from different periods in geological history—the researchers determined that as these great land masses continued to pull apart, Greenland began to break away from Baffin Island about 55 million years ago. This created a narrow ocean basin, now known as Baffin Bay, by about 36 million years ago, when Greenland stopped moving away from North America.

The formation of Baffin Bay and the Labrador Sea, enabling water to flow between the Arctic and Atlantic oceans, triggered dramatic climate changes in this region. By studying

A diver explores one of the many underwater caves in the Caribbean Sea, *below left,* where previously unknown species have existed unchanged for millions of years. An entirely new class of crustaceans that live in these caves was described in autumn 1985. Their scientific name, *Remipedia,* comes from Greek words meaning *paddle-foot,* and refers to the many paddle-like legs on the animal's trunk, *below right.*

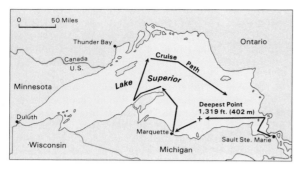

Exploring Lake Superior

Scientists at Michigan State University in East Lansing used the *Johnson Sea-Link II, right,* a two-person research submarine, to explore the bottom of Lake Superior, *above,* in three stages during the summer of 1985. During this first successful exploration of the bottom of a large freshwater lake, scientists discovered that freshwater fish can exist at depths of 402 meters (1,319 feet) and found that sediments on the lake bottom contain microorganisms, providing new insights into the lake's ecology.

Oceanography

Continued

fossil remains in these cores, the researchers concluded that about 15 million years ago the polar regions of the Atlantic Ocean were much warmer than they are now.

Origin of the Tyrrhenian Sea. The *Resolution* moved its operations to the Mediterranean Sea in January 1986. It drilled 11 holes in the floor of the Tyrrhenian Sea, an arm of the Mediterranean Sea that lies between Italy and the islands of Sardinia, Sicily, and Corsica. The ship took core samples of the sea floor in water depths between 2,000 and 3,000 meters (6,600 and 9,800 feet).

Analysis of the cores revealed the origin of the Tyrrhenian Sea. The cores showed that the land in the south of Italy was originally linked to a larger land mass that included present-day Corsica, Sardinia, and Sicily. About 9 million years ago, the land in the south of Italy began to break away from the larger land mass, and a small shallow bay formed between them. After several million years, the shallow bay became a deep basin.

Some 5.5 million years ago, the narrow passage that linked the Mediterranean Sea to the Atlantic Ocean closed, and the Mediterranean dried up. This caused a dry desert climate in the region. After about 500,000 years, the passage to the Atlantic reopened, and ocean waters refilled the Mediterranean and the deep basin, which became the Tyrrhenian Sea.

Life at deep-sea vents. Research showing how a diverse community of marine organisms that live near deep-ocean, hot-water vents obtain food energy from chemical compounds was reported in March 1986 by marine biologists at the University of California at Santa Barbara. In 1977, oceanographers first discovered these communities surrounding openings on the deep-sea floor, where seawater heated in Earth's crust spews out. Scientists had thought that sunlight was required to sustain life, but sunlight does not reach the deep-sea vents. Because *photosynthesis,* the process by which plants use energy from sunlight for growth, is not possible around the

Finding the *Titanic*

At about 1 A.M. on Sept. 1, 1985, there was a knock on the door of my cabin on the Woods Hole Oceanographic Institution's research vessel *Knorr*, which was exploring the waters about 800 kilometers (500 miles) south of Newfoundland, Canada. The ship's cook stuck his head in the doorway and said, "The guys in the van [control room] think you should come down."

I rushed down to the van and looked at the video monitor, which was displaying images of the ocean floor some 3,700 meters (12,500 feet) below us. On the screen was a picture of an enormous ship's boiler with a distinctive pattern of rivets. The picture was being returned by video cameras aboard the *Argo*, an unmanned robot submarine controlled by a cable connected to the *Knorr*.

"That's it!" I exclaimed. We had done it. We had found the *Titanic*, a supposedly unsinkable British luxury liner that had struck an iceberg and gone to the bottom in April 1912. More than 1,500 people died in the tragedy.

The wreckage remained undiscovered for 73 years mainly because the distress signal radioed from the sinking ship had not contained precise information about the ship's location. To have a reasonable chance of finding the *Titanic*, an explorer would have to cover at least 250 square kilometers (100 square miles) of ocean floor. In a manned research minisubmarine, it would be like crawling around the ocean floor with a flashlight. But I believed that the *Argo* could find the *Titanic*.

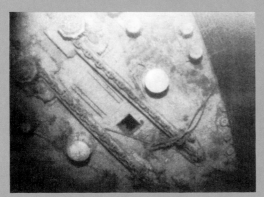

Found on Sept. 1, 1985, the luxury liner *Titanic* rests on the floor of the Atlantic Ocean. The ship struck an iceberg and sank in 1912.

To improve our ability to explore in deep water, I had begun to design the *Argo* for the U.S. Navy in 1980. I intended the 5-meter- (16-foot-) long vessel to be capable of descending 6,000 meters (20,000 feet) below the surface. Equipped with powerful lights, video cameras, and *sonar devices*, which use sound waves, it could locate objects underwater.

By August 1985, the *Argo* was completed and ready for testing. The Navy and Woods Hole, which built the craft, approved a test in the area where the *Titanic* sank. The test period was not long enough to ensure a successful search by the *Argo* alone, however, so I enlisted the aid of deep-sea researchers at IFREMER—France's institution for ocean exploration. They had worked with me on an earlier project.

We set out in June, and the search was scheduled to run until early September. An IFREMER research ship towed the *Sar*, an unmanned vessel equipped with sonar and a device for analyzing the metallic content of objects found by the sonar. The *Knorr* towed the *Argo* and the *Angus*, an older unmanned submersible vessel housing three 35-millimeter cameras. The IFREMER oceanographers hoped to locate the *Titanic* in July. The *Knorr* would then bring the *Argo* and the *Angus* to the site to photograph the wreckage.

Bad weather hampered the French ship's operations. By August 6, it had covered 80 per cent of the search area and had not found the *Titanic*.

On August 15, we boarded the *Knorr* for the final phase of the exploration. First, we eliminated potential targets detected earlier. Then we concentrated on looking for a trail of debris such as those left by airplanes and ships falling to the ocean floor. Many pieces of debris are too small to be seen by sonar, but the debris trail could easily be seen by *Argo*'s cameras. This strategy led to the discovery of the boiler.

Ironically, it was the *Knorr*'s *fathometer*, an ordinary sonar device that is standard on all fishing vessels, that detected the *Titanic*'s hull, while we were maneuvering near the boiler. Working around the clock, we then guided the *Argo* over the *Titanic*—beginning at the bow—and had it take detailed video pictures of the sunken liner. These showed the ship to be in remarkably good condition and surprisingly free of marine growth. On September 5, the *Angus* took close-up photos of the *Titanic*.

Finding the *Titanic* ended a 73-year-old mystery. But, more important, it began a new phase in underwater exploration—exploring with robot divers—that will help us in our continuing quest to learn more about the planet on which we live.   [Robert D. Ballard]

Oceanography
Continued

vents, the organisms that live there must rely on some other source of energy to produce their food.

The University of California researchers attached a chemical analyzer called a Scanner to the outside of the research submarine *Alvin.* During 1985, they took some 10,000 measurements of chemicals in the water near vents along the Galapagos Rift Valley in the eastern Pacific Ocean.

The pattern was clear. Organisms living near the vents rapidly used up sulfur and oxygen. Water surrounding clusters of mussels and smaller organisms had lower sulfide and oxygen concentrations than water in nearby areas where there was little or no marine life. Water samples from areas with the greatest density of animals contained almost no sulfides.

These measurements, the first chemical tests performed on location around the vents, provided convincing evidence that vent communities in the darkest ocean depths convert the sulfur and oxygen from hot-water vents into food energy.

Atlantic vents. Marine geologist Peter Rona and his colleagues aboard the National Oceanic and Atmospheric Administration vessel *Researcher* in the summer of 1985 located a cluster of some 11 *black smokers*—volcanic formations resembling chimneys that vent extremely hot mineral-rich water from beneath the seabed. The smokers were found along the Mid-Atlantic Ridge, a system of volcanic peaks and valleys that extends along the mid-ocean floor of the Atlantic Ocean.

Their discovery marked the first time that oceanographers have located hot vents in an area where sea-floor ridges are pulling apart slowly. Most hot-water vents have been discovered along ridges where new sea floor is being produced rapidly. The discovery of hot-water vents on these slow-spreading centers indicates that these regions may add far more to the ocean's chemistry and temperature than scientists had thought. [Feenan D. Jennings and Lauriston R. King]

In WORLD BOOK, see OCEANS; TECTONICS.

Paleontology

What appear to be some of the oldest fossils ever found were reported in February 1986 by geologists Gary R. Byerly, Donald R. Lower, and Maud M. Walsh of Louisiana State University in Shreveport. The fossils were discovered in rocks dated at 3.4 billion to 3.5 billion years old near Barberton, South Africa, about 300 kilometers (185 miles) east of Pretoria. Similar fossils of about the same age were discovered in 1979 in Australia. Both groups are at least 200 million years older than the oldest previously known fossils.

The fossils found were ancient *stromatolites,* layered rock formations from 1 to 20 centimeters (0.4 to 8 inches) tall created by sediments trapped on mats of sticky algae. Not only are these stromatolites among the oldest known fossils, they are also only about 300 million years younger than the world's oldest known rocks. The existence of these fossils indicates that very early in Earth's history, algae were already advanced enough to form mats and other complicated structures instead of growing only as solitary cells.

Ancient corals. A debate over whether the unknown, extinct creatures that formed honeycomblike skeletons of so-called "tabulate corals" were corals or sponges was settled in July 1985 by paleontologist Paul Copper of Laurentian University in Sudbury, Canada. Found in rocks from the later Paleozoic Era—about 500 million to 230 million years ago—tabulates had traditionally been classified as corals. Recently, however, some scientists have argued that tabulates might represent a type of sponge.

Copper settled the issue by finding the first fossilized tabulate skeleton containing the preserved bodies of corals that once inhabited it, in 430-million-year-old rocks in Quebec, Canada. The creatures, which had about 12 tentacles surrounding a central mouth, closely resembled the soft bodies of living corals found today.

Oldest squid. A West German paleontologist announced in November 1985 the discovery of the fossilized remains of the oldest known squid. Wilhelm Stürmer of Erlangen found the

294

Dinosaur Discoveries

Dinosaur fossil bones uncovered in Alaska, Texas, and Canada and reported in 1985 and 1986 extended the known range of the prehistoric creatures and represented time periods from which few dinosaur fossils have ever been found.

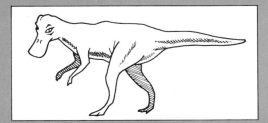

The jawbone of a plant-eating duckbilled dinosaur, *top,* similar to a hadrosaur, *above,* was found in Alaska, farther north than any dinosaur bone ever discovered.

A scientist, *top,* uncovers fossil bones of a previously unknown plant-eating dinosaur, *above,* from a site in Texas where many 100-million-year-old fossils were found.

A penny-sized footprint of the smallest known dinosaur, a sparrow-sized creature, was found at a 200-million-year-old site on the Bay of Fundy in Nova Scotia, Canada, where scientists discovered the largest collection of animal fossils ever found in North America.

Paleontology

Continued

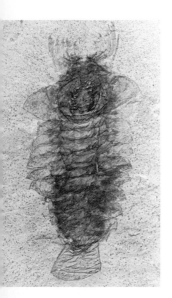

The fossil of a marine arthropod found in 530-million-year-old rock in British Columbia, Canada, may represent a distant ancestor of scorpions, among the first land animals. The fossil animal, which is only 7 centimeters (2¾ inches) long, has been nicknamed "Santa Claws" because of the five pairs of claws attached to its head.

fossil in 390-million-year-old black slate from West Germany. Scientists have found few fossils of squids, because their soft bodies usually deteriorate rapidly after death. Stürmer's squid evidently was buried very soon after death and its tissues were quickly replaced by iron pyrite, also known as "fool's gold." Despite its great age, Stürmer's squid, which has tentacles with hooks and what may be suckers, closely resembles a species of squid found today off the western coast of Africa.

Primitive mammal fossil. The oldest mammal fossil found in Australia was described in November 1985 by Australian paleontologists from the University of New South Wales, the Australian Museum in Sydney, and the Queensland Museum in Brisbane. The fossil, which was found in the early 1980's at Lightning Ridge in New South Wales, is part of a right jawbone containing three teeth. It is about 113 million years old, at least 85 million years older than any other mammal fossil found in Australia. The fossilized jawbone is believed to have belonged to a *monotreme* (egg-laying mammal) about the size of a badger. As such, it is the oldest monotreme fossil ever found.

More on mass extinctions. The link between a mass extinction at the end of the Cretaceous Period about 65 million years ago and the collision of a meteorite with Earth was strengthened by discoveries of ancient "ashes" in several places around the world. In October 1985, chemists at the University of Chicago reported finding grains of carbon in 65-million-year-old sediments in Spain, Denmark, and New Zealand. The scientists contended that the soot was produced by massive forest fires triggered by a meteorite impact. According to their theory, the fires created huge clouds of soot that blocked sunlight and sharply and suddenly cooled temperatures on Earth, causing the extinction of the dinosaurs and many other animal species.

Gradual extinction. Another study, published in May 1986, however, concluded that the dinosaurs died out gradually and that if a meteorite impact did occur at the end of the Cretaceous Period, it was not the major

reason for the dinosaurs' extinction. The study, by a team of scientists headed by paleontologist Robert E. Sloan of the University of Minnesota in Minneapolis, also argued that some dinosaur species survived into the Tertiary Period that followed.

Sloan and his colleagues based their conclusions on an analysis of dinosaur fossils found in layers of sediment from the Hell Creek Formation—several hundred meters of sediment deposited by ancient streams in eastern Montana. According to Sloan's team, dinosaurs began to die out gradually in Montana; Wyoming; and Alberta, Canada, about 7 million years before the end of the Cretaceous Period. The scientists also reported finding the last of the dinosaur fossils in sediments 1.3 meters (4 feet) above the layer of iridium at the Cretaceous-Tertiary boundary believed to have been laid down during the meteorite impact. The sediments above the iridium layer were deposited 40,000 years after the Tertiary Period began.

The scientists did not dispute the theory that a meteorite impact took place. But they argued that other factors, including climate changes, the extinction of plant species eaten by vegetarian dinosaurs, and competition from mammals, were chiefly responsible for the dinosaurs' extinction.

Vertebrate extinction pattern. Most scientists studying mass extinctions have concentrated on the reasonably complete fossil record of marine *invertebrates* (animals without backbones). In August 1985, paleontologist Michael J. Benton of Queen's University in Belfast, Northern Ireland, reported finding six periods of mass extinction in the fossil record of land-dwelling vertebrates (amphibians, birds, reptiles, and mammals). These periods roughly coincide with six of the eight periods of marine extinctions identified in 1983 by paleontologists David M. Raup and J. John Sepkoski, Jr., of the University of Chicago. Benton reported, however, that fewer land-dwelling animals died off during these periods than marine animals. In addition, he found no evidence of a regular cycle of extinctions.   [Carlton E. Brett]

In WORLD BOOK, see DINOSAUR; FOSSIL; PALEONTOLOGY.

Physics, Fluids and Solids

A group of seven researchers from Temple University in Philadelphia, Boston University, and Los Alamos National Laboratories in New Mexico reported in June 1985 on a material that becomes a *superconductor* at extremely low temperatures in the presence of a magnetic field. A superconductor conducts electricity without resistance. A normal superconductor loses its superconductivity in a strong magnetic field.

The researchers found that an alloy known as cerium-lead-3 becomes a superconductor at a temperature of 0.2 K when placed in a magnetic field of 14 tesla. Absolute zero is equal to 0 K (−459.67°F. or −273.15°C). A field of 14 tesla is 140,000 times as strong as Earth's magnetic field.

The researchers observed also that the alloy's *specific heat*—the amount of heat needed to raise the temperature of one gram of the alloy one Celsius degree—increased enormously when it was cooled down to 4 K, and reached a maximum around 1.1 K. The alloy, like all metals, stores heat energy in the form of vibrations of its atoms and its *free electrons*—electrons that can move from one atom to another freely and are responsible for electric current. At 1.1 K, the electrons can store 1,000 times more heat energy than they do at 5 K. Electrons that were 1,000 times as massive as ordinary electrons would store this much heat energy, so physicists call the alloy a *heavy-electron metal*, even though its electrons have normal mass.

In recent years, researchers have found several other heavy-electron metals. Scientists suspect that the so-called heavy electrons are responsible for the superconductivity of some of these materials in strong magnetic fields.

Physicists compare this superconductivity to the *superfluidity*—the ability to flow with no mechanical resistance—of a form of helium known as He-3 at a very low temperature. Superfluid He-3 can flow effortlessly through a pinhole, for example. The superfluid helium atoms and the heavy electrons have the same amounts of

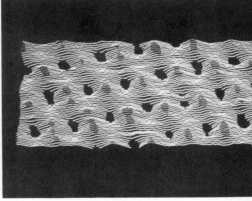

A new and smaller scanning tunneling microscope, *left*, can sweep a needlelike probe back and forth less than one-millionth of a millimeter above the surface of a material. The device produces an electric current that a computer converts to a three-dimensional image of the surface. Areas that look like hilltops, *above*, are locations of atoms in a graphite surface.

Physics,
Fluids
and Solids

Continued

A new electron-microscope technique shows regions within a material called *magnetic domains*. In a domain, individual atoms align with one another like tiny bar magnets. This line-up of "atomic magnets" can point in various directions in neighboring domains. The photo shows four domains in an area about ten-millionths of a meter wide. One looks like a light-colored wedge, another like a dark hill, and the medium-gray areas represent two domains that happen to point in the same direction.

spin, and researchers think that this spin may be responsible for both superfluidity and superconductivity. The essential difference between He-3 and heavy electrons is their electric charge. He-3 atoms are electrically neutral and therefore form a superfluid, while heavy electrons carry an electrical charge and therefore form a superconducting electric current.

Magnetic domains. In early 1985, researchers at Hitachi Limited's Central Research Laboratory in Tokyo reported the first images of *magnetic domains*—tiny regions of a magnetized material in which the magnetic fields point in the same direction. The researchers produced the pictures with a *scanning electron microscope* and a *spin-polarization detector.*

In ordinary photography with a scanning electron microscope, the microscope sweeps a narrow beam of electrons over the object to be photographed. These electrons knock other electrons—called *secondary electrons*—out of the outer layers of the object. An electron detector then measures the flow of secondary electrons and produces an electric current whose strength is proportional to the number of secondary electrons. The detector sends the current to an electronic device that translates the current into signals for a televisionlike screen. The number of secondary electrons depends upon the structure of the scanned object, so the signals construct an image of the scanned object on the screen.

The Hitachi researchers used an effect described in 1982 by physicist John Unguris and colleagues at the National Bureau of Standards (NBS) laboratory in Gaithersburg, Md. An electron spins around its own axis, and the NBS scientists discovered that secondary electrons ejected from a magnetized material retain the spin orientation, or spin polarization, they had in the material. The spin orientation of a secondary electron emitted from a given domain in a magnetized material is directly related to the direction of the magnetic field in that domain. So by counting secondary electrons and determining their spin orientations, the Hitachi researchers were able to produce images of magnetic domains.

To determine spin orientation, the researchers used a *Mott detector*, an electronic machine about 1 meter (39 inches) long. They connected this machine to an electron microscope so that the stream of secondary electrons flowed into the machine. Inside the machine, the electrons were directed toward a thin gold film. The electrons interacted magnetically with nuclei of atoms in the film and scattered to one side of the film or the other, depending upon the electron's spin orientation. From the difference between the number of electrons collected by electrical devices at the two sides of the film, the researchers calculated the spin direction of the beam.

Unguris and his NBS colleagues announced in the summer of 1986 that they had developed a fist-sized spin-polarization detector. The new detector is easier to connect to an electron microscope and requires less power than does the Mott detector used by the Hitachi researchers.

Important applications of magnetic domain photography include the study of permanent magnets and of magnetic materials used for the recording of digital data on computer disks and tapes. A strongly magnetic material has large domains with magnetization in one particular direction and small domains with magnetization in other directions. When a material is magnetized or demagnetized, the boundaries between domains move, increasing or decreasing the total area of magnetization in one direction. By making these boundaries visible, researchers can discover factors that make materials strong permanent magnets. Scientists already have found that certain impurities in the crystal structure of magnetic materials make boundary motion more difficult.

Quasicrystals. In October 1985, five researchers at Cornell University in Ithaca, N.Y., and two scientists at Sandia National Laboratories in Albuquerque, N. Mex., announced independently that they had obtained *quasicrystals* by bombarding a thin film of an alloy of aluminum and manganese with a beam of xenon *ions* (charged atoms). The bombardment with ions rearranged atoms in the alloy to form a quasicrystal.

IBM scientists use two laser beams to encode data on a tiny sliver of an experimental material that can store 100 billion characters or bits of computer data per square inch (6.45 square centimeters).

A quasicrystal is a form of solid matter discovered in 1984 by physicist Dan Schechtman and his colleagues of Israel Institute of Technology in Haifa during experiments conducted at the NBS laboratory in Gaithersburg.

Until Schechtman's discovery, solid matter was known to exist in only crystalline and glassy forms. The atoms that make up crystal substances, such as table salt, are arranged in a repeating pattern called the *unit cell*. The distance between unit cells is the same throughout the crystal. Physicists call this arrangement *periodic*.

In glassy substances, such as ordinary glass and certain plastics, the atoms are not arranged in an orderly fashion. Instead, they occupy random positions.

A quasicrystal has unit cells that do not form a periodic pattern. Schechtman obtained quasicrystals by dropping molten drops of a manganese-aluminum alloy on a spinning metal disk and cooling them rapidly.

Also in October, physicist Leonid Bendersky of Johns Hopkins University in Baltimore announced that he and his colleagues had used the spinning-disk technique at the NBS laboratory to produce an aluminum-manganese quasicrystal that differed geometrically from Schechtman's.

Theorists have not yet been able to visualize the structure of a quasicrystal. The unit cell of Schechtman's quasicrystal, for example, is the *icosahedron*, a solid with 20 faces that are equilateral triangles. It is not possible to tightly pack a given space with building blocks of this shape.

In February 1986, physicist Per Bak of Brookhaven National Laboratory on Long Island, N.Y., published a mathematical analysis of the problem of determining the position of the atoms in a quasicrystal made up of icosahedrons. He showed that the problem has an infinite number of solutions. In other words, mathematics cannot determine the positions of the atoms. Bak assumes that the unit cells are *deformed* (pressed out of shape) so that they fit together perfectly to fill a given space.   [Alexander Hellemans]

In WORLD BOOK, see CRYSTAL; ELECTRON MICROSCOPE; MAGNET AND MAGNETISM; PHYSICS.

Physics, Subatomic

Two beams of subatomic particles collided with a record-breaking combined energy of 1.6 trillion electron volts in the Tevatron particle accelerator at Fermi National Accelerator Laboratory (Fermilab) near Chicago in October 1985. (One electron volt is the amount of energy an electron gains when it moves across an electric potential of 1 volt.) The Tevatron is so powerful that researchers who will use it to probe the fundamental forces of the universe hope for a few surprises.

Subatomic, or particle, physics has been free of surprises for nearly a decade. All experiments have merely confirmed the *Standard Model*, the current concept of matter and forces, without doing much to close certain gaps in our knowledge.

The Standard Model depicts matter as being made up of two kinds of building blocks: *leptons*, including the electron, and *quarks*, pointlike particles that make up protons and neutrons—which in turn make up atomic nuclei. Three forces are required to account for the behavior of leptons and

quarks: the *electromagnetic force*, which is responsible for the behavior of electrons; the *strong force*, which binds quarks together in sets of three to form protons and neutrons; and the *weak force*, which is responsible for certain kinds of radioactivity.

The three forces are now well understood, due in large measure to ongoing experiments at particle accelerators throughout the world. (The force of gravity, the fourth of the fundamental forces, plays no significant role in the phenomena that can be studied with accelerators.) In the Special Reports section, see MIND-BOGGLING MYSTERIES OF MATTER.

The main problem in particle physics today lies in understanding why different subatomic particles have the masses they do. Ever since Albert Einstein developed his famous equation $E = mc^2$ in 1905, it has been clear that mass represents "frozen" energy. Einstein's equation says that the amount of energy "frozen" in a particle equals the particle's mass times the speed of light *squared* (multiplied by itself).

A huge cylindrical collider detector awaits installation in the Tevatron particle accelerator at Fermi National Accelerator Laboratory (Fermilab) near Chicago. Later, on Oct. 13, 1985, the device detected a head-on collision of subatomic particles moving with a world-record combined energy of 1.6 trillion electron volts.

"OK, Donaldson, what's all this nonsense I hear about you detecting gravity waves?"

Physics, Subatomic

Continued

In the Standard Model, a new force called the *Higgs interaction* is said to be the source of this energy. Subatomic particles theoretically acquire mass by interacting with particles called *Higgs bosons*. No such particle has ever been observed, however. Without some experimental data on this particle and its force, there is little hope of progress on the problem of mass and "frozen" energy.

Insights from new machines? Progress in particle physics has usually come from the development of bigger and more powerful accelerators. These "atom smashers" accelerate a beam of particles to a speed approaching the speed of light, then collide the beam with a stationary target or with another beam moving in the opposite direction. New particles form in many of these collisions.

Most newer accelerators collide two beams, because a head-on collision is much more powerful than the collision of a moving particle with a stationary one. And most colliding-beam machines collide a beam of matter parti-

cles with a beam of their *antimatter* counterparts—particles that are exactly the same but have opposite electric charge. Much of the collision energy "freezes out" immediately, forming a vast swarm of new particles. With powerful new machines, scientists may find clues about the Higgs boson.

The Tevatron, which collides protons and antiprotons, was scheduled to become fully operational in late 1986.

Another large atom-smasher, the SLAC Linear Collider at the Stanford Linear Accelerator Center in Palo Alto, Calif., was scheduled to start up in early 1987. This machine will collide electrons with their antimatter counterparts, *positrons*. Japan's first colliding beam accelerator, Tristan, also is scheduled to begin operating in 1987. Two other such machines are under construction in Western Europe and one in the Soviet Union.

Mystery particle. Nuclear physics is a changing field. For years, its main goal was to map the structures of nuclei, and study simple reactions affecting

Physics, Subatomic

Continued

one or perhaps a few nuclear particles. Nuclear physicists have nearly completed this task and are now turning their attention to collisions of two heavy nuclei. These collisions must take place at high energies to overcome the mutual repulsion of the nuclei—a result of each nucleus' positive electric charge.

This research is still in its infancy, but it has already given birth to a mystery, which scientists in 1986 tried to explain. Collisions at the UNILAC accelerator of the Society for Heavy Ion Research in Darmstadt, West Germany, since 1983 have been producing positrons whose energy level cannot be accounted for by the Standard Model.

This mysterious effect occurs when heavy nuclei meet with just enough energy to overcome their mutual repulsion. They touch gently, momentarily forming an atom with a "double nucleus." If the number of protons in the combined nucleus exceeds 173, the electric field in its vicinity is strong enough to produce an electron and a positron by the conversion of electric

energy to mass. Electrons have a negative charge, so the electron is trapped in an orbit near the positively charged nucleus. The positron has a positive charge, so it is ejected from the vicinity of the nucleus.

According to the Standard Model, positrons produced in this manner should have a wide range of energies, and most of the positrons observed in the UNILAC experiments do have such a range. But several independent groups of experimenters working at UNILAC have reported that about 25 of every 1 million collisions produce positrons of a single well-defined energy level.

Physicists theorized that one possible source for such a positron would be an electrically neutral particle, produced in the collision, that is more than three times as heavy as an electron. The neutral particle would break up quickly into an electron and a positron. If this were the case, the electron might be created far enough from the nucleus to avoid becoming trapped in orbit. To test the idea of the neutral

Thick metal "doughnuts" called resonators, installed in a new section of the superconducting accelerator at Argonne National Laboratory near Chicago, boost electrically charged atoms to speeds up to 50,000 kilometers (31,000 miles) per second. This is 50 per cent faster than they can travel in the accelerator alone. Researchers began to use the new equipment in October 1985.

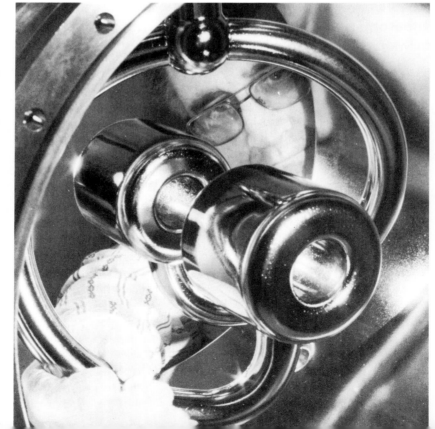

particle, researchers in 1986 looked for electrons in company with the positrons, and they found some.

It is hard, however, for physicists to interpret this result, because there is no place in the Standard Model for such a heavy neutral particle. Research is continuing in hopes of learning more about the mystery particle.

Space law verified. Much of the recent research in atomic physics, the study of the motions of electrons in atoms, has involved *lasers* and *masers*, sources of pure and concentrated light or radio waves. The beam from a laser or maser consists of a stream of identical waves, which can serve as an extremely precise standard for measuring both distance and time. In the Special Reports section, see THE FABULOUS LASER.

In 1985, researchers at the Time and Frequency Division of the National Bureau of Standards in Boulder, Colo., used a hydrogen maser to test a fundamental law of physics. This law states that all directions in space are *equivalent*. In other words, a moving object responds to forces in precisely the same fashion, no matter in which direction it moves.

Radio waves transmit the electromagnetic force. So, to determine how a moving object reacts to this force, the Boulder scientists for many days shot various radio waves from the maser into beryllium atoms. They monitored the frequency of the waves absorbed by electrons in the atoms.

The electrons absorbed best at a frequency of about 303 million waves per second. Throughout the experiment, this number varied by no more than 0.0001 wave per second. If all directions in space were *not* equivalent, the physicists might well have detected a variation in the frequency of the waves as Earth's rotation turned the experimental equipment round and round relative to the rest of the universe.

The result of the Boulder experiment was 300 times more precise than any previous test of the uniformity of space.   [Robert H. March]

In WORLD BOOK, see ATOM; PARTICLE ACCELERATOR; PARTICLE PHYSICS.

Psychology

Teen-agers of the 1980's in the United States are smarter than those of the previous two decades, according to conclusions drawn in 1985 by researchers who follow the College Board's Scholastic Aptitude Test (SAT) scores. Average SAT scores declined dramatically during the 1960's and 1970's, but this trend appears to have reversed according to psychologist Robert B. Zajonc of the University of Michigan in Ann Arbor.

In a report presented at the annual meeting of the American Association for the Advancement of Science in June 1985, Zajonc suggested that a rise in test scores that began in 1980 may be related to changes in family size. The birth rate in the United States declined during the 1960's, leading to smaller families. Children born to small families, states Zajonc, have an intellectual advantage over those born to large families. An only child, for example, benefits intellectually by being exposed primarily to the adult intelligence and language of his or her parents. A child born into a large family, however, is exposed primarily to the intellect and language of other children. The current upswing in SAT scores should continue for another 16 to 18 years, because the birth rate continued to decline during the 1970's, according to Zajonc. But then, he predicts, SAT scores will begin to decline again because the birth rate and family size have been rising since 1980.

Left-handers' brains. Left-handed people differ from right-handed people in the size of the corpus callosum, the band of nerve fibers that connects the left and right *hemispheres* (halves) of the brain. This finding was reported in August 1985 by psychologist Sandra Witelson of McMaster University in Hamilton, Canada, who studied 42 patients suffering from terminal cancer. Examination of their brains after death revealed that the corpus callosum was about 11 per cent larger in left-handers and *ambidextrous* people (those who use both hands equally well) than in right-handers.

This size difference may have something to do with the division of tasks

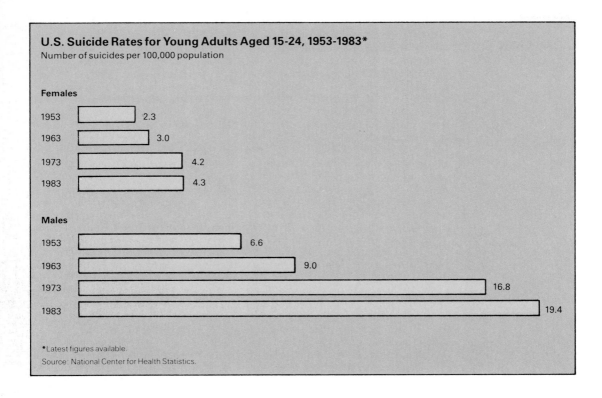

U.S. Suicide Rates for Young Adults Aged 15-24, 1953-1983*

Number of suicides per 100,000 population

Females

1953	2.3
1963	3.0
1973	4.2
1983	4.3

Males

1953	6.6
1963	9.0
1973	16.8
1983	19.4

*Latest figures available.

Source: National Center for Health Statistics.

Psychology

Continued

Youth Suicides Soar

Since the early 1950's, the rate of suicide has tripled among young men and nearly doubled among young women in the United States. Psychologists and other experts are uncertain about what is causing this alarming trend. Although young men have a higher rate of death from suicide, suicide attempts occur more often among young women.

between the hemispheres. In most right-handers, the left hemisphere specializes in language. In left-handers, however, language, visual, and spatial tasks tend to be shared by both hemispheres, and this might require a larger corpus callosum to handle the increased communication between the right and left brain.

"Bigger" does not necessarily mean "better," according to Witelson. A larger corpus callosum and less hemispherical specialization might be better for certain *cognitive* (knowledge-related) skills but worse for others. More research is needed to see if there is a link between corpus callosum size and particular skills. See also NEUROSCIENCE. In the Special Reports section, see OUR "TWO BRAINS": FACTS AND MYTHS.

The brain's dictionary. Psychologist John Hart, Jr., and his colleagues at Johns Hopkins University and the University of Maryland Hospital in Baltimore reported in August 1985 on a medical case that provides a clue to the way that knowledge is organized in

the brain. This finding was based on their work with a patient identified as "M.D.," who suffered a stroke that damaged a part of the left hemisphere of his brain. As a result, he suffered a complete loss of his ability to understand and use words. Eighteen months after his stroke, however, M.D. had almost totally recovered and was able to perform well on a standard language test. But he still had trouble with the names of fruits and vegetables.

The researchers worked with M.D. for more than a year and found that when he was shown various objects or drawings of objects he could name almost all of them. When shown fruits and vegetables, however, he could name only about two-thirds of them correctly. When given photographs of a variety of items and asked to sort them by category, his only mistakes involved fruits and vegetables.

The researchers also used a test in which M.D. was shown pictures of two objects, and the name of one object was said aloud to him. He was then asked to point to the picture of that

Psychology

object. Surprisingly, M.D. was able to point immediately to the correct pictures of all the fruits and vegetables after hearing their names. Also, he was able to categorize the written names of fruits and vegetables—the same fruits and vegetables whose pictures he could not name or categorize.

As a result of these tests, the researchers concluded that M.D. still knew as much as he ever did about fruits and vegetables. But because he was unable to name them just by seeing them, he could not gain access to information about them stored in his brain. Because M.D.'s stroke affected only two related categories of words, the researchers concluded that the brain's "dictionary," which contains about 75,000 words in an adult, is organized according to categories that can be disturbed by damage to specific areas of the brain.

Temperament and heart disease. Children with certain personality traits may be more likely than other children to develop into the aggressive, hostile, competitive adults whose life style can lead to heart disease, according to a November 1985 report by psychologist Laurence Steinberg of the University of Wisconsin at Madison. Adults with such a behavior pattern—called type A behavior—may be more likely to develop coronary artery disease than are people with a more relaxed attitude.

Steinberg's work was based on a study of a group of 133 people since their infancy in 1956. The group contained roughly equal numbers of boys and girls. Steinberg reported that, among both the boys and girls studied, those who had a high level of physical activity and suffered moodiness during childhood were more likely to exhibit type A behavior in adulthood. In addition, boys—but not girls—who had low activity levels and suffered moodiness were likely to develop type A behavior in adulthood.

Steinberg addressed the question of why low activity level in boys but not in girls would be related to adult type A behavior. He concluded that it may be connected with the different ways boys and girls are brought up. Parents, teachers, and others may encourage boys with low activity levels to develop a strong drive for achievement and success in an effort to make up for their more passive nature. But they may permit girls exhibiting a low level of activity to remain relatively passive.

Steinberg cautioned, however, that not every child with the temperament he described will grow up to be a type A adult. According to Steinberg, it is more likely that family and school pressures act in combination with certain traits of personality and temperament to encourage the development of type A behavior.

Dreamers in distress. For many years, psychologists, psychiatrists, and other scientists have debated the function and the psychological importance of dreaming. In recent years, some prominent scientists have suggested that dreams have no psychological significance. In 1981, biologist Francis H. C. Crick, winner of the 1962 Nobel Prize in physiology or medicine, proposed that dreams have no meaning, but simply rid the brain of unneeded associations stored in networks of brain cells. In March 1986, psychologists Ronald J. Brown and Donald C. Donderi of McGill University in Montreal, Canada, gave evidence for the psychological significance of dreams when they reported the results of studies showing that recurring dreams may be related to psychological distress.

The researchers studied 67 people—30 people who were currently experiencing a recurring dream, 18 who had experienced a recurring dream in adulthood but not during the previous year, and 19 others who had never had a recurring dream as adults. All 67 people were given standard tests of psychological functioning. The researchers found that those in the group experiencing recurrent dreams were more likely than the people in the other two groups to have high levels of anxiety, depression, stressful life events, and minor physical complaints. Those in the group that no longer had recurring dreams appeared to be experiencing the least psychological distress—even less than the people who had never experienced a recurring dream. This finding supports the idea that a recurring dream stops when some type of psychological conflict has been resolved. [Robert J. Trotter]

In WORLD BOOK, see PSYCHOLOGY.

Weight reduction may be an effective treatment for patients with *hypertension* (high blood pressure) and increased heart size, according to a study reported in February 1986 by researchers at the University of New South Wales in Sydney, Australia. People suffering from hypertension have an increased risk of developing *left ventricular hypertrophy (LVH)*—an enlargement of the left ventricle of the heart. Such an enlargement has been associated with increased rates of heart attack and stroke. Most hypertensive people are also overweight, a condition that, of itself, can lead to LVH. The combination of hypertension and increased heart size doubles the risk of death from stroke or heart attack compared with the risk for patients with hypertension alone.

The researchers divided 41 hypertensive and overweight adults into three groups. The first group followed a weight-reduction program; the second group was treated with a drug that lowers blood pressure; and the third group received no treatment.

After six months, patients in the weight-reduction group had lost an average of about 8 kilograms (17 pounds). The drop in their blood pressure was significantly greater than that of the untreated group and slightly greater than that of the group treated with drugs. Patients in the weight-reduction group also showed a substantial decrease in heart size. This decrease was directly related to their degree of weight loss. Neither of the other groups showed any change in heart size. These results indicate the benefits of weight reduction in controlling blood pressure and preventing or reversing LVH.

Premature mortality and the draft. United States veterans of the Vietnam War have had increased mortality rates during the years since their military service, according to a report published in March 1986 by epidemiologist Norman Hearst and his colleagues at the School of Medicine of the University of California in San Francisco. Previous studies had indicated that U.S. troops who served in Vietnam had higher rates of drug and alcohol abuse, depression, marital problems, criminal arrests, and other psychological problems than similar groups who did not serve in Vietnam.

Hearst and his team examined the death records of 14,145 men in California and Pennsylvania. These men had been eligible for the military draft from 1970 to 1972, when a draft lottery system was in effect. The lottery divided young men—the year they became age 20—into a draft-exempt group and an eligible group.

Men in the eligible group had a 4 per cent higher overall death rate during the years 1974 to 1983 than did those in the exempt group. The difference in mortality was entirely explained by a 13 per cent increase in suicide and an 8 per cent increase in deaths due to motor vehicle accidents. The eligible group had slightly lower mortality only from cirrhosis of the liver. There was no difference between the death rates of eligible and exempt groups from other causes of death.

The researchers then calculated the death rates for 1974 to 1983 among men who actually served in the military and among those who were eligible but did not serve. They found that the death rate from suicide was 65 per cent higher among veterans than among those who did not serve. The veterans' death rate from motor vehicle accidents was 49 per cent higher.

The San Francisco study cannot explain why these high rates of death occurred 2 to 13 years after service in Vietnam. But the findings have important implications for prevention by identifying a large group of men who have an increased risk of premature death. This underlined the importance of community support and assistance for Vietnam veterans.

Smokeless tobacco hazards. A dramatic increase in the use of smokeless tobacco (snuff and chewing tobacco) was reported in April 1986 by researchers at the Massachusetts Department of Public Health in Boston and several other medical institutions in the United States. The use of moist snuff, for example, increased by 55 per cent from 1978 to 1984.

The report showed a heavy increase in the use of smokeless tobacco by young people in particular. Various surveys have shown that between 8 and 36 per cent of male high school

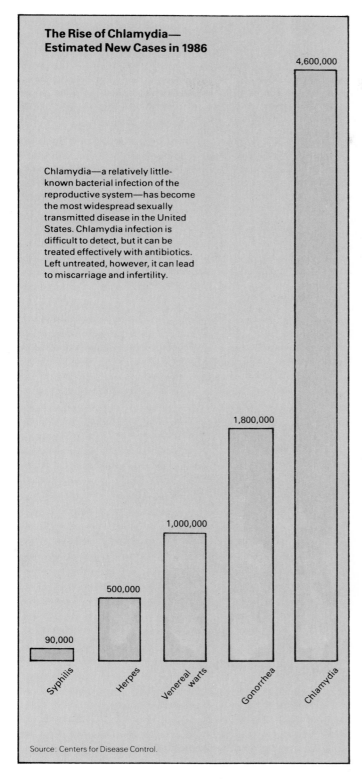

**The Rise of Chlamydia—
Estimated New Cases in 1986**

Chlamydia—a relatively little-known bacterial infection of the reproductive system—has become the most widespread sexually transmitted disease in the United States. Chlamydia infection is difficult to detect, but it can be treated effectively with antibiotics. Left untreated, however, it can lead to miscarriage and infertility.

4,600,000

1,800,000

1,000,000

500,000

90,000

Syphilis

Herpes

Venereal warts

Gonorrhea

Chlamydia

Source: Centers for Disease Control.

and college students are regular users. People under age 21 account for 3 million of the 10 million smokeless tobacco users in the United States. And substantial numbers of children aged 8 and 9 years have begun to use these products.

This trend was cause for considerable concern, because smokeless tobacco use increases a person's risk of developing cancers of the mouth and throat. Smokeless tobacco has also been linked to cancer of the esophagus, larynx, and pancreas and to gum disease and high blood pressure. Both snuff and chewing tobacco contain nicotine and are addictive. In reaction to the great increase in smokeless tobacco use, the U.S. Congress passed a law in February 1986 that requires health warning labels on smokeless tobacco packages and bans television and radio advertising of these products.

Colon cancer and physical activity. Physically inactive people have a higher risk of developing colon cancer than do physically active people, according to a study published in May 1986. Epidemiologist Maria Gerhardsson of the National Institute of Environmental Medicine and the Karolinska Institute in Stockholm, Sweden, analyzed health data on 1.1 million Swedish men, aged 20 to 64, covering a period of 19 years.

The men were classified according to the amount of physical activity involved in their job. There were 89 active occupations (involving sitting less than 20 per cent of the time) and 41 sedentary jobs (sitting more than 50 per cent of the time).

Gerhardsson found no difference between the active and sedentary groups in the incidence of rectal cancer. But there was a 40 per cent higher incidence of colon cancer among the sedentary workers.

Physical activity stimulates the movement of material through the colon. As a result, exposure time to potentially hazardous dietary substances in the colon is reduced for active people. Such a decrease in the time dietary residues spend in the colon may reduce the incidence of colon cancer in active people. [Michael H. Alderman]

In WORLD BOOK, see PUBLIC HEALTH.

Science Education

The drive for excellence in science education in the United States received much public attention during 1985 and 1986. Surveys by public opinion analyst Daniel Yankelovich and Robert E. Yager, professor of science education at the University of Iowa in Iowa City, showed that public support for science and for science education has increased dramatically. The current level of interest in science and science teaching actually exceeds the enthusiasm that followed the Soviet Union's launching of *Sputnik 1*, the first artificial satellite, in 1957. After *Sputnik*, many Americans became concerned about the Soviet lead in the space race and called for better science education to help close the gap.

Public interest in science education in the United States in the mid-1980's could be traced to a desire for greater economic security. Many Americans believe that if students receive better science instruction, they will be better equipped as adults to hold jobs and otherwise compete economically in an age of science and technology.

Textbook decision. In September 1985, the California Board of Education decided to reject all seventh- and eighth-grade science textbooks submitted by publishers for use by public schools in the state. The board claimed that the books lacked adequate treatment of evolution and human reproduction. In California, as in many other states, schools may not spend state funds on textbooks the state has not approved. Science educators hailed the California decision as an important reversal of a trend that began in the early 1970's among textbook publishers who hoped to satisfy conservative groups by avoiding discussion of evolution and certain other topics. In December 1985, the California board approved 10 revised biology textbooks submitted by publishers.

Cooperative projects. The National Science Foundation (NSF), an independent federal agency that supports both scientific research and science education, continued to emphasize cooperative projects in which schools, private industry, and states provided

Drawing by Lorenz; © 1986 The New Yorker Magazine, Inc.

"That is the correct answer, Billy, but I'm afraid you don't win anything for it."

Science Education

significant funds to supplement NSF support. For example, seven corporate sponsors took part in the second annual National Science Week from May 11 to 17, 1986, with the NSF serving as coordinator. National Science Week provided a wide range of science-related activities, most of which were aimed at junior high and high school students. The NSF plans a third Science Week in April 1987.

The National Science Teachers Association (NSTA), the world's largest association for science teachers, sponsored and supported the Triangle Coalition for Science and Technology Education, a three-way partnership involving education, science, and industry. The coalition played a major role in planning and executing National Science Week.

A national conference held in June 1985 under NSTA sponsorship at Phillips Exeter Academy in Exeter, N.H., established the importance of teachers in science education. Forty-five outstanding secondary teachers met with 12 national leaders from education and industry to discuss problems in science education.

The report of the Exeter conference, *Science and Technology Education for Tomorrow's World*, was published and distributed by the NSTA. The report emphasized the role teachers must play in educational reform. "The top-ranked problems—goals, curriculum, instruction, professional issues—are all areas over which teachers have direct influence," the report said.

National forum. The American Association for the Advancement of Science (AAAS), the world's largest federation of scientific organizations, organized the National Forum of School Science, a meeting held in October 1985 in Washington, D.C., for more than 200 science teachers, school administrators, scientists, and others. The forum, which focused on science teachers and instruction, was so successful that the AAAS planned to hold similar annual forums in 1986, 1987, and 1988.   [Robert E. Yager]

In WORLD BOOK, see EDUCATION; SCIENCE PROJECTS.

Science Fair Awards

Winners in the 45th annual Westinghouse Science Talent Search—the oldest and largest science student competition in the United States—were announced by Science Services of Washington, D.C., on March 3, 1986.

The 40 finalists, selected from a total of 1,219 high school seniors, spent five days in Washington. The winners were selected after interviews designed to indicate their potential for scientific creativity. The top 10 winners shared a total of $115,000 in scholarships presented by Westinghouse Electric Corporation. Each of the remaining 30 finalists received a cash award of $1,000.

First place and scholarships of $20,000 each were awarded to two students who tied for the top honor—Wendy K. Chung of Miami and Wei-Jing Zhu of Brooklyn, N.Y.

Chung, 17, of Miami Killian Senior High School, won for her study of the Caribbean fruit fly *Anastrepha suspensa*, which attacks more than 80 species of fruit in Chung's home state of Florida. Chung determined at which stage of ripeness the fly is most likely to lay its eggs in fruit, and she suspects that some chemical produced in the fruit either repels or attracts the flies at various stages of ripeness.

Wei-Jing Zhu, 16, of Brooklyn Technical High School won for his project on algebraic number theory. Zhu developed different representations for a class of numbers of the form $(a + bi)$ where i is the square root of -1.

Second place was not awarded because of the two first-place awards.

Third place and a $15,000 scholarship went to Yoriko Saito, 18, of Homewood High School in Homewood, Ala., for her project in biochemistry. She used tomato plants infected with the tumor-causing bacterium *Agrobacter tumefaciens* in experiments to change the plants' genetic structure to make them more resistant to disease, drought, and herbicides.

Fourth place and a $10,000 scholarship went to George J. Juang, 17, of Benjamin N. Cardozo High School in Queens, N.Y., for his physics project. Juang examined how a *colloid* (a sus-

Wei-Jing Zhu, left, of Brooklyn, N.Y., and Wendy K. Chung of Miami, Fla., tied for first place in the 1986 Westinghouse Science Talent Search.

Science Fair Awards

Continued

pension of solid particles in a liquid) could be analyzed in *phase conjugation* devices. A phase conjugation device is a mirrorlike apparatus that seems to reverse a beam of laser light passing through a substance, creating an effect much like running a film backwards.

Fifth place and a $10,000 scholarship went to Anh Tuan Nguyen-Huynh, 17, of University High School in Chagrin Falls, Ohio. He studied how magnesium and vitamin C prevent an antischizophrenic drug from being taken up by cells in the brain.

Sixth place and a $10,000 scholarship went to Jessica L. Boklan, 17, of Roslyn High School, East Hills, N.Y., for her math project. Boklan found equations that could generate all reversal products for two- to four-digit numbers. Reversal products result from pairs of equal-digit numbers with products equal to the product of their reversals. For example, a three-digit reversal product would be $693 \times 264 = 462 \times 396$.

Seventh place and a $7,500 scholarship went to William E. Bies, 17, of Mt. Lebanon High School in Pittsburgh, Pa., for his astronomy project that involved creating a computer model showing what might cause the spiral arms in spiral galaxies.

Eighth place and a $7,500 scholarship went to Mary E. Meyerand, 17, of Glastonbury High School in Glastonbury, Conn., for building an underwater energy device to generate electric power from the motion of ocean waves. Her device would be placed on the sea floor where it would not be destroyed by storms.

Ninth place and a $7,500 scholarship went to Andrew L. Feig, 18, of University High School in Los Angeles for his immunology project. Feig produced immune molecules called antibodies for a protein created by a gene and thought to play a role in a common childhood cancer.

Tenth place and a $7,500 scholarship went to Allen W. Ingling, 17, of Buckeye Valley High School in Delaware, Ohio, for creating a computer-controlled instrument used to diagnose color blindness.   [Irene B. Keller]

Space Technology

On Jan. 28, 1986, a giant fireball destroyed the United States space shuttle *Challenger* and killed its seven-member crew (see Close-Up). The U.S. National Aeronautics and Space Administration (NASA) grounded its remaining shuttle orbiters, leaving only a fleet of nonreusable rockets for launching payloads into space. Then on April 18, an Air Force Titan rocket carrying a secret military satellite exploded seconds after liftoff from Vandenberg Air Force Base in California. And on May 3, a NASA Delta rocket carrying a $57.5-million weather satellite was deliberately destroyed for safety reasons when its main engine shut down after liftoff from Cape Canaveral, Florida. The three catastrophes brought the U.S. space program to a halt. Neither NASA nor the Department of Defense could launch any commercial, military, or scientific payloads into space until investigations determined the causes of the failures.

Delayed launches. The space shuttle program began encountering problems on July 12, 1985, when the launch of the orbiter, *Challenger*, was aborted on the launching pad at Cape Canaveral. Computers detected a sluggish valve in one of *Challenger*'s three main engines and automatically shut the engines down to ensure safety.

The launch was rescheduled for July 29. This time, *Challenger* lifted off successfully, but 5 minutes and 45 seconds into its flight, *Challenger*'s computers again shut down one main engine. *Challenger* was flying high enough and fast enough to achieve a safe orbit, but the altitude was lower than planned and inhibited the use of some scientific instruments.

The scientific instruments included infrared, solar, and X-ray telescopes that were mounted in *Challenger*'s cargo bay. The telescopes were carried into space to furnish astronomers and solar physicists with observations of the sun, the stars, and galaxies free of interference from Earth's atmosphere.

Another space shuttle mission, originally scheduled for Dec. 18, 1985, was delayed several times due to bad weather and technical problems. It was finally launched on Jan. 12, 1986. During the flight, the crew of the orbiter *Columbia* deployed a communications satellite but failed in an attempt to photograph Halley's Comet.

Satellite "jump start." On Aug. 27, 1985, the shuttle *Discovery* was launched on a seven-day mission that deployed a U.S. Navy satellite, and communications satellites for the Australian government and a private U.S. company. The highlight of the mission, however, was the "jump start" repair of a disabled U.S. Navy communications satellite, *Leasat 3*, that had been launched from *Discovery* in April 1985. *Leasat 3* had failed to reach the correct orbit because a timing system for the upper stage of its booster rockets malfunctioned. Astronauts William F. Fisher and James D. Van Hoften rendezvoused with the satellite, brought it inside *Discovery*'s cargo bay for repairs, and redeployed it.

Fisher and Van Hoften inserted safety plugs to prevent accidental activation of the satellite, which was loaded with rocket fuel. They then installed a remote power unit that in effect acted as a "jump start," activating the timing system.

Although the astronauts succeeded in repairing *Leasat 3*, the new Navy *Leasat 4* satellite that they launched malfunctioned after it reached its correct orbit. *Leasat 4* is orbiting at 35,900 kilometers (22,300 miles) above Earth and so is beyond the reach of the shuttle orbiters and repair.

Joint Spacelab mission. On Oct. 30, 1985, the shuttle *Challenger* was launched on an eight-day joint mission with West Germany. During the mission, West Germany was responsible for operating Spacelab, a pressurized cabin in *Challenger*'s cargo bay, while NASA was responsible for shuttle flight operations. Nearly 80 scientific experiments were conducted in Spacelab, which is designed for conducting experiments under the unique conditions of weightlessness in space.

Other U.S. missions. Among other highlights of the U.S. space program during the year was the launch and retrieval of an X-ray satellite from the orbiter *Discovery* during a mission that lasted from June 17 to 24, 1985. The *Spartan* X-ray observatory gathered data about the center of the Milky Way galaxy over a three-day period during *Discovery*'s flight.

The *Challenger* Disaster

The United States space program suffered the worst disaster in its history on Jan. 28, 1986, when the space shuttle *Challenger* was destroyed in a giant fireball about 73 seconds after liftoff from the John F. Kennedy Space Center at Cape Canaveral, Florida. The seven-member crew—mission commander Francis R. Scobee; pilot Michael J. Smith; mission specialists Ronald E. McNair, Ellison S. Onizuka, and Judith A. Resnik; payload specialist Gregory B. Jarvis; and teacher-observer Christa McAuliffe—perished in the disaster. See DEATHS OF SCIENTISTS.

A 12-member commission, appointed by U.S. President Ronald Reagan on February 3 to investigate the cause of the disaster, placed the blame on a leak in a joint in one of the shuttle's two solid-fuel booster rockets. This allowed a 2760°C (5000°F.) plume of gas to escape about 58 seconds into the flight. The plume burned a hole in the bottom of the shuttle's external fuel tank, which contained highly explosive liquid oxygen and liquid hydrogen.

In its final report, issued on June 9, 1986, the presidential commission found that the leak in the right solid-fuel booster rocket was due to the failure of primary and backup rubber seals known as O-rings. The failure of the O-rings, in turn, was due to a combination of cold temperatures at the launch site and design deficiencies at the joints.

Shuttle booster rockets are built in segments that are bolted together to form a stack. To prevent hot gases within the rocket from escaping at the joints connecting the segments, each joint contains two O-rings, resembling giant rubber washers, that fit into grooves filling a narrow gap at the joint. Putty material packed around the inside of the joint provides protection against the high temperatures created when the rockets are fired.

In addition to its insulating role, the putty was designed so that it would push into the joint as the rocket ignited. Air trapped in the joint ahead of the putty would be forced against the O-ring seals, helping them to fit tightly in their grooves. The commission learned that cold temperatures can affect how the putty exerts pressure on the O-rings. Cold temperatures, such as occurred on the morning of the tragic launch, also harden the rings, making it more difficult for them to fill their narrow grooves. The effect, according to one investigator, is like "trying to shove a brick into a crack."

The commission also learned that examinations of boosters recovered after earlier launches had shown a flaw in the basic design. Internal forces within the boosters at the time of ignition cause stretching and bulging at the joints. When this happens, the backup seals are totally ineffective for a few milliseconds. If the putty in a booster does not work properly because of cold temperatures and the primary seal also fails, the hot gas in the booster can push past the seals and burn through the joint.

The commission concluded that this is what happened during the *Challenger* launch. The temperature at Cape Canaveral on the morning of the launch was 2°C (36°F.), the coldest temperature ever for a shuttle launching. Photographs show a series of smoke puffs emerging from the joint within a second after ignition, while the shuttle was still on the launching pad. The investigators concluded that the smoke came from a burning O-ring.

The commission also criticized the communications and decision-making process within the National Aeronautics and Space Administration (NASA). Engineers had noted deficiencies in the joint design as early as 1977, but these concerns were not passed along to top management until 1985.

The commission found that NASA officials at George C. Marshall Space Flight Center in Huntsville, Ala., in charge of overseeing the booster rockets, and officials at Morton Thiokol Incorporated, the manufacturer of the rockets, had treated the problem as an engineering issue that needed correcting. But they decided the booster was safe enough to use until the joint design could be improved.

Morton Thiokol engineers testified that they believed the cold temperatures expected for January 28—launch day—could affect the joint's performance. They told investigators that on the evening of January 27, they argued with Marshall officials to delay the launch. Morton Thiokol management reportedly overruled its engineers, however, and approved the launch. According to the presidential commission, Marshall officials involved in the January 27 discussions did not inform key launch officials at NASA of the serious questions raised about the cold weather.

The shuttle disaster was a major setback for the U.S. space program. It forced the delay of launching important commercial, military, and scientific satellites until the booster rockets could be redesigned and until other safety flaws found by the commission were corrected. And it created a crisis of confidence within NASA that might take much longer than engineering problems to repair.   [Craig P. Covault]

Black smoke emerges (circle) from a joint on the right solid-fuel booster rocket within a second after ignition while *Challenger* is still on the launching pad, *left,* on Jan. 28, 1986. About 73 seconds later, gas leaking from the joint causes the explosion, *above,* that destroys *Challenger* and its crew.

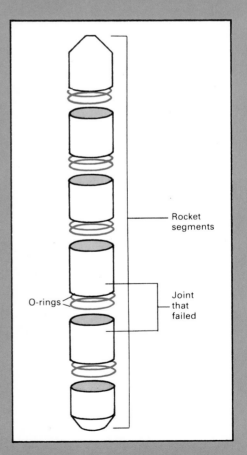

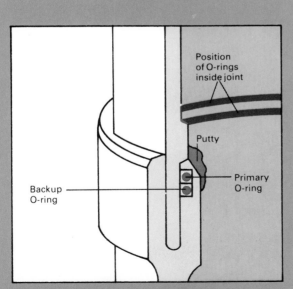

The problem was traced to O-rings designed to seal the joints where rocket segments came together, *right*. The O-rings and putty inside, *above,* stiffened by the cold, failed to keep hot fuel from burning through.

Space Technology

Continued

The new space shuttle orbiter, *Atlantis*, made its maiden flight from Oct. 3 to 7, 1985, reportedly carrying a payload for the U.S. Department of Defense. A second *Atlantis* mission, which began on Nov. 26, 1985, and lasted for eight days, demonstrated how large structures could be assembled in space by astronauts working outside the orbiter. Two spacewalks by Army Lieutenant Colonel Sherwood C. Spring and Air Force Major Jerry L. Ross demonstrated construction techniques that may be used to build a manned space station in the 1990's.

Soviet space program. The Soviet Union on June 6, 1985, launched the *Soyuz T-13* spacecraft carrying two cosmonauts on a dangerous mission to repair the *Salyut 7* space station, which had been crippled by a power failure. Cosmonauts Vladimir Dzhanibekov and Viktor Savinykh docked their *Soyuz* to the *Salyut* two days after launch and found a dark and frozen space station. During the next 10 days, the cosmonauts—wearing their space suits for warmth—fixed the *Salyut*'s broken electrical system, putting the station back into operation.

On Sept. 17, 1985, the Soviets launched an additional crew of three cosmonauts to the *Salyut 7* station. The new crew assisted the two cosmonauts already on board in carrying out further repairs. Two cosmonauts returned to Earth on Sept. 25, 1985, leaving the other three crewmen on board the *Salyut*. This was the first crew change in space.

The remaining three cosmonauts encountered trouble in November 1985 when one of the cosmonauts became seriously ill. On November 21, all three cosmonauts abandoned the space station because of the illness and returned to Earth.

On Feb. 19, 1986, the Soviet Union launched a new space station named *Mir*, the Russian word for *peace*. *Mir* is a more modern version of the *Salyut 7*, and the Soviets intend it to be the first permanently manned space station. On March 13, the Soviets launched a two-man cosmonaut crew to the new space station.

In a November 1985 test of construction techniques in space, astronaut Sherwood C. Spring fastens aluminum tubes together while standing on the remote-controlled arm of the shuttle *Atlantis*. Such techniques may be used to assemble a manned space station in the 1990's.

Space Technology

Continued

Probing planets and comets. Several countries carried out scientific space probes between June 1985 and June 1986. The European Space Agency (ESA), Japan, and the Soviet Union launched probes to rendezvous with Halley's Comet. The Soviet Union sent probes to the surface of the planet Venus. *Voyager 2*, launched by NASA in 1977, flew by the planet Uranus.

On June 10 and June 15, 1985, the Soviet *Vega 1* and *Vega 2* spacecraft dropped meteorological balloons into the atmosphere of Venus. The spacecraft also dropped two landing craft onto the planet's surface to sample its soil. The two balloon experiments marked the first time that meteorological balloons like those used on Earth were employed to study the atmosphere of another planet. After dropping the balloons and landers, *Vega 1* and *Vega 2* left Venus and continued on their principal mission—flying to meet Halley's Comet.

On Sept. 11, 1985, NASA's *International Cometary Explorer* became the first spacecraft to fly by a comet when it traveled through the *coma* (a vast gas cloud) surrounding the nucleus of Comet Giacobini-Zinner about 71 million kilometers (44 million miles) from Earth. The spacecraft made observations supporting the theory that comets are made of ice and dust.

On Jan. 24, 1986, the *Voyager 2* spacecraft flew by Uranus, sending back to Earth stunning photographs of the planet's outer atmosphere, rings, and moons. See ASTRONOMY, SOLAR SYSTEM (Close-Up).

In mid-March 1986, two Japanese spacecraft studied Halley's Comet from afar, while the Soviet Union's *Vega 1* and *Vega 2* spacecraft and the ESA's *Giotto* spacecraft flew close by, returning the first images of a comet's *nucleus*, its core of ice and dust. A comet's nucleus cannot be seen from Earth because the coma obscures it from our view. The *Vega* and *Giotto* images showed the nucleus to be shaped like a peanut and about 24 kilometers (15 miles) long—somewhat larger than expected. [Craig P. Covault]

In WORLD BOOK, see SPACE TRAVEL.

Zoology

Birds of a feather *do* flock together and for good reason—they are able to catch more fish that way, according to a February 1986 report by researchers in Sweden. Zoologist Frank Götmark and his colleagues at the University of Göteborg reached that conclusion after studying a dozen black-headed gulls in captivity. They found that gulls in groups caught more fish than solitary gulls.

The scientists observed gulls feeding on a school of 350 small fish in a shallow indoor pool. The researchers tested the gulls individually and in groups of three and groups of six. They counted the birds' attempts to catch fish as well as the number of fish caught. Each gull nabbed 10 to 30 fish in three minutes when hunting alone but caught twice as many when hunting with five other birds. Groups of three caught more fish than lone gulls but did not do as well as groups of six.

Flocks did better because of their effect on the fish, the scientists concluded after studying videotapes of the experiments. They found that when the gulls hunted together, the school of fish broke into groups that were half the size of groups hunted by a single bird. The fragmentation of the school apparently increased the vulnerability of the individual fish. The videotapes also revealed that the more gulls there were in a group, the more likely it was that a fish trying to escape from one bird would be driven toward another.

The platypus's sixth sense. More than its wide snout and egg-laying habits distinguish Australia's duck-billed platypus from other mammals, Australian and West German scientists reported in January 1986. The platypus feeds on small animals living in streams, and the researchers discovered that, like certain fish and amphibians, the platypus has a "nose" for electricity. It hunts by homing in on electric fields produced by its prey.

Zoologist Henning Scheich and his colleagues at the Technical University in Darmstadt, West Germany, working with scientists from the Australian National University, studied the under-

Zoology

Continued

water behavior of four platypuses in a laboratory pool filled with muddy, murky water. The investigators observed that the animals kept their eyes, ears, and nostrils shut tight while submerged but could still find prey. The scientists theorized that specialized nerve endings in the platypus's bill pick up these brief low-voltage pulses.

To confirm their theory, the scientists placed a 1.5-volt battery in the mud at the bottom of the pool. In a series of tests, the platypuses all performed well at detecting the battery.

The researchers studied a platypus bill with an electron microscope and found that it contained a network of very fine nerve endings. When a platypus encounters slight changes in voltage, these nerve cells apparently send a signal to the animal's brain.

The ear of the mantis. The Cyclops was one of a race of mythical giants with one huge eye in the center of the forehead. The praying mantis is also a cyclops of sorts—it has one ear in the center of its body, biologists David D. Yager and Ronald R. Hoy of Cornell University in Ithaca, N.Y., reported in February 1986.

Once considered deaf, praying mantises were thought to depend solely on sight and smell to find mates and evade predators. Yager and Hoy, however, discovered that the insect reacts to a wide range of frequencies and intensities, including *ultrasonic* sounds (sounds that are too high for the human ear to perceive). Upon close inspection, the researchers found that the mantis has an ear—actually two eardrums situated within a single deep groove—in the center of its abdomen. The researchers said the mantis's ear may help the male mantis find females to mate with.

Male mantises court at night, flying along odor trails left by females. But the insects may also "call" to each other with weak ultrasonic signals produced by rubbing their wings against their abdomen.

Elephant rumbles. Communication at sound frequencies beyond the range of human hearing is not confined to the world of insects and bats. Even el-

A male takin, a little-known animal native to the mountains of China, feeds on the tips of tree branches. Photos of takins were published for the first time in the Western world in autumn 1985. Close relatives of musk oxen, takins weigh up to 293 kilograms (650 pounds) and stand as tall as 127 centimeters (50 inches) at the shoulder. Zoologists think there are several thousand takins living in China's mountain forests.

A chameleon, fitted with special glasses that change the apparent distance of objects, stalks its prey. While wearing the glasses, the chameleon shoots out its tongue to the exact spot where the glasses make an insect appear to be, rather than where the insect is actually located. The experiment shows that chameleons, far from being hit-or-miss hunters, use their tongues with pinpoint accuracy.

Zoology

Continued

ephants produce sounds that human beings cannot hear, other Cornell University researchers reported in February 1986. Biologist Katherine Payne and her colleagues discovered that elephants make *infrasonic* noises (too low for the human ear to perceive) apparently to communicate with other members of the herd. Finback whales also produce infrasonic calls, but no land mammal had been known to make these low-frequency sounds.

Payne first suspected that elephants make inaudibly low sounds during a visit to a zoo. While watching the elephants, she several times felt a throbbing in the air, much like the vibrations produced by distant thunder.

Payne and her fellow researchers later returned to the zoo, where they used ultrasensitive sound-recording equipment to capture the inaudible throbs on tape. They noted that the vibrations occurred when a spot on an elephant's forehead fluttered. The fluttering forehead movements evidently produced the rumbling sounds.

The scientists theorized that ele-

phants use infrasonic sounds for various kinds of communication. Adult elephants, for example, seem to answer young calves with these sounds. And male elephants may listen for low-frequency signals from distant females that are ready to mate.

Prairie dog infanticide. Despite their apparent sociability, even prairie dogs have their dark side. Researchers at Princeton University in New Jersey reported in November 1985 that *infanticide* (the killing of babies) accounts for half the deaths of pups in a prairie dog colony. Adult prairie dogs often kill—and sometimes eat—pups.

The Princeton scientists, headed by biologist John L. Hoogland, spent seven years observing a colony of prairie dogs in Wind Cave National Park in South Dakota. They kept track of individual prairie dogs by putting tags on the animals' ears. They also took blood samples from the prairie dogs to determine the genetic relationships among all the members of the colony.

During the period of the research project—from 1978 through 1984—

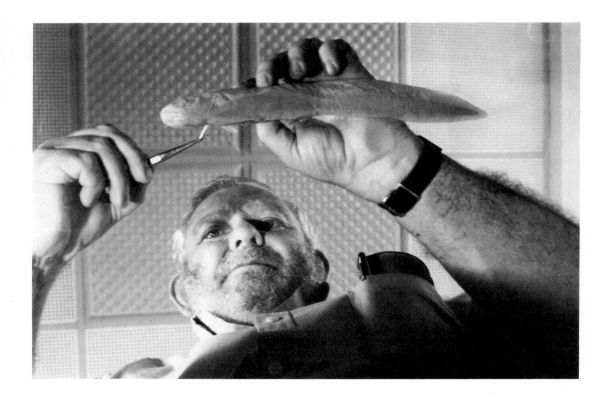

Zoology

Continued

Marine biologist Richard H. Rosenblatt of the Scripps Institution of Oceanography in La Jolla, Calif., examines a newly discovered type of eelpout, an eellike saltwater fish. The eelpout was found at a hot-water vent on the floor of the Pacific Ocean about 1,600 kilometers (1,000 miles) west of Central America.

761 young were born and 73 were killed. Males killed some of the offspring, but nursing females did most of the killing. In some cases, these marauding females protected their own pups while killing other mothers' pups. In other instances, mothers killed their own offspring or abandoned them, allowing them to be killed by neighboring females. Hoogland theorized that the purpose of some—or all—of the killings may have been to reduce overcrowding.

The killers were almost always related to the pups' mothers. In most animal societies, aggressive behavior of this sort is directed against unrelated individuals. Hoogland said prairie dogs may kill their own kin simply because it is easier than stalking and killing unrelated animals.

Leggy "lungs." Crabs have more than one way to catch a breath of fresh air, Australian zoologist David Maitland of the University of New South Wales in Kensington reported in February 1986. Some crabs breathe underwater through gills, and a few have lungs—

but sand-bubbler crabs "inhale" through membranes on the back surface of their legs.

Scientists had known for some time that sand-bubbler crabs, which are common on many tropical and subtropical beaches, breathe air. When the tide comes in, these round-bodied crustaceans burrow into the sand, trapping a pocket of air with them. It was not known, though, how the crabs—which have gills but not lungs—take the air into their bodies.

In laboratory experiments, Maitland tested the respiratory function of the sand-bubbler's leg membranes. He compared the amount of oxygen crabs used before and after he applied coats of paint to the membranes. One coat of paint reduced the crabs' oxygen use by almost two-thirds. A second coat caused the crabs to suffocate.

Maitland found that the sand-bubbler crab's leg membranes work much like lungs. Blood drifts through the crab's body, collects in the legs, and then flows through ever finer channels. When the blood finally flows di-

The Plight of the Condor

The California condor, one of the world's most endangered birds, is fighting against all odds to survive as a species. By mid-1986, only three of these vultures remained in the wild—lone sentinels of a vanishing breed that thousands of years ago commanded the skies over much of North America. The three survivors—all males—have become the focus of a heated debate over how best to protect them to ensure the survival of the species.

Many wildlife experts, including those at the United States Fish and Wildlife Service as well as the Los Angeles Zoo and San Diego Wild Animal Park, argue that the three condors should be captured and placed in "protective custody" at the two zoos, where a government-sponsored captive-breeding program has been in effect since 1979. There are 24 condors in captivity, 12 in Los Angeles and 12 in San Diego.

Other experts, however, including officials of the National Audubon Society and a number of scientists, believe that the three wild condors should be left to fly free in their natural habitat—the rolling hills and canyons of southern California.

There is a great sense of urgency on both sides. Although the condor's numbers have been diminishing dramatically since the mid-1940's, the bird's future has never seemed so bleak.

Once the condor ranged as far east as Florida; as far north as British Columbia, Canada; and as far south as Mexico. Its spectacular 3-meter (9½-foot) wingspan enables it to soar on air currents to heights of 4,600 meters (15,000 feet) and to glide downward at speeds up to 130 kilometers (80 miles) per hour. But hunting, the growth of cities, environmental pollution, and the illegal collection of condor eggs have taken a grim toll.

During the winter of 1984-1985, 6 of 12 wild condors disappeared and are presumed dead. This course of events so alarmed the Fish and Wildlife Service that on Dec. 17, 1985, it reversed its long-standing policy of leaving some condors in the wild and ordered the capture of the remaining 6 wild condors. The decision was attacked by the National Audubon Society, which obtained a court order preventing the agency from carrying out its plan.

The Audubon Society argued that removing the condors from the wild would imperil their habitat, which is under pressure from developers, and reduce the chances of reestablishing the bird in the wild. In addition, the society argued that without wild condors, there would be no "guide birds" for condors released from the captive breeding program to imitate and learn from. Finally, the society pointed out that not one condor egg has been produced in captivity—the captive breeding program is totally dependent on eggs brought in from the wild by trained biologists.

Even as both sides argued in court, there was mixed news from California. On Jan. 18, 1986, a wild female condor died after swallowing lead shot embedded in a carcass it had eaten. And in early March, a condor egg was found destroyed beneath its nest. But on June 6, a condor chick hatched at the San Diego Park. Because the three remaining condors in the wild are male, a female condor, captured in June, may be returned to the wild to ensure egg production. (A fourth male condor was captured in May.)

Debate also continued over plans to purchase a refuge for the condors. In 1984, at the urging of the Audubon Society, the U.S. government agreed to buy a 5,700-hectare (14,000-acre) ranch northwest of Los Angeles. The ranch land includes one of the condor's prime foraging areas. The Fish and Wildlife Service has delayed the purchase, however, contending that if the remaining wild condors are captured, the refuge would be unneeded.

Meanwhile, other experts argue that the problem of whether to buy the ranch can wait until the remaining wild condors are safe in captivity. They argue that the loss of a single bird in the wild hastens the day of extinction. With each bird's death, the gene pool gets smaller. Already, they say, the condor may be "functionally extinct." That is, it may have reached the point where its numbers—in the wild and in captivity—are too small to ensure the survival of the species. [Larry B. Stammer]

A biologist restrains a newly captured wild condor, trapped as part of an effort to preserve this endangered species.

Zoology

Continued

rectly under the membrane, it absorbs oxygen and releases carbon dioxide through the pores of the membrane.

Untrustworthy birds. Even birds have tricksters in their ranks, according to Charles Munn, a biologist at the Bronx Zoo in New York City. Munn made that discovery while studying the behavior of insect-eating birds in the Amazon rain forests of Peru. He noticed that two species of birds that often act as sentinels and warn other birds of approaching danger frequently sounded false alarms in order to grab another bird's prey. His observations added to the growing body of evidence that animals may not always be as straightforward as they seem.

Two species of insect-eating birds that live in groups inhabit the forests where Munn did his research. One species hunts in the *upper canopy*, or treetops; the other type hunts in the *lower canopy*—the bushes and smaller trees. While they feed, the flocks must keep an eye out for bird-eating hawks. They are aided by the two sentinel birds—the ant shrike, which serves as

a lookout for the lower-canopy birds, and the shrike-tanager, which keeps watch for the upper-canopy birds.

When either of these sentinel birds gives a sharp call, the other birds freeze and then dart for cover. In return for providing these warnings, the sentinels rely on the other birds to flush out insects for them. The sentinel birds will not steal an insect from another bird's bill, but they often try to outmaneuver birds that are pursuing an insect. Munn found that a sentinel bird was most likely to give a false alarm when competing with another bird for an insect.

The false calls were shorter than the real alarms—usually just a few notes to distract a nearby rival. But the duped birds could not afford to ignore any such "warnings." "The potential penalty for ignoring even one alarm call might be death," Munn said, "so it is not surprising that flock birds seem to take all alarm calls seriously."

[William J. Bell and Elizabeth Pennisi]

In WORLD BOOK, see ANIMAL; ZOOLOGY.

Science You Can Use

In areas selected for their current interest, *Science Year* presents information that the reader as a consumer can use in making decisions—from buying products to caring for personal health and well-being.

Video Systems: New Choices for Home Moviemakers

Home moviemaking has changed rapidly in the past few years. In a field once dominated by film, video is quickly gaining the upper hand. In 1985, Americans bought about 400,000 video *camcorders* (combination camera-recorders), according to the Electronic Industries Association, compared with fewer than 75,000 Super 8 film cameras.

Why are so many people choosing video over film? The answer is largely convenience. About 28 million American households had video cassette recorders (VCR's) by 1986, all hooked up to their TV sets and ready to play video cassettes. Video is more convenient than dragging a film projector and movie screen out of the closet. Video also allows you to see your recorded movies immediately, without making a trip to a film developer and waiting for them to finish their job. You can also record over a video movie if you do not want to save what you've shot.

Film still has its advantages, however. The start-up costs are a lot lower. You can get a simple Super 8 film camera for less than $150, and the cheapest silent and sound projectors for about $150 and $300, respectively. But the least expensive video movie equipment will set you back about $1,000. Film is also a lot easier to edit. You simply cut up the pieces of developed film and splice them back together in the order you want. Editing with video involves copying the information recorded on one videotape to a second videotape by using two VCR's and by monitoring your effort with two TV's and a lot of patience.

Home video moviemaking didn't really take off until the introduction of the camcorder in August 1983. Camcorders are compact and "self-sufficient." They contain a camera, a recorder, and a battery for the recorder—all in one unit. By 1985, video manufacturers had introduced camcorders using four different methods for taking video pictures. These are Beta; VHS; VHS-C, a small-cassette format compatible with VHS VCR's; and 8-millimeter (8-mm), which uses a cassette as small as an audio tape. Thus, camcorders were available to match the format of any consumer VCR.

Prior to the camcorder, the only home movie video systems available were two-piece units—a video camera, which translates scenes into electronic signals, and a battery-powered, portable VCR, which lays down those signals on videotape. The portable VCR—connected to the camera by a cable—is usually hung from the shoulder with a strap. As a result, it is bulkier and heavier than a camcorder, weighing 5 to 10 pounds or more. The separate cameras add another 2 to 6 pounds. These separate video cameras and portable VCR's are still available. They have remained popular because they have many features that can't be found on camcorders, such as time-lapse photography; stereo sound; and the ability to put titles directly on the video picture.

Purchasing a portable VCR and camera, instead of a camcorder, also could be less expensive for the consumer who does not have a tabletop VCR at home. Unlike camcorders, most portable VCR's can replace a tabletop VCR because they perform the same functions. Most portables come in two pieces—the recorder section and the tuner-timer section. The recorder section goes out with the camera on the shoots. The tuner-timer section stays at home. When attached to the recorder section and the TV antenna, the tuner-timer can be programmed to record your favorite TV programs.

Portable VCR's range in price from about $500 to $1,000, about $200 more than comparable tabletop VCR's. Add to this a separate camera that costs from $400 to about $1,000, and you can purchase a video system for

Making Home Movies		
Format:	**Advantages**	**Disadvantages**
Film	Start-up costs inexpensive, ranging from $150 to $450. Easy to edit. Excellent color and picture detail. Small, lightweight, and easy to handle.	Waiting time for developing. Requires setup of projector and screen. Limited choice of models. About 2½ minutes of shooting time per film cartridge.
Video	No developing needed. Viewed on TV screen. Up to 8 hours shooting time per tape.	Expensive, ranging from $650 to over $2,000. Difficult to edit. Color and picture quality not as good as film. Generally heavier than film cameras.
Varieties of video movie equipment:	**Advantages**	**Disadvantages**
Camcorder	Light and easy to carry—eliminates need to carry extra weight of portable VCR pack on your shoulder as required with separate video camera.	Expensive, ranging from $1,000 to $1,800. Lacks range of features available on separate video cameras.
Separate video camera	Offers wide range of features, such as fade-in, fade-out; stereo sound; time-lapse recording; and the ability to put titles directly on video picture. Relatively cheaper than combination of camcorder and tabletop VCR.	Extra weight of portable VCR pack.
8-mm camcorder	Very lightweight and easy to handle. Simple to operate.	Expensive, about $200 to $300 more than half-inch video camcorders.

less than the cost of both a tabletop VCR and a camcorder.

The camcorder cannot replace a tabletop VCR. Although a camcorder can play back recordings on a TV, it does not have the tuner-timer section that comes with a portable or tabletop VCR, though some can work with optional tuner-timers.

The great advantage of camcorders lies in their weight and size. Camcorders range in size from the VHS and Beta models, weighing from about 5 to 8 pounds, to smaller 8-mm and VHS-C units, weighing between 1½ and 5 pounds.

Many camcorder models, including some 8-mm models, use adapters to play back tapes on your TV. You hook the camcorder to the adapter, which is hooked up to your TV. None of the Beta camcorders, however, can play back directly on your TV. This is because of the recording process they use. To view the tape on your TV, you must take the recorded tape from the camcorder and play it on a separate Beta VCR. The tiniest 8-mm camcorder—the Handycam made by the Sony Corporation of America—requires a special VCR made for 8-mm tapes. The Handycam and the separate 8-mm VCR are sold as a unit.

Video cameras and camcorders come with slightly different options that you should consider before you make your purchase decision. These options include, for example, various pickup devices and viewfinders.

Video cameras and camcorders offer two kinds of *pickup devices*, the part of the camera that converts incoming light to electronic signals. The pickup device lies directly behind a video camera's lens, so that light entering through the lens strikes the pickup device. The most common type of pickup device is a tube, ranging from one-third to two-thirds of an inch in diameter. Although bigger tubes mean bigger cameras, they also mean better pictures, because bigger tubes collect more light. The advantage of a tube is that it allows you to shoot in dim light—even by candlelight with some advanced models. Its chief disadvantage is that it can be permanently damaged if it is aimed at an extremely bright light source, such as the sun.

The other type of pickup device is a solid-state computer chip with thousands of microscopic photosensors, known either as a charge-coupled device (CCD) or a metal oxide sensor (MOS). These pickups are much smaller than tubes and thus enable manufacturers to build smaller and lighter cameras and camcorders. For a number of years, manufacturers shied away from using computer chips because they performed poorly in low light and reproduced color inadequately in comparison with tubes. Marked improvements have been made in these areas, however, so more and more cameras and camcorders are now using chips, which can't be damaged by bright lights.

Video *viewfinders* also come in two varieties: electronic and optical. An optical viewfinder resembles those found on film cameras. They allow you to see approximately what you are shooting, though not exactly as it will later appear on your TV. Electronic viewfinders, however, are actually tiny TV tubes perched on top of the camera. Electronic viewfinders have two advantages. First, they allow you to see what you are recording exactly as it will appear on your TV screen. Secondly, they enable you to play back the scenes you've just recorded in the middle of a shooting session. If you don't like a scene you've just taped, you can rewind the recorder to the scene's beginning and tape it over. Most electronic viewfinders show the image in black and white, but a few show color.

Finally, there are special options to consider when you're shopping for a video camera or camcorder. For example, some camera models offer autofocus, which automatically focuses the lens, eliminating the need to adjust the focus manually when your subject moves closer or farther away. Because the sensors used in autofocus can sometimes be fooled by background objects, you may also want the ability to manually override the autofocus in certain situations.

Video and film both have advantages and disadvantages, which makes choosing between them a matter of trade-offs. Judging from video sales, however, Americans are letting their choice be known.   [Jennifer Stern]

What to Look for in a Videotape

With more than 28 million video cassette recorders (VCR's) installed in American homes by 1986, more and more people were shopping for blank videotape to record their favorite TV programs or to use with video cameras for making home movies. They had a wide selection to choose from. At least 20 companies were manufacturing videotape in 1986. Tapes come in three formats, in a variety of lengths, and in several different grades. How does the owner of a VCR go about choosing a tape that has both good quality and is well suited to his or her needs?

Some of the choices are fairly obvious. Beta, VHS, and 8-millimeter (8-mm) are the three basic formats used in VCR's made for consumers. *Format* refers to the method by which picture and sound signals are recorded on videotape. You simply choose the cassette format that matches the format of your VCR. Beta and VHS both use tape that is one-half inch wide. Beta cassettes are considerably smaller than VHS cassettes, however, and the cassettes are not interchangeable.

The newest video format is 8-mm. It uses tape that is about one-third inch wide and is packed in a cassette only a little larger than an audio cassette.

Choosing the tape length that best suits your needs is also relatively easy. VHS tapes are labeled from T-30 to T-160. At the standard play (SP) speed, T-30 will record for 30 minutes, and T-160 will record for 160 minutes. Recording time is doubled at the slower, long play (LP) speed and is tripled at the even slower, extended play (EP) speed. So, a T-160 tape recorded at LP yields 320 minutes of recording time, and recorded at EP it yields 480 minutes, or 8 hours, of recording time. Generally, tapes that are recorded at faster speeds will produce a sharper picture than tapes that are recorded at slower speeds.

Beta tapes are labeled differently. A tape labeled L-125 will record for 30 minutes at the Beta II speed and 45 minutes at the slower Beta III speed. A tape labeled L-830 will record for 200 minutes at Beta II and 300 minutes at Beta III. The 8-mm tapes come in 15-, 30-, 60-, 90-, and 120-minute lengths and are labeled MP-15, MP-30, and so on.

Shorter tape lengths are generally most convenient for making home movies with a video camera or camcorder. Most home moviemakers have found that a 30-minute or 60-minute tape allows sufficient time for capturing a child's birthday party, a family reunion, or some other special event. The longer tape lengths, especially the popular two-hour cassettes, are best for taping TV programs.

The third and last consideration in deciding what tape to choose concerns quality. Most companies that manufacture videotapes have been licensed by the developers of the three VCR formats. These licensed companies have demonstrated the ability to make tape and produce cassettes that are up to the developers' standards. Not all the tape cassettes being sold are from licensed companies, however. Consumers who purchase an unlicensed tape risk harming their VCR's with poorly made tapes or cassettes. Residue from such tapes may damage the video recording and playback heads, and poorly made cassettes may jam in a VCR.

To avoid these misfortunes, choose cassettes with the official Beta, VHS, or 8-mm logo on the package, rather than cassettes with labels such as "B-type," "V-type," or "V.H.S." Only licensed companies can display the Beta logo, which has the word Beta above the Greek letter beta; or the VHS logo, which consists of the capital letters VHS, without periods. The official 8-mm logo has the numeral 8 in a box.

Tape manufacturers offer up to four different grades of tape—usually labeled standard grade, high grade, extra high grade, or pro. The variety allows you to tailor your tape selection

Tape Care Tips

- Keep tapes away from dust and tobacco smoke.
- After each use, store your tape cassettes in plastic sleeves. Cardboard sleeves shed paper dust onto tape cassettes.
- Store cassettes away from high temperatures, preferably no more than 70°F. and out of direct sunlight. Never leave tapes in a hot car.
- Store recorded tapes away from TV sets, stereo speakers, and other appliances that produce magnetic fields, which can erase the recorded images on your tapes.
- Store cassettes upright, never flat, with the loaded cassette reel below the unloaded one to prevent damage to tape edges and reels.
- Store the tape so that only the plastic leader is exposed to the air. Do this by rewinding the tape or playing it all the way through.
- Exercise tapes you don't play very often by playing them or fast forwarding and then rewinding them— about twice a year.

to your recording and budget needs.

Tape grade refers to the quality of the materials making up the tape itself. If you could examine a tape microscopically, you would see two and sometimes three layers. One layer is a polyester base film. The second layer consists of tiny metal oxide particles mixed with a gluelike substance that binds the particles to the base film. High-grade tapes also have a third layer called a backcoating that helps ensure the tape will run smoothly through the VCR.

The higher the grade of videotape, the better each element of the tape is likely to be. As a general rule, higher grades of tape last longer and produce better pictures.

Selecting the grade of tape you want ultimately depends on how special the recording will be to you. For a home movie of "baby's first steps," you might want an extra-high-grade or pro video cassette because such tapes will last longer and will provide a better picture. For taping the daily soap operas for one-time viewing, standard-grade tape is fine. If you plan to record TV programs at the slow VCR speeds, however, you may want to use higher-grade tape. At those speeds, the video heads lay down much less information on each given area of tape surface, so a tape that can retain as much information as possible is best.

Though they are small and inexpensive—averaging about $5 each in 1986—videotapes should not be taken for granted. Poor-quality tapes or tapes that are improperly cared for could damage the surface of the recording heads inside a very expensive piece of equipment—your VCR. And you could lose your recorded programs at the same time.   [Jennifer Stern]

Contact Lenses: Keeping an Eye on New Advances

About 70 per cent of the people living in the United States require some type of vision correction. Of these, about 19 million people, mostly in the 20- to 40-year-old age group, have chosen to wear contact lenses.

Contact lenses are plastic eyeglasses that are worn directly on the eye. About the size of a person's little fingernail, contact lenses rest on a thin layer of tears that float on the surface of the *cornea*, the transparent outer tissue of the eyeball.

Each year, about 2 million to 3 million Americans become contact lens wearers. Most are likely to wear one of four common types: hard contact lenses, gas-permeable hard lenses, daily-wear soft lenses, or extended-wear soft lenses. Special types of contact lenses are also available for people who need bifocals to correct *presbyopia* (a blurring of objects close to the eye caused by aging), or who need to correct *astigmatism* (blurred vision caused by a defect in the shape of the cornea).

Daily-wear soft lenses are currently the most commonly worn contact lenses. In the United States, about 13.3 million people were wearing this type of lens in 1986, but extended-wear soft lenses have also become popular.

There are a number of reasons for wearing contact lenses rather than ordinary eyeglasses. For people who are very *near-sighted* (images of distant objects appear blurred), ordinary eyeglasses make images appear smaller than they are, while side—or peripheral—vision is distorted. With contact lenses, however, the size of images appears normal, and side vision is not affected. Contact lenses are also better than ordinary eyeglasses for people who have had cataracts removed. Otherwise, the ability to correct vision is about the same for ordinary eyeglasses and contact lenses. Most of the people who wear contact lenses probably do so because they believe it improves their appearance.

Only ophthalmologists, optometrists, and opticians are legally qualified to fit contact lenses in the United States. An ophthalmologist is a medical doctor trained to recognize and treat eye diseases. An optometrist is a licensed, nonmedical professional who is trained to examine eyes and to prescribe and fit glasses and contact lenses. An optician is someone who makes and sells eyeglasses and contact lenses that have been prescribed by optometrists or ophthalmologists.

Standard hard contact lenses were introduced in the 1950's. These lenses do not absorb water and will not allow tears or air to pass through them. This can create a problem because both tears and air provide oxygen that the cornea needs to remain healthy. If the cornea does not receive enough oxygen, it will become swollen, and the contact lens will feel uncomfortable. If the contact lens is not removed, the eye will become red and painful.

Hard lenses have other disadvantages. They must be worn according to a strict schedule with a gradual increase in wearing time. These lenses also may "pop out," and it is not uncommon for foreign bodies to get underneath them. On the positive side, however, hard lenses are durable, easy to handle and clean, and are relatively inexpensive.

In order to overcome the disadvantages of hard contact lenses, other types of lenses were invented. Gas-permeable lenses, introduced in 1979, offer greater comfort and longer wearing time than do standard hard lenses. They are called *gas permeable* because they allow oxygen and carbon dioxide to pass through them. Although these lenses are somewhat flexible, they are still considered hard lenses. And as with ordinary hard lenses, visual sharpness, durability, and ease of handling and care are other advantages of these lenses.

Daily-wear soft contact lenses, introduced in 1971, not only allow air to pass through but also absorb water.

Characteristics of Various Types of Contact Lenses

Common Types of Contact Lenses

Lenses	Characteristics
Hard	**Hard plastic:** Prevent tears and air from passing through. Cause initial discomfort and require period of adjustment. Must be worn according to a regular daily schedule with an average wearing time of 8 hours. May pop out. Easy for foreign bodies to get trapped between the lens and eye. Cause blurred vision—ranging from a few minutes to several hours—when removed and replaced by glasses. Are durable, lasting up to 10 years. Provide clear, sharp vision. Easy to handle and clean. Relatively inexpensive. **Gas permeable:** Allow some air to pass through. Are more flexible than ordinary hard lenses but less pliable than soft ones. Provide sharp vision. Are durable and easy to handle and clean.
Soft	**Daily wear:** High water content allows tears and air to pass through. Very comfortable and easy to adjust to. Strict wearing schedule not required. Vision not as sharp as with hard lenses. Lens not as durable as hard, requiring replacement after about two years. Must be handled carefully; rip easily. Require greater attention to cleaning. Must be stored in disinfecting solution. **Extended wear:** Very high water content—about 15 to 25 per cent more than daily-wear soft lenses—allows tears and air to pass through readily. Extremely comfortable. Can be worn during sleep and for extended periods, ranging from a week to a month. More prone to build-up of deposits. Less durable, requiring replacement sometimes as often as twice a year. Can be torn easily. Can lead to serious eye infection if strict hygiene is not followed. Frequent, follow-up eye examinations required. Expensive.

Special types of lenses

Bifocals		Toric
Concentric (Far vision, Near vision) Crescent (Far vision, Near vision)	Bifocal contact lenses come in two basic designs: concentric and crescent. The various parts of the lens contain corrections for near and far vision, but the lines separating the corrections are not visible as they are in most bifocal eyeglasses.	Toric lenses are soft lenses designed to correct astigmatism. People with astigmatism have an irregularly shaped cornea. The toric lens is curved in a way that compensates for this shape. In addition, added plastic is often placed in the lower part of a toric lens to weight it down and prevent it from rotating.

The water content can vary from 30 per cent to 40 per cent. Because of this, soft lenses are extremely comfortable. They can be worn after the first fitting for many hours, and a strict wearing schedule is unnecessary. Soft lenses have several disadvantages, however. For example, visual sharpness is not as crisp as it is with hard lenses. Foreign particles and natural secretions from the eye build up on soft lenses, and they are not as durable as hard lenses. Soft lenses must be disinfected and stored in a saline solution, and they are more time-consuming to clean.

Extended-wear soft lenses were approved by the federal Food and Drug Administration (FDA) in 1980 and became widely available in 1981. They are thinner than daily-wear soft lenses, have a higher water content of about 55 to 80 per cent, and are made of a slightly different material that allows more oxygen to reach the cornea. Because of this, they are even more comfortable than daily-wear soft lenses and can be worn for extended periods, including during sleep.

People who wear such lenses, however, must follow strictly the schedule for removal and cleaning called for by their contact lens specialist. Frequent follow-up eye examinations after the initial fitting are extremely important.

There may be greater risks with extended-wear lenses than with other types of contact lenses. It appears that people sometimes disregard the disinfecting, cleaning, and removal schedule because the lenses can be worn for extended periods. As a result of this casual attitude, the oxygen supply to the cornea is reduced for a longer period than would be the case with soft lenses that are removed daily.

Cases of corneal ulcers have been reported among people with extended-wear lenses. A corneal ulcer occurs when the outer layer of the cornea is worn down and bacteria invade the tissue. The resulting infection can scar the cornea—sometimes permanently—and an unchecked infection can cause loss of sight. Anyone who experiences such symptoms as redness of the eye, pain, a discharge from the eye, or reduced vision should remove the lens immediately and seek medical care.

The special types of lenses for presbyopia and astigmatism are relatively new. Both are considered difficult to fit. Bifocal lenses for presbyopia come in two designs: crescent-shaped and concentric-shaped like a bull's-eye. Both designs combine prescriptions for near and far vision.

In the crescent design, the top part of the lens contains the correction for distance, and the crescent-shaped segment at the bottom of the lens contains the correction for near vision. As the eye gazes ahead, it looks through the part of the lens that corrects for distance, and when the eye gazes down—as for reading—it looks through the part that corrects for near vision. Similarly, in the concentric design, the innermost ring is for distant vision, and the outermost ring for near vision.

A soft contact lens with a special shape for correcting astigmatism became available in 1980, and there are now several designs. One type consists of a gas-permeable hard lens at the center fused to a soft lens that surrounds it. This combination provides sharp vision with the hard lens and comfort with the soft lens.

Finally, tinted soft lenses are now available in green, blue, aqua, and violet. These lenses can change the color of a blue or green eye.

New contact lens designs and improvements are constantly becoming available. Soon to be released are "soil-resistant" soft lenses that prevent the build-up of foreign particles. Now available in Europe are disposable, extended-wear soft lenses that come in "six packs." After three months, the wearer discards the worn lens and inserts a new one, free of secretion build-up. These lenses, however, still pose problems with quality control, sterility, and comfort.

In the experimental stage is the "instant contact lens." A drop of a special liquid containing a patient's prescription would be placed on the eye. Instantly, the drop would harden into a contact lens offering perfect comfort, fit, and vision.

With constant improvements being made, contact lenses continue to grow in popularity. As they do, people are finding fewer reasons for wearing eyeglasses.   [Spencer E. Sherman]

Matching Pots and Pans to Your Cooking Needs

For thousands of years, people have made cooking utensils out of two kinds of materials—metals and ceramics. Copper, tin, and iron have been traditional favorites among the metals; and earthenware, stoneware, and glass among the ceramics. Modern cooks can also choose from such innovations as stainless steel, aluminum, ceramic-metal hybrids, and "nonstick" resin coatings.

Ideally, pots and pans should offer two characteristics. They should conduct heat well, so that they heat evenly and do not burn food. And their surfaces should be chemically unreactive, so that the flavor, color, and nutritional value of the food are not harmed by the utensil during cooking. But even today, no single material gives ideal cooking performance.

Cooking can be broadly defined as the transfer of energy from a heat source to food. When we cook on the stove or in the oven, we first heat the pan that contains the food, and the pan then transfers the heat energy to the food itself. This process of heat transfer is called *conduction*, the movement of heat through a material by the motion of a material's molecules, atoms, or subatomic particles.

Metals are very good heat conductors because of the movement of the subatomic particles called *electrons* that orbit the nuclei of metal atoms. In a metal, the outer electrons are held loosely and can break free of their orbit and move easily throughout the metal. When heat is applied to a metal pan, these mobile electrons transfer heat energy readily from one spot to another.

Ceramics, on the other hand, are very poor conductors of heat. Ceramics consist of varous oxide molecules, and the electrons in such molecules cannot move about as easily as those in metals and therefore cannot easily transmit energy from one point to the next. Heat is conducted through ceramics by the vibrations of whole molecules or groups of molecules. This is a much slower process than occurs in metals.

These basic properties of metals and ceramics help determine their roles in the kitchen. Because they are good heat conductors, metal pots and pans can be heated directly on the stovetop, but ceramic utensils are best suited to slow heating in an oven.

The mobility of electrons that makes metals good conductors of heat also gives them the disadvantage of reacting chemically with food molecules when heated. Fresh metal surfaces can react with pigment molecules in food or give light-colored foods a grayish cast. They can also hasten the destruction of vitamins and impart a metallic flavor to the food. The tightly bound electrons in ceramic materials, on the other hand, do not react readily with food and so do not affect food quality.

When metals are exposed to the air, their surface atoms undergo a spontaneous reaction with oxygen in the air to form stable metal oxides. These metal oxides form a natural protective coating, but it is extremely thin and easily scratched through or worn away.

Although all metals are good heat conductors, some are better than others. Copper is the best conductor, but copper has three significant disadvantages. It is relatively expensive, and it tarnishes quickly. Most important, unlined copper utensils can be a health hazard, because copper from the unlined surface can react with the food being cooked. And too much copper in the diet can cause gastrointestinal problems, even damage to the liver.

To overcome this drawback, copper utensils are usually lined with a thin coating of tin, but tin has its own problems. Tin has a low melting point of about 450°F., a temperature sometimes reached in cooking. Tin is also susceptible to wear.

Aluminum boasts a heat conductivity second only to copper's. It is nontoxic and relatively inexpensive. Alu-

Picking Pots and Pans

Types	Cost	Heat Conduction	Reaction with Food	Other Qualities
Aluminum	Relatively inexpensive	Excellent heat conductor, second only to copper	Can discolor food	Surface easily pitted
Cast iron	Inexpensive	Heats slowly but holds heat for long periods of time	Tends to discolor some foods, unless properly "seasoned"	Corrodes easily
Ceramic	Relatively inexpensive	Poor heat conductor. Best for oven cooking. Good for keeping cooked foods warm	None	Resists corrosion, but cracks and shatters easily
Combinations of metals	Relatively expensive	Improves heat conduction, does not develop hot spots that can burn food	None	Resists corrosion
Copper	Expensive	Best heat conductor available. Heats evenly and never develops hot spots	Unlined copper readily reacts with food, sometimes adversely	Tarnishes easily
Stainless steel	Relatively expensive	Inefficient heat conductor. May develop hot spots, depending on thickness	None	Resists corrosion

minum is also a lightweight metal, which makes aluminum cookware easy to handle. But its thin, weak oxide coating is worn through easily during cooking, so that light-colored foods tend to turn gray or black.

To overcome this problem, manufacturers introduced anodized aluminum utensils. Anodized aluminum is made by placing the metal in a solution of sulfuric acid and passing an electric current through the solution. This electrochemical process forms a thick oxide coating on the aluminum surface.

Cast iron, an alloy of iron and about 3 per cent carbon, is another popular metal for utensils. It is not as good a conductor of heat as copper or aluminum, but an iron pan will absorb more heat and hold it longer than an aluminum pan of the same thickness.

The advantages of cast iron are its low cost and its harmlessness. The human body absorbs only a fraction of the iron it ingests when food is cooked in cast iron, and most people can actually benefit from additional dietary iron. The biggest disadvantages of iron are its tendencies to make light-colored foods turn gray and for the metal to rust.

Stainless steel was developed in the late 1800's in order to overcome iron's rust problem. Stainless steel is an alloy of various metals, including chromium, iron, carbon, and manganese. Chromium is the chief ingredient and the secret behind stainless steel's rust resistance.

Stainless steel has two important drawbacks, however. It is much less efficient at conducting heat than is iron. And it is relatively expensive. For these reasons, stainless steel utensils are usually made fairly thin, and this results in a tendency to develop *hot spots*—heat is distributed unevenly so food cooks unevenly.

Earthenware, stoneware, and glass are all ceramics—mixtures of oxide compounds of silicon, aluminum, and magnesium. Earthenware is made by molding and drying clays. Stoneware is made from clays that are high in silica, the major component of sand. Stoneware is baked at a high temperature, so that it turns partly to glass. It is less porous than earthenware and much more durable. Glass consists almost entirely of silica.

Ceramic materials resist corrosion and tend not to react with food molecules, but they are poor heat conductors. They are also brittle. Both metals and ceramics expand when they are heated, but being poor conductors, ceramics cannot distribute direct heat quickly and evenly. When a ceramic pot is placed on a stovetop, the part of the pot directly over the flame or electric element expands while nearby areas do not. This creates stresses that can build up until the utensil cracks or shatters. Heat-resistant glass contains small amounts of compounds that reduce the effect of heat expansion. This glass is more resistant to heat shock but not immune. Ceramic materials are therefore limited primarily to the even heat of oven cooking.

Efforts to create the ideal pan with good heat conduction and a surface that does not react with food have led to utensils made of various combinations of materials. For example, coating the underside of a stainless steel pan with a layer of copper, or sandwiching a copper or aluminum plate between two stainless steel layers in the bottom of the pan, reduces stainless steel's problem of hot spots while retaining its protection from rust.

Coatings of a material that does not react with food can be applied to the surfaces of iron, steel, or aluminum utensils. Enamelware, for example, is made by fusing powdered glass onto iron or steel utensils. These thin ceramic layers are easily chipped, however, so enamelware should be treated with some care.

Resins developed in the 1960's are another major class of protective coatings. The "nonstick" Teflon and Silverstone coatings are carbon-fluorine compounds that do not react with food and are very easy to clean. They are fairly easily scratched, however, and food can stick in the scratches.

Choosing the right cookware is a matter of matching your kitchen habits with utensils of the appropriate quality, convenience, and price. The better your pots and pans are suited to your cooking needs, the less trouble it will be for you to prepare the foods that you enjoy.   [Harold McGee]

Home Medical Tests: What You Should Know

Many medical tests that were once performed in a doctor's office can now be performed in your home. Since the early 1980's, drug companies have introduced a variety of home medical tests. Sales of such tests in the United States reached $535 million by the end of 1985, and industry experts predicted $1 billion in sales by the early 1990's. What kinds of tests are available, and what should consumers know about them?

All of the home medical tests are nonprescription, sold over the counter in drugstores. Two basic types of test kits are available to the general public—*diagnostic* tests and *monitoring* tests. A diagnostic test determines whether a certain condition, such as a pregnancy, or a disease, such as strep throat, has taken hold in your body. A monitoring test checks a known condition. One

such test, for example, determines the *blood sugar* (glucose) level in a person with diabetes.

Home medical tests must receive approval from the federal Food and Drug Administration (FDA) before the tests can be sold. Home medical tests must meet the standards of tests used by professional laboratories, according to FDA requirements. By mid-1986, the FDA had approved 76 different brands of home medical tests for monitoring or diagnosing eight basic conditions: blood pressure; glucose levels in blood or urine; hidden blood in the stool; gonorrhea; pregnancy; *ovulation* (the release of a woman's egg from the ovary); strep throat; and urinary tract infections.

The most widely available tests or kits on drugstore shelves in 1986 were those for pregnancy, ovulation, hidden

Home Medical Tests		
Condition	**Processing time**	**Cost**
Blood pressure	Immediate	From $30 to $60
Hidden blood	Immediate	From $6 to $8
Glucose monitoring	Immediate	From $10 to $100
Gonorrhea	Two or three days	From $14 to $20
Pregnancy	15 minutes to an hour	About $11
Ovulation	Two hours	From $30 to $60
Strep throat	Four hours	About $10
Urinary infections	Four hours	About $10

blood, glucose monitoring, and blood pressure. The tests for urinary tract infections, gonorrheal infections, and strep throat were available in only some parts of the United States as drug companies tested them to determine consumer interest.

Blood-pressure kits and the latest ovulation detection kits in 1986 ranged in price from $30 to $60. Other home tests ranged from $6 to $11.

The first home test was introduced in 1941. It enabled diabetics to detect the presence of urinary glucose. Medical tests for any other condition had to be performed in a doctor's office or a medical laboratory.

The tests required chemicals and equipment too complicated or too bulky to be used at home by the typical consumer. Many tests involved growing cultures under laboratory conditions and required two or three days before results were available.

The scientific breakthrough that made home tests possible for a variety of medical conditions occurred in 1975 when scientists produced the first monoclonal antibodies, now the basic ingredient in most home tests. A monoclonal antibody is a *clone* (copy) of an *antibody* (a substance produced by the immune system) that reacts to a specific *antigen*, or identifying molecule, on a substance foreign to the body.

In 1977, soon after this breakthrough, the first home pregnancy test was introduced. This test contained monoclonal antibodies for a hormone that is present only in the urine of pregnant women. If the hormone is present, the monoclonal antibodies react to another ingredient in the test. With the most recent tests, this reaction causes a color change in the urine. The color change usually becomes apparent within an hour. No special laboratory equipment or time-consuming process is required, making the test simple enough to be performed at home.

By the early 1980's, drug companies were introducing a variety of home medical tests using monoclonal antibodies. Ovulation kits, for example, have monoclonal antibodies that react to a specific hormone that surges in quantity just before ovulation. Again, a color change alerts the user to impending ovulation. Unlike pregnancy tests, which claim an accuracy rate of 99 per cent, the ovulation tests are labeled "predictive." They tell the user when she is most likely to ovulate—and therefore, most likely to become pregnant.

Tests for hidden blood in the stool also use monoclonal antibodies, embedded in a pad of tissue paper. Color changes in the paper indicate the presence of hidden blood. Mere traces of blood found in feces can mean ulcers, hemorrhoids, colitis, diverticulitis, or polyps. Hidden blood can also be an early symptom of cancer of the colon and rectum, the second-largest cancer killer in the United States after lung cancer.

The monitoring tests used by diabetics rely on chemicals that react to the presence of glucose rather than on monoclonal antibodies. In most tests, a person with diabetes dips a stick or a strip of paper into a few drops of urine or blood and matches the resulting color to a chart to determine his or her glucose level. Some companies have introduced easy-to-read computerized meters that flash a digital readout of the blood glucose levels when the strip is inserted in the meter.

The medical community's reaction to home medical tests has been mixed. Many physicians and medical associations have expressed concern about some diagnostic tests, for example. They warn that such tests often do not tell whether a person actually has a particular condition. Other tests or a physical examination that can be performed only by a doctor are often needed in conjunction with a particular home test. The physicians' concern is based on the fear that if someone obtains negative results from a home test kit, it may keep that person from seeing a physician and a condition may go undetected.

A negative result on a home pregnancy test should not be considered as proof without a pelvic examination by a physician, according to Louise Tyrer, vice president for medical affairs for the Planned Parenthood Federation of America. A spokesman for the American College of Obstetricians and Gynecologists also cautioned that the "pregnancy tests have to be carefully done." In a small percentage of cases, the tests show negative results though the woman is pregnant. Likewise, some tests show positive results though there is no pregnancy, according to the spokesman.

The American Cancer Society (ACS) has expressed similar concern about home tests for hidden blood. The ACS believes the test should be used only in conjunction with a doctor's examination. The ACS has warned that the home tests for hidden blood are not diagnostic tests for colorectal cancer, but merely tests for blood in the stool. While blood in the stool can be an early warning signal for colorectal cancer, other types of tests are used to actually diagnose colorectal cancer, and these must be done under the supervision of a physician. Nevertheless, an ACS spokesman stated that "anything that gets people to go to a doctor if

they normally wouldn't is a good thing."

A similar view was echoed by James Sammons, executive vice president of the American Medical Association, during testimony before the FDA in October 1985 on the safety and effectiveness of home medical tests. If properly implemented, Sammons told the FDA, the tests "can be a positive step toward continued improvement in the health of the American people. . . .We see this technology as one which can lead individuals to greater personal involvement in decisions regarding prevention, detection, and treatment of disease." There were, however, some areas of concern, Sammons added, about the ability of the home-test user to interpret results correctly and act upon them.

Many other physicians see the home tests as a positive development that encourages people to become involved in caring for their health and detecting early symptoms of disease. "The home test stimulates the consumer to check something early; to get some information on whether they need to see a physician," says Edward Langston, a physician and the chairman of the Committee on Drugs and Devices for the American Academy of Family Physicians. "My experience with the stool blood tests has been positive. They are very helpful. I have had patients come in for diagnosis because of them." The academy's official position states that the tests can be done reasonably well at home, but should be done along with a physician's examination.

Most of the home tests provide a toll-free telephone number that is answered by a health professional. Instructions that come with the tests urge the consumer to call if there are any questions about the results of the tests. Pamphlets included with the tests also urge the consumer to see a physician if the test results are positive.

Some home medical tests appear to have the potential to lower health costs, while providing some health benefits. But the tests may have negative results for the consumer if they are used as a substitute for a physician's diagnosis. As the variety of tests grows, so do these potential risks and benefits.   [Judy Alsofrom]

People in Science

The work of science is carried out in many places, including government-supported institutions and even the military services. This section presents two government-supported research settings and the people who work in them. It begins with the story of an admiral in the United States Navy whose career was intimately involved with the development of computer science. It continues with the story of one of the most famous research establishments in Europe and its great scientists, past and present.

This pioneer in the development
of computing continues to inspire
students and professionals alike.

Grace M. Hopper

BY GINA KOLATA

Rear Admiral Grace Murray Hopper points to a white clock
mounted on the wall of her office, where it is surrounded by a vast
array of plaques and framed awards. This is no ordinary clock—it
runs backward. She keeps it there, she says, to remind everyone
who comes into her office that she refuses to listen to the phrase
"but we've always done it that way." That phrase, she says, is "the
worst in the English language."

Until she retired at the end of August 1986, Admiral Hopper was,
at age 79, the Navy's oldest officer on active duty. She pioneered in
the development of computer programming, and her long and distinguished career parallels the rise of the age of computers. She
worked on the first large-scale computer and was instrumental in
developing the popular computer language COBOL. She even had
a hand in inventing the term *debugging* a computer. Her numerous
honors and awards include more than 40 honorary degrees and
election to the National Academy of Engineering. The Association
for Computing Machinery has dedicated an achievement award—

Opposite page:
Speaking to a group of
high school students,
Rear Admiral Hopper
holds up a piece of wire
to illustrate the distance
a signal in a computer
can travel in one-bil-
lionth of a second.

the Grace Murray Hopper Award—to her. Prior to retirement, Admiral Hopper was Special Adviser to the director of the Naval Data Automation Command in Washington, D.C.

Hopper's numerous accomplishments are a testament to her conviction that one should never let preconceived notions of how things have to be done stand in one's way. A woman in a "man's world," Hopper received a Ph.D. degree in mathematics at a time when few women even went to college. Throughout her career, Hopper has repeatedly surprised her colleagues and supervisors by doing things that they said could not be done. Even in retirement, she plans on lecturing to students and computer professionals throughout the United States, reading mountains of material to keep up with developments in her field, and continually learning new things. "The day I stop learning is the day I die," she says.

Grace Murray was born on Dec. 9, 1906, in New York City. By all accounts, she was a mischievous and determined child. "I love a good gadget," she says, and she particularly enjoyed learning how mechanical devices work. When she was about 7 years old, she took apart so many clocks trying to figure out how they work that her parents finally gave her a clock of her own to tinker with, telling her to leave the rest of the clocks alone.

She was also adventurous and daring. When she was 18, her neighborhood was visited by a young man who made his living taking people up for a short ride in an airplane—for a stiff fee. The plane was "made of wood, linen, and wire," Hopper recalls. "I squandered all my money—it cost $10—and went up in the plane."

The oldest of three children, Grace grew up in the city but spent summers at her family's vacation home in Wolfeboro, N.H. Her parents held views that were unconventional for the early 1900's and encouraged her to shun the customary feminine roles of the time. Her father, insurance broker Walter Fletcher Murray, was, she remarks, "ahead of his time." He believed that Grace and her younger sister should have the same opportunities as their brother, and he urged them to go to college. He also insisted, Hopper says, that each of the girls work for at least a year after completing their education—just to be sure they were able to support themselves.

With her family's encouragement, Grace attended Vassar College, in Poughkeepsie, N.Y., where she studied mathematics, physics, and economics. "If I had known I would be in computers, I couldn't have made a better choice," she remarks. But she thought at the time that she would either teach mathematics or work as an *actuary*, analyzing statistics for an insurance company. She graduated from Vassar in 1928, a member of the Phi Beta Kappa honor society. She then entered graduate school at Yale University in New Haven, Conn. Two years later, she married Vincent Foster Hopper, whom she had met in Wolfeboro. (They were divorced in 1945.) Ever the one to defy expectations, she had married before completing her

The author:
Gina Kolata is a senior writer for *Science* magazine.

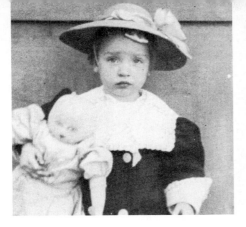

As a child, Hopper dutifully clutches a doll, but her early fascination with gadgets led to her work with computers.

A backward-running clock on Hopper's office wall symbolizes her belief in not being bound by conventions.

education and supporting herself as her father had wanted. In 1934, Grace Hopper received a Ph.D. in mathematics from Yale. After graduate school, she taught mathematics at Vassar and at Columbia University's Barnard College in New York City.

Then, in late 1941, the United States entered World War II. It was a time of intense patriotism. "You have to understand," she stresses, "*everybody* joined something in World War II. Hopper, in 1943, at age 37, was determined to join the Navy.

But there were stumbling blocks. First, she was a mathematician. The government had identified mathematics as a crucial occupation and had decided that mathematicians could make their greatest contribution to the war effort as civilians. To join the armed services, Hopper would have to be released from her civilian job or be unemployed for six months. Hopper managed to get released from her job at Vassar by threatening to quit and remain unemployed for six months if Vassar refused to let her go. The second stumbling block was her weight. She weighed only 105 pounds, and the Navy required that recruits of her height—5 feet 6 inches—weigh at least 121 pounds. Hopper managed to get a waiver, however, and finally, in December of 1943, she was sworn in.

Hopper completed midshipmen's school six months later and was commissioned as a lieutenant junior grade in the WAVES (*Women Accepted for Volunteer Emergency Service*)—the Women's Reserve of the U.S. Naval Reserve. She was ordered to report to the Bureau of Ordnance Computation Project at Harvard University in Cambridge, Mass. It was an assignment that was to change her life.

On a Monday morning in early July 1944, Grace Hopper walked into the basement of Harvard's Cruft Laboratory and saw, for the first time, a computer. It was the Mark I, the first large-scale computer. Hopper reacted with delight. "It was the biggest gadget I had ever seen. It was 51 feet long, 8 feet high, and 8 feet wide and was enclosed in a glass case. I wanted to find out how it worked."

The Mark I, or ASCC (*Automatic Sequence Controlled Calculator*), was a far cry from the computers of today. It weighed about 5

The Mark I, or Automatic Sequence Controlled Calculator, *top,* was the first large-scale computer. During the mid-1940's, at the beginning of her Navy career, Hopper worked with the Mark I's designer, Howard H. Aiken (seated next to Hopper), *above,* programming the computer to perform complex calculations needed by the Navy.

tons, had more than 750,000 parts, and contained about 500 miles of wire. Today, all its circuits could be contained on a microprocessor chip smaller than a thumbnail. The Mark I was built by International Business Machines Corporation (IBM) at a cost of about $1-million and was driven by a 5-horsepower motor. Information was fed into the computer on punch cards and paper tape. The Mark I's operations were controlled chiefly by *electromechanical relays*—magnetically operated switches similar to the mechanism in a doorbell. When the Mark I was operating, the clacking of these relays sounded like a roomful of people knitting. The Mark I could do three additions or subtractions a second. It could multiply numbers in 4 seconds and divide them in 10 seconds. Today's computers are about a billion times faster.

The Bureau of Ordnance Computation Project was run by Navy Commander Howard H. Aiken, a Harvard professor who had originally conceived of the design for the Mark I while a graduate student at Harvard in 1937. The project's goal was to use the computer in making the extremely complex calculations needed to operate the new armaments being used in the war. For example, Hopper was asked to use the machine to calculate the area covered by a minesweeping device towed by a ship. To do this, Hopper and her colleagues had to develop methods of *programming* the computer.

Programming involves writing instructions that permit a computer to perform a particular task. A computer program spells out exactly what operations the computer must perform, in what order the steps must be performed, and which locations in the computer's memory will be used. Hopper and her programming colleagues—Ensigns Robert V. D. Campbell and Richard M. Bloch—had to write these programs in what is called *machine language*—that is, in "language" that the machine could "understand." Since any computer is basically a large number of switches, the instructions must indicate how these switches should be set for the performance of each task. Each task requires a different pattern of switch settings. Instructions

A moth taped in a Navy logbook remains as evidence of the first actual debugging of a computer. On Sept. 9, 1945, while Hopper was working with the Mark II, the moth got caught in a relay switch, causing the computer to stop. Hopper and her colleagues removed the dead bug and preserved it in their logbook.

in machine language are written as a long series of digits representing the "on" or "off" settings of the switches.

Hopper, Campbell, and Bloch not only wrote the programs for the Mark I but also—along with four assistants—repaired the computer and kept it running. When they suspected a failure in a switch inside the computer, they would turn off all the lights and Hopper would take out a small mirror from her purse. Then they would use the mirror to look for electric sparks in the computer that identified the failed part.

In 1945, Hopper and the Harvard group began building the Mark II, successor to the Mark I. It was then that the famous debugging incident occurred. As Hopper tells the story, it was summer and quite hot, so they had opened all the windows in the small building dating from World War I in which they were working. The computer stopped, and the scientists, as usual, began looking for the failed relay. The problem, they discovered, was a moth that had flown in and, as Hopper puts it, "had been beaten to death by the relay. The operator got a pair of tweezers. Very carefully, he took the moth out of the relay, put it in the logbook, put Scotch tape over it, and wrote 'first actual case of bug being found.'"

From then on, whenever Aiken came by to check on their progress and asked, as he always did, "Are you making any numbers?" Hopper and her colleagues would tell him they were debugging the computer. The moth that they took out of the computer that day was preserved and is now on display at the Naval Museum at the Naval Surface Weapons Center in Dahlgren, Va.

After the war ended in 1945, Hopper requested a transfer from the Naval Reserve to active Navy duty, but she was 40 years old, two years over the age limit. Vassar offered Hopper her teaching job back and the title of full professor, but, she says, "I decided that computers were more fun." She remained in the Naval Reserve and stayed on at Harvard as a research fellow, working with the Mark II and later with the Mark III.

The ENIAC (*E*lectronic *N*umerical *I*ntegrator *A*nd *C*omputer), built in 1946 by engineers John W. Mauchly and J. Presper Eckert, Jr., represented a major advance in computer design. In 1949, Hopper joined the computer company founded by Eckert and Mauchly to produce computers for business and commercial use.

In the meantime, the commercial computer industry was being born. It began during World War II with the work of engineers John W. Mauchly and J. Presper Eckert, Jr., of the University of Pennsylvania's Moore School of Electrical Engineering. In 1943, they began building the world's first fully electronic digital computer—called ENIAC (*E*lectronic *N*umerical *I*ntegrator *A*nd Computer). Unlike the Mark I, the ENIAC was designed for business and commercial use as well as for scientific and military purposes.

The ENIAC was completed in 1946. It was a huge machine—100 feet long, 10 feet high, and 3 feet deep. It weighed 30 tons. Instead of relays, it used about 18,000 vacuum tubes. Information was entered into and retrieved from the computer on punch cards. The ENIAC could process information much faster than the Mark I, performing 5,000 additions or subtractions per second. But setting the ENIAC up to solve a problem was very time consuming. The only way to change the machine's instructions was by manually resetting many of its 6,000 dials and switches and plugging in various specialized sections of the machine that were wired to perform certain mathematical operations. Despite such drawbacks, the ENIAC was a major advance in computer design.

Later in 1946, Eckert and Mauchly left the University of Pennsylvania and started their own company, the Eckert-Mauchly Computer Corporation, to build computers for general use. Grace Hopper joined the young company in 1949 as senior mathematician.

Most people involved in the development of computers during the 1940's believed that the need for such devices was quite limited.

345

They thought that, for the most part, computers would be needed only for certain military and scientific uses and that a handful of computers would be able to meet these needs. In starting a company to build computers for business use, Eckert and Mauchly took a great risk. And in joining the firm, Grace Hopper characteristically was siding against the conventional wisdom of the time.

The Eckert-Mauchly Computer Corporation began by building a computer called BINAC (*BIN*ary *A*utomatic *C*omputer). The BINAC was ordered by Northrop Aircraft Corporation to help in developing a guided missile. When Grace Hopper joined the Eckert-Mauchly Computer Corporation in 1949, one of her first tasks was to help teach Northrop employees how to use the computer.

The BINAC was the first computer to use magnetic tape for processing and storing information. It also stored programs in its memory. This made it possible to change instructions without resetting thousands of switches and dials. The BINAC was compact compared with other computers of the day. It contained 3,500 vacuum tubes and could perform 3,500 additions or subtractions per second. Its memory held up to 512 "words" of machine language.

In 1950, Eckert-Mauchly was bought by Remington Rand, and later, in 1955, it merged with Sperry Corporation. Throughout this time, the young firm was building still another computer, called UNIVAC I (*UNIV*ersal *A*utomatic *C*omputer), which was based on the BINAC.

"Those were precarious days," Hopper recalls. "We used to say that if UNIVAC I didn't work, we were going to throw it out one

During the early 1950's, *above left,* Hopper (standing) works on the development of the UNIVAC (*UNI*Versal *Au*tomatic *C*omputer). UNIVAC was the first commercially available computer. During the 1960's, *above,* Hopper instructs servicemen in the use of COBOL (*CO*mmon *B*usiness *O*riented *L*anguage). COBOL, a programming language for business use, was developed in 1959, based largely on Hopper's earlier work in programming.

345

side of the factory, which was a junkyard, and we were going to jump out the other side, which was a cemetery!" As it turned out, they did not need to take such drastic action.

The UNIVAC I, the first commercially available computer, was a great success. It was relatively small, measuring 14½ feet long, 7½ feet high, and 9 feet wide. It could hold a thousand machine language "words" in its memory and perform about 3,000 additions or subtractions a second. It used magnetic tape for receiving, storing, and processing information.

One of the greatest factors hampering the acceptance of computers in the business world was the difficulty and slowness of programming the machines to perform business functions. Highly trained mathematicians were needed to write programs in machine language, and the supply of such qualified people was small. The solution to this problem lay in the development of *programming languages* that would enable programmers to write instructions in a simpler form than the digits of machine language. The key person in the early development of programming languages was Grace Hopper. It was in this area that she made her greatest contribution to the development of computing as we know it.

While working on the Mark I and its successors at Harvard, Hopper and her colleagues had developed a method of simplifying and speeding up the writing of programs. Certain operations of the computer, called *subroutines*, were necessary parts of many different

Surrounded by awards and mementos of a long and distinguished career, Hopper works in her office at the Washington, D.C., Navy Yard.

programs. Such subroutines, for example, involved solving certain classes of equations or classifying and sorting data. Rather than re-create these sections of the programs each time they were needed, the programmers copied the machine language from notebooks in which they had recorded these common subroutines. This speeded up programming, but it was still a slow process, and the programmers often made mistakes in copying.

In 1952, while working on the UNIVAC I, Hopper developed a way of programming the computer to copy the subroutine for itself. In so doing, she invented the *compiler*—a system of translating simple instructions into machine language. Hopper recorded the subroutines, in machine language, on magnetic tape. Then, when she was writing a program and came to a point where she needed to use a subroutine, she did not have to copy the subroutine in machine language. Instead, she merely instructed the computer to locate the needed subroutine on the tape and put it in the program.

Hopper then devised a way of using the compiler system to put many subroutines and other instructions together to produce an entire program. This enabled people to write programs—requiring hundreds of subroutines—in a kind of shorthand, which the system then translated into machine language. The compiler system performed the same sort of function as a person simultaneously translating into English a speech given in French, as the speaker is talking.

President Ronald Reagan congratulates Hopper on her promotion to commodore on Dec. 15, 1983.

Hopper and project manager Eva M. Sebastian break ground for the Grace M. Hopper Navy Regional Data Automation Center in San Diego, Calif., on Sept. 27, 1985.

But Hopper soon discovered a difficulty in using the compiler. When the compiler was translating each step, or operation, in the program, one after another, it frequently came to a place where the program had to skip ahead. At operation 20, for example, the program might say "Go to operation 46." But at operation 20, the computer had not yet encountered operation 46. The computer would not even know where in its memory to find operation 46. It would be as if the French speaker whose talk was being simultaneously translated said, "Insert here an English translation of the third sentence that I shall say in the next paragraph of my speech."

At this point, Hopper got an inspiration. As an undergraduate at Vassar, she had played on the basketball team. She remembered how the girls had solved the problem of getting the ball down the court. Under the rules in girls' basketball then, the players could dribble the ball only once. And they could not take a step while holding the ball. So a player who had the ball but was far from the basket would pass the ball to a teammate and then run as fast as she could to the basket so that the teammate could throw the ball back to her when she got there.

Hopper's idea was to program what she called a "neutral corner"—a place in the computer's memory—to perform the function of the teammate who received the ball and then passed it back. The neutral corner could keep little memos about where the program was "going." When the compiler got to operation 20, for example, it inserted an instruction to jump to the neutral corner. Then it continued translating the program. When it reached operation 46, it inserted an instruction in the neutral corner to jump to operation 46. Thus, when the program was running, and it reached operation 20, it would jump to the neutral corner. Then the instruction in the neutral corner caused it to jump to operation 46. This clever solution kept the program intact and allowed the compiler to run smoothly despite the need to jump ahead of itself at times.

Hopper and her colleagues created the compiler "in a back corner of the room," she says, because no one in the company's management believed it could be done. "We had to sell management on the idea that we could do it," Hopper remarks. "Selling is always a problem, but eventually we got a budget and got the project going. Then we had to sell it to the customers. We had to change people's minds."

During the mid-1950's, Hopper and her staff were at work creating a language that would be suitable for programming computers to perform tasks for business, such as automatic billing and calculating payroll checks. To be acceptable to people, the programming language had to be easy to use. Taking her concept of the compiler a step further, Hopper suggested a radical idea. "I proposed we write computer languages in English sentences. No one thought it was possible. They said computers couldn't understand English. But we did it anyway." This was the beginning of FLOW-MATIC, the first computer language to use English-language instructions. FLOW-MATIC was well received by business and provided the basic pattern for later programming languages used for data processing. FLOW-MATIC was soon being used by several organizations, including Du Pont Company, Metropolitan Life Insurance Company, United States Steel Corporation, and Westinghouse Electric Corporation.

By the late 1950's, computer professionals, including Hopper, were becoming concerned that programming languages might become another Tower of Babel. Four such languages, including FLOW-MATIC, had already been proposed. So, on May 28, 1959, about 40 computer experts from industry, the government, and the University of Pennsylvania met at the Pentagon in Washington, D.C., to discuss the problem. They formed a committee known as CODASYL (COnference on DAta SYstems Languages) to develop a single, general-purpose computer language for business use. Hopper was a technical adviser to the executive committee, and her influence and contribution to the effort were substantial.

The language developed by CODASYL was modeled very closely after FLOW-MATIC. It is called COBOL (COmmon Business Oriented Language), and it had a tremendous impact on the growth of computing. COBOL became the standard programming language used in the business world and in the U.S. Department of Defense and has remained in wide use.

Since 1946, in addition to her civilian work, Hopper had been in the Naval Reserve, consulting and lecturing for the Navy. On Dec. 31, 1966, the Navy retired her with the rank of commander—after 23 years of service. "It was the saddest day of my life," she laments. Her retirement lasted only seven months, however. She was recalled to active duty on Aug. 1, 1967, to help standardize computer languages. "I was delighted," she says.

She returned to active duty immediately and was asked to help with a problem the Navy was having with COBOL. At that time, there were many different versions of COBOL. Although there

Hopper chats with admirers after addressing an audience of high school students in April 1986. She has given about 200 speeches a year, never failing to impress upon her listeners the value of exploring new paths and not just continuing to do things "the way they have always been done."

were standard specifications for COBOL, they were open to different interpretations, and different manufacturers interpreted them differently. Consequently, one manufacturer's version would not run on another manufacturer's computer. Hopper and her colleagues definitively interpreted the standards and enforced them for the Navy so that each COBOL program the Navy bought could be run on all of the Navy's computers. At that point, the General Services Administration, the federal agency responsible for the government's property and equipment, asked Hopper's group to standardize COBOL for the entire U.S. government.

When Hopper was recalled to active duty in 1967, she was asked to serve for a period of six months. But her contribution proved to be so vital that those six months became nearly 20 years. She was elevated to captain by President Richard M. Nixon in 1973, and 10 years later was made commodore. In November 1985, Congress changed the title of all commodores to rear admiral.

When asked to characterize her most important achievement during her long and distinguished career, Hopper replies that her greatest contribution has been "all the young people I've trained."

"Hopper was fantastic to work with," says computer specialist Richard C. Fredette, who worked with her in the Pentagon from 1967 to 1975. "She gave me good basic direction and then let me go off and accomplish wild and woolly things. She was always very encouraging and was always looking forward to the future. Because of her, I look forward constantly."

The future of computing, says Hopper today, is going to involve much greater use of *computer networks*—groups of connected computers. Part of the reason for this, she says, is that we are reaching limits in our attempts to make computers faster. By way of explanation, she likes to hand out "nanoseconds" when she gives her talks. These are small pieces of wire—11.78 inches long—that represent the maximum distance that anything, including signals in a computer, can travel in a *nanosecond* (one-billionth of a second). Today's computers add and subtract in nanoseconds. The next fastest order of speed would be to add and subtract in a few *picoseconds*—trillionths of a second. But signals may not be able to travel far enough in a few picoseconds to locate two numbers in a computer's memory, bring them to the unit that adds or subtracts them, and then store the result back in the memory. Therefore, the next step, Hopper explains, is to make more use of computer networks. In a computer network, several computers work simultaneously on different parts of a problem and then put the parts together to reach the solution.

Hopper also sees a bright future for "expert systems"—computers programmed with the knowledge of an expert in a particular field. Among the best-known expert systems are programs that contain medical information that can help doctors diagnose illnesses.

Admiral Hopper uses every opportunity to communicate her vision of the future of computing. She is constantly on the go, traveling across the United States and to other nations to participate in computer conferences and to give speeches. She has given about 200 speeches a year to audiences ranging from computer professionals to schoolchildren. "The bulk of students today are the brightest and most eager to learn we've ever had," she says. She tells them to learn techniques of problem solving and to look always to the future. "The future is what's important. My part of the history of computing has already happened," she says.

Everywhere she goes, she shares the lessons learned from "what has happened" during her long and distinguished career. Perhaps the most important lesson she teaches her enthusiastic audiences is to take chances—to explore new directions and not simply continue doing things "the way they have always been done." She also never misses an opportunity to share her motto: "A ship in port is safe, but that is not what ships are built for."

For further reading:

Blair, Marjorie. "Through the Looking Glass with Grace Hopper." *Electronic Education*, January 1984.

Gilbert, Lynn, and Moore, Gaylen. *Particular Passions*. Crown, 1981.

Johnson, Steve. "Grace Hopper: A Living Legend." *All Hands*, September 1982.

Mompoullan, Chantal. *Voices of America: Interviews with Eight American Women of Achievement*. United States Information Agency, 1984.

Zientara, Marguerite. *The History of Computing*. CW Communications, 1981.

West Germany's leading research
organization has survived
many years of crisis and war.

The Max Planck Society at 75

BY ALEXANDER DOROZYNSKI

In 1986, the scientists of the Max Planck Society for the Advancement of Science celebrated the 75th anniversary of the society, the leading organization for scientific research in West Germany. They had good reason to celebrate, because their organization had survived a stormy past. The society had made it through World War I and the terrible years of Adolf Hitler and World War II, only to come close to being dismantled as a Nazi organization that had served the German war effort. Saved largely through the efforts of a British chemist—Bertie K. Blount, then an army colonel—the society went on to reemerge as a world-renowned center of research.

Throughout the 1900's, the Max Planck Society has employed many of the world's leading scientists. Since 1914, members of the society have won 22 Nobel Prizes. The most recent winner, in 1985, was Klaus von Klitzing, a physicist at the Max Planck Institute for Solid State Research in Stuttgart, one of 60 separate institutes supported by the society. Stuttgart lies in the valley of the Neckar River, and the area is often called West Germany's Silicon Valley because, like its counterpart in California, it is a center for electronic research and manufacturing. When von Klitzing's prize was announced in October 1985, the normal quiet of the institute's labo-

Opposite page, top: Scientists at the Kaiser Wilhelm (now the Max Planck) Institute for Chemistry in Berlin, Germany, work with equipment that was state-of-the-art in 1913. *Opposite page, bottom:* A scientist at the Max Planck Institute for Biochemistry in Martinsried, West Germany, in 1986 carries on the tradition of research excellence begun 75 years before.

ratories was disturbed by popping champagne corks, cheers, and toasts to the 42-year-old physicist, whose research into electrical conductivity has important applications in computer design.

The Max Planck institutes range in size from the huge Max Planck Institute for Plasma Physics near Munich, with a staff of nearly 1,000, to the tiny Max Planck Institute for Mathematics in Bonn, with a staff of 10. The institutes work in a wide variety of fields in the natural and social sciences and the humanities. The society's stated objective is to operate research institutions "for the benefit of the public." It does not attempt to cover all areas of research but instead focuses on promising new leads and tries to supplement university and other institutional research. Over the years, the society has concentrated on certain areas, especially biochemistry, medical research, and plasma physics.

The Max Planck Society was founded in 1911 to ensure that Germany would not lag behind other great nations in the natural sciences. The emperor of Germany, Kaiser Wilhelm II, presided at the founding ceremonies and donated a site in the imperial domain of Dahlem, now a residential district in West Berlin. The organization was originally named after him—the Kaiser Wilhelm Gesellschaft zur Förderung der Wissenschaften (Kaiser Wilhelm Society for the Advancement of Science). To ensure the society's independence, Germany's financial leaders gave it a generous endowment.

The founder and first president of the Kaiser Wilhelm Society was Adolf von Harnack, a theologian who would now be called a science policymaker. Harnack had an idea that was unusual for his time. He proposed setting up institutes devoted entirely to research, where scientists could pursue their investigations free from the teaching duties they would have at a university. This proposal represented a radical break from German tradition, which held that teaching and research should not be separated.

Ten years later, there were 14 Kaiser Wilhelm institutes, working in areas ranging from brain research and cell chemistry to iron and leather research. In 1930, Harnack died, and German physicist Max K. E. L. Planck was elected his successor. Planck was then 72 years old and one of the world's most renowned and respected scientists. In 1900, he had proposed the idea of tiny bundles of energy called *quanta* to explain why light was emitted by certain heated objects. Planck's idea revolutionized physics by leading to the development of a field called *quantum mechanics*, which describes the structure of the atom and the interactions of subatomic particles, the tiny units of matter that make up atoms. For that work, Planck was awarded the Nobel Prize in physics in 1918. He thus joined the society's long line of Nobel Prize winners, which began with Max T. F. von Laue, who received the physics award in 1914 for his discovery that X rays could be *diffracted* (bent) by the atoms in crystals, thus proving that X rays are waves.

The author:
Alexander Dorozynski
is a free-lance writer
based in Paris.

The Max Planck Society was established in 1911 at a founding session in Berlin, *above*. The society was originally named after the emperor of Germany, Kaiser Wilhelm II. The emperor (wearing cap) visits the first research institute, *right,* in 1912 with the society's founder and first president, Adolf von Harnack (wearing chain of office).

Soon after Planck took office, one of the most difficult periods in the society's history began. In 1933, the Nazi leader Adolf Hitler became the head of Germany's government. Hitler declared that Germans and certain other peoples of northern Europe, called *Aryans*, were superior to all other peoples. The Nazis used these beliefs to justify brutal persecution of Jews, Gypsies, and others said to be non-Aryans.

The Kaiser Wilhelm Society, which was partially supported by government funds, came under pressure to enforce the official Nazi policy of removing non-Aryans from key positions. Chemist Fritz Haber, a 1918 Nobel laureate who was Jewish, resigned in 1933 as director of the Institute for Physical Chemistry and Electrochemistry after two of his Jewish department heads had been dismissed. And a 1922 Jewish Nobelist, Otto Meyerhof, director of the Institute for Physiology, fled Germany in 1938. Karl Neuberg, director of the Institute for Biochemistry—who also was Jewish—was forced into early retirement and eventually, in 1939, compelled to leave Germany. Between 1933 and 1940, nearly one-third of the scientists and directors at the Kaiser Wilhelm institutes were dismissed on political or racial grounds.

Planck at first hoped that the new regime would, "like all storms, be short-lived." He requested and was granted an audience with Hitler in May 1933 to defend Jewish scientists and try to convince Hitler of the damage being done to German science. But the Nazi leader refused to listen. "A Jew is a Jew," he said, and when Planck insisted, Hitler went into a violent fit of anger. Hitler never changed his anti-Jewish policies, and in 1937, Planck resigned.

In 1939, World War II began. Germany and the other Axis powers, mainly Italy and Japan, fought the Allies, which included Australia, Canada, France, Great Britain, the Soviet Union, and the United States.

In 1940, the Kaiser Wilhelm Society suffered a blow to its independence when the Nazi government stepped in and appointed the society's president, an officer formerly elected by the organization's members. The new president was Albert Vögler, who was not a scientist but a leader of the war industry and head of a large German steel company.

In addition, the Kaiser Wilhelm Institute for Physics was forced to devote itself to Germany's atomic research program. Physicist Werner K. Heisenberg, who had won the Nobel Prize in 1932, directed these efforts. The Kaiser Wilhelm physicists were moved to the cellars of an old brewery in southwest Germany. They made little progress in developing an atomic bomb, however, because they lacked uranium and other materials.

Planck, meanwhile, suffered personal tragedy during the war. An Allied bombing raid destroyed his home in Berlin and everything he owned. Planck's son Erwin took part in an unsuccessful attempt on Hitler's life on July 20, 1944, and was hanged in January 1945.

The Allies defeated Germany in 1945 and divided the country into four military occupation zones, with the French, the British, the Soviets, and the Americans each occupying a zone. General Lucius D. Clay, military governor of the U.S. zone, wanted to have the Kaiser Wilhelm Society dismantled because of its activities during the war. The society would probably have perished without the efforts of the British chemist Blount, who had studied in Germany before the war. Blount argued in London on behalf of the society, and the British agreed to give it a new start, provided it be renamed after Max Planck.

In 1945, Planck, then 87 years old and grieving over the death of his son, was persuaded to resume the presidency of the society for a year while the organization was in transition. His successor was Otto Hahn, the 1944 Nobel Prize winner in chemistry. Hahn also became the first president of the renamed and reconstructed Max Planck Society for the Advancement of Science, officially established in 1948. Since then, the Max Planck Society has played a major role in rebuilding West German science and has grown rapidly to become one of the world's leading research organizations. The soci-

President Max Planck speaks to the Kaiser Wilhelm Society on its 25th anniversary, *above,* which came during the period of Nazi rule, one of the worst times in the history of the society. Planck and Albert Einstein are honored at a 1929 awards ceremony, *left,* but honors soon turned to oppression. Planck was horrified by Nazi persecution of Einstein, whom he helped recruit for the society, and other leading Jewish scientists.

ety's network of research institutes expanded quickly during the 1960's and early 1970's, a time when West German and other European universities were plagued by political unrest. Now there are 60 Max Planck institutes, with a total staff of about 10,000 people, of whom 4,000 are scientists.

Two Max Planck institutes are in other countries. The Max Planck Institute for Psycholinguistics, which studies how people acquire and use language, is in Nijmegen, the Netherlands. The Hertziana Library, a center for research on art history, is in Rome.

The society puts special emphasis on cooperation with the European Community (EC or Common Market). Several Max Planck institutes have participated in research projects with the European Space Agency, an organization of Western European nations that built the Spacelab orbiting laboratory and now launches commercial satellites. The European Incoherent Scatter Scientific Association (EISCAT) is a geophysical research institution that operates two radar systems to study the scattering of radio waves in the high atmosphere. EISCAT is supported jointly by the Max Planck Society and by science organizations in Finland, France, Great Britain, Norway, and Sweden. Max Planck institutes are also involved with the European Laboratory for Particle Physics (CERN—formerly the European Organization for Nuclear Research) near Geneva, Switzerland, the world's largest center for the study of subatomic particles.

In addition, the society promotes links with research centers abroad. It has cooperation agreements with the Chinese Academy

After World War II, British chemist Bertie K. Blount, *below,* persuaded the Allies to give the Kaiser Wilhelm Society a new start, provided it be renamed after Max Planck. At ceremonies in 1948, *below right,* Otto Hahn, standing at the right, becomes the first head of the renamed and reconstructed Max Planck Society for the Advancement of Science.

of Sciences and joint projects with the National Science Foundation of the United States.

The Max Planck Society has an annual budget of 1 billion Deutsche marks (about $430 million), which is about 2 per cent of the total yearly spending for research and development in West Germany. In the past 10 years or so, however, the organization's rapid growth has come to a stop. Society President Heinz A. Staab points out that the budget has stayed the same for about 15 years, while personnel and equipment costs have increased steadily. Because of inflation, this amounts to a steady decrease in funding.

A southward drift of high-technology research and industry in West Germany has also posed some problems. There is now a disproportionate concentration of institutes in the southern part of the country. There are 10 institutes in and around Munich, and the southern cities of Tübingen, Freiburg, Stuttgart, and Heidelberg each have 2 or more. In addition, the administrative headquarters are in the Residenz in Munich, a complex of buildings that was once the residential palace of the rulers of the state of Bavaria.

The Max Planck Society gets nearly 90 per cent of its funding from the federal government and the 11 states plus West Berlin that make up the Federal Republic of Germany. The south's large share of institutes displeases some northern states.

In spite of such problems, most Max Planck scientists find no reason to complain. "On the whole, we have good working conditions, money, and time," says Klaus Kühn, director of the Connective Tis-

The Max Planck Society headquarters are in the Residenz in Munich, *left,* once the residential palace of the rulers of Bavaria. Society President Heinz A. Staab, *above,* has his office there.

sue Research Department at the Institute for Biochemistry in Martinsried, a suburb of Munich. "It's a privilege to be here, and you pay for it with work."

Max Planck scientists like to describe the structure of their organization as "democratic." The basic units of the Max Planck Society are its institutes. A typical institute, with a staff of 200 to 300, is headed by a board of directors, who elect one of their number as the managing director, usually for a term of several years. In some cases, an institute may be founded around a particular scientist, who becomes its director.

The members of the Max Planck Society hold an annual meeting, at which they vote on major policy decisions and changes in the society's bylaws. There are two chief kinds of members: *scientific members*, scientists who belong to the boards of directors of the various institutes; and *supporting members*, individuals and corporations whose contributions help support the society.

The central decision-making body of the Max Planck Society is called the Senate. The Senate decides on the founding, closing, and reorganization of institutes, appoints scientific members, and drafts budgets. There are about 50 senators, of whom two-thirds are Max Planck Society scientists. The remaining third of the Senate seats are reserved for officials of state and federal governments and for journalists, members of labor unions, and representatives of industries and universities.

The Senate elects the society president for a six-year term, renewable only once. The president has great power, drafting basic science policy outlines and chairing the Senate and the annual membership meeting. The president generally handles important or sensitive matters, such as smoothing out internal conflicts, persuading a scientist to retire, and discouraging or encouraging a scientist who wishes to create a new institute.

In addition to this "democratic" system that allows members to participate in the decision-making process with a minimum of outside interference, the Max Planck Society has a built-in mechanism for flexibility and quality control. This adaptability and accountability contrasts with the more rigid structure of German and other European university research centers, where many researchers have lifetime tenure. At the Max Planck institutes, scientists do not hold lifetime jobs. The institutes themselves are dispensable and renewable. A researcher, even an institute head, is generally given a limited contract. If the research is not satisfactory, the contract may not be renewed. Even if an institute's work is extremely good, the institute may be closed if its particular line of research no longer need be pursued.

The result of such policies is a high rate of turnover. Between 1972 and 1982, for example, the Max Planck Society closed 17 institutes and independent departments and began the process of

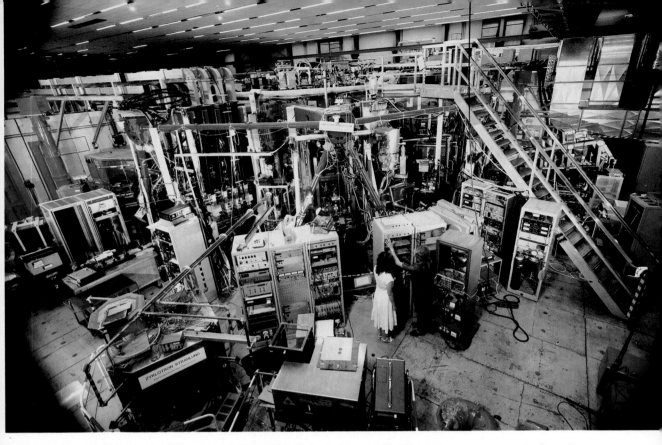

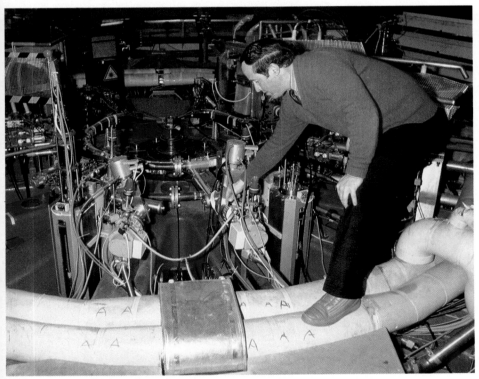

At the Institute for Plasma Physics near Munich, scientists work with an experimental nuclear fusion device called the tokamak, *above*. Physicist Karl H. Steiner, *left,* makes an adjustment on the tokamak's upper section.

Scientists in the connective tissue unit of the Institute for Biochemistry study a connective-tissue protein called collagen. Biochemist Klaus Kühn and his colleague Ulrike Mayer, *above,* examine results of a test that breaks down the protein molecules into their ''building blocks,'' called amino acids. Another researcher, *right,* runs tests to analyze the amino acids.

closing 3 others. In the same period, 7 new institutes and 8 new independent project groups, some the forerunners of institutes, were founded.

The Institute for Physics illustrates the many changes that an institute may go through in its lifetime. It was created in 1917 in Berlin. Its first director was the great German-born physicist Albert Einstein, whom Planck helped recruit from Switzerland to head the institute. After World War II, the institute was rebuilt in Göttingen with Werner Heisenberg, who had headed Germany's atomic research program during the war, as its director. The institute moved in 1958 to Munich, where it now has three subunits: the Werner Heisenberg Institute for Physics, which investigates the properties and interactions of subatomic particles; the Institute for Astrophysics, which conducts research into astronomical bodies; and the Extraterrestrial Physics Institute, which studies the outer reaches of Earth's atmosphere and interplanetary space.

In 1960, Heisenberg, jointly with the Max Planck Society, founded a private nuclear fusion research center, which was fully integrated into the society in 1971 as the Max Planck Institute for Plasma Physics. Since its founding, the plasma physics institute has grown rapidly to become the largest in the Max Planck Society. It now has eight scientific divisions and a staff of about 1,000. Its mission is to develop a nuclear fusion reactor that will produce energy by the controlled fusion of the nuclei of hydrogen atoms. Atomic energy today is produced by fission, the splitting of atoms, and generates large quantities of radioactive waste. Fusion, which creates the energy of both the sun and the hydrogen bomb, may someday provide an almost unlimited source of energy with little radioactive waste. But scientists have not yet succeeded in harnessing fusion to produce usable energy. In the Special Reports section, see THE FABULOUS LASER.

Nuclear fusion can occur only in a hot, gaslike substance called *plasma*, made up of free electrons and free nuclei. Because it has special electrical and magnetic properties, plasma is often called "the fourth state of matter," after solids, liquids, and gases. For fusion to occur, plasma must be heated many millions of degrees, and scientists have yet to develop a container that can hold such superhot plasma for very long.

A major area of research at the Institute for Plasma Physics is the development of ring-shaped devices called *tokamaks*, in which hot plasma is confined in a magnetic field. The tokamak's main magnetic field is generated by large coils surrounding its containing walls, but the device also passes a strong current through the plasma, inducing an additional magnetic field in the plasma that helps to confine it inside these "magnetic bottles."

When will fusion energy become available to the world? "If all goes on schedule, experiments will continue until the year 2005 or so and a demonstration reactor should be ready in about 2020," says institute physicist Karl H. Steiner. "But if there's a surprise—a good surprise—it may be earlier."

Another example of the metamorphosis of an institute is the Max Planck Institute for Biochemistry in Martinsried, near Munich. Its origin can be traced to the Kaiser Wilhelm Institute for Experimental Therapy established in Berlin in 1912. In 1973, the Max Planck Institute for Biochemistry merged with the Institute for Protein and Leather Research and the Institute for Cell Chemistry. This merger created the second-largest Max Planck institute, with a staff of 600.

The biochemistry institute's range of research is much broader than its name implies, extending beyond biochemistry to include biophysics, virology, cell biology, genetics, and other biological sciences. At the Gene Center, a joint research venture of the institute and the University of Munich, scientists are working with a technique called *recombinant DNA technology* that can alter the hereditary material of living things. This new technology, also called *gene-splicing* or *genetic engineering*, already is used in drug production and agriculture.

The work of the institute's Connective Tissue Research Department focuses on a fibrous protein called *collagen*, the chief substance making up the connective tissues that link, support, and enclose the other organs and tissues of the human body. Scientists in the department, headed by Klaus Kühn, study how collagen is formed in the body and how collagen formation is disrupted in certain diseases. Because changes in the body's collagen are one of the chief physical signs of old age, their studies eventually may help medical science find ways to better control the aging process.

Throughout its turbulent history, the Max Planck Society has succeeded in preserving one of its most important advantages—its independence. With the exception of Vögler, who was appointed by the Nazi government, all the society's presidents have been elected by its own Senate. To this day, says President Staab, there is no outside interference in the selection of researchers hired by the society. The success of the society's research programs is often attributed to this independence and to the shrewd selection of projects and of scientists to carry them out.

The Max Planck Society has, to some extent, backed away from Adolf von Harnack's original idea of separating research from teaching. Today, nearly one-fourth of the society's scientists also teach part-time in universities. Many feel that this trend will continue, and that the society may become less independent and more integrated within the West German scientific establishment. But most observers agree that the prestige of the Max Planck Society is so great that no government would risk tampering with a magnificent organization honed not only by crisis and war but also by enormous success that, apparently, has not spoiled it.

World Book Supplement

Revised articles reprinted from the 1986 edition of *The World Book Encyclopedia.*

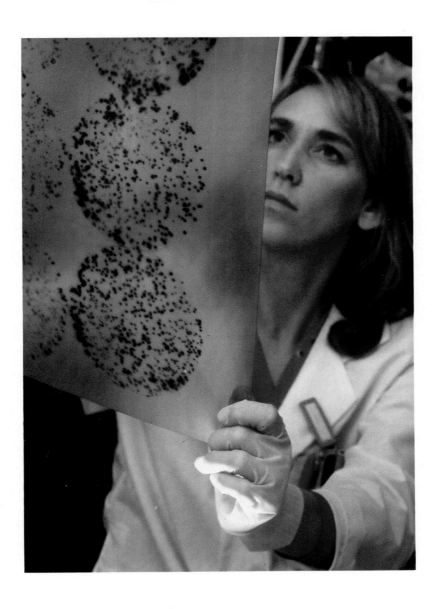

© Jim Pickerell

Civil Engineers Inspecting a Building Site

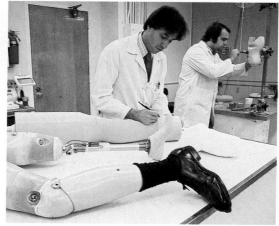
© Dan McCoy, Black Star

Biomedical Engineers Designing Artificial Limbs

The Field of Engineering includes a broad range of activities—from planning and supervising large construction projects to designing and producing aids for the physically handicapped.

ENGINEERING

ENGINEERING is the profession that puts scientific knowledge to practical use. The word *engineering* comes from the Latin word *ingeniare*, which means *to design* or *to create*. Engineers use principles of science to design structures, machines, and products of all kinds. They look for better ways to use existing resources and often develop new materials. Engineers have had a direct role in the creation of most of modern *technology*—the tools, materials, techniques, and power sources that make our lives easier (see TECHNOLOGY).

The field of engineering includes a wide variety of activities. For example, engineering projects range from the construction of huge dams to the design of tiny electronic circuits. Engineers may help produce guided missiles, industrial robots, or artificial limbs for the physically handicapped. They develop complex scientific equipment to explore the reaches of outer space and the depths of the oceans. Engineers also plan our electric power and water supply systems, and do research to improve automobiles, television sets, and other consumer products. They may work to reduce environmental pollution, increase the world's food supply, and make transportation faster and safer.

In ancient times, there was no formal engineering education. The earliest engineers built structures and developed tools by trial and error. Today, special college training prepares engineers to work in a certain branch or field of engineering and standards of quality and performance guide them on the job.

The Branches of Engineering

Most of the specialized fields of engineering developed since about 1750. Before that time, engineering

The contributors of this article are Margaret L. A. MacVicar, Professor of Physical Science at the Massachusetts Institute of Technology, and Edith H. Fine, an educator and author.

dealt mostly with the construction of buildings, roads, bridges, canals, or weapons. As people gained more knowledge of science and technology during the 1700's and 1800's, engineers began to specialize in certain kinds of work.

Today, new fields of engineering are continually emerging as a result of scientific and technological breakthroughs. At the same time, the boundaries between the various fields are becoming less and less clear-cut. Numerous areas of engineering overlap, and engineers from different specialties often work closely together on projects. The following section discusses the major branches of engineering, as well as some of the smaller specialized fields.

Aerospace Engineering involves the design, production, and maintenance of commercial and military aircraft. Engineers in the aerospace field also play an essential role in the development and assembly of guided missiles and all types of spacecraft. Aerospace engineers help build wind tunnels and other testing equipment with which they carry out experiments on proposed craft to determine their performance, stability, and control under flight conditions. Aerospace research ranges from efforts to design quieter and more fuel-efficient commercial aircraft to the search for new materials that can withstand the high radiation levels and extreme temperatures of space flight.

In order to design strong, safe vehicles, aerospace engineers must know and put into practical use the principles of *aerodynamics*, the study of the forces acting on an object due to air moving past it (see AERODYNAMICS). They must also have a thorough understanding of the strength, elasticity, and other properties of the materials they use and be able to predict how they will behave during flight. Aerospace engineers work closely with electrical engineers in developing guidance, navigation, and control instruments and with mechanical engineers in designing suitable engines. They also assist civil engineers in planning airport facilities.

Biomedical Engineering applies engineering techniques to health-related problems. Biomedical engineers develop aids for the deaf and blind. They cooperate with physicians and surgeons to design artificial limbs and organs and other devices and machines that assist or replace diseased or damaged parts of the body. Biomedical engineers help provide a wide variety of medical tools, from instruments that measure blood pressure and pulse rate to surgical *lasers*, concentrated beams of light that can be used to perform delicate operations. Some biomedical engineers specialize in programming computer systems to monitor a patient's health or to process complex medical data. Others cooperate with architects, doctors, nurses, and other specialists to plan hospitals and community health centers.

In choosing materials for artificial aids and organs, biomedical engineers must understand the physical and chemical properties of the materials and how they interact with each other and with the body. One of the chief areas in biomedical engineering research focuses on the development of materials that the human body will not reject as foreign substances. In their work, biomedical engineers often use principles of biology, chemistry, and medicine and of electrical, materials, and mechanical engineering. See BIOMEDICAL ENGINEERING.

Chemical Engineering deals with the large-scale processing of chemicals and chemical products for industrial and consumer uses. Chemical engineers are concerned with the chemical processes that change raw materials into useful products. They plan, design, and help construct chemical plants and equipment and work to develop efficient and economical production methods. Chemical engineers work in many industries, including the manufacturing of cosmetics, drugs, explosives, fertilizers, food products, fuels, plastics, and soaps.

Chemical engineers must know how to handle and transport large quantities of chemicals. They have to understand such problems as heat transfer from one substance to another, absorption of liquids and gases, and evaporation. They control such processes and operations as distillation, crystallization, filtration, mixing, drying, and crushing.

The work of chemical engineers relies heavily on principles of chemistry, physics, and mathematics. Chemical engineers consult with electrical, mechanical, and industrial engineers in the design of plants and equipment. Some chemical engineers work closely with environmental engineers in seeking safe disposal methods for hazardous by-products of chemical processing.

Civil Engineering, the oldest of the main branches of engineering, involves the planning and supervision of such large construction projects as bridges, canals, dams, tunnels, and water supply systems. Civil engineers also cooperate with architects to design and erect all types of buildings. Other civil-engineering projects include airports, highways, levees, irrigation and sewerage systems, pipelines, and railroads.

Civil engineers work to build strong, safe structures that meet building codes and other regulations and are well suited to their surroundings. They are responsible for surveying and preparing building sites and for selecting appropriate materials. Civil engineers must also understand the use of bulldozers, cranes, power shovels, and other construction equipment.

Some civil engineers specialize in the study of the physical characteristics of soils and rocks and the design of foundations. Others concentrate on the management

© David R. Frazier

An Aerospace Engineer at an assembly plant checks over a guided missile while a worker looks on. Aerospace engineers also play a key role in the production of airplanes and spacecraft.

© Hans Namuth, Photo Researchers

A Chemical Engineer uses laboratory tests to determine which processing methods are the most economical and efficient. The best methods will later be adapted to large-scale chemical plants.

© Sepp Seitz, Woodfin Camp, Inc.

Electrical Engineers develop a wide variety of electrical and electronic devices. These electrical engineers are reviewing a greatly enlarged design for a single tiny electronic circuit.

of water resources, including the construction of flood control and irrigation systems, hydroelectric power plants, and water supply and sewerage systems. Still others are concerned with designing transportation systems and methods of traffic control. Many civil engineers are involved in city planning and urban renewal programs (see CITY PLANNING; URBAN RENEWAL).

Electrical Engineering deals with the development, production, and testing of electrical and electronic devices and equipment. Electrical engineers design equipment to produce and distribute electricity. This equipment includes generators run by water power, coal, oil, and nuclear fuels; transmission lines; and transformers. Electrical engineers also design and develop electric motors and other electrical machinery as well as ignition systems used in automobiles, aircraft, and other engines. They work to improve such devices as air conditioners, food processors, and vacuum cleaners.

Electrical engineers who specialize in electronic equipment are often referred to as *electronics engineers*. Electronics engineers play an essential role in the production of communications satellites, computers, industrial robots, medical and scientific instruments, missile control systems, and radar, radio, and television sets. Some engineers in the electronics field develop master plans for the parts and connections of miniature *integrated circuits*, which control the electric signals in most electronic devices (see INTEGRATED CIRCUIT). Many electronics engineers design, build, and program complex computer systems to perform particular tasks. Telecommunication, the transmission and reception of messages over long distances, is another major specialty of electronics engineering (see TELECOMMUNICATION).

Environmental Engineering concerns efforts to prevent and control air, water, soil, and noise pollution. Environmental engineers develop equipment to measure pollution levels and conduct experiments to determine the effects of various kinds of pollutants. They design air pollution control devices and operate water purification systems and water treatment plants. They also develop techniques to protect the land from erosion and from pollution by chemical fertilizers and pesticides.

Environmental engineers are specialists in the disposal of hazardous wastes from factories, mining operations, nuclear power plants, and other sources (see HAZARDOUS WASTES). They work to clean up unsafe dump sites created in the past and do research on new storage and recycling techniques. Environmental engineers are also involved in the development of cleaner and more reliable forms of energy and in developing ways to make the best present and future use of natural resources. Environmental engineers work with agricultural and mining engineers to develop production techniques that do the least possible damage to the land. They assist civil engineers in the design of water supply, waste disposal, and ventilation systems and chemical and nuclear engineers in waste disposal.

Industrial Engineering applies engineering analysis and techniques to the production of goods and services. Industrial engineers determine the most economical and effective ways for an organization to use people, machines, and materials. An industrial engineer may select the location for a plant or office, determine employee re-

Gary Milburn, Tom Stack & Assoc.

Environmental Engineers are concerned with preventing and controlling pollution. These engineers are checking for leakage and contamination at a dump site for hazardous wastes.

© Cameramann International Ltd.

An Industrial Engineer uses a computer to design an automated robot for an assembly line. Industrial engineers are continually working to improve the production of goods and services.

© Odyssey Productions

Metallurgical Engineers separate metals from their ores and prepare them for use. The engineers above are supervising the pulverizing of silver ore, one step in obtaining the pure metal.

quirements, select equipment and machinery, lay out work areas, and plan steps in operations. Industrial engineers also develop training and job evaluation programs and work-performance standards, and help determine wages and employee benefits. They work to solve such problems as high costs, low productivity, and poor product quality.

Mathematical models developed on computers enable industrial engineers to simulate the flow of work through an organization and to evaluate the effects of proposed changes. Industrial engineers also use data-processing systems to aid in financial planning, inventory control, and scheduling. Their work often requires a knowledge of economics, psychology, and personnel management. Industrial engineers work in a wide variety of businesses and industries, including banks, construction and transportation firms, government agencies, hospitals, and public utilities.

Materials Engineering deals with the structure, properties, production, and uses of various materials. Materials engineers work with both metallic and non-metallic substances. They try to improve existing materials and develop new uses for them, as well as to develop new materials to meet specific needs. *Mining* and *metallurgical* engineering are major subdivisions of materials engineering. Mining engineers work closely with geologists to locate and appraise deposits of minerals. They decide how to remove the ore from the ground as cheaply and efficiently as possible. Mining engineers have to know about civil, mechanical, and electrical engineering in order to plan shafts and tunnels, ventilate mines, and select mining machinery.

Metallurgical engineering deals with separating metals from their ores and preparing them for use. In *extractive* metallurgy, engineers remove metals from their ores and refine them to a pure state. Engineers in *physical metallurgy* develop methods for converting refined metals into useful finished products. See METALLURGY.

Other materials engineers specialize in the production and uses of such synthetic materials as ceramics and plastics (see CERAMICS; PLASTICS). Materials engineers help develop new materials for the aerospace, biomedical, construction, electronic, and nuclear fields. They cooperate with chemical, industrial, and mechanical engineers in working out the complex processes that convert raw materials into finished products.

Mechanical Engineering involves the production, transmission, and use of mechanical power. Mechanical engineers design, operate, and test all kinds of machines. They develop and build engines that produce power from steam, gasoline, nuclear fuels, and other sources of energy. They also develop and build a wide variety of machines that use power, including air-conditioning, heating, and ventilation equipment; automobiles; machine tools; and industrial-processing equipment. Mechanical engineers are involved in every phase in the development of a machine, from the construction of an experimental model to the installation of the finished machine and the training of the workers who will use it.

Mechanical engineers work in many industries, such as power generation, public utilities, transportation, and all types of manufacturing. Many mechanical engineers concentrate on research and development because new types of machinery are continually in demand. Mechanical engineers are involved in almost every other branch of engineering, whenever a new or improved machine, device, or piece of equipment is required.

Nuclear Engineering is concerned with the production and applications of nuclear energy and the uses of radiation and radioactive materials. Most nuclear engineers design, construct, and operate nuclear power plants that generate electricity. They handle every stage in the production of nuclear energy, from the processing of nuclear fuels to the disposal of radioactive wastes from nuclear reactors. They also work to improve and enforce safety standards and to develop new types of nuclear energy systems.

Nuclear engineers also design and build nuclear engines for ships, submarines, and space vehicles. They develop industrial, medical, and scientific uses for radiation and radioactive materials. Some nuclear engineers specialize in designing and constructing *particle accelerators*, devices that are used in scientific studies of the atom and in creating new elements (see PARTICLE ACCELERATOR). Others specialize in the development of nuclear weapons. Nuclear engineers also play a role in the development of radiation sources, detectors, and shielding equipment. The work of nuclear engineers frequently overlaps with that of electrical, environmental, mechanical, and materials engineers.

Other Specialized Fields focus on even more specific areas of engineering than do the major branches. This section describes a few of the more important specialties.

Acoustical Engineering deals with sound. The work of acoustical engineers includes designing buildings and rooms to make them quiet; improving conditions for listening to speech and music in auditoriums and halls; and developing techniques and sound-absorbing materials to reduce noise pollution.

Agricultural Engineering involves the design of farm buildings, agricultural equipment, and erosion control, irrigation, and land conservation projects. Agricultural engineers are also concerned with the processing, transporting, and storing of agricultural products.

Computer Engineering involves the development and improvement of computers, storage and printout units, and computer information networks. Computer engineers design the features of computer systems to suit particular operations.

Marine Engineering concerns the design, construction, and repair of ships and submarines. Marine engineers are also involved in the development of port facilities.

Ocean Engineering involves the design and installation of all types of equipment used in the ocean. The products of ocean engineers include oil rigs and other offshore installations, marine research equipment, and breakwater systems used to prevent beach erosion.

Petroleum Engineering deals with producing, storing, and transporting petroleum and natural gas. Petroleum engineers locate oil and gas deposits and try to develop more efficient drilling and recovery methods.

Textile Engineering is concerned with the machinery and processes used to produce both natural and synthetic fibers and fabrics. Engineers in this field also work to develop new and improved textiles.

Transportation Engineering involves efforts to make transportation safer, more economical, and more efficient. Engineers in this field design all types of transpor-

Mark Antman, Image Works

A Mechanical Engineer makes adjustments to a wind turbine. Mechanical engineers are involved in every phase in the development of a machine, from its design to its final installation.

© Cameramann International Ltd.

A Nuclear Engineer, *foreground,* monitors the central control room of a nuclear power plant. Nuclear engineers also help process nuclear fuels and dispose of radioactive wastes from reactors.

tation systems and develop related facilities for reducing traffic problems.

History

The history of engineering is the record of human ingenuity through the ages. Even in prehistoric times, people adapted basic engineering techniques from things that were available in nature. For example, sturdy sticks became levers to lift large rocks, and logs were used as rollers to move heavy loads. The development of agriculture and the growth of civilization brought about a new wave of engineering efforts. People invented farming tools, designed elaborate irrigation networks, and built the first cities. The construction of the gigantic Egyptian pyramids at Giza during the 2500's B.C. was one of the greatest engineering feats of ancient times (see PYRAMIDS). In ancient Rome, engineers built large aqueducts and bridges and vast systems of roads. During the 200's B.C., the Chinese erected major sections of the monumental Great Wall of China (see GREAT WALL OF CHINA).

Early engineers used such simple machines as the inclined plane, wedge, and wheel and axle. During the Middle Ages, a period in European history that lasted from the A.D. 400's to the 1500's, inventors developed machines to harness water, wind, and animal power. The growing interest in new types of machines and new sources of power to drive them helped bring about the Industrial Revolution of the 1700's and 1800's (see INDUSTRIAL REVOLUTION). The role of engineers expanded rapidly during the Industrial Revolution. The practical steam engine developed by the Scottish engineer James Watt in the 1760's revolutionized transportation and industry by providing a cheap, efficient source of power. New ironmaking techniques provided engineers with the material to improve machines and tools and to build bridges and ships. Many roads, railroads, and canals were constructed to link the growing industrial cities.

Distinct branches of engineering began to develop during the Industrial Revolution. The term *civil engineer* was first used about 1750 by John Smeaton, a British engineer. Mechanical engineers emerged as specialists in industrial machinery, and mining and metallurgical engineers were needed to supply metals and fuels. By the late 1800's, the development of electric power and advances in chemical processing had created the fields of electrical and chemical engineering. Professional schools began to be founded as the demand for engineers steadily increased.

Since 1900, the number of engineers and of engineering specialties has expanded dramatically. Artificial hearts, airplanes, computers, lasers, nuclear energy, plastics, space travel, and television are only a few of the scientific and technological breakthroughs that engineers have helped bring about in this century. Because science and technology are progressing and changing so rapidly, today's engineers must study throughout their careers to make sure that their knowledge and expertise do not become obsolete. They face the challenging task of keeping pace with the latest advances while working to shape the technology of the future.

Engineering Careers

The field of engineering offers a broad range of job opportunities. Engineers may work in factories, offices, and government laboratories or at construction sites. Some engineers are involved in the research and development of new products. Others are responsible for turning plans and specifications for new structures, machines, or systems into reality. Still others use their background and training to sell and service technical equipment. Many engineers work on projects in teams that include scientists, technicians, and other engineers. But some engineers act as independent consultants who sell their services to people who need engineering assistance. Engineers may also hold teaching positions or move up into management positions in business.

Certain abilities and traits help qualify a person for an engineering career. Engineers must have technical aptitude and skill in mathematics and the sciences. They should be curious about the "how" and "why" of natural and mechanical things and creative in finding new ways of doing things. Engineers need to be able to analyze problems systematically and logically and to communicate well—both orally and in writing. They should be willing to work within strict budgets and meet tight deadlines for completing projects. Skill in directing and supervising other workers is also important.

Education and Training. For students considering a career in engineering, the most important subjects to take in high school are mathematics and science courses and English. Typically, the mathematics courses should cover algebra, geometry, trigonometry, and introductory calculus. Chemistry and physics are important sciences for students to take. Helpful electives include foreign languages; economics, history, and other social studies courses; and composition and public speaking.

To enter the engineering profession, most students complete a four-year bachelor's degree program at a college or university. In addition to a course of study in their chosen engineering fields, engineering students must take several advanced mathematics and science courses. Most undergraduate degree programs also include courses in such subjects as economics, history, languages, management, and writing to equip students with the skills that will be needed in their later work as engineers. Many programs require the completion of an independent study or design project, including a formal report, before graduation.

Undergraduate engineering students often take part in *internships* or *cooperative education* programs in which they alternate between going to school and working for nearby companies as special engineering trainees. These programs give students the benefit of practical experience while studying for their degrees.

Graduate study gives the engineering student additional preparation for a professional career. Some engineering students study for another year after receiving a bachelor's degree. They undertake a program of advanced course work in a specialized field and earn a master's degree. The completion of an original research project called a *thesis* is part of most master's programs. Engineering students who want to teach at a college or university or do advanced research may then study three to five more years to earn a doctor's degree.

Some universities, junior and community colleges, and technical institutes offer two-year and four-year degree programs in certain specialized areas of engineering technology, such as computer maintenance and electronics. Engineering technology programs prepare students for basic design and production work in engineering rather than for jobs that require extensive knowledge of science or mathematical theory. *Engineering technicians*, graduates of the two-year programs, and *engineering technologists*, graduates of the four-year programs, form an important part of engineering teams.

Registration and Licensing. In the United States, laws affecting the registration and licensing of engineers vary from state to state. In general, engineers must be registered if they offer their services to the public or if they are involved in construction. The usual requirements for registration are that the engineer must (1) be a graduate of an approved engineering school, (2) have four years of applicable engineering experience, and (3) pass a state examination. Each state has a board of engineering examiners that administers the licensing laws.

In Canada, engineers must be registered before they can practice. Each province has an association that administers the licensing requirements.

Professional Organizations and Standards. Many of the specialized fields of engineering have their own professional societies. The societies publish technical articles and help members keep up to date. They also grant awards to outstanding engineers, work to promote public understanding of engineering, and encourage young people to become engineers. Many engineering societies prepare standards for procedures and sponsor research of general interest.

Other engineering organizations include the Accreditation Board for Engineering and Technology (ABET) and the American Association of Engineering Societies (AAES). The ABET and the AAES are administrative organizations composed of several engineering societies. The ABET reviews and accredits courses of study in engineering and engineering technology. It also provides guidance material for high school and college students. The AAES helps its member societies coordinate their activities and exchange information. The ABET has its headquarters in the United Engineering Center, 345 E. 47th Street, New York, NY 10017. The AAES is at 415 Second Street NE, Washington, DC 20002.

Many professional engineers in the United States observe a code of ethics called *Canons of Ethics of Engineers*, which is recognized by the ABET. The code tells how engineers should conduct themselves in dealing with the public, with clients and employers, and with other engineers. Professional societies specializing in one area of engineering often have additional rules governing the professional behavior of engineers in that specialty.

In Canada, the Canadian Council of Professional Engineers, headquartered in Ottawa, Ont., assists the provincial licensing associations in coordinating their activities. The council's accreditation board evaluates engineering courses of study, faculties, and facilities at Canadian colleges and universities. The council also judges the academic qualifications of foreign engineers who are seeking immigration to Canada. The council works closely with the ABET in the United States.

MARGARET L. A. MacVICAR and EDITH H. FINE

Some Engineering Societies

American Institute of Aeronautics and Astronautics
1633 Broadway, New York, NY 10019

American Institute of Chemical Engineers
345 E. 47th Street, New York, NY 10017

American Institute of Mining, Metallurgical, and Petroleum Engineers
345 E. 47th Street, New York, NY 10017

American Nuclear Society
555 N. Kensington Avenue, La Grange Park, IL 60525

American Society of Civil Engineers
345 E. 47th Street, New York, NY 10017

American Society of Mechanical Engineers
345 E. 47th Street, New York, NY 10017

Engineering Institute of Canada
2050 Mansfield Street, Montreal, PQ H3A 1Z2

Institute of Electrical and Electronics Engineers
345 E. 47th Street, New York, NY 10017

Institute of Industrial Engineers
25 Technology Park/Atlanta, Norcross, GA 30092

Society of Women Engineers
345 E. 47th Street, New York, NY 10017

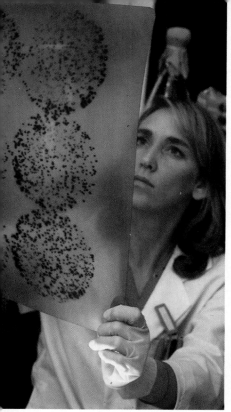

An Astronomer Readying His Telescope

© Jonathan Blair, Woodfin Camp, Inc.

© Hank Morgan, Photo Researchers

A Biologist Studying a Photo of Viruses

Cindy Rymer, Click/Chicago

Archaeologists Working at a Dig

© Sepp Seitz, Woodfin Camp, Inc.

Mathematicians Solving Problems

The World of Science consists of many fields of study. For example, scientists may investigate the structure of galaxies or the way tiny organisms function. They may explore the remains of past cultures or prove mathematical statements. New areas of scientific research are continually emerging.

SCIENCE

SCIENCE covers the broad field of knowledge that deals with observed facts and the relationships among those facts. The word *science* comes from the Latin word *scientia*, which means *knowledge*. Scientists study a wide variety of subjects. For example, some scientists search for clues to the origin of the universe. Other researchers examine the structure of molecules in the cells of living plants and animals. Still others investigate why we act the way we do, or try to solve complicated mathematical problems. But in whatever field they work, all scientists explore the workings of the world.

Scientists use systematic methods of study to make observations and collect facts. They then work to develop theories that help them order or unify related facts. Scientific theories consist of general principles or laws that attempt to explain how and why something happens or happened. Science advances as scientists accumulate more detailed facts and gain a better understanding of these fundamental principles and laws.

A theory developed by a scientist cannot be accepted as part of scientific knowledge until it has been verified

Joseph W. Dauben, the contributor of this article, is Professor of History and the History of Science at the City University of New York.

by the studies of other researchers. In fact, for any knowledge to be truly scientific, it must be repeatedly tested experimentally and found to be true. This characteristic of science sets it apart from other branches of knowledge. For example, the *humanities*, which include religion, philosophy, and the arts, deal with ideas about human nature and the meaning of life. Such ideas cannot be scientifically proved. There is no test that tells whether a philosophical system is "right." No one can determine scientifically what feeling an artist tried to express in a painting. Nor can anyone perform an experiment to check for an error in a poem or a symphony.

Science also differs from other types of knowledge in that scientific progress depends on new ideas expanding or replacing old ones. Great works of art produced today do not take the place of masterpieces of the past. But the theories of modern scientists have revised many ideas held by earlier scientists. Repeated observations and experiments lead scientists to update existing theories and to propose new ones. As new discoveries continue to be made, even many recent scientific theories will become outdated and will have to be replaced by better theories that can explain more facts. In this way, scientific knowledge is always growing and improving.

The Importance of Science

Science has enormous influence on our lives. It provides the basis of much of modern *technology*—the tools, materials, techniques, and sources of power that make our lives and work easier. The term *applied science* is sometimes used to refer to scientific research that concentrates on the development of technology. The discoveries of scientists also help shape our views about ourselves and our place in the universe.

To Everyday Life. Modern science and technology have changed our lives in many dramatic ways. Airplanes, automobiles, communications satellites, computers, plastics, and television are only a few of the scientific and technological inventions that have transformed human life. Research by nuclear physicists has led to the development of nuclear energy as a source of power. Agricultural output has soared as scientists have developed better varieties of plants and highly effective fertilizers. The development of antibiotics and other new drugs has helped control many infectious diseases. Studies in anatomy and physiology have led to amazing new surgical techniques and to the invention of lifesaving machines that can do the work of such organs as the lungs, kidneys, and heart.

Although scientific and technological achievements have benefited us in numerous ways, they have also created serious problems. The rapid growth of industrial technology, for instance, has resulted in such grave side effects as environmental pollution and fuel shortages. Breakthroughs in nuclear research have led to the development of weapons of mass destruction. Some people fear that advanced biological research will produce new disease-causing bacteria or viruses that resist drugs. People are also concerned that computerized information systems may eventually destroy personal privacy.

The harmful effects of some technological applications of science have led some people to question the value of scientific research. But science itself is neither good nor bad. The uses that businesses, governments, and individuals choose to make of scientific knowledge determine whether that knowledge will help or harm society. For a more detailed discussion of the benefits and side effects of technology, see TECHNOLOGY.

To Philosophical Thought. Science has greatly affected the way we view ourselves and the world around us. In ancient times, most people believed that natural events and everything that happened to them resulted from the actions of gods and spirits. For example, they thought that angry gods and evil spirits caused disease by invading or attacking the body.

The ancient Greeks were among the first peoples to begin to use systematic observation and reasoning to analyze natural happenings. As scientific thinking gradually developed, nature came to be seen less and less as the product of mysterious spiritual forces. Instead, people began to feel that nature could be understood and even controlled through science.

Over the years, scientific findings have increasingly influenced philosophical and religious thought about the nature of human beings and their place in the universe. In the mid-1500's, for example, the Polish astronomer Nicolaus Copernicus proposed that the earth and the other planets travel around the sun. Although his theory was later proved to be correct, it stirred strong opposition among philosophers and religious leaders of the time. They had long believed that the earth and the people on it had special importance because the sun, stars, and planets revolved around the earth.

The theories developed by the British naturalist Charles Darwin in the mid-1800's also aroused bitter philosophical and religious debates. Some philosophers and religious leaders opposed Darwin's idea that all species of plant and animal life *evolved* (developed gradually) from a few common ancestors. They felt that this theory of evolution contradicted the belief that God created human beings and gave them special emotional and intellectual gifts. These debates continue today. During the late 1800's and early 1900's, the Austrian physician Sigmund Freud developed a theory that unconscious motives control much of human behavior. His research and writings have raised serious questions about the extent to which people have free will and are responsible for their behavior. See EVOLUTION (Acceptance of Evolution); FREUD, SIGMUND (His Influence).

Since 1900, new scientific theories have begun to alter philosophical views about the nature of reality and the limits of our ability to observe it accurately. In 1905, for instance, the German-born physicist Albert Einstein published his special theory of relativity. The theory dramatically changed some of the most basic ideas about time, space, mass, and motion. For example, it stated that observations of space and time are not absolute. They are affected by the motion of the observer. See RELATIVITY.

The Branches of Science

Scientific study can be divided into four major groups: (1) mathematics and logic, (2) the physical sciences, (3) the life sciences, and (4) the social sciences. Within these main categories are many smaller groupings of closely related specialties. For example, anthropology, psychology, and sociology are *behavioral sciences* included in the category of the social sciences. Geology, meteorology, physical geography, and physical oceanography are grouped together as the *earth sciences* within the category of the physical sciences.

As scientific knowledge has grown and become increasingly complicated, many new fields of study have emerged. At the same time, the boundaries between scientific fields have become less and less clear-cut. Numerous areas of science overlap, and it is often hard to tell where one science ends and another begins. For instance, both chemistry and physics deal with atomic structure. Both paleontology and geology study the age of rocks in the earth. Many of the most important scientific advances have resulted from the exchange of ideas and methods among different branches of science.

In some cases, sciences have come to overlap so much that *interdisciplinary* fields have been established. Such fields combine parts of two or more sciences. For example, *biochemistry* combines areas of biology and chemistry in studying the chemical processes that occur in living plants and animals. *Economic geology* draws upon economics and geology in investigating the distribution of such natural resources as gold, silver, and petroleum.

WORLD BOOK has separate articles on many of the branches of science discussed in this section. For a complete listing of these articles, see the *Related Articles* at the end of this article.

Mathematics and Logic are not based on experimental testing. But they can be considered part of science because they are essential tools in almost all scientific study. Mathematics enables scientists to prepare exact statements of their findings and theories and to make numerical predictions about what will happen in the future. Logic provides the basis for all scientific reasoning.

Mathematics has a number of major branches. *Arithmetic*, which furnishes the basis for many of the other branches of mathematics, is the study of numbers and of methods for calculating with numbers. *Algebra* involves solving *equations*, mathematical sentences that say two expressions are equal. In algebraic equations, letters are used to represent unknown quantities. *Calculus* is used to solve problems dealing with changing quantities. *Geometry* concerns the mathematical relationships of points, lines, angles, surfaces, and solids in space. *Probability* deals with the likelihood that an event will occur. *Statistics* is used to analyze large amounts of numerical information for significant trends.

Scientific reasoning depends on both *deductive logic* and *inductive logic*. In using deductive logic, a scientist reasons from known scientific principles or rules to draw a conclusion relating to a specific question. The accuracy of the scientist's conclusion depends on the accuracy and completeness of the principles or rules used. Inductive logic requires a scientist to make repeated observations of an experiment or an event. From the many observations, the scientist can form a general conclusion. See DEDUCTIVE METHOD; INDUCTIVE METHOD.

The Physical Sciences examine the nature of the universe. They study the structure and properties of nonliving matter, from tiny atoms to vast galaxies. The physical sciences include (1) astronomy, (2) chemistry, (3) geology, (4) meteorology, and (5) physics.

Astronomy is the study of comets, meteors, galaxies, planets, stars, and other objects in space. Astronomers map the locations of heavenly bodies and investigate the physical and chemical processes that occur in celestial objects. They also study the structure, composition, size, and history of the universe.

Chemistry studies natural and artificially created substances to determine their composition and structure and the changes that occur when they combine and form other substances. Chemists take molecules apart and put them together in new ways. They try to find out why chemical reactions occur and how they can be controlled. *Organic chemistry* deals with most compounds containing the element carbon, and *inorganic chemistry* concerns all other compounds. *Radiochemistry* investigates radioactive substances and their uses. *Stereochemistry* examines the different chemical properties that result when compounds of the same formula differ in the relative position of their atoms in three-dimensional space. *Physical chemistry* studies the effects of light, heat, and other forms of energy on chemical processes.

Geology investigates the composition, structure, and history of the earth. Geologists analyze how such forces as earthquakes, volcanic eruptions, and wind or water erosion change the earth's surface. They also study meteorites and materials brought back from the moon. Branches of geology include *petrology*, the study of rocks; *mineralogy*, the study of minerals; and *seismology*, the study of earthquakes. *Geochronology* seeks to determine the age and history of the earth and its parts.

Meteorology is the study of the earth's atmosphere and the conditions that produce weather. Meteorologists try to predict the weather. They work to develop improved instruments for collecting data about the atmosphere. They also seek better techniques to make weather forecasting more exact. *Climatologists* analyze weather trends to determine the general pattern of weather that makes up an area's climate.

Physics is concerned with matter and energy. Physicists study mechanics, heat, light, sound, electricity, magnetism, and the properties of matter. *Atomic physics* involves the study of the structure and properties of atoms, and *nuclear physics* focuses on the makeup and behavior of the nuclei of atoms. *Particle physics* deals with the nature of electrons, protons, and other tiny bits of matter smaller than atomic nuclei. *Cryogenics* examines the behavior of matter at extremely low temperatures, and *plasma physics* investigates the behavior of ionized gases at exceptionally high temperatures. *Solid-state physics* studies the properties of extremely pure crystals and other solid materials.

The Life Sciences, also called the *biological sciences* or *biology*, involve the study of living organisms. There are two main fields of the life sciences. *Botany* deals with plants, and *zoology* with animals. Botany and zoology are further divided into various branches, each of which can be subdivided into areas of special study. Most major branches of the life sciences apply equally to plants and animals. Many of the branches, such as anatomy and physiology, overlap with, and contribute greatly to, the study of medicine. See MEDICINE.

Anatomy examines the structure of living things. Anatomists investigate the parts of organisms and how the parts are related. *Histology* deals with tissues, and *cytology* with the fine structures of individual cells. *Comparative anatomy* studies similarities and differences in the body structure of animals and provides clues to how certain animals might have evolved.

Physiology deals with the normal functions of living things and their parts. For example, physiologists study how nerve fibers transmit impulses and how organisms take in and use food. *Biochemistry* examines the chemical processes that are involved in the actions of the different parts of plants and animals. *Biophysics* investigates the

© Chuck O'Rear, Woodfin Camp, Inc.

Modern Technology plays a key role in almost every area of scientific research. The physicist above is using *lasers* (concentrated beams of light) in measuring airstream velocity.

physical processes involved in the functioning of the various parts of living things.

Other Branches. The field of *genetics* is concerned with how plants and animals pass on characteristics to their offspring. *Molecular biology* examines the structure and function of proteins and other large molecules essential to life. *Paleontology* investigates the forms of life that existed in prehistoric times. *Taxonomy* involves the classification of living things. *Sociobiology* deals with the biological basis for the social behavior of people and other animals. *Ecology* focuses on the relationships living things have to one another and to their environment.

Some life sciences concentrate on certain kinds of organisms. For example, *bacteriology* is the study of bacteria, and *ornithology* is the study of birds. Some other life sciences investigate the organisms that live in a specific environment. *Marine biology,* for instance, studies the plants and animals of the sea.

The Social Sciences deal with the individuals, groups, and institutions that make up human society. They focus on human relationships and the interactions between individuals and their families, religious or ethnic communities, cities, governments, and other social groups. Social scientists attempt to develop general "laws" of human behavior. But their task is difficult because it is hard to design controlled experiments involving human beings. Social scientists must therefore rely heavily on careful observations and the systematic collection of data to arrive at their conclusions. The use of statistics and mathematical models is important in analyzing information and developing theories in the social sciences. The main branches of the social sciences include (1) anthropology, (2) economics, (3) political science, (4) psychology, and (5) sociology.

Anthropology investigates the origin and development of human cultures and of human physical characteristics. Anthropologists study various groups of people to determine their similarities and differences. They compare the arts, beliefs, customs, daily life, inventions, languages, social relationships, and values of different cultures. *Archaeology* traces the development of cultures by studying the things that earlier peoples made and used.

Economics examines how people produce goods and services, how they distribute them among themselves, and how they use them. Economists deal with problems in such areas as management and labor relations, the setting of wages and prices, and the use of natural resources. They use computers and statistical analysis to construct mathematical models that enable them to determine how various economic systems work and to predict the effect of changes in the systems.

Political Science studies forms of government, political parties, pressure groups, elections, and other aspects of politics. Political scientists try to develop theories about political power and behavior and seek to discover what kinds of government may benefit people the most under given circumstances. They also measure public opinion.

Psychology involves investigation of mental processes and behavior. *Physiological psychologists* study how the nerves and the brain work. *Behavioral psychologists* observe and record the ways in which people and other animals relate to one another and to the environment. They use systematic methods to examine people's thoughts, feelings, and personality traits. Psychologists also explore the causes of mental disorders.

Sociology studies the nature, origin, and development of human society and community life. Sociologists investigate the interrelationships among individuals and groups in a society. They examine cultural influences, standards of behavior, and other factors that can affect general social conditions. They also explore the causes of crime, divorce, poverty, and other social problems.

How Scientists Work

Scientific research is a creative process that can involve a variety of techniques. Important advances may result from patient hard work or sudden leaps of imagination. Even chance can play a role in the scientific process. For example, Sir Alexander Fleming, a British bacteriologist, discovered penicillin accidentally in 1928, when he noticed that a bit of mold of the genus *Penicillium* had contaminated a laboratory dish containing bacteria. Examining the dish, Fleming saw that the bacteria around the mold had been killed.

Scientists use a number of methods in making discoveries and in developing theories. These methods include (1) observing nature, (2) classifying data, (3) using logic, (4) conducting experiments, (5) forming a *hypothesis* (proposed explanation), and (6) expressing findings mathematically. Most scientific research involves some or all of these steps.

Observing Nature is one of the oldest scientific methods. For example, the ancient Egyptians and Babylonians studied the motions of heavenly bodies and so learned to predict the changes of seasons and the best times to plant and harvest crops. In the 1830's, Charles Darwin carefully observed plants and animals in many parts of the world while serving as a naturalist with a British scientific expedition aboard the H.M.S. *Beagle.* Study of the specimens collected on the voyage helped Darwin develop his theory that modern species had evolved from a few earlier ones.

Classifying Data can reveal the relationships among observed facts. In the mid-1800's, Dmitri Mendeleev, a Russian chemist, classified the elements into families or groups in a chart called the *periodic table.* On the table, elements with similar properties appeared at regular intervals. Gaps in the table indicated elements that were not yet known. Scientists later proved the importance of Mendeleev's systematic classification when they discovered the existence and chemical properties of new elements that filled the gaps.

Using Logic enables scientists to draw conclusions from existing information. In the late 1800's, a German physicist named Wilhelm Wien studied the relationship between temperature and the energy radiated by heated solids and liquids. After studying many specific examples, he noted that multiplying the temperature of a heated solid or liquid by the wavelength of greatest intensity radiated at that temperature always produced the same number. Although Wien could not test all solids and liquids, he used inductive reasoning to conclude that this number was a *universal constant* which was the same for all heated solids and liquids, regardless of their physical or chemical makeup.

Conducting Experiments is a major tool in developing and testing scientific theories. The Italian astronomer and physicist Galileo was one of the first scientists to recognize that systematic experimentation could help reveal the laws of nature. In the late 1500's, Galileo began performing carefully designed experiments to study the basic properties of matter in motion. By rolling balls of different weights down inclined planes, he discovered that all objects fall to the ground with the same *acceleration* (rate of increase in speed), unless air resistance or some other force slows them down. In the early 1600's, William Harvey, an English physician, used the experimental method to learn how blood circulates through the body. He made careful studies of the human pulsebeat and heartbeat and *dissected* (cut up) human and animal corpses for examination. Harvey concluded that the heart pumps blood through the arteries to all parts of the body and that the blood returns to the heart through the veins.

Forming a Hypothesis requires talent, skill, and creativity. Scientists base their proposed explanations on existing information. They strive to form hypotheses that help explain, order, or unify related facts. They then use experimentation and other means to test their hypotheses. The discovery of the planet Neptune in the mid-1800's resulted from the formation of a hypothesis. Astronomers noticed that Uranus, which they thought was the most distant planet, was not always in the position predicted for it by the laws of gravitation and motion. Some astronomers concluded that the laws did not hold at such great distances from the sun. But others hypothesized that the variations in the orbit of Uranus might be caused by the force of gravity from an unknown planet. By calculating where such a planet would have to be located to affect the orbit, astronomers eventually discovered Neptune.

Expressing Findings Mathematically can yield valuable insights about how the world works. Galileo used mathematics to express the results of his experiments with falling bodies and to enable him to determine the distance an object would fall in a certain amount of time. The English scientist Sir Isaac Newton developed a mathematical theory of gravitation in the 1600's that explained many types of motion, both on the earth and throughout the universe. In the early 1900's, the German-born physicist Albert Einstein found that mass is related to energy by the equation $E = mc^2$. The equation states that *energy* (E) is equivalent to *mass* (m) multiplied by the *speed of light squared* (c^2). Einstein's equation later provided the basis for the development of nuclear energy.

The History of Science

From earliest times, people have been curious about the world around them. Thousands of years before civilization began, people learned to count and tried to explain the rising and setting of the sun and the phases of the moon. They studied the habits of the animals they hunted, learned that some plants could be used as drugs, and acquired other basic knowledge about nature. These achievements marked the beginnings of science. They were among the first attempts to understand and control nature. In general, mathematics and medicine were the first sciences to develop, followed by the physical sciences, life sciences, and social sciences.

Early Civilizations. The sciences developed by the peoples of the first civilizations dealt chiefly with practical matters. For example, mathematics was used to record business and government transactions. Astronomy provided the basis for keeping time and determining when to plant and harvest crops. As early as 3000 B.C., the Egyptians studied the heavens to forecast the arrival of the seasons and to predict when the annual flooding of the Nile River would occur. The Egyptians used geometry to establish property lines and to make the measurements needed to build huge pyramids. They also learned some anatomy, physiology, and surgery through embalming their dead.

In ancient Babylonia, the people used a system of counting in units of 60, which is the basis of the 360-degree circle and the 60-minute hour. They understood fractions, squares, and square roots. They also developed complicated mathematical models of the motions of the planets and other heavenly bodies. Their detailed observations of the heavens enabled them to predict eclipses of the sun and moon and other astronomical events.

The Chinese and Indian civilizations developed a little later than the Egyptian and Babylonian cultures. By the 1300's B.C., the Chinese had mapped the major stars in the heavens and, like the Babylonians, succeeded in predicting eclipses. The ancient Chinese had their own system of mathematics. They also developed acupuncture and other medical practices that have been handed down almost unchanged to the present. Medicine in ancient India dealt with the prevention as well as the treatment of illness. Indian surgeons performed many kinds of operations, including amputations and plastic surgery. Early Indian mathematicians invented the Hindu-Arabic numerals that we use today.

The earliest advanced cultures in the Americas also had a working knowledge of astronomy and mathematics. One of the first major civilizations was that of the Olmec Indians of Mexico, who developed a counting system and a calendar between 1200 and 100 B.C. By about A.D. 250, the Maya of Central America and Mexico were studying the motions of the sun, moon, stars, and planets from observatories. They used their astronomical knowledge to develop religious and civil calendars. The Maya also had an advanced mathematical system. During the 1400's, the Aztec Indians of Mexico and the Inca Indians of Peru ruled powerful empires. Carvings on a famous "Calendar Stone" left behind by the Aztec represent the regular motions of the heavenly bodies, as well as religious symbols and symbols for the days of the month. The Inca used mathematics in constructing buildings and roads.

Ancient Greece. The Greeks left the greatest scientific heritage of all the ancient peoples. They stressed the importance of developing general theories about the workings of the world and were the first to begin systematically to separate scientific ideas from superstition.

About 400 B.C., a Greek physician named Hippocrates taught that diseases have natural causes and that the body can repair itself. He was the first physician known to consider medicine a science apart from religion. During the 300's B.C., Aristotle, one of the greatest Greek philosophers, studied many areas of science. Aristotle gathered vast amounts of information about the variety, structure, and behavior of animals and plants. He showed the need for classifying knowledge and recognized the importance of observation. He also developed deductive logic as a means of reaching conclusions.

Greek mathematics was more advanced than that of any other ancient culture. The Greeks became the first people to separate mathematics from purely practical uses and to develop systematic methods of reasoning to prove the truth of mathematical statements. By 300 B.C., Thales, Pythagoras, Euclid, and other Greek mathematicians had perfected geometry as a single logical system. The Greeks believed that the study of mathematics could yield absolutely certain and eternal knowledge. For example, once a principle of geometry was proved, it remained true for all time.

Some Greek scientists had an interest in practical affairs. During the 200's B.C., for instance, the Greek mathematician and inventor Archimedes performed experiments in which he discovered the laws of the lever and the pulley. The discoveries led to the construction of machines that could easily move heavy loads.

The Greeks mapped the stars and measured the size of the earth with surprising accuracy. The astronomers used the circle, which they considered the perfect mathematical form, as their model for the heavens. They worked out various mathematical models and mechanical systems that explained the motions of the planets in terms of circular paths. In the A.D. 100's, Ptolemy, one of the greatest astronomers of ancient times, presented his ideas and summarized those of earlier Greek astronomers in the *Almagest*. In this work, Ptolemy stated that the sun and the planets moved around the earth in circular orbits. Astronomers accepted versions of Ptolemy's *geocentric* (earth-centered) theory of the universe for more than 1,400 years.

Although the ancient Greeks made many important scientific advances, their approach to science had limitations. Believing mathematics to be eternally true, unchanging knowledge, the Greeks never saw that it could be used to analyze the physics of motion and other constantly changing properties of nature. Nor did the Greeks discover the importance of testing their observations systematically. Many of their conclusions were false because they were founded on "common sense" instead of experiments. For example, Aristotle mistakenly thought, on the basis of common sense, that heavier objects fall to the earth faster than lighter ones.

Ancient Rome. By the A.D. 100's, the city of Rome had conquered much of the known world, including the areas of Greek civilization. The Romans were excellent architects, engineers, and builders. But they contributed little to theoretical science. Under Roman rule, scholars continued to accept the scientific knowledge of the Greeks. Many Roman physicians came from the Greek-speaking world, and the Romans employed Greek tutors or sent their children to Athens and other centers of Greek learning for advanced education.

Although the Romans themselves made few scientific discoveries, vast encyclopedias of scientific knowledge were written under Roman rule. In a 37-volume work called *Natural History*, the Roman author Pliny the Elder gathered the scientific learning of his day. A Greek geographer and historian named Strabo described all parts of the known world in his 17-volume *Geography*.

The Greek physician Galen, who practiced medicine in Rome during the A.D. 100's, developed the first medi-

Highlights in the History of Science

Hippocrates taught that diseases have natural causes.

Archimedes discovered the laws of the lever and the pulley.

Ptolemy proposed that the earth is the center of the universe.

c. 400 B.C.   c. 300 B.C.   200's B.C.   A.D. 100's

Euclid organized geometry as a single system of mathematics.

Galen developed the first medical theories based on experiments.

Granger Collection

Egyptian Geometry dealt with surveying land and other practical matters. This papyrus from the 1500's B.C. shows calculations of the area of a field.

Fresco (1510-1511);
The Vatican, Rome
(SCALA/Art Resource)

Aristotle, *right,* the great Greek philosopher, studied many areas of science in the 300's B.C. He emphasized careful observation in his scientific studies.

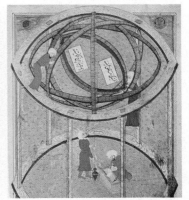

Granger Collection

Arab Astronomers of the A.D. 800's and 900's mapped the heavenly bodies. The Arabs also made major advances in mathematics, medicine, and optics.

SCIENCE

cal theories based on scientific experiments. Galen dissected animal corpses for study and greatly advanced the knowledge of anatomy. However, he had many false notions about how the human body works.

The Middle Ages was a 1,000-year period in European history that began in the A.D. 400's. For hundreds of years after this period began, little scientific investigation took place in Europe. Most scholars were more interested in *theology*, the study of God, than in the study of nature. They relied on Greek and Roman writings for scientific information and saw no need to make observations of their own. Aristotle, Euclid, Galen, and Ptolemy were considered the authorities on science. But many of the ancient works used by European scholars of the Middle Ages were poorly preserved. Errors were introduced as copies were made, and the contents of the works were often inaccurately summarized.

Meanwhile, Arabs in the Middle East preserved much of the science of ancient Greece and Rome. They carefully translated many Greek and Roman texts into Arabic. Through their conquests, they came into contact with Persian astronomy, history, and medicine and with the Indian system of numbers and decimal numeral system.

Arabic scientists also made important contributions of their own in astronomy, mathematics, medicine, optics, and other sciences. An Arab mathematician named Al-Khowarizmi organized and expanded algebra in the early 800's. Avicenna, an Arab physician of the late 900's and early 1000's, produced a vast medical encyclopedia titled the *Canon of Medicine*. It summed up the medical knowledge of the day and accurately described meningitis, tetanus, and many other diseases. During the early 1000's, an Arab physicist known as Alhazen recognized that vision is caused by the reflection of light from objects into our eyes. In spite of their many scientific achievements, the Arabs did not use experimental methods or develop the instruments or applied mathematical techniques that were necessary to the development of modern science.

During the 1000's, European scholars began to show a renewed interest in science. Many major Arabic scientific works were introduced into Europe and translated into Latin, the language of learning in the West. The Hindu-Arabic number system also spread to Europe, where it stimulated the development of mathematics and began to be used in business. Some theologians of the 1100's and 1200's, such as Peter Abelard of France and Thomas Aquinas of Italy, started systematic efforts to bring Christian teachings into harmony with rediscovered scientific ideas. During the 1100's, the first European universities were established. In time, universities were to play a vital role in the growth of science.

Relatively few medical advances occurred in Europe during the Middle Ages. Physicians relied on the teachings of Galen, rather than make new discoveries based on their own observations and studies. Epidemics frequently swept across Europe. In the mid-1300's, for example, a terrible outbreak of bubonic plague called the Black Death killed about a fourth of Europe's population. To treat or prevent diseases, many people continued to depend on magic and superstition.

The Rebirth of Science in Europe began in 1543 with the publication of two books that broke scientific tradi-

Leonardo da Vinci studied anatomy, astronomy, botany, and geology.

c. 1500

Johannes Kepler established astronomy as an exact science.

1609

William Harvey published his theory of how the blood circulates.

1628

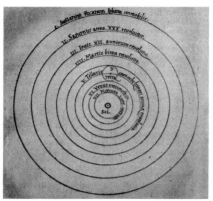

© Jay M. Pasachoff

The Sun-Centered Theory is shown in this diagram from *On the Revolutions of the Heavenly Spheres* (1543) by Nicolaus Copernicus of Poland. His work revolutionized astronomy.

Granger Collection

Andreas Vesalius wrote the first scientific text on human anatomy. His book, *On the Fabric of the Human Body*, appeared in 1543.

Granger Collection

A Pendulum Clock from 1641 was designed by the Italian scientist Galileo, who saw the need for precise scientific instruments.

tion. One book was written by the Polish astronomer Nicolaus Copernicus, and the second by Andreas Vesalius, an anatomist born in what is now Belgium.

Copernicus' book, called *On the Revolutions of the Heavenly Spheres*, challenged Ptolemy's view that the earth was the center of the universe. Ptolemy's geocentric theory required a complicated series of circular motions to account for astronomers' observations of how the planets appeared to move. Copernicus realized that if the earth and other planets traveled around the sun, a less complicated arrangement of circles could explain the observed motions of the planets. But his *heliocentric* (sun-centered) theory still did not accurately predict the motions of all the planets.

During the 1500's, a Danish astronomer named Tycho Brahe observed the motions of the planets far more precisely than they had ever been observed before. Brahe's work enabled Johannes Kepler, a German astronomer and mathematician, to lend new support to the heliocentric theory in 1609. Kepler used intricate calculations to show that the theory could explain the movements of the planets if the planets orbited the sun in *elliptical* (oval) paths rather than circular ones. The elliptical shape of the orbits would also make it easier to account for the movements of the planets. Kepler's work marked the start of modern astronomy.

The second tradition-breaking book published in 1543 was Vesalius' *On the Fabric of the Human Body*. In this work, Vesalius laid out in detail the most precise anatomical knowledge of the day. Vesalius based the book on observations he made in dissecting human corpses. His book gradually replaced the texts of both Galen and Avicenna.

The Scientific Revolution. During the late 1500's and early 1600's, scholars and scientists increasingly realized the importance of experimentation and mathematics to scientific advances. This realization helped bring about a revolution in science. The great Italian scientist Galileo stressed the need for carefully controlled experiments. In his research, Galileo used observation and mathematical analysis as he looked for cause and effect relationships among natural events. He recognized that experimentation could lead to the discovery of new principles. For example, Aristotle had taught that the heavier an object is, the faster it falls to the ground. Galileo questioned that idea. He set up experiments to find the true laws of falling bodies and proved that Aristotle was wrong. Through experimentation, Galileo discovered many basic principles of mechanics.

Galileo also saw the need to extend the range and power of the human senses with scientific instruments. He improved such instruments as the clock and telescope. With the telescope, Galileo found convincing evidence supporting Copernicus' heliocentric theory.

Another remarkable scientist of the 1600's was Sir Isaac Newton of England. Newton used the findings of others to develop a unified view of the forces of the universe. In his book *Principia* (1687), he formulated a law of universal gravitation and showed that both objects on the earth and the heavenly bodies obey this law. Newton's studies of lenses and prisms laid the foundation for the modern study of optics. Newton and Gottfried Leibniz, a German philosopher, independently developed a new system of mathematics, calculus.

Robert Hooke used the microscope to uncover the world of cells.

Adam Smith published the first complete work on classical economics.

Mid-1600's   Early 1700's   1776

Robert Boyle helped establish the experimental method in chemistry.

Carl Scheele and Joseph Priestley independently discovered oxygen.

Mary Evans Picture Library

Bettmann Archive

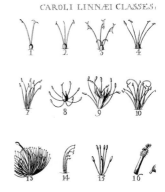

CAROLI LINNÆI CLASSES.

Hunt Institute for Botanical Documentation, Carnegie-Mellon University

Experiments with Prisms conducted in the 1600's by Sir Isaac Newton of England began the modern study of optics. Newton demonstrated that sunlight is a mixture of light of all colors.

Human Vision was explained in geometric terms by René Descartes, a French philosopher of the 1600's. He held that mathematics was a model for all sciences.

Scientific Classification was begun by Carolus Linnaeus of Sweden in the 1700's. In this plate, he grouped plants by sexual parts.

379

SCIENCE

The scientific revolution also extended to many other areas of science. Modern physiology began in the early 1600's with the work of William Harvey, an English physician. Harvey performed careful experiments and used simple mathematics to show how blood circulates through the human body. In the mid-1600's, an English scientist named Robert Hooke pioneered in the use of the microscope to study the fine structures of plants and animals and uncovered a new world of cells. Also in the mid-1600's, Robert Boyle, an Irish scientist, helped establish the experimental method in chemistry. Boyle introduced many new ways of identifying the chemical composition of substances.

In addition to scientific discoveries, new ideas about the philosophy and methods of science arose during the 1600's. The French philosopher René Descartes proposed that mathematics was the model all other sciences should follow. He believed that mathematics yielded absolutely certain conclusions because the mathematical process started with simple, self-evident truths and then used logic to move, step by step, to other truths.

The English philosopher and statesman Francis Bacon viewed experience as the most important source of knowledge. He thought that by collecting all the observable facts of nature, a person could discover the laws which govern the universe. In his book *The New Atlantis* (1627), Bacon described a research institution equipped with many tools of modern science, including laboratories, libraries, and printing presses. Bacon's ideas inspired the creation of the Royal Society in London in 1660 and of the Academy of Sciences in Paris in 1666.

These societies were among the first institutions whose chief aim was to promote science.

Some theologians of the 1600's supported science because they believed that it helped reveal the wonders of God's creation. They also felt that scientific discoveries could be used to improve the quality of human life. But many other theologians were deeply upset by the development of scientific laws that seemed to govern the physical world without divine assistance. They opposed the heliocentric theory and condemned other scientific ideas that they believed contradicted traditional beliefs about human beings and their place in the universe.

The Age of Reason, also called the *Enlightenment*, was a philosophical movement that greatly affected the development of science during the late 1600's and the 1700's. The leaders of the movement insisted that the use of reason was the best way to determine truth. They felt that everything in the universe behaved according to a few simple laws, which could be expressed mathematically. The philosophers of the Age of Reason developed many rules of scientific study that are still used.

Great efforts were made during the Age of Reason to circulate the results of the scientific research of the times. Many scholars gathered, organized, and published this knowledge. The most famous reference work was the 28-volume *Encyclopédie* (1751-1772) edited by two French authors, Denis Diderot and Jean d'Alembert. The *Encyclopédie* contained reports on much of the science and technology of the day. See AGE OF REASON.

One of the major scientific achievements of the 1700's was the creation of modern chemistry. Scientists developed the techniques necessary for isolating and studying gases in their pure forms. They discovered many chemi-

---

Antoine Lavoisier discovered the nature of combustion.

James Clerk Maxwell developed his electromagnetic theory.

○ 1777   ○ 1830   ○ 1860's

Charles Lyell showed that the earth has changed slowly through the ages.

Bettmann Archive

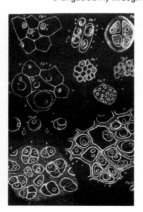

Granger Collection

Michael Faraday, shown in his laboratory at the Royal Institution in London, produced a current with a moving magnet in 1831.

Drawings of Cells made by Theodor Schwann of Germany in the 1830's helped prove cells make up all organisms.

Beak Adaptations in finches on the Galapagos Islands were noted by the British naturalist Charles Darwin. Darwin used such species variations to support his theories of evolution, which he set forth in *The Origin of Species* (1859).

cal substances, including chlorine, hydrogen, and carbon dioxide. Oxygen was discovered by the Swedish chemist Carl Scheele in the early 1770's and independently by the English chemist Joseph Priestley in 1774. By 1777, Antoine Lavoisier of France had discovered the nature of *combustion* (burning). He showed that combustion results from the rapid union of the burning material with oxygen. Lavoisier also proved the law of the conservation of matter. This law states that matter cannot be created or destroyed but only chemically changed in form. Lavoisier also helped work out the present-day system of chemical names.

Major advances occurred in biology during the 1700's. A Swedish naturalist and botanist named Carolus Linnaeus devised a systematic method for naming and classifying plants and animals in the mid-1700's. His method, with many alterations, is still used. Two French naturalists, Comte de Buffon and Georges Cuvier made great advances in the study of fossils and of comparative anatomy and did much to prepare the way for the scientific investigation of evolution.

In 1776, the Scottish economist Adam Smith published *The Wealth of Nations*, the first systematic formulation of classical economics. The first systematic studies of electricity were also conducted during the 1700's. In the American Colonies, Benjamin Franklin proved in 1752 that lightning is electricity when he performed his famous experiment of flying a kite during a thunderstorm. In the late 1700's, two Italian scientists, Luigi Galvani and Count Alessandro Volta, made some of the first experiments with electric current.

Scientific Advances of the 1800's. Scientific expeditions traveled to all parts of the world during the 1800's.

Their purpose was to expand geographical knowledge and to study the plants and animals they found. From 1831 to 1836, Charles Darwin worked as a naturalist with a British expedition aboard the H.M.S. *Beagle*. The *Beagle* visited places throughout the world, and Darwin studied plants and animals everywhere it went. While on the voyage, Darwin read the works of a British geologist named Charles Lyell. Lyell believed that the earth had been changed slowly and gradually by natural processes over long periods of time. Darwin began to wonder whether life on the earth had also evolved through natural processes.

Darwin set forth his theories of evolution in *The Origin of Species* (1859). In this book, Darwin gave evidence that plants and animals had changed their characteristics through the ages. He explained how these changes might have occurred through *natural selection*. In this process, the organisms best suited to their environment are the ones most likely to survive and leave descendants. Darwin's ideas helped explain the basic similarities—or unity—among all living organisms because they evolved from common ancestors. The theory of evolution became one of the most intensely debated scientific issues of the late 1800's. The theory aroused especially fiery opposition among religious leaders who believed that it conflicted with the Biblical account of the Creation. See EVOLUTION.

Another important unifying idea in the biological sciences was the theory that all living things are made up of cells. The theory was proposed by two German scientists, Matthias Schleiden and Theodor Schwann, in the

---

Dmitri Mendeleev published his periodic table of the elements.

Marie and Pierre Curie isolated the element radium.

Sigmund Freud established the field of psychoanalysis.

1869   1879   1898   c. 1900

Wilhelm Wundt founded one of the first psychology laboratories.

Paul Ehrlich originated the treatment of diseases with chemicals.

Bettmann Archive

Granger Collection

Granger Collection

Gregor Mendel, an Austrian monk, discovered the basic laws of heredity in the mid-1800's. He studied the inheritance of various traits in garden pea plants.

Louis Pasteur of France started modern microbiology in the mid-1800's with his discovery that certain kinds of microscopic organisms cause disease.

Max Planck, a German physicist, advanced his quantum theory in 1900. The theory states that energy is given off in a stream of separate units called *quanta.*

1830's. Their idea had been influenced by a German philosophical movement called *Naturphilosophie*. This movement emphasized the unity of all things in nature and of all forces in the universe.

Physical scientists of the 1800's also tried to produce a unified, complete view of the laws of nature. The Russian chemist Dmitri Mendeleev helped systematize the study of chemistry when he published his periodic table in 1869. In the 1840's, James P. Joule, an English physicist, showed that heat is a form of energy. He was also one of several scientists to advance the law of the conservation of energy. This law states that energy cannot be created or destroyed but only changed in form.

The physicists Michael Faraday of England and Joseph Henry of the United States found independently in 1831 that a moving magnet can produce an electric current. In the 1860's, James Clerk Maxwell, a Scottish mathematician and physicist, worked out the mathematical equations for the laws of electricity and magnetism. Maxwell's electromagnetic theory stated that visible light consists of waves of electric and magnetic forces. It also proposed the existence of invisible waves composed of the same forces. In the 1880's, Heinrich Hertz, a German physicist, produced electromagnetic waves that fitted Maxwell's theory. His work led to the development of radio, radar, and television.

During the late 1800's, several important scientific discoveries began to reveal a new picture of the physical universe. In the 1700's, the idea that matter consists of small particles that cannot be divided began to gain acceptance. In 1803, an English chemist named John Dal-

ton had used the idea of indivisible particles, or atoms, to explain the way elements combine and form compounds. But in the 1890's, the picture of atoms as solid objects began to fade. Scientists discovered electrons and natural radioactivity. These discoveries suggested that atoms have some kind of internal structure.

Several new sciences had their beginnings in the 1800's. In the 1830's, the French philosopher Auguste Comte started the study of sociology. Comte developed the theory of *positivism*, which held that social behavior and events could be observed and measured scientifically. In the mid-1800's, Gregor Mendel, an Austrian monk, discovered the basic statistical laws of heredity that laid the foundation for the science of genetics. The French chemist Louis Pasteur started modern microbiology in the mid-1800's with his studies of fermentation and disease. He found that certain microscopic organisms can produce disease in people and other animals.

Many scientists of the 1800's studied the relationship between the physiology of the nervous system and human behavior. In 1879, Wilhelm Wundt, a German philosopher, founded one of the first laboratories of experimental psychology in Leipzig, Germany. In the late 1800's and early 1900's, the Austrian physician Sigmund Freud established the field of psychoanalysis by introducing the idea that mental illness could be understood in terms of competing, unbalanced forces in the unconscious mind.

Science in the Early 1900's. Revolutionary advances in physics marked the beginning of the 1900's as scientists continued to challenge existing ideas. In 1900, Max Planck, a German physicist, advanced his quantum theory to explain the spectrum of light emitted by certain

---

Ernest Rutherford put forth his theory of atomic structure.

Jonas Salk produced the first effective polio vaccine.

| 1911 | 1928 | 1953 | 1957 |

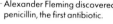
Alexander Fleming discovered penicillin, the first antibiotic.

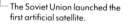
The Soviet Union launched the first artificial satellite.

Granger Collection

Historical Pictures Service

© Bar-Brown, Camera Press Ltd.

Albert Einstein, a German-born physicist, revolutionized scientific thinking about space and time with his special theory of relativity, published in 1905.

Enrico Fermi and his co-workers at the University of Chicago achieved the first controlled nuclear chain reaction in 1942, starting the atomic age.

A Ladderlike Model of DNA, the substance that controls heredity, was built by James Watson of the United States, *left*, and Francis Crick of England, *right*, in 1953.

heated objects (see QUANTUM MECHANICS). The theory states that energy is not given off continuously, but only in separate units called *quanta*. In 1905, another German physicist, Albert Einstein, showed that light may be regarded as consisting of individual energy units, which he called *photons*. That same year, Einstein published his special theory of relativity. His theory revised many of the ideas of Newtonian physics and offered scientists new ways of thinking about space and time. See RELATIVITY.

Research into the structure of the atom expanded rapidly. In 1911, the British physicist Ernest Rutherford theorized that the mass of an atom is concentrated in a tiny nucleus, which is surrounded by electrons traveling at tremendous speeds. But his theory did not deal with the arrangement of electrons. In 1913, a description of electron structure was proposed by Niels Bohr, a Danish physicist. Bohr suggested that electrons could travel only in a set of definite orbits around the nucleus.

Bohr's original picture of the atom soon proved to be inadequate, though many of the ideas behind it were correct. By 1928, a complete description of the arrangement of electrons had been obtained with the help of other physicists, especially Erwin Schrödinger and Wolfgang Pauli of Austria, Paul Dirac of England, and Max Born and Werner Heisenberg of Germany. The discovery of the neutron and other atomic particles followed this early work. Chemists used the new information about atoms to improve their ideas about chemical bonds. They produced many new compounds and developed a variety of plastics and synthetic fibers.

Great progress was also made by social scientists of the early 1900's, as they began to rely more heavily on statistical analysis and scientific research methods. In the biological sciences, a number of physician-scientists showed the importance of vitamins in the human diet. Their achievements helped conquer such nutritional diseases as beriberi and scurvy. The German physician and chemist Paul Ehrlich founded the field of chemotherapy, in which diseases are treated with chemicals. In 1928, Alexander Fleming, a British bacteriologist, discovered penicillin, the first of many antibiotics.

The work of numerous scientists began to establish the importance of genetics as a separate branch of biology. About 1901, a Dutch scientist named Hugo de Vries extensively described *mutations*—changes in hereditary material of cells. About 1910, Thomas Hunt Morgan, an American biologist, and his associates proved that *genes* are the units of heredity and that genes are arranged in an exact order along the length of cell structures called *chromosomes*. Morgan mapped the location of genes on the chromosomes of fruit flies and identified the genes responsible for such specific traits as eye color and wing shape. In the mid-1920's, an American geneticist named Hermann J. Muller discovered that mutations could be produced by treating an organism with X rays.

Achievements of the Mid-1900's. Science continued to make great strides in all fields during the mid-1900's. One of the most important breakthroughs in nuclear physics occurred in the late 1930's, when Otto Hahn and Fritz Strassmann of Germany and Lise Meitner and Otto Frisch of Austria discovered the possibility of releasing energy by splitting atoms of uranium. The Italian-born physicist Enrico Fermi and his co-workers

Researchers developed the first successful recombinant DNA procedure.

◯ 1974   ◯ 1981

The United States launched the *Columbia*, the first reusable manned spacecraft.

NASA

Fermilab

© John Marmaras, Woodfin Camp, Inc.

Space Exploration began to open new frontiers of scientific research during the 1960's. In 1969, astronauts of the U.S. Apollo 11 mission became the first human beings to walk on the moon.

Tracks Made by Atomic Particles from a *particle accelerator,* a device that speeds up the particles, enable physicists to study the most basic units of matter.

Genetic Engineering, which is used to alter an organism's genetic makeup, may one day help in treating hereditary diseases.

achieved the first controlled nuclear chain reaction in 1942 at the University of Chicago. Intensive research during World War II (1939-1945) led to the use of nuclear energy in weapons.

Physicists discovered new elementary particles in the mid-1900's. They also established the existence of *antiparticles*, which have electric charges or other properties that are the reverse of ordinary atomic particles (see ANTIMATTER). Chemists expanded the periodic table through the creation of new radioactive elements (see TRANSURANIUM ELEMENT). Anthropologists made new discoveries about the distant past of human beings. Geologists explained many of the changes that occur in the earth's crust with their theory of *plate tectonics* (see TECTONICS). Medical science developed the Salk and Sabin polio vaccines and introduced organ and tissue transplants and other new surgical techniques. Two biologists, James D. Watson of the United States and Francis H. C. Crick of Great Britain, proposed a model of the molecular structure of *deoxyribonucleic acid* (DNA), the substance that carries genetic information.

The space age began in 1957, when the Soviet Union launched the first artificial satellite to circle the earth. In 1969, two U.S. astronauts became the first human beings to walk on the moon (see SPACE TRAVEL). Astronomers also greatly expanded their knowledge of the size, structure, and history of the universe with the use of radio telescopes to collect and measure radio waves given off by objects in space. Using radio telescopes, astronomers discovered *pulsars*, *quasars*, and other previously unknown objects in space (see PULSAR; QUASAR). Radio astronomers also found evidence to support the theory that the universe began with an explosion called the *big bang* (see COSMOLOGY [The Big Bang Theory]).

Science also made important contributions to technology during the mid-1900's. Physicists invented the transistor, which revolutionized the electronics industry and enabled manufacturers to produce portable battery-powered radios and TV sets, pocket-sized calculators, and high-speed computers. Similarly, the invention of *lasers* (concentrated beams of light) promised great advances in communications, electronics, medicine, and weapons (see LASER).

Science of Today and Tomorrow. Scientific progress is faster today than ever before. This progress is reflected not only by the many discoveries made each year but also by the thousands of scientists involved in research and by the vast sums of money spent on scientific work. As the number of scientists has grown, cooperation and communication among them have become increasingly important. Many recent achievements have resulted from scientists working in research teams. Hundreds of scientific journals, professional societies, and computerized information systems make it possible for scientists to exchange information quickly and easily.

Increasingly powerful and advanced equipment is helping scientists in many different fields expand our knowledge about the world. For example, *particle accelerators*, which speed up the movement of the particles that make up atoms, have enabled physicists to create and study *quarks* and other basic units of matter (see PARTICLE ACCELERATOR; QUARK). Chemists and molecular biologists have developed *nuclear magnetic resonance*

spectroscopy and other advanced techniques that can reveal fine details of the structure of molecules (see NUCLEAR MAGNETIC RESONANCE). Improvements in computers have enabled mathematicians to solve problems at previously unheard of speeds. New telescopes, satellites, orbiting observatories, and space probes have provided astronomers with information about distant reaches of the universe.

A process called *genetic engineering* has become a valuable tool in genetics research. In this process, an organism's hereditary makeup is altered. Geneticists have engineered bacteria to produce human *insulin*, a hormone used to treat diabetes, and human *interferon*, a protein that fights viral diseases. See GENETIC ENGINEERING.

Scientists still have many new areas to explore. Through genetic engineering, for example, they hope to find new ways to diagnose and treat hereditary diseases. Astronomers are only beginning to investigate the idea of the *inflationary universe*—that is, the idea that the universe expanded extremely fast in the first fraction of a second following its origin in the big bang explosion. Physicists are working to develop *grand unified theories* that would explain the interactions between the elementary particles of atoms and the fundamental forces of the physical world.

The science of today and tomorrow promises to continue to improve our understanding of the universe and to give us ever greater control over nature. But at the same time, serious debates have arisen over such science-related issues as whether it is moral to interfere in the genetic makeup of human beings or to use lasers for destructive purposes. In the future, scientists and nonscientists alike will have an increasing responsibility to ensure that the best possible uses are made of knowledge from scientific research.

JOSEPH W. DAUBEN

Questions

What is an *interdisciplinary* science?

What are some methods scientists use in making discoveries and developing theories?

Who was one of the first scientists to recognize that systematic experimentation could help reveal the laws of nature?

What are some ways in which modern science and technology have changed our lives?

Why are mathematics and logic essential tools in almost all scientific study?

What people preserved much of the science of ancient Greece and Rome during the Middle Ages?

What characteristics set science apart from other branches of knowledge?

How did the discovery of electrons and natural radioactivity during the late 1800's begin to reveal a new picture of the physical universe?

What were the limitations of Greek science?

What marked the rebirth of science in Europe in 1543?

Additional Resources

Level I

ASIMOV, ISAAC. *More Words of Science*. Houghton, 1972. *Please Explain*. 1973.

COHEN, I. BERNARD. *From Leonardo to Lavoisier, 1450-1800*. Scribner, 1980.

Growing Up with Science: The Illustrated Encyclopedia of Invention. Ed. by MICHAEL DEMPSEY. Stuttman, 1984.

Level II

GOLDSTEIN, THOMAS. *Dawn of Modern Science: From the Arabs to Leonardo da Vinci*. Houghton, 1980.

MARKS, JOHN. *Science and the Making of the Modern World*. Heinemann, 1983.

Index

This index covers the contents of the 1985, 1986, and 1987 editions of SCIENCE YEAR, The World Book Science Annual.

Each index entry gives the edition year and a page number, for example, 87-123. The first number, 87, indicates the edition year, and the second number, 123, is the page number on which the desired information begins.

There are two types of entries in the index.

In the first type, the index entry (in **boldface**) is followed immediately by numbers:
   Paleontology, 87-294, 86-252, 85-246
This means that SCIENCE YEAR has an article titled Paleontology, and that in the 1987 edition the article begins on page 294. In the 1986 edition, the article begins on page 252, and in the 1985 edition it is on page 246.

In the second type of entry, the boldface title is followed by a clue word instead of by numbers:
   Obesity: Close-Up, 85-292; nutrition, 87-288; psychology, 86-302
This means that there is no SCIENCE YEAR article titled Obesity, but that information about this topic can be found in a Close-Up in the 1985 edition on page 292. There is also information on this topic in the Nutrition and Psychology articles of the 1987 and 1986 editions on the pages given.

When the clue word is "il.," the reference is to an illustration only:
   Chameleon: ils., 87-90, 317
This means there are illustrations of this animal in the 1987 SCIENCE YEAR, on pages 90 and 317.

The various "See" and "See also" cross-references in the index direct the reader to other entries within the index:
   Horticulture. See **Agriculture; Botany;** and **Plant.**
This means that for the location of information on horticulture—look under the boldface index entries
   Agriculture, Botany, and **Plant.**

Index

A

A, Vitamin: Close-Up, 85-292

Absolute dating: human fossils, Special Report, 86-198

Accelerator, Particle. See **Particle accelerator.**

Acetaminophen: drugs, 87-252

Acetylcholine: memory, Special Report, 86-177

Acid rain: environment, 87-262, 86-269; meteorology, 87-281

Acne: skin, Special Report, 85-77

Acquired Immune Deficiency Syndrome. See **AIDS.**

Adapter: Consumer Science, 87-324

Addiction: neuroscience, 86-291

Adhesives: Consumer Science, 85-325

Adjuvant: vaccines, Special Report, 86-150

Adolescent: nutrition, 85-293

Aerial photography: remote sensing devices, Special Report, 87-171

Aerobic exercise: Consumer Science, 86-328

Africanized honeybee: agriculture, Close-Up, 87-214

Aging: medicine, 86-278; skin, Special Report, 85-77. See also **Old age.**

Agriculture, 87-212, 86-212, 85-212; Close-Up, 85-269; genetic engineering, 87-263; New World archaeology, 87-220. See also **Botany; Climate.**

Agrobacteria: genetic engineering, 86-274

AIDS: Close-Up, 86-306; immunology, 86-275, 85-273; public health, 85-306; Special Report, 87-112

Ain Ghazal: Old World archaeology, 87-223

Air pollution: environment, 87-262, 86-269, 85-267

Airplane safety: lightning, Special Report, 87-79; Special Report, 86-111

Alamo: archaeology, 86-221

Alcoholic beverage: diet and cancer, Special Report, 86-60

Alcoholism: neuroscience, 87-285

Algae: botany, 86-235; environment, 87-261, 85-268; il., 87-238; oceanography, 86-258; Patrick, Ruth, 85-352; Yellowstone, Special Report, 86-52

All-in-one package: computer, 86-242

Allergy: medicine, 85-279

Alphanumeric display: Consumer Science, 86-334

ALS (amyotrophic lateral sclerosis): neuroscience, 86-289

Altazimuth mount: Consumer Science, 86-323

Aluminum cookware: Consumer Science, 87-330

Alvin: (submarine): oceanography, 87-294

Alzheimer's disease: memory, Special Report, 86-176

Ames test: diet and cancer, Special Report, 86-56

Amiga: computer hardware, 87-244

Amino acids: chemistry, 85-235; molecular biology, 87-284; vaccines, Special Report, 86-147

Amnesia: memory, Special Report, 86-169

Amphipithecus mogaungenis: anthropology, 87-216

Amygdala: memory, Special Report, 86-170

Anasazi Indians: remote sensing devices, Special Report, 87-178

Andromeda galaxy: *IRAS,* Special Report, 85-52

Anesthesia: psychology, 85-304

Angiogenin: medical research, 87-273; molecular biology, 87-283

Angiogram: medical imaging, Special Report, 85-156

Angonoka tortoise: il., 87-96

Animal: memory, Special Report, 86-178. See also **Zoology.**

Animal navigation: monarch butterfly, Special Report, 87-14

Anodized aluminum: Consumer Science, 87-332

Anorexia nervosa: psychology, 86-302; eating disorders, Special Report, 87-59

Antelope: zoo, Special Report, 85-181

Anthropoid: anthropology, 87-216; Madagascar, Special Report, 87-90

Anthropology, 87-216, 86-215, 85-215; books, 85-231; human fossils, Special Report, 86-194. See also **Archaeology.**

Antibiotic: agriculture, 86-213; dentistry, 85-275; drugs, 87-251

Antibody: AIDS, Special Report, 87-114; anthropology, 86-216; bone marrow, Special Report, 85-38; vaccines, Special Report, 86-143

Anticlotting agent: chemistry, 86-238

Antifrost bacteria: agriculture, 87-213

Antigen: AIDS, Special Report, 87-114; bone marrow, Special Report, 85-34; vaccines, Special Report, 86-143

Antigenic determinant: vaccines, Special Report, 86-147

Antioxidant: diet and cancer, Special Report, 86-62

Antitumor substance: zoology, 85-318

Aperture: Consumer Science, 86-322

Apparent brightness: galaxies, Special Report, 87-47

ARC (AIDS-related conditions): AIDS, Special Report, 87-123

Archaeology, New World, 87-219, 86-220, 85-219; Aztecs, Special Report, 87-30; books, 87-236; Mammoth Cave, Special Report, 85-141; Port Royal, Special Report, 86-96; remote sensing devices, Special Report, 87-169. See also **Anthropology.**

Archaeology, Old World, 87-222, 86-217, 85-217

Archaic site: New World archaeology, 87-221

Argo: oceanography, Close-Up, 87-293

Artificial blood cell: medical research, 87-275

Artificial insemination: zoo, Special Report, 85-181

Artificial intelligence: Special Report, 85-187

Artificial skin: skin, Special Report, 85-82

ARV (AIDS-associated retrovirus): AIDS, Special Report, 87-117; immunology, 86-275

Asteroid: paleontology, 86-252

Astigmatism: Consumer Science, 87-327

Astronaut: deaths, 87-249; People in Science, 86-339

Astronomy, Extragalactic, 87-225, 86-229, 85-227; books, 86-233; galaxies, Special Report, 87-45; shadow matter, Special Report, 87-184

Astronomy, Galactic, 87-228, 86-226, 85-224; books, 86-233, 85-231; *IRAS,* Special Report, 85-41

Astronomy, Solar System, 87-231, 86-223, 85-221; books, 86-233; Halley's Comet, Special Report, 86-28; planetary atmospheres, Special Report, 85-127. See also **Space Technology.**

Atari ST Series: computer hardware, 87-245

Atherosclerosis: Close-Up, 85-279

Atlantic blue crab: il., 87-254

Atlantis (spacecraft): space technology, 87-314

Atmosphere: planetary atmospheres, Special Report, 85-127. See also **Climate; Meteorology; Weather.**

Atom: laser, Special Report, 87-145; particle accelerator, Special Report, 85-100; shadow matter, Special Report, 87-186. See also **Physics, Subatomic.**

Atom smasher. See **Particle accelerator.**

Atomic Vapor Laser Isotope Separation (AVLIS): energy, 87-258

Australopithecus: anthropology, 85-215; human fossils, Special Report, 86-196

Autofocus: Consumer Science, 87-324

Automation: agriculture, 86-214; electronics, 87-257

Automobile: Close-Up, 85-259; electronics, 85-262

Awards: Nobel Prizes, 87-286, 86-308, 85-308; Science Fair Awards, 87-309, 86-309

Axon: memory, Special Report, 86-172; neuroscience, 87-284

Aye-aye: Madagascar, Special Report, 87-89

Aztecs: Special Report, 87-28

B

B₆, Vitamin: nutrition, 86-293, 85-291

B cell: AIDS, Special Report, 87-114;

Index

Index

Globular cluster: galaxies, Special Report, 87-53

Glomar Challenger: oceanography, 85-252

Glue: Consumer Science, 85-325

Gluon: particle accelerator, Special Report, 85-110; shadow matter, Special Report, 87-189

Glycosides: monarch butterfly, Special Report, 87-15

Goldstein, Allan M.: science awards, 86-310

Gondwanaland: Madagascar, Special Report, 87-86

Gracile australopithecine: human fossil, Special Report, 86-203

Graft-versus-host disease: bone marrow, Special Report, 85-36

Grand Unified Theories: birth of universe, Special Report, 85-91

Grass: ecology, 87-253, 85-255

Gravitational lens: astronomy, 86-230, 85-227

Graviton: shadow matter, Special Report, 87-189

Gravity: birth of universe, Special Report, 85-90; seismic tomography, Special Report, 87-198; shadow matter, Special Report, 87-184; Yellowstone, Special Report, 86-51

Great Nebula of Orion: il., 87-49

Great Temple of the Aztecs: Special Report, 87-28

Greece, Ancient: Old World archaeology, 87-223

Greenhouse effect: environment, 85-268; meteorology, 87-280

Gulf ridley sea turtle: oceanography, 85-254

Gull: zoology, 87-315

Gum disease. See **Periodontal disease.**

H

Habituation: memory, Special Report, 86-178

Hailstone: meteorology, 85-255

Halley's Comet: astronomy, 87-231, 85-222; Special Report, 86-28; space, 87-315

Hammerhead shark: il., 86-18

Handycam: Consumer Science, 87-324

Hanfmann, George M. A.: deaths, 87-248

Hard contact lenses: Consumer Science, 87-327

Hard X rays: laser, Special Report, 87-155

Hardware (computer). See **Computer Hardware.**

Hauptman, Herbert A.: Nobel Prizes, 87-286

Heart, Artificial: medicine, 86-283

Heart attack: Close-Up, 85-279; medicine, 85-279

Heart disease: nutrition, 86-291, 85-290; psychology, 87-305

Heart transplant: Close-Up, 86-282

Heat lightning: lightning, Special Report, 87-77

Heavy-electron metal: physics, 87-297

Heavy element: galaxies, Special Report, 87-53

Heavy ion accelerator: physics, 86-301

Heavy metals: botany, 87-238

Heavy noble gas: planetary atmospheres, Special Report, 85-133

Heavy nucleus: physics, 85-294

Helper T cell: AIDS, Special Report, 87-114; public health, 85-306

Hemisphere (brain): brain, Special Report, 87-158; psychology, 87-303

Hemophilia: molecular biology, 85-288

Heparin: chemistry, 86-239

Hepatitis: vaccines, Special Report, 86-145

Heredity: medicine, 85-276. See also **Genetic Engineering; Genetics.**

Herodium: il., 87-180

Herpes: immunology, 87-271; vaccines, Special Report, 86-143

Herschel, William: galaxies, Special Report, 87-46; Mars, Special Report, 87-128

Hessian fly: il., 87-212

Hidden Cave (Nevada): archaeology, 86-220

Hierarchical theory: astronomy, 87-226

Higgs interaction: birth of universe, Special Report, 85-97; physics, 87-300

High blood pressure. See **Hypertension.**

High-speed photography: biomechanics, Special Report, 85-114

Hippocampus: memory, Special Report, 86-170

HLA antigen: bone marrow, Special Report, 85-34

HMSA (hydroxymethanesulfonate): environment, 87-263

Hologram: computer graphics, Special Report, 87-111; laser, Special Report, 87-149

Home exercise equipment: Consumer Science, 86-328

Home medical tests: Consumer Science, 87-333

Home moviemaking: Consumer Science, 87-322

Hominid: anthropology, 87-217, 85-215; human fossils, Special Report, 86-196; Old World archaeology, 86-217

Homo erectus: anthropology, 86-215; il., 86-209

Homosexuals: AIDS, Special Report, 87-115

Honeybee: agriculture, Close-Up, 87-214

Hontoon Island: New World archaeology, 87-221

Hopper, Grace M.: People in Science, 87-339

Hormone: diet and cancer, Special Report, 86-60; medicine, 87-278

Horticulture. See **Agriculture; Botany; Plant.**

Hot spring: Yellowstone, Special Report, 86-51

Household cement: Consumer Science, 85-326

HTLV-III (virus): AIDS, Special Report, 87-117; Close-Up, 86-306; immunology, 86-275, 85-273

Hubble, Edwin P.: galaxies, Special Report, 87-48

Hubble Space Telescope: galaxies, Special Report, 87-54

Huizilopochtli: Aztecs, Special Report, 87-30

Human fossils: anthropology, 86-215, 85-215; Special Report, 86-194

Human sacrifice: Aztecs, Special Report, 87-32

Huntington's disease: genetics, 85-271; neuroscience, 85-289

Hurricane: coral reef, Special Report, 85-27

Hybridization: molecular biology, 87-282

Hydrogen: galactic astronomy, 87-229; galaxies, Special Report, 87-55; Halley's Comet, Special Report, 86-32; planetary atmospheres, Special Report, 85-132

Hydrogen sulfide: *Alvin*, Special Report, 86-77; Thames, Special Report, 86-159

Hydrotropism: botany, 87-238

Hydroxyl radical: meteorology, 87-280

Hypertension: drugs, 86-247, 85-241; public health, 87-306

I

Ibuprofen: drugs, 85-242

Icon: computer hardware, 87-244

Imaging: biomechanics, Special Report, 85-125

Immune system: AIDS, Special Report, 87-113; bone marrow, Special Report, 85-36; immunology, 85-273; skin, Special Report, 85-78; vaccines, Special Report, 86-143

Immunology, 87-270, 86-275, 85-273. See also **Immune system.**

Imprinting: oceanography, 85-254; zoo, Special Report, 85-179

Inbreeding: zoo, Special Report, 85-171; zoology, 85-319

Indian, American: anthropology, 86-216; Aztecs, Special Report, 87-28; Mammoth Cave, Special Report, 85-143; New World archaeology, 87-219, 86-220, 85-219; remote sensing devices, Special Report, 87-178

Indirect immunofluorescence: dentistry, 87-250

Indole: Special Report, 86-64

Indri: Madagascar, Special Report, 87-90

Industrial pollution: Thames, Special Report, 86-160

Infanticide: zoology, 87-317

Infantile amnesia: memory, Special Report, 86-171

Inference engine: computer software, 87-246

Index

Index

Index

Index

Acknowledgments

The publishers of *Science Year* gratefully acknowledge the courtesy of the following artists, photographers, publishers, institutions, agencies, and corporations for the illustrations in this volume. Credits should read from top to bottom, left to right on their respective pages. All entries marked with an asterisk (*) denote illustrations created exclusively for *Science Year*. All maps, charts, and diagrams were prepared by the *Science Year* staff unless otherwise noted.

Cover
   © Jeff Smith
3   Brent Jones*
4   ARDEA; National Research Council of Canada; © Chuck O'Rear, West Light
5   Tom Sever; © Hans Namuth, Photo Researchers
7   Dartmouth College; Dan Miller*; Fermi National Accelerator Laboratory; University of California; University of Michigan; Missouri Botanical Garden; New York State Educational Department
10   © Thomas Ives; Mary Anne Enriquez*; Joe VanSeveran*
11   Frans Lanting; David Hizer, Aspen; Abel Image Research
12–14   Frans Lanting
16   L. P. Brower; Frans Lanting; Frans Lanting
17   Frans Lanting
18   Jeff Foott, Tom Stack & Assoc.
19   L. P. Brower
20   Jeff Foott, Tom Stack & Assoc.; L. P. Brower; L. P. Brower
21–22   L. P. Brower
23   Frans Lanting; L. P. Brower
24–25   L. P. Brower
26   L. P. Brower; Monarca A. C.
28   National Institute of Anthropology and History, Mexico City
29–31   David Hizer, Aspen
33   © British Library; American Museum of Natural History; From the *Codex Borhonicus*
34   Robert Addison
37–38   David Hizer, Aspen
39   Richard Townsend; David Hizer, Aspen
40   David Hizer, Aspen
41   National Institute of Anthropology and History, Mexico City
42   David Hizer, Aspen; National Institute of Anthropology and History, Mexico City
44   © David F. Malin, Anglo-Australian Telescope Board
48   Rob Wood, Stansbury, Ronsaville, Wood Inc.*
49   © Hale Observatories; © California Institute of Technology
50–51   © Hale Observatories
52   Rob Wood, Stansbury, Ronsaville, Wood Inc.*
54   © National Optical Astronomy Observatories
55   Optical photograph from the National Geographic-Palomar Sky Survey; X-ray contours from the Smithsonian Observatory; Rob Wood, Stansbury, Ronsaville, Wood Inc.*
58–66   Guy Wolek*
70   © Thomas Ives
72   Granger Collection
73   Roberta Polfus*
74   © Robert E. Pelham, Burce Coleman Inc.
75   © Thomas Ives
77–78   Roberta Polfus*
80   Mary Evans Picture Library
82   National Aeronautics and Space Administration
83   Philip W. Brown and Philip L. Hazlett, National Aeronautics and Space Administration; National Aeronautics and Space Administration
84   Bruce Coleman Inc.
88   Russell A. Mittermier; © Joy Spurr, Bruce Coleman Inc.; Kjell B. Sandved, Bruce Coleman Inc.; © Russ Kinne, Photo Researchers
90   John Visser, Bruce Coleman Inc.; E. R. Degginger, Animals Animals/Earth Scenes; S. C. Bisserot, Bruce Coleman Inc.
91   Sara Woodward*
92   Liz and Tony Bomford, ARDEA; Zig Leszczynski, Animals Animals/Earth Scenes
93   © Joy Spurr, Bruce Coleman Inc.; Russell A. Mittermier; © Ted Schiffman
94   Russell A. Mittermier
95   © Joy Spurr, Bruce Coleman Inc.
96   Russell A. Mittermier; Rod Williams, Bruce Coleman Inc.

98   Abel Image Research
100   McDonnell Douglas Corporation; General Electric
101   Massachusetts Institute of Technology Museum
102   National Research Council of Canada
103   Richard J. Feldmann, National Institutes of Health
104   Chrysler Corporation
105   S. Van Baerle and D. Kingbury, Computer Graphics Research Group, Ohio State University (Rainbow); © 1985 Paramount Pictures Corporation
106   John F. Hawley, California Institute of Technology
108   Art Matrix
109   International Business Machines
110   Richard J. Feldmann, National Institutes of Health
112   Louise Gubb, Gamma/Liaison
115–116   Scott Thorn Barrows*
117   Scott Thorn Barrows*; Barromes/Pytkowic, Gamma/Liaison; Centers for Disease Control
118   © Dennis Brack, Black Star; David Powers, University of California at San Francisco; Sichov, Sipa
119–120   Scott Thorn Barrows*
121   © Michel Steboun, Black Star
122   © Arthur Gloor, Animals Animals/Earth Scenes
124   Scott Thorn Barrows*
126   National Air and Space Museum, Smithsonian Institution; Jet Propulsion Laboratory
130   The Viking Press, Inc.; Brown Bros.
131   U. S. Geological Survey
132   National Aeronautics and Space Administration; Kim Poor*; National Aeronautics and Space Administration; Kim Poor*
133   Jet Propulsion Laboratory; Kim Poor*; National Aeronautics and Space Administration
136   National Space Science Data Center; National Aeronautics and Space Administration
137   National Aeronautics and Space Administration
138   National Aeronautics and Space Administration; Kim Poor*
139–140   Kim Poor*
142   © Jeff Smith
145   Hughes Aircraft Company; © Dan McCoy, Rainbow; Spectra-Physics
146   Mary Anne Enriquez*
148   © Chuck O'Rear, West Light
149   © Charles Falco, Science Source
150   © Chuck O'Rear, West Light
151   General Motors Corporation; U.S. Department of Agriculture
152   Mary Anne Enriquez*; Department of Defense
153   Mary Anne Enriquez*
154   Brian Quintard, Lawrence Livermore National Laboratory; Gary Stone, Lawrence Livermore National Laboratory; Brian Quintard, Lawrence Livermore National Laboratory
156–165   Joe Rogers*
168   Tom Sever
173   Aerofilms Limited; National Aeronautics and Space Administration; Tom Sever; R. E. W. Adams, University of Texas at San Antonio
174–175   Tom Sever
176   Laboratory of Anthropology, Museum of New Mexico (Charles A. Lindbergh)
177–180   Tom Sever
182–194   Joe VanSeveran*
196   Terri Murphy*
199   Granger Collection
200   Terri Murphy*; U.S. Geological Survey
201   Terri Murphy*
202   Terri Murphy*; Terri Murphy*; Adam Dziewonski, Harvard University
203   Adam Dziewonski, Harvard University; Robert Paz, California Institute of Technology